CW00551259

ISBN 978-0-9932164-6-6

A N T E N N A   P U B L I C A T I O N S

THE GYPSY SWITCH
AND OTHER RITUAL JOURNEYS

The Story of One Woman becoming part of the Sacred Landscape of Britain

by
Jill Smith

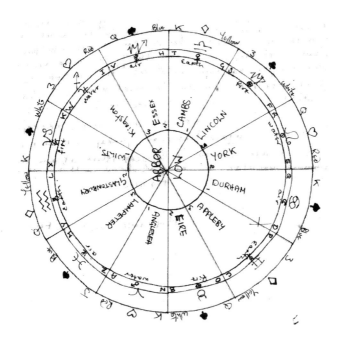

This book is dedicated to the memory of Lynne (Sinclair) Wood, who often understood what I was doing better than I did myself.

CONTENTS

FOREWORD

I'm not a writer, but felt I had to write this foreword, as Jill's work and story (which are more or less the same thing) have an heroic quality to them - a quality that is a rare commodity in an increasingly commodified artworld.

I first got to know Jill's work through the ritualistic performances she made at sacred Neolithic sites around the UK. These rituals articulated my own thoughts about these places, managing to appear simultaneously futuristic and ancient.

It's not often that you come across an artist who is so dedicated to their vision that they go on a journey around Britain, and this is what this book is about - The Gypsy Switch, the year-long journey Jill took in 1984-85 when she began even deeper artistic research into the human relationship with place.

The Gypsy Switch exactly coincided with the national battle, and trauma, of the miner's strike, and what Jill did could not have been further away from the aspirational consumer lifestyle of Thatcher's Britain. As she explains in this book, Jill lived very simply - often in the open air - and she found a natural kinship with the Greenham Common women, Earth mystics, spiritual feminists, and radical pagans. She even spent time with the anarchist punk group CrAss.

It was a remarkable journey that has ended on the Isle of Lewis, where Jill was drawn to be close to the standing stones that have inspired her now for nearly 40 years.

Jeremy Deller

INTRODUCTION

In setting out to write this book I intended it to be solely about how I travelled the year long Gipsy Switch journey round Britain in 1984-85 not long after giving birth to my fourth child in a tipi in Wales. Initially I travelled this in a horse-drawn waggon with a few other people, but when they all dropped out I carried on alone, completing the circle, walking for three and a half months with a rucksack on my back, my son on my front and a bag in each hand.

In the years since I have often been asked "How did you do it with a baby?" People have wanted to know about what actually happened on a day-to-day level, with all the mundane practicalities, as well as the deep spirituality of the experience.

But they didn't just want to know about The Gipsy Switch. For several years before that journey I had made pilgrimages through the landscape, sleeping out with no tent, in all weathers and at all times of year. They wanted to know how I did that as well. I felt the need to explain that I was not some super-human being, some Amazon, but an ordinary woman who had for a few years lived an extraordinary life.

As I wrote I found the story was not just about the landscape journeys but about a time in my life of enormous emotional, psychological and physical upheaval as I drifted apart from my marriage and family, needing time alone with the ancient sacred places of our land, realising my real self had become lost in my childhood and, having walked away from everything I had owned and become, slowly rebuilding and re-discovering that original true self.

I learned of The Gipsy Switch when talking about the stone circle Arbor Low in Derbyshire with a friend, Stephanie Smith. She explained that this was the hub of the journey and sent me a diagram of it which showed a circle round England and Wales, touching Ireland, with 12 named places corresponding to the 12 signs of the zodiac. In travelling it one would move round a zodiac on the earth as the sun travelled through the zodiac in the heavens. I knew immediately it was something I must undertake one day, but that I would have to wait for the right time and circumstances in my life to arise.

At that time I was known as Jill Bruce, working in a Performance Art partnership with my then- husband, the late Bruce Lacey, carrying out spectacular celebratory, ceremonial, ritual performances all over the country, but most particularly at the Albion Faires in East Anglia. We always worked in

Scorpio in the Glastonbury Terrestrial Zodiac journey

a circle, celebrating natural cycles and also travelled the country in our yellow ex-GPO truck visiting ancient Neolithic and Bronze Age sites, performing at them, then showing documentation in subsequent gallery exhibitions.

The concept of 'journeying', in the sense of travelling between sites and linking them back into an ancient network by the energy of one's human movement, became increasingly important to me, as was the concept of not only celebrating the cycles of nature but also living their energy and becoming part of them. All this became a spontaneous form of 'self-initiation', the understanding of which came later.

I had become excited by the concept of 'terrestrial zodiacs' which were being much written about at the time. In the 1930s Katherine Maltwood discovered giant figures in the Somerset landscape, formed by rivers, streams, field edges and ancient earthworks, which represented the zodiac signs in the correct order and positions when a map was laid under a planesphere of the stars. She linked it to Arthurian legends and a quest for the Holy Grail. It is thought that John Dee, alchemist and advisor at the court of Queen Elizabeth knew of it. It was much disputed, but rang a deep truth in me, and in 1977 Bruce and I journeyed round it in 4 days, celebrating 3 signs a day, it seeming to have its own reality; one somehow just slightly out of step with the surrounding mundane world. Many such zodiacs were being discovered all over Britain in the '70s; how many real, how many the fruits of active imaginations, I don't know, but it did seem there might be a zodiac of zodiacs right round the land. Maybe this was The Gipsy Switch.

Mrs Maltwood's friend Mary Caine later wrote extensively about these zodiacs and had found one in her own area – Kingston-on-Thames near London. This turned out to be a named place on the Gipsy Switch. I knew of one at Bury-St-Edmunds in Suffolk, another near Hebden Bridge in Yorkshire and one at Pumpsaint in Wales. This latter was very close to another place on the Switch – Lampeter.

At several fairs, especially a Tree Fair at Rougham in Suffolk, we performed zodiac celebrations, for which I painted 12 wooden discs with the appropriate signs on them. These would become part of my Gipsy Switch journey.

So when I was given the diagram of the Switch I was extremely interested. At the time I understood it to be a year's journey which Irish travellers had made, moving round a cycle of horse fairs. For Gemini it included Appleby – the great annual horse fair to which gipsies still travel from all over the land.

Recently I corresponded with Stephanie Smith and she attempted to discover the history of the diagram. Eventually it seemed likely that someone had originally linked together information from many Gipsy stories and given them form, although I was told it had come from 'an old Gipsy man' at Glastonbury. It then passed through several hands which added other New Age glosses to it. These meant little to me and indeed, it didn't matter much to me whether it was a traditional journey or not – it was a concept which fitted completely into what I then felt to be my 'work' and of fundamental importance.

The idea of moving round the land continuously for a year as the sun moved through the zodiac in the sky; to be the human link between the heavens and the earth, perhaps even helping a little towards restoring some balance our ancient ancestors held which has been lost in modern life, seemed like some form of personal destiny which must be fulfilled.

Travelling from sacred site to sacred site had also made me aware of how the sites themselves had been linked into a whole rich network. For a lot of our existence as humans we were hunter- gatherers (or perhaps more rightly gatherer-hunters) moving through a landscape with which we had a deep physical and spiritual relationship. We were dependant on our knowledge of it: its physical features, its water sources, the life cycles of its plants and animals; but also had a deep spiritual and shamanic relationship with it, giving back as well as taking, tending it and creating some form of harmony and balance which kept both it and us well.

Virgo in a zodiac performance at Rougham Tree Fair

In travelling their Dreaming Paths this is what Australian Aboriginal people did for tens of thousands of years (perhaps even rejecting settled farming when this was realised as a possibility). I am sure it is how our own ancestors lived, but this relationship became lost when people settled and started farming and 'owning' land, becoming even more lost as time moved on.

To those peoples the night skies were as present and powerful as the day. Living as I do now in the Western Isles of Scotland in a place with no street lights it can be a shock to realise the intensity and depth of the blackness of night; the brilliance and apparent closeness of stars, the astonishing light of the moon and the wonder as it changes shape night by night. The heavens were as much a part of our ancestors' reality as the earth. The night skies held the realms of their creation ancestors and their goddesses and gods. Maybe movements of constellations, of moon and sun at specific times created 'bridges' to the realms of the ancestors and gods, giving them access to the earth; and the spirits of the dead the opportunity to return to their ancestral 'homes in the sky'.

So, this is my story, not only of these landscape journeys, but of how I didn't just step from a warm house to suddenly take up this very different way of life but underwent a long process of being more and more outdoors, even 'rejecting' houses for a while, until it simply became how I lived, how I felt most natural and normal. It is the story of hardship, both physical and emotional, as much as of intense spiritual experience; difficulties with some

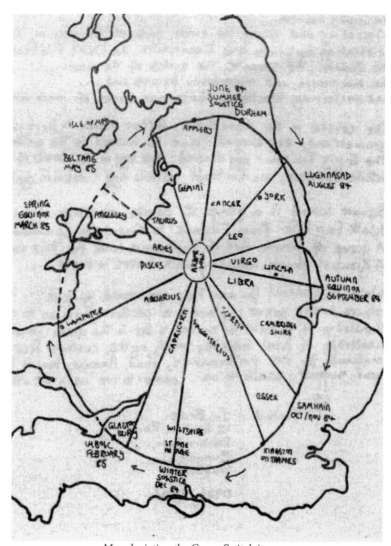

Map depicting the Gypsy Switch journey

people as well as the extraordinary kindness and help given by so many more. It includes my doubts and insecurities as well as the heights and the joys.

It is based almost entirely on the diaries and writings I did at the time, so contains the views, feelings and knowledge which unfolded as I journeyed, rather than necessarily how I perceive things now.

Any comments I make from the perspective of now I think I have made clear.

This was, in a way, the high point of my life; the most intense and extraordinary time. Perhaps you can't live at that intensity for too long. I am more settled and calm now. I did these things at a time in my life when it became possible and am so glad I just seized the moment. I hope to give people the idea that if the right circumstances crop up in their own lives, then they too can do something similar. It is possible.

My undying gratitude to Rupert White for turning my manuscript into a physical book, and my dream into reality, when I no longer had the heart or energy to pursue literary agents or larger-scale publishers. My enormous thanks to Lois Darley for hours of scanning and computer help. My thanks to Stephanie Smith for giving me the original plan of The Gypsy Switch; to all the people both named and unnamed in the text who offered help, food, water, places to stay and restored my faith in human nature; and to Simant Bostock, Janet Jenkins, Poppy Palin and Karen Taylor for reading an earlier manuscript, offering suggestions and helping me believe it was all worthwhile.

PART 1

Chapter 1: The Slow Move Out Onto the Land

So, how did it all begin? I wasn't a country girl but born in North London, living in the city for my first 37 years, gradually moving nearer to the centre, though I did start out in a place which almost edged onto the country, being brought up by my maternal grandparents after both my parents died of cancer aged 36 when I was 2.

In those days it was thought best if a child forgot, so I was told nothing of my parents, even that they had existed, so did indeed forget what little I had remembered of them and grew up feeling strange and isolated and somehow different from other children. Something was missing but I didn't know what. Somewhere inside me there was a sense of abandonment and confusion. My 2-year old questions weren't answered and this led to my never asking anything or expressing my feelings.

My grandparents' house had a big back garden where I played on my own throughout the year and in the summer lay for hours on the grass gazing at the sky. There were fruit trees I climbed and a big oak tree I sat in which overlooked a playing field. To one side of this was a golf course and beyond that an endless expanse which blended into countryside. The back fence had a little door in it which, as I grew older, I would sometimes sneak through to take a short cut to the bus stop. This was in Green Dragon Lane. I first went to a school called Merryhills and walked to it down World's End Lane which had trees and a ditch on one side and on the other some 'countryside'. These places must have been old but the roads where I lived were part of a suburb built between the wars as part of the expansion of the edges of London.

Like most children in those days, I spent much of my life outdoors, playing in the road, which had little traffic, and on an 'island' covered in trees and shrubs. With my aunt and uncle and three cousins I'd go out into the country to trainspot steam engines and have picnics at dramatic places like Ivinghoe Beacon.

As I grew older I would go cycling and picnic with school-friends in fields with no barbed wire and nothing to stop us but a wooden gate; small fields with hedges and trees and real thatched hay- stacks and no gigantic combine harvesters as tall as a house. It sounds like history but feels just a few years ago to me.

We always went on holiday to Walton-on-the-Naze in Essex. As a child I loved playing all day on the beach and catching shrimps, but growing older became bored by it as my friends went off to exotic places like Cornwall – or even abroad. But Walton still had some elemental places to walk, especially on wild and windy cliff-tops.

Much of the time I was very alone. Growing up with old people full of unspoken grief was strange. My grandparents had also lost their first daughter aged six in 1911 in quite traumatic circumstances, as she died of peritonitis during an operation on the kitchen table; but none of this was spoken of, certainly not to me, so it wasn't until I was an adult that I had much understanding of their situation. They weren't like parents to me, but over-protective guardians forbidding me from doing most of what I found interesting.

All I wanted was to be an actress, imagining a dynamic and colourful life far from the endless cream paint and net curtains of the grey and colourless suburbs. I wanted adventure and excitement and a life which was 'different'. I didn't find getting on with people that easy in 'real life', but on stage I could be anyone and do anything.

In 1959 I went on a local youth club trip to Norway. The boat journey took a couple of days and I sat outside watching the 'molten ice' of the wake for hours. The whole trip plucked at ancient memory deep within me, though I didn't realise this at the time. We walked through a freezing stream of glacial melt-water, and on a fjord boat trip I sensed real trolls in the forests on the surrounding mountainsides. It was unlike anything I had experienced in England and I was thrilled by the drama of this landscape.

Living now on the Isle of Lewis I am acutely aware of being among people who truly belong to the land of their birth, who know their family histories and genealogies and how those are deeply related to place. Many people, in England especially, no longer 'belong' anywhere. They move around, have no roots, no sense of family history being of place and I think we are the worse for it. I know little of where my own people are from, and although I still feel some connection to London – the place that was there before the city perhaps – I have no sense of belonging to it and do not really know where I am 'from'.

When I was 17 I began an unsatisfactory relationship with the artist Bruce Lacey which quickly destroyed my dreams and cut me off from my friends. Our first child was born in 1961 and I lived alone with him as an 'unmarried mother' in dingy bedsits for four and a half years. As I grew older and moved

Jill and Bruce doing their 'Fred Astaire and Ginger Rogers' dance in The Electric Element

closer to the centre of London I seemed to forget my early relationship with the edges of countryside. Swiss Cottage, South Kensington, Crouch End, Stroud Green, Palmers Green and then on a road between the Holloway and Caledonian Roads – Mackenzie Road - which was a rat-run for lorries which regularly drove into and smashed up parked cars and our Bedford Dormobiles. By then I was living with Bruce, getting married in 1967, and by 1969 having 3 children, Kevin, Tiffany and Saffron. The house was a condemned wreck, due to be demolished to make way for a park; rooms above a shop which had been a Rediffusion sub-station, with broken banisters and a front door straight onto

15

the street where sometimes people were knifed or shot. There was a tiny back garden which was so overgrown and full of junk you could hardly move in it so I hung the washing on a line from the kitchen window.

The children had one bedroom at the top of the house. Bruce and I didn't have a bedroom, just slept in the living room. If I came home exhausted from work and Bruce had a crowd of people round I had to go and lie on the floor of the children's room. There was no bathroom, but we had a pink Victorian hip-bath in the kitchen, filled from a wonderful Ascot which I'd still rather have than a temperamental modern computerised boiler. Saffron was born there – a wonderful family occasion – but it is strange now the house is demolished to think the place of her birth is just air. In the '60s all this had a strange glamour for being so different from the grey regimentation of the suburbs. But no countryside. Dusty pavements. No trees. No grass even.

Then we moved to Hackney. This was before East London 'happened', though may have been at the beginning, as we were caretakers of a SPACE artists' studio (Martello Street). A 'creeping Islingtonitis' was drifting over from Highbury, but our area was still pretty working-class and we were opposite the All Nations Club.

Kevin now had a room of his own, with Tiffany and Saffron sharing another. Bruce and I still had no bedroom, still sleeping in the living room. There was still no bathroom, still the old pink hip-bath in the kitchen filled from the same old Ascot which we had taken with us. Bruce had a huge studio and storage space for his vast collection of eccentricities, but never created an area for me so I could have my 'own space'. All I got was a cupboard under the stairs with barely room for a chair. When Bruce created a dark-room, worked out how to process films and print pictures, then got bored with it, I was able to take over and spent hours, days, weeks, in its dark, in the red light, with the smell of chemicals and the magic as the images appeared on the paper. It was a chance to be alone with my own mind and dreams.

This part of my life is a whole other story, but things began to stir in me. The children walked to their primary school across the now famed London Fields. When I walked over to Broadway Market, which was then a thriving local street market, on a few days each year the London plane trees came alive in a very particular way, with identities which reached out and communicated with me.

This was by now the '70s, but in the '60s there had been a couple of occasions when I had travelled across country to Wales. Firstly, on a train passing through Wiltshire, the whole landscape throbbed with an intensity I'd never previously experienced. I sensed the spirits of an ancestral Neolithic people rising up from the ground – rather like the army of skeletons in Jason and the

Argonauts – crying out to me that they hadn't been ignorant savages but people with an ancient wisdom which had now been forgotten. It was as though they were telling me it was my duty, my role in life, to let people today know about them.

The second occasion was when driving along the A4, before the M4 was built, when suddenly out of the dusk loomed the vast bulk of Silbury Hill. At school my history lessons began with the Romans and we were taught nothing of what had gone before. I knew of Stonehenge but had no idea the whole of Britain was covered with ancient Neolithic and Bronze Age stone circles and earthworks, and knew nothing of the civilisation which had raised them.

Not long after this we went on a family holiday exploring Avebury, West Kennet and other sites in Wiltshire and Dorset. One day we climbed onto Windmill Hill which overlooks Silbury and Avebury and here I experienced what felt like a memory, as though I had become again a member of an ancient group of nomadic people who travelled here annually to meet up with many other tribes. I felt strongly connected to the West Kennet long barrow, as though it were 'our place', but looking down towards the Avebury area saw a tribe of very different people erecting the great stones of the circle. They seemed to have come from somewhere else and it was as though this signalled the beginning of the end of our old ways.

Stonehenge was then a much more pleasant place to visit than now. Although there was an entrance building and a tunnel under the road, once you emerged there was no path round the stones and you could wander about as you wished. We went on to Woodhenge, originally a structure of great wooden posts and while there, someone told us of an archaeological dig at nearby Durrington Walls, a henge monument which was due to have a road built either through it or very close. One of the archaeologists showed us a post-hole which was being excavated. It had a slope, where the great post was put in at an angle then hauled upright. In it were objects, including an antler pick, which had been hurriedly thrown in to prevent the pole from toppling over. So the archaeologist said. Antler picks must have been prized tools and nowadays I would rather think it was an offering made to whatever totemic being was probably carved on the pole. It was awesome to feel this immediate contact with the person who had put it there all those thousands of years before.

These were intense and unexpected experiences, yet none of it fitted in to the life I was leading at the time. Having worked for an agency which employed 'resting' actresses (Problem Ltd.) doing mainly cleaning work and child care, I then worked for 7 years as a market and social research interviewer. With no car, I often trudged over several pages of the London A-Z in a day.

During these years Bruce became quite a well-known artist.

I had been to RADA, but left when I had Kevin, missing my moment of glory in the Vanbrugh Theatre in front of potential agents and producers. In the years since I had only had occasional small parts on TV and in short films (mainly by Bob Godfrey), hadn't been able to get my acting life going and was bursting with a desperate urge to express my latent creativity. I was a huge fiery Leo who had somehow become tamed and was desperate to burst out of my cage.

As we moved into the '70s there was a great expansion of possibility in the arts. With eccentric musicians, the Alberts, we wrote our own version of The Three Musketeers, toured it (very successfully in France and Belgium) and eventually ended up at the Royal Court Theatre with Rachel Roberts (then married to Rex Harrison) as Madame de Winter. Bruce was D'Artagnan and I was Constance Bonacieux. There was a chance here to write my part, make my own costume and feel I was being a bit more artistic.

Another show with the Alberts began a big change in my life. For The Electric Element each person in the cast wrote their own scene based on their personal fantasy. There were Pirates, Russians, dopplegangers and much else. These themes were linked together by the story of a Professor (Bruce) who invented a machine (the Materialiser) which drew in The Most Beautiful Woman in the Universe (me!!!). She almost immediately disappeared and he spent the rest of the show seeking her through all the other variations in time and space, often encountering a woman who resembled her but didn't recognise him. Eventually they were re-united, doing a kind of Fred Astaire and Ginger Rogers dance in front of a huge golden fan. This was choreographed by the very patient Eleanor Fazan who directed the show at the Theatre Royal, Stratford East.

The key point for me was that when I finally appeared, dressed in gold, I declaimed a great speech invoking the goddess, which I had adapted from a passage in Apuleius' The Golden Ass. Speaking this each night had an effect on me which bore fruit some years later.

The show gave me the opportunity to create fantasy personalities for myself, having all my life sought an identity, as though I could put one on like a coat. I made my own costumes and got a firm which made wigs for shop-window dummies to create several great golden-orange structures which I wore on my head.

Around this time I entered 5 of the wonderful Andrew Logan's Alternative Miss World competitions. These grew from intimate but exotic parties in his studio spaces to vast extravaganzas which he still holds every few years. I made my costumes for these and absolutely adored doing them. The contestants were/are both men and women and I enjoyed the moment when, one year when I was thin, brown, muscular and very glamorous, being chatted up by a gay man who didn't know which gender I was.

Jill appearing in an early Andrew Logan's Alternative Miss World

Somewhere amongst all this we began to get interested in subjects like magic, mythology and alchemy and as I read about these it was as though some deep, ancient and long-forgotten memory began to wake within me.

We began doing short performance pieces, many in outdoor situations, evolving some which were 'comically alchemical'. One involved bringing down the nose-cone of an alien space-craft, opening it up with much spectacle to reveal a squat green Martian which I had made from slabs of cake, sculpted, covered in marzipan and painted with food colour. Brightly costumed, I cut up the Martian and gave out portions to the watching crowd. It was one of several subsequent cake sculptures which, along with other food events, I began to develop as 'The Picnic as an Art form'.

One year, for one of the Alternative Miss Worlds, I decided my swimwear costume should be made of seaweed. I went by train to my childhood holiday resort of Walton to collect a bucket of seaweed from the beach. I had been an adventurous teenager, sneaking off all over the place, usually to see a film or play starring Sir Laurence Olivier, on whom I had a great crush, but in all the

19

years with Bruce I'd never gone anywhere on my own, except for the market-researching. This journey had a profound effect on me as I re-connected with my elemental childhood self.

After The Electric Element Bruce and I decided to work on our own together without The Alberts. We became a Performance Art duo called 'Galactic Theatre' which we registered as a business name, or often just 'Bruce Lacey and Jill Bruce'. (I had tried to remain Jill Smith when I joined the actors' union Equity, but there was already an actress with a similar name so I quickly plumped for Jill Bruce). Our first show was 'Stella Superstar and Her Amazing Galactic Adventures', a mixture of live action, film, slide sequences, special effects and music, involving, of course, a lot more spectacular costumes and fantasy personalities. We toured the country with it, packing our three ton truck with sets and acting as our own roadies. I got very strong carrying huge speakers and structures made from 8'x4' three- quarter ply, sniffing haughtily at sexist blokes who asked 'Can I give you a hand with that, love?' Once we had thus proved ourselves to the then Arts Council of Great Britain (ACGB), we applied for finance and for 5 years received a 'guarantee against loss' from the Performance Art branch of the Fine Art Dept.

In 1976 my 96-year old grandmother had an operation which she sailed through, but following which she was sent to a convalescent home. Bruce and I used to visit and get her walking around the garden, for she was terrified of ending up in an old people's home and was afraid my uncle (her only remaining child) and aunt were plotting with the matron to put her into one. She'd always pleaded with me 'don't let them put me in a home, Jill' so when the day came for her to leave, she sat with her hat on, clutching her handbag, and demanded to be taken home. I said I'd go and stay with her until I was confident she could get around the house ok, make herself cups of tea safely and so on.

Mine was a strange family which didn't express emotions or talk about feelings, and as she and I sat silently for hours in armchairs on either side of the fireplace her need to communicate was so great that I began to find her thoughts coming into my own head, not something I was at all used to. Eventually she might make some remark which echoed exactly what I had heard in my mind, so I knew it wasn't imagination. Then, as I (in my mid-30s) woke up each morning in my old childhood bedroom, I felt like an old woman, as though she was desperately trying to communicate her own experience.

For my birthday Kevin gave me a copy of John Michell's 'A View Over Atlantis' and as I sat reading it avidly it seemed to re-open a whole new understanding of the world and how it worked: that the earth had a life-force and living energy flowing through it. I'd already been feeling this without rationalising it, and now it all came to the surface.

Back, Bruce and Jill (in wig), front, left to right - Tiffany, Kevin and Saffron

Then, as I sat watching my Grandmother's TV, on came a programme with Mary Caine talking about Katherine Maltwood's discovery of the Glastonbury Terrestrial Zodiac. I was totally mesmerised, as though bits of a jigsaw puzzle were starting to come together to form a loose image, even though I didn't have the full picture on the box. When I thought my grandmother could cope, I returned home, but my life had somehow changed.

Initially I got deeply into the concept of 'leys' and 'ley-hunting' and we started to visit more Neolithic and Bronze Age sites. It was hard to understand the effect all this was having on me: I was connecting with those ancient ancestors, those people who built the structures of stone and earth, and was experiencing the 'power of place'.

I began to find London itself very powerful, sensing the ancient energy points there long before the city, and my relationship with it changed, even though on a day-to-day level I felt trapped and oppressed by it. We got out of London to perform, but it took hours to free ourselves of the city with its snarled up roads and motorways, and hours to get back home when we were tired.

1976 was the year of The Great Drought. At a Science Fiction fair we met someone who asked if we'd like to perform at the last Barsham Faire in Suffolk. It sounded interesting but was 'medieval', with no electricity, so we turned ourselves into 'The Elemental Co-ordinators', and began to work out a whole new way of performing. I made some costumes (dedicated to earth, air, fire and water) and planned how we could work in a circle. Some time before, when stranded in Wales by motorways completely blocked by snow I had done some spontaneous 'sympathetic magic' which had worked, so we had the idea that our performances, our honouring of and working with the ancient elements, could have an actual effect in the physical world.

At the faire I went into a kind of retreat, working out a sequence of events which seemed to come from some deep memory inside me, as though I was waking up and remembering things from my ancient ancestral past. We didn't use words, it was all visual - using lots of 'props', objects, movement and bits of spectacle like coloured smoke, fire and water, banging things for noise and blowing conch shells. However it all felt somehow powerfully real.

Well, the Elemental Co-ordinators did co-ordinate some aspect of the elements –the drought ended, it poured with rain and flooded the fair. (And of course that MP bloke got all the credit!)

The faire had a deep effect on me in other ways. Walking around at night seemed to bring back memories of past lives when I too had lived like this. Stalls lit by candles and lamps, people gathered round fires with medieval music and medieval clothes. I felt oddly out of place and had a desperate longing to actually live this way. The spirit and energy of 'the faire people' appeared to be part of a creative community where everyone pulled together; a world I wanted to belong to.

It was strange returning to London after such an overwhelming experience. I had become dissatisfied with living in the city anyway, but now it was a dissatisfaction with a whole way of life, even though our 'life style' was very basic, austere and unlike that of most people we knew. For all our 'philosophy' of living as we wished without having to earn extra money to pay for treats which made up for the drudge of working, I lived in a constant state of stress and anxiety trying to make ends meet and it slowly wore me down. I couldn't analyse it into clear thoughts in those days; couldn't untangle or understand my feelings and dreaded what might come next, worrying how we would shift all our belongings when we had to leave each home, and filled with a muddle of unexpressed emotions churning around inside me.

Realising how many millennia-old skills were being lost incredibly rapidly in the 20th century I began to learn how to bake my own bread, loving the feel of something living in my hands as I kneaded the dough, and to learn about plants and herbs and trees, trying to incorporate wild food into some of our meals. I was trying to bring something lost back into our life.

The Barsham Faires gave way to the Albion Fairs in East Anglia. They were no longer medieval but still to a large extent non-electric and performing at them became a large part of our life. Each fair had a theme – earth, air, fire and water; sun, moon, rainbow, trees, zodiac.... In preparation for each I found myself going into long periods of meditative space where I would connect deeply with the theme, then emerge with a structure and ideas for the performance.

The Moon Fair affected me deeply. I am a fiery Leo and had always been a Sun person, not really connecting with the moon and dark night. Living in London one rarely saw them amongst the tall buildings and sodium-lit streets anyway. Discovering the energy and cycles of the moon as our powerful 'sister' enabled me to enter fully into the reality of being a woman, learning how the moon affected the rhythms of my own body and its watery dark depths, waking up to my real identity as a woman, and in this there was a powerful and real magic which at times manifested in our performances. Each performance was a story and, in a way, a journey. What I didn't realise at the time was that I was also on a journey of spiritual development and a self-initiation into the deep mysteries of woman-hood and woman magic, and our human interaction with the rhythms of the earth and universe.

At ancient sites we would sit waiting for the sun to rise and this was my first experience of being out with the creatures of the night and those which awoke with the day, knowing that cold hour which comes before dawn, colder than the rest of the night; the chill breeze which stirs everything as the thought of the sun's rising blows across the land.

Jill and Bruce at the Albion Rainbow Fair

I discovered the need to shape these trips into journeys with a purpose, feeling the sites weren't separate from each other but linked into a living network which had once needed humans to keep the links alive and tend the sacred landscapes. I began taking 'gifts' from one site to the next to link them back into a powerful network. I would take water from sacred wells (such as Chalice Well in Glastonbury) with which to anoint ancient stones to bring back some of that original connection to the life-force from which modern life had severed them. We would do our ceremonies 'for real' and then re-enact them for the camera, creating documentation to display on the walls of galleries in later exhibitions. We drove to the ancient sites in our truck full of props and costumes without pre- planning what we would do, but let the site speak to us, then evolved something we felt the place wanted.

For several years I celebrated my birthday at Waylands Smithy long barrow on the Ridgeway Path in Berkshire. I sent out invitations and people came from all over. I called the events 'A Smith at the Smithy', a picnic where everything had something to do with 'Smith' – Granny Smith apples, Smiths crisps, John Smiths beer etc. In early August it was also a celebration of the place, the Celtic festival of Lughnasadh/Lammas and the harvest. With our children we would stay there a few days, camping near the long barrow and sometimes we

24

would lie on the barrow itself for hours watching the Perseid meteor shower which comes at that time of year. I loved that site, with its tall trees arching over the barrow. These were blown down in the great wind of 1987, leaving it bare and more as it must have originally been, when it was surely a white gash of chalk gleaming in the sun and moonlight, a walk away from the magnificent Uffington white horse.

In 1978 my grandmother died aged 98. It was the first time I'd sat with someone as they died. I was glad she had lived long enough for us to become close, for had she died when I was a teenager I would probably have hated her for ever, as she had by then become something of an ogre in my life, ridiculing all I cared about and forbidding me from doing anything which was normal for my age; but time and my own maturity had enabled me to understand her and the ways in which she sometimes behaved. I had known I would be left half her 'estate', but was surprised to realise it might be enough to buy somewhere in East Anglia. It wasn't anywhere near enough to buy a place in London, but I was pretty desperate by then to get out of the city.

Years before, when Bruce and I were first looking for somewhere to live together, we had gone further and further from London in our search. It was amazing what had still been available in the mid-60s: in one place a row of houses with no electricity or track to them were going for £50 each. A little thatched cottage called 'Dingle Dell' caught my heart. I had £1,000 left to me from when my parents died, but Dingle Dell cost £1,200 and there was no way I could borrow the extra £200, so that dream had to be abandoned. We then found an old Co-op shop and abattoir in Bungay, Suffolk which we could have rented for £5 a week. An architect friend of Bruce's drew up plans for us to have it converted, but in the end we just chickened out of being that far from London. In 1966/67 Bruce didn't know how he would get work out of the city and I still had a townie's irrational fears of the country, with visions of Tiffany, who was then a baby, lying dead in a ditch or something. We didn't in the end pursue it, went back to London and rented the place between the Holloway and Caledonian Roads where Bruce had to climb on the roof to mend it.
Had we moved to Bungay then, maybe we would have been in at the birth of the Barsham Faires. But it seems we had to go through a whole process of change in London to come to the point where we were the Elemental Co-ordinators and were ready to live in East Anglia.

So in 1978/79 we looked at what was available for my new lot of money. One place was full of chickens, the owner pointing out that it had a very good roof and suggesting we could build new walls. Eventually, though, we found two little semi-detached cottages with lots of out-buildings, a small animal yard and one and a fifth acres of land which included the remnants of an old orchard. Brentwood Farm was right on a busy road, the B1135 between Wymondham and Ashwellthorpe , and seemed perfect. After a protracted, and I'm not sure

25

properly legal, telephone auction, it became mine, but as we were married – ours.

Well, we had our three-and-a-half ton ex-GPO truck and I bought a little yellow Morris 1000, also ex- GPO, which for the first time in decades brought me a little independence, though I could only find my way around London by following familiar bus routes. Every weekend we would drive a load from London, late on a Friday night, up the M11 and A11 in convoy to the little place which had once been an 11-acre farm. We unloaded everything and drove back on the Sunday so Tiffany and Saffron could go to school on Monday. There was no electricity, no running water - just a well outside at the back. We would arrive late at night in the dark, light oil-lamps and candles and sit round a card-table to eat and talk. Some of those weekends were the happiest of my life at that time.

In the late '70s factory farming was spreading like a disease over an East Anglia which had used horses only a decade or two before. A local farmer owned the land on either side of our place and had to bring his tractors and other equipment out onto the road from one field to get into the next. He bought the 11-acre farm so he could turn it into one big field and wouldn't have to go out on the road between the two, selling off the buildings and little bit of land to us. One weekend during our move we arrived to find that he had grubbed up and burned all the trees from the old orchard. All that were left were the few on our little patch. There wasn't even any wood left which we could have used on our fire. It was heartbreaking.

After three and a half months, everything had gone from Hackney and we made our final move. Kevin was about 17 by then and wanted to stay in London. He and I didn't have a good relationship when he was a teenager and I wasn't in the mental state to sort any of it out, not really understanding my own reactions to things. Tiffany was nearly 13, having a good social life in Hackney, going to ice-skating and lots else and with a place in what was then a very desirable comprehensive. She never understood why we had to leave London, but I had to put the money I'd received into property or would have had to spend it on rent and it would have been gone. Saffron had been having a bad time at school anyway, so maybe it was better for her. She was just 10 and when we moved she went to a little school round the corner. The day when we finally left London Tiffany kept listening to Capitol Radio until the signal finally faded to nothing. She vowed she would return as soon as she was old enough, but as I write she hasn't.
I had lived all those years having to rent places, never having any security (especially in bed-sits I'd been thrown out of several times, the most spectacular being just after Kevin was born) and had all that time longed to own my own place. We had never before had enough capital to buy anywhere, and being poor and self-employed, couldn't get a mortgage.

There was a lot wrong with my life really: things I had dreamed of had crumbled to dust. I wasn't very happy in my relationship with Bruce, but we were creative together and the years had flown by. I kept thinking 'if only this were different, if only that were different, then everything would be alright. If only we had our own house, our own bedroom, if only, if only, if only...

Was this the dream coming true? Would I be happy at last? I had such dreams of how it would be in the little cottages with the bit of land and the few fruit trees...would this be the last 'if only'?...

Chapter 2: In the Country at Last.

At first it was amazing. Having performed the cycles of nature for several years I was now becoming a true part of them; drawing water from the well rather than a tap, drinking it to become part of my body, then peeing it out onto the earth so it became part of Her body again, returning what I had taken with thanks. This was what humans had done until so recently in our existence, being a complete part of the whole. Around this time I began to think of the earth as She, the Mother, the mother I had never had maybe.

But of course, Tiffany and Saffron wanted a more 'normal' life. Bruce plumbed in running water and wired the place for electricity. I cried the first time the electric light was switched on and shone into those corners of the little cottages which had never seen anything but sunlight, moonlight, oil lamps and candles; which had nurtured their mysterious shadows and secrets since the day they were built. The house with no water or electricity had been perfect for me; now a bit of my dream had been chipped away.

Bruce made a door between the two cottages so it became one house. At one side there was a little kitchen garden which I should have started to cultivate before doing anything else, but I felt driven to have a go at a bigger bit of land which had been part of a small field. We turned one fifth of an acre into a paddock and in another fifth I decided to grow food.

Although it had been a tiny farm, there had been chemicals used on the land and even though small, I knew it would take years to become 'clean'. Initially it was very hard to dig: by hand, by foot, by spade, learning it all from a book. I dug the rows for potatoes by moonlight, needing to get it done, and planted vegetables which had to fight huge battles with weeds, slugs, birds etc. I had taken on too big a space for a beginner, doing it on my own. I had dreamed that the whole family would work on it together but it didn't turn out like my dream.

We bought a goat, Sarny Sou, a British Saanen, and I fell in love with her, feeling she was almost human, or had been, or would be in her next incarnation. I developed a complex relationship with her, as though she were my mother, my self and my child. She was like a mother, giving me milk; like my self worrying about losing my breast milk when my daughters were tiny; and like my child, for she was dependent on me to feed and look after her. I loved going out in the cold early mornings, giving her a bowl of soaked sugar-beet pulp and burying my face in her warm flank as I milked her.

We had some bantam chickens in a long run which had occasionally to be moved, and I did need help with that. There was an enormous amount of fruit on the trees: cooking apples, eating apples and tiny little red Robin Pea pears. We had not long joined the Common Market and they had 'banned' many indigenous British fruits from general sale. There was a weekly auction in Wymondham and people were eager to buy any of this traditional produce which was dying out quite fast. I planted some plum trees. There were lots of blackberries. I made gallons of wine and pounds and pounds of jam – mixing just a little of some other fruit with the Bramleys. When the vegetables grew, I made pickle. When there was a glut of eggs I made lemon curd. I pickled walnuts (one of my favourite foods) and even pickled ash keys. I believed that if I didn't use everything which Nature provided then she might not give it again.

And I made the best bread ever. There was a scullery and a very basic kitchen with a tiled floor. In the wall of the kitchen was an oven fuelled by wood. I learned to tell its temperature from the heat of the metal door. Although at times it was stressful there did seem to be so much I wanted from life at last coming together.

Bruce set up a smithy in one of the outbuildings and we started to learn blacksmithing. I was a Leo. I was a Smith, and particularly good at keeping the fire at the right heat. We made things for our performances and I did surprisingly well, my arms still being strong in those days.

Although this is jumping on a bit, towards the end of my time there I began to learn basket-making from an apprentice of one of East Anglia's famed makers – Ronnie Woods. On my maternal grandfather's side, basket-making had been my family's trade in London. A & G Walden Bros. Of St John Street, EC1, they had made industrial baskets for hospitals, the GPO and had various Government contracts. As a child I had gone for days to 'the office' and can still remember the smell of the willow soaking in huge tanks.

Our performances changed in subtle ways. Instead of buying materials from shops and garden centres we could now use things from our own land: food I'd grown, eggs from our chickens, milk from our goat, water from our well, and our own earth, it all becoming even more real and powerful. In London I had made costumes of artificial fabrics bought from market stalls, but now made them from natural materials such as unbleached cotton and muslin. I dyed them - tie-dyeing, sew-dyeing, dipping etc, having the space outdoors for this now, and it became my new art-form. Eventually I dyed some of them with natural stuff: onion skins, walnut husks etc. One year I even grew woad but though I did have the complex recipe for turning it into a dye-stuff, I sadly never got round to doing that.

A Moon performance for the Albion Moon Fair

Back in the early '70s I had started to go blonde to better fit in with my then brightly coloured clothes and Biba make-up. Now I bleached it almost white and dyed it temporary colours to go with the theme of each fair – the Rainbow one being especially stunning. As a Leo I worked with fire a lot and often wore it on my head.

When we travelled around the country I took Sarny Sou in the back of my Morrie. She would never sit down so I had to drive very carefully, especially on roads with lots of roundabouts, but I couldn't take her more than 100 miles or her milk would go down. We kept her first daughter (Gina) and she would happily sit down in the van as she'd done it all her life. We took them to all the fairs, being away maybe a week or more.

Although we were performing at most of the fairs, we never did become part of 'the fair people', living quite a way north of the Waveney Valley where most of them were based. Sandra and Andy Bell, who seemed to be at the core of the whole East Anglian scene, were planning to move away to begin a very different life. Maybe being part of something had all been an illusion. Even at the fairs we were never really part of the social scene, having to stay in our own area with all our performance structures, props and 'Palaeolithic tent', not able to go and have a wild rave at the evening events and the beer tent. Our children had more of a social life there than we did. Bruce didn't want me just disappearing off on my own to have a good time, so there wasn't much opportunity for fun and things were not really how I had thought they would be.

Bruce went to events in Norwich, meeting new people, but they weren't really people I related to and I began to find others with whom I had more in common. I was becoming isolated from my own family, living in a world inside my own head with interests which seemed to be pulling me in other directions, things happening to me on a really fundamental level. Calling it spirituality sounds too much of the mind; this was more a deep learning at the very core of my being: my body, my spirit, my heart, my soul, my absolute relationship with the vastness of everything; with the earth, plants, trees, animals and birds; with sky, weather, sun, rain and wind; with the patterns and movements of moon, stars and the dark night sky; with the cycles of growth and decay, and the powerful energy which flows through the land. It was as though the whole of nature was teaching me, as though I was receiving direct transmission from everything about everything.

It wasn't rational. It wasn't just in my head. It was crazy and wild. I struggled to make any sense of it, and though it was a fantastic experience, it was tough. My 'woman magic' and identity as a woman were also becoming more alive and I was drawn to people who could understand this world inside me.

The power of Neolithic and Bronze Age sites and their network across the land became part of my being. My awareness of those ancestors, those wise people who had constructed that network, called me powerfully to become even closer to them. I needed more and more to be by myself. My little yellow van gave me the freedom to drive off for a bit and sit with my own head, often writing reams, both to myself and others, trying to fathom it all out. I would go for walks alone, seeing and sensing everything with this new awareness and began to realise how much Bruce had kept me in a cage, not wanting me to have any sort of life apart from him. I needed time on my own and to be in the company of others who understood and most of all I needed to be with the ancient and sacred places of the land; and I no longer wanted to be at those places with

Cailleach, West Kennet

Bruce. His energy seemed to conflict with that of the land and with the state in which I now found myself.

Another thread entered my life at this point. I was introduced to the Dzog Chen (Tibetan) Buddhist teachings which were being taught to Westerners by the late Tibetan master Namkhai Norbu Rinpoche. These seemed to resonate with me clearly, not seeming in any way alien. Norbu had left Tibet at the same time as the Dalai Lama, becoming a Professor at Naples University. People discovered he was a Dzog Chen master and after much soul-searching he decided to pass on the teachings to Westerners. I liked the fact that he wasn't all dressed up, sitting on a throne, expecting thousands of prostrations before him. He just sat on a chair in ordinary Western clothes, making himself accessible. These teachings are known as the 'direct path'. You get it all thrown at you and it is your responsibility to commit to the teachings and work with them.

I was introduced to the teachings before receiving transmission from him, but this did get me into the routine of celebrating each dark and full moon, giving a shape and pattern to the rhythm of my new life and helping to ground the enormous upheaval which was going on in my reality.

An important event also was meeting Lynne (Sinclair) Wood, an Australian artist who had been in Britain a few years, visiting Neolithic and other sacred sites. She took me down to West Wales to meet the Swedish goddess-artist Monica Sjoo who was living there at the time. This began to focus my sense of the earth being 'She' into a concept of 'goddess' and the politics of being a woman, enabling me to find the strength of the woman-spirit within me. I didn't have a concept of Goddess as a kind of female God, nor have I ever taken on the vast world-wide pantheon of goddesses, apart from a few who seem to personify the spirit of place, and I use the word very little now, but at the time it was a way of clarifying my new way of relating to things.

It became difficult for me to be in the house, especially in the evenings as the others sat watching television with the electric light on. I loved cooking, especially with the food I was growing, but after supper just wanted to be outside on my own, watching the sun set, the moon rise and the twilight turn to dark. I no longer wanted to sleep indoors and began spending the nights under the little goat shelter we'd built in the paddock. (The goats went into the small animal yard at night). I wanted just to be in a sleeping-bag on the earth, feeling the shape of it beneath me as I curled my body round its humps and bumps. For the first time I watched dew form - in the silence even hearing the sound of it - and sometimes watching that dew turn to frost.

To begin with I wore clothes inside the sleeping-bag with a couple of coats on top, then as summer grew took more and more clothes off, after a while not even wanting to sleep under the shelter, and it became a form of sacred experience. For one year (1980) I photographed every sunrise moment from the same spot, whether it was clear enough to actually see or not. I would stand there, knowing it was coming, and all of nature would become still and silent and watch and wait with me. They too knew it was coming. It was awesomely beautiful, as though we shared a secret which then became manifest. In flat East Anglia there was a single tree on the horizon and as the position of the sunrise moved first north and then south with the turning of the year, so the tree moved one way and then the other across my photographs. The colours changed. The local farmer grew rape seed and it blazed brilliant yellow, then faded. It was a deep experience to watch that movement, that cycle, and be part of it. I later exhibited the photographs in a long line round the walls of a Norwich gallery. They were mounted on black Canford paper and I kept them

Front of the invitation card for our second exhibition at the Acme gallery

with me through many subsequent moves, finally putting them on a bonfire
when I left our home on Lewis in 1996. They had become by then too buckled
and damaged to exhibit, but I still have the 35mm slides on which they were
originally photographed.

The moon's movements are much more complex than those of the sun and I hadn't even begun to understand them, but at least I was now watching the crescent grow from dark, become so quickly full and bright out there in the country, then shrink through the waning crescent to dark again.

Reading back over fragments written in old diaries I am surprised to realise how stressed I was in 1981, suffering what now seems to be clinical depression. I was totally lacking in energy, exhausted, unable to cope with all the work we were doing: all the fairs and that year, a major exhibition at the Serpentine Gallery in London, the smaller one in the Norwich, then another major one at the Acme gallery in Covent Garden. Since then, I have forgotten how I felt at that time, remembering only the positive. Little survives of what I wrote, but I seem to have been overwhelmed, worried sick about the goats, wanting simply to be with the earth, my plants, trees and animals; rushing about here, there and everywhere, but needing just to be still, feeling claustrophobic and trapped. I wanted desperately to go off on my own, to drive off and get away, yet at that point not seeming able to. I would be totally down, unable to do anything at all, then suddenly full of a new energy and happiness, able to do everything which had to be done, and my goodness, so much did get done that year!

The Serpentine exhibition (Cycles of the Serpent) was a bad experience. We created a serpentine structure out of long poles and in and on it placed objects, photos etc. about the turning cycles of the year as we lived them at Brentwood Farm. I had a lot of personal writing in it; lots of photographs of the plants, vegetables, fruit, goats, chickens and the important events in our country calendar. I made 'ladies' representing the elements (and me), and dressed them in my costumes.

Bruce asked for some display stands and exhibited our goat and horse shit as 'sacred objects' (we were looking after a friend's pony). I felt uncomfortable about this but didn't say anything and of course the media seized on it, there was a huge hoo-ha and the whole exhibition was ridiculed. I had put so much of my self into it and then had it turned into a joke. Bruce, the comedian, the professional British eccentric, had got publicity but destroyed my dream. I think this was one of many 'last straws' of the relationship as far as I was concerned. I often felt our performances were treated as a joke, and the more they became real for me, the more I wanted to withdraw from them being perceived that way.

However, later in the year, the Acme exhibition was filled with a massive energy which strengthened my ability to be myself. For years I had felt trapped in my marriage and working relationship, with no real friends or life outside it, but feared walking away into a void. But after the Acme I started to have a life of my own, went out with others and got to know many more people. It was at this point that the Dzog Chen teachings and Goddess concepts became a big part of my life, bringing a different focus and direction to all my random craziness, which now started to fall into some kind of pattern and shape. But it was only a start.

During the winter of '81/'82 I was swept along by a tide of inevitability, no longer having to make decisions. I flew free of the cage and just followed where there seemed no doubt. I can't now find records of exactly what I did or where I went, but made my first excursions into the landscape alone. In the early days I drove to them in my Morrie van but then began to go off on foot. Previously I had been driven everywhere by Bruce, and hadn't travelled on public transport, apart from London buses and underground, and that one train journey to get the seaweed, so finding out how to get about on my own without driving was a huge challenge.

Going to Avebury and the West Kennet long barrow by train and bus, I felt so liberated, so much more in control of my life. I slept for the first time in West Kennet and realised it was like the vagina and womb of the earth: the old winter mother receiving and holding the spirits of the dead, maybe from there enabling their birth into another dimension: a place of death and rebirth and for shamanic initiation - a different kind of death and rebirth. I was finding myself so completely at one with the earth that I became the earth, so being inside the long barrow was like being inside my own body, the ancient ancestral body of the Winter Hag. There was nothing to fear, for how could I fear my own body, how could I fear the body of the Great Mother?

The Tibetan Dzog Chen teachings seemed so familiar that I thought the Neolithic belief-system of these islands could have come from the same roots as that of the pre-Buddhist Bon religion of Tibet. Here too perhaps the bones of the ancestors had been excarnated, used as sacred objects, put in the long barrow and taken out for ceremonies; femurs used for thigh-bone trumpets, skulls used as bowls or skinned over to make drums. This was the winter, the night and the dark, and outside were the black skies and stars. And this was my reality now.

There were not so many visitors to the long barrow in those days, at least not in the winter dark. A few groups turned up in the evening, surprised to find me there, but then I would have the place to myself. I half-slept, half-dreamed and had things that were more visions than dreams. I saw a group of elders dressed in white sitting in a circle chanting, with a line of light from the outside shining along the 'vagina' of the barrow to the centre of their circle. I was close to those ancestors, those ancient people who gathered for the ceremonies of the night, who had called out to me all those years before.

One of the panels of documentation on the Acme gallery walls during our exhibition

I had a sleeping-bag and rug and wore lots of clothes, by now used to being outdoors. Aware of the cold I was learning to wrap it around me like a blanket so the essential 'me' stayed warm on the inside and wasn't cold. It was a form of practice. I had little to eat or drink, so these nights out became like vision quests. I was in an altered state of reality anyway (no drugs!) but this was becoming my norm.

In the mornings I would walk to the top of the hill where the ancient Ridgeway Path meets the A4, because in those days there was one of my 'best caffs in Britain'. It was a truck-drivers cafe where they would stay over-night, so was open early for breakfast and late into the evening. They didn't seem to mind if I sat there for hours drinking tea, thawing out, coming into the day, before walking back to Avebury and, if I was going home, the Swindon bus and the train back to London. I returned often to Avebury and other places in Wiltshire and Berkshire during this time of discovery.

It was very strange for my daughters who didn't understand at all what was going on. I didn't myself, though it seemed everything I was doing just had to be. I had no way of putting it into words or communicating it to them. I'd been a brilliant mother to babies and little children, maybe because I had had a mother until I was two, but I'd had no role model for motherhood of teenagers and hadn't learnt the right communication skills. To them I was becoming a different person, but I felt that at last I was becoming the real me. It was a very difficult time and the intervening years haven't made it any easier. That was one very sad aspect my new life, even though I was making friends with people who understood without my having to explain.

When it came near mid-winter and Christmas I heard there was to be a retreat with the Tibetan master, Norbu, in Sardinia. I knew I had to go, to receive transmission of the practices I'd been doing without it, which hadn't been correct, though my practice was becoming powerful, strong and clear. I had one last thing inherited from my parents which might be of some value, put it in an auction and got a couple of hundred pounds.

Sardinia was warm in winter and as I was now rejecting buildings almost completely I just slept outside. Sardinia had many houses and buildings which were 'organic' in shape, with no straight walls or corners and I adored them. It was good to be there when there were no tourists.

The teachings were quite advanced, but made absolute sense, and many practices I used straight away to help me with difficult situations in life. Even though many years later I have got out of the way of formal practice, some essence of those Sardinia teachings stays as a fundamental part of me and has got me through some really hard times since. Anyone wishing to know more about the teachings should contact the Dzog Chen community for direction.

I returned to an incredibly cold winter in England and got flu!

It was the first time I'd left my family for Christmas. They must have thought I was being incredibly selfish but I felt I had no choice. For so many years I had carried the burden of Christmas alone, spending months preparing for it with little money, buying the same number of presents for each child, spending the same amount on each and becoming exhausted by the whole thing. It felt like an enormous relief not to have to do it all that year, though I'm sure I'd bought presents and set a lot of it up before I left.

By now I was getting to know the sacred places of the land on a very deep level, including those in East Anglia. Here there were old churches which had been built on the much older sacred sites of a pre-Christian people and were full of ancient power. It was a potent time.

My air costume on one of the 'ladies' on our structure at the Serpentine gallery. The zodiac discs which would later form part of the Gypsy Switch journey.

1982 came. Once again I did the Arts Council application for our Guarantee Against Loss. We had to give them the schedule of all we planned to do in the forthcoming year, and then stick to it, even if we wanted to go off in a different direction. This time we were turned down. On one level it was totally shattering, as the money had not only provided all the costs for our performance work, but had paid to keep our vehicles on the road and a percentage of our telephone and electricity bills. But on another level, although it scared me, it also freed me from being trapped in my working partnership with Bruce. I was no longer tied to a year-long schedule of work with him. I was free.

I organised a lovely exhibition with a group of artists at a small gallery in Brighton and in preparation spent some nights out on the Downs and in the great earthwork of Chanctonbury Rings, which was covered by a huge canopy of trees. It was a terrible shock to return some years later to find nearly all of them had fallen in that same wind of 1987 which brought down the trees at Waylands Smithy, but there again, it probably looked more as it had in the days when it had been built. It had been utterly magic there in the dark, under that whispering canopy; a memory I shall never forget.

While we were living in London, I had been strongly pulled to visit the Callanish Stones on the Isle of Lewis in the Western Isles of Scotland, but we had never gone. In 1980 and '81 a group of artists and photographers we knew went there and stayed some weeks each time. They had tried to persuade us to join them, but some of their strange stories had put us off and in hindsight I am very glad I didn't go then; with Bruce.

One year, when they returned, I was sitting with Saffron in a tent at the 'Faerie Faire' in Norfolk when one of the artists – Keith Payne – called by and told us of a mountain which could be seen from the Callanish stones : 'The Sleeping Beauty' resembled the profile of a sleeping woman and every 19 years, at the major southerly lunar standstill, the low rising moon emerges re-born from her body. Hearing about this affected me deeply and from that moment, not only Callanish, but this sleeping mountain, began to fill my awareness, calling me strongly to go to them.

In 1982 Keith and the writer John Sharkey were about to set off on a journey up the whole of the Outer Hebrides, visiting all the ancient sites in the Islands, writing a book to be called 'The Road Through The Isles' (Wildwood 1986). A whole group of people including Monica, and Lynne who had been part of the '80/'81 group, were going to meet up with them at Callanish for the Summer Solstice. It seemed as though this was the time I must go to the Islands and the mountain: the call was so strong I could no longer resist. However, it was so overpowering I felt I couldn't just pop up there like a tourist, believing this to be the greatest pilgrimage of my life. I heard of a concept, originally Lynne's, which seemed to be the journey I must make. I was by now perceiving the whole of Britain as the body of a great creation ancestress lying in the sea; the body of the great goddess, the body of Albion.

It was thought that certain key sites right up her body - from toe-tip to brow - corresponded to specific places in one's own body. I felt them to be not so much chakras but the 'places' in a Dzog Chen purification practice I'd been doing. It all rang totally true and the form of the pilgrimage I must make to finally reach Callanish at the Brow of Britain. I needed journeys to have a shape, structure and purpose, and this was perfect, absolutely what I must do. I would rise up through these sites in the body of the land, carry out the purification practice at each and in the places in my own body. I would link them into a line of light and carry it to Callanish. I was going to the Islands at last.

The sites were:

Feet: Boscawen-Un in Cornwall; Base/genitals: Avebury in Wiltshire; Centre/solar plexus: Arbor Low in Derbyshire; Heart: Castlerigg in Cumbria; Throat: Twelve Apostles in Dumfries and Galloway; Brow: Callanish on the isle of Lewis.

I also felt I must pause at Glastonbury on the way.

Chapter 3: Awakening

My life changed completely over that winter of '81 and the early months of '82. A friend said later that it had been like watching a butterfly emerge from a chrysalis, but my real self was emerging - from my own shadow; a shadow I had lived in for much of my life.

It was a heady time, a time of massive expectation, excitement and crazy wildness as a totally different experience of reality unfolded, my earlier perceptions seemingly having been covered in endless veils, all the veils now flying off. I was experiencing everything with such glorious intensity that it was hard to keep hold of any part of my previous normality.

Nowadays, it has all been absorbed into a more balanced sense of the real, yet it is hard sometimes not to feel a little envious of 'her': that vibrant me of the early '80s But I know what pain went with it and wouldn't want to live through that again.

I became more and more an outdoor person; rejecting even a tent to sleep in. In a tent I felt as cut off from the outside as if in a house: I wanted to lie watching the moon and stars and to feel the breeze on my face. When I visited people I often slept in their gardens, and once, when staying with Lynne in London, as I rolled out my sleeping-bag on her floor, dried leaves fell out and she said it was as though I had come from the realm of faerie.

Builders merchants sold different thicknesses of wide plastic sheeting and I bought several yards of a kind which was thick enough so I wouldn't put my finger through it, yet thin enough to fold up small and not take up much space in my rucksack. I had to use this when it rained, making a kind of bag in which I could lie with all my stuff, tucking it round me with just a little hole near the ground which I could hold open to breathe.

I spent much of the early months of '82 with my Dzog Chen community friends. I would drive up to the A11, turn left and whizz down to London in my little van. That junction, so clear in my memory, has now been by-passed and to travel up the new road and not see it is quite disorientating. I spent time with people with whom I now seemed to have much in common; freed from the constraints of my marriage I began to make new friends and form friendships with people who had previously only been acquaintances.

As Spring moved towards Summer, I began to prepare for my great pilgrimage. I wasn't going to drive, didn't have time to walk all the way and hadn't yet learned the skills of hitching. At nearly 40, finding my way was exciting. I discovered the wonder of National Express coaches, which were very cheap, and would turn up at a bus/coach station, ask how to get somewhere, buy a ticket and be off. I would get near to each site on my journey, walk the last miles in pilgrimage, then stay for several days, immersing myself completely in the spirit of the place.

Seeing the whole of Britain as a giant figure lying sleeping in the ocean, I felt the Great Mother waiting for me to travel her huge body and the compulsion towards the journey was enormous, as though I were following some path laid out for me many lifetimes before. I stepped onto it and travelled with no uncertainty, not questioning anything of what I intended to do.

What would I take? Bruce gave me an old canvas rucksack which was just a big bag without any sort of frame, not long and thin like modern ones which cling to your back. If you pack these with the weight close to you and high up it makes the load feel much lighter and easy to carry, but the old one was heavy, hard to pack efficiently and dragged down on my neck, shoulders and back.

However, it was what I had.

In 'researching' my own past I found a list I made when preparing to leave. What I eventually took was close to this and similar to the lists I make today, even for much lesser journeys. I had no tent. I took one or two folded sheets of the plastic, a sleeping-bag, and a woven cotton rug which I would roll up and tie on top of the rucksack. Nowadays I wear good strong boots and thick socks when I'm walking, needing to support my ankles, but on that journey all I had was a pair of little black cotton shoes with a buttoned strap. They were very popular at the time – were they tai chi shoes?

Sometimes I wore thin socks with them, but mostly just my bare feet inside. I wore two skirts, which was how I dressed anyway: a long cotton one to my ankles and a knee-length wrap-around one tied over the top. I took some trousers, though I can't remember what they were like - I don't think there were combat trousers or even jogging bottoms in those days. I took knickers, but didn't always wear them (less washing) and had given up wearing a bra. I had a few t-shirts and one jumper and a lovely patchwork padded cotton jacket which had faded from being out in the sun so much.

I had a scarf made from 'Ancient Smith' tartan bought years before in Edinburgh but no gloves or hat. The list says 'toothbrush/paste, soap, flannels, washing powder, talc, deodorant; Anne French Skin Milk, which I used most

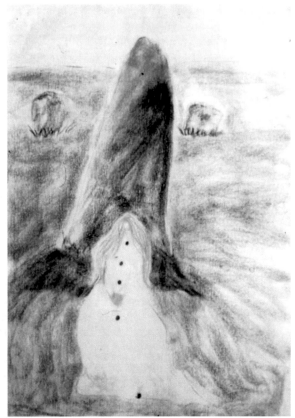

My image of the Frock Maiden at Boscawen Un circle in Cornwall

of my life as a cleanser; cotton wool, mascara, mirror, comb'. I seem also to remember taking green eye-shadow. I took a road map of Britain, buying OS maps of each area as I got to it. A sharp knife, needles and cotton, Elastoplast, elastic bands, Post Office book, money, scissors, exercise books to write in, pens, drawing book, plain postcards, envelopes, stamps, information on phases of the moon, address book and personal letters. I took my old Pentax camera which had become part of me and which had documented everything I'd done for years. I knew though, that I didn't want to document this journey, didn't want to experience everything through the camera lens, but directly with all my senses. I would just photograph the journey of what I called 'The Frock' and thought that when it was over I would try to create drawings of all I had experienced as a way of sharing it with others.

A big part of what I aimed to do was to carry out the Dzog Chen practice of purification at each site, this being also my own personal spiritual journey.

Having pretty well given up public performance I no longer felt the need for elaborate costumes; however, for this journey I made a kind of 'frock' from unbleached muslin. It covered my head and face as well as my body. Onto each place, which would correspond when I was wearing it to the places on my body I would purify during the practice, I sewed a felt disc in the appropriate Tibetan colour, and on each drew the appropriate Tibetan symbol. I intended to do the practice in each place on the land, wearing the 'frock', then remove the disc, leave it somewhere on or near the site and replace it with some little plant, an exchange which felt vitally important to me.

So, I also took: The Frock, nightlights and matches, 'any relevant rocks', and plastic bags and labels for small objects I would collect on my way. When making journeys between sites, I would take some small thing from one place as a gift to the next, in order to make that link and help re-awaken the flow of life and energy between one place and another, and keep tiny but potent things for use on altars, performance pieces, exhibitions or future journeys, but never to in any way endanger the sites or their ecology.

My list also said: bottle of water and 'food as I come by it'. I collected 'ephemera' en route: bus tickets, timetables, paper bags with interesting addresses on, and little packets of sugar which, sadly, in the intervening years, have dissolved and turned some of the other things into a sticky mess.

Still living at Brentwood Farm, when I set off I imagined I would return, though I could only see a future as far as the journey, could not even imagine what would come after. We had been planning the second Faerie Faire at Lyng; I had booked all the performers, and made a promise that I would come back for it, seeing this journey as a longer version of what I had been doing for months.

I didn't feel I was walking out on my family or abandoning my daughters, as they had their home and their father and our lives had become very separate anyway. I think, naively, I imagined they might be proud of me, might think it exciting to have a mother who went off on such adventures, rather than being dull, boring and grey. I thought it was about time Bruce took on some of the routine, day- to-day things of being a parent; things which had always been left up to me. And as I say, I felt I had no choice.

I was worried about leaving Sarny Sou. She'd had kids that Spring and wasn't well. I had taken her to the vet who said she had some retained placenta but he couldn't do anything about it. Gina had also had kids but rejected them, and Sarny Sou had taken on feeding those as well as her own. I had to trust the others to look after her.

45

So, on the 19th of May 1982 I set off for London. At dawn on the 21st I went with my friend Julia to Primrose Hill where we did a lot of Tibetan practice and sat quietly as the sun rose high through the mist of a very hot day. My bag was heavy and I quickly got blisters on my feet as I travelled to Victoria Coach Station and found there was a bus to the South West within an hour. I was desperate to escape the clutches of London, on a wave, being carried by a momentum beyond my control. The coach was unbearably hot and I dozed off into a strange state of otherworldlyness. I got to Exeter and waited for another coach to Penzance, chatting for a long time with a guy with a surfboard who worked on the St. Ives beach for the summer. By the time we reached Penzance it was fully dark and raining that fine, misty rain which gets into everything, but which was a relief from the heat of the journey. A taxi driver did his best to dissuade me from walking, but I knew this had to be my first pilgrimage. I had to shake off the reality of the speeding coach and settle myself into the state of Cornwall.

It was Dark Moon night as I walked 3 or 4 miles in the unbelievable blackness. I put a plaster on my foot and it didn't hurt any more. It had seemed fitting to have a pain in my foot down in this foot of Britain. I plodded on relentlessly, uphill, downhill, hardly able to see where I walked. There were powerful smells in the wet. I later wrote: "the rank, dank, sickly-sweet perfume of over-full blossom, rose-like, faintly corrupt, and wood-smoke from late night chimneys. The lush vegetation clung to me silently as I passed and tears of cold ran down my legs. Occasional passing car lights created white circular rainbows in the magical mist". Carrying my heavy load I hoped I would get thin and strong as I travelled.

I went up the lane to the Boscawen-Un circle, but in the dark with no torch couldn't find it. I had tried to keep my only pair of shoes free of puddles, but the lane was muddy so I took them off and walked bare-foot, ankle-deep in mud and cattle shit. I knew there was no point in hunting for the gap through to the circle, so found a wider, grassy bit of path and lay down there to sleep, removing my wettest things. I spent the night in a half sleep, half waking state with no more rain. I was here in the toe of Britain. My journey had begun.

The light came early and I was pleased to realise I could just lie down and sleep anywhere on the earth. The circle was easy to find in the daylight. The wet grass washed the mud from my feet and after a while a wind came up and I dried my wet clothes on gorse bushes.

I was excited, the blood pounding through my body and making my head hurt. I was overwhelmed by what I was doing and what lay ahead of me. To begin with the circle overpowered me and I found it hard to enter, but after a while that feeling eased and I began my practice and made my exchanges. I photographed the Frock under the central leaning stone, then put it on and

46

walked round the circle. As I carried out my practice it seemed the place in me and the place in the land became one. I removed the 'feet' disc from the Frock and found a place to leave it, then asked if I could take a gorse flower and sewed it on to the frock in the place where the disc had been.

Everything became as it should be. I saw my whole journey stretch ahead of me like a line of light snaking up Britain. I knew if I took it stage by stage, day by day, I would eventually get to the brow.

The sky was clear and blue. I sat outside the circle in a slight trance until evening. There were only two lots of visitors to the stones and I marvelled at how people make quite difficult journeys to sites, then having got there, don't seem to know what to do, and leave.

That night I slept under the central slanting stone and had vivid dreams. At one point I felt an animal jump on me, but there was nothing there. I had completely stepped out of every aspect of the life I had known and into this intense and totally different reality.

The next day I felt, as I still do, that down in the toe of Britain I was cut off from the rest of the land, so was anxious to get on with my journey. I packed up and walked back to Penzance. It was a glorious day. I bought post-cards and got coaches: Penzance to Plymouth; Plymouth to Exeter; Exeter to Taunton, and from there decided to walk in pilgrimage to Glastonbury.

To begin with it was a dual carriageway and endless houses, but after a while I was on the A361 and got as far as West Lyng, which, reminding me of the Faerie Faire at Lyng in Norfolk, seemed an appropriate place to stop. I'd walked 7 miles in two and a half hours, which didn't seem bad; my blistered feet not seeming to trouble me on the rest of the journey. I hopped through a gap in a hedge so I could sleep completely hidden in the long grass at the edge of a field. I always seemed to find these perfect places to sleep, tucking myself away where no-one would see me. I would sit (writing) until dusk came, as though I were just having a rest, then as it grew dark lie down, and in the morning be sitting up again (after picking the slugs off my neck) before anyone was about.

When I first woke I panicked about what I was doing, but after cleaning my teeth and having a basic wash with water from my bottle, this soon passed and I was on my way by 7.10am.

Walking on, I experienced with such intensity every flower I passed, every tree, every cloud, everything which seemed to be so vibrantly new, really as though I were being re-born, seeing it all with new eyes, seeing so much I had never noticed before – and all this without drugs! Osier beds, chats with basket-makers, Burrow Mump in the wind near a bridge where old men stood timelessly as they had for decades, soulful pansies in front gardens, stones on milk-bottle tops to deter birds from pecking, lines of pollarded willow trees like crazy Strewel Peters or maiden goddesses gone mad, a great grey heron rising from a ditch and flapping melancholically into a wood, an old hawthorn tree creaking as I passed, and they were making hay in Somerset while the sun shone.

In the reality of the journey, I was somehow separate from the 'normal' world I walked through. Still quite overwhelmed I wrote..."my life is changing with this journey...I have left things I will never return to...am slowly, slowly shedding layers and layers of past experience, layers of my past life as I rise through the land. The change is fundamental yet subtle, hard for anyone to understand without knowing how restricted I have been. As I rise I shed limitations and decades of conditioned response, yet it is in a way frightening. Freedom can be frightening when it is new".

I became happy in a way I had rarely known. I was enjoying myself. I love Somerset and began to have what felt like past-life memories – of being a child, maybe a boy, maybe of many childhoods in the rolling greenness of that area. I would walk a bit, then sit and have some water, eat anything I might have with me, write about what I was feeling and send postcards to friends. I bought a lot of postcards.

At one point I phoned home. I can't remember what was said, but this was when I realised I had actually left, that I wouldn't return and would have to find somewhere else to live when the journey was over. I worried then about my daughters and all I had left behind and a kind of chill ran through me. It hit me that I would have to spend the rest of my life alone, that now I really was alone.

I climbed a high, steep hill and slept near a row of trees before walking on to Glastonbury the next day.

Glastonbury was an important place to me. Bruce and I had been to the Tor many times for the Summer Solstice and it had been part of several smaller journeys I'd already made. It seemed the place to pause and assess what I was doing, to clarify things before moving on with a new sense of purpose; to slow down a bit. In later years I would sit by the Chalice Well and realise that all my past journeys were still going on somewhere, still vibrantly alive in some other bits of the multiverse.

I slept two nights on the Tor: the first in a hollow smelling of sheep piss and in cloud which kept rising and falling so that sometimes I was above 'the mists of Avalon' watching birds fly up and then back down into it again. In a way, I was flying too. Another night I slept at the foot of the Tor by some (I think) chestnut trees and dreamed there were horses on the Tor. I visited my beloved Chalice Well, which was a much more informal place in those days, lying for hours on the grass making 'days-eye' chains.

A friend, Ian, came from Cardiff to give me a lift to Avebury and we had an amazing day at nearby sites; places I'd never been to before, places I think I might never find again, as though they were in the realm of faerie. We saw a fox and a badger, walked near East Kennet and along an ancient dyke- way, picnicked in an otherworldly field and discovered a kind of bower with energy so intense it almost sent me spinning right up to the Hebrides there and then.

Ian drove me to Avebury and said goodbye. I walked across the circle to a solitary stone, lit a nightlight and fell asleep, only to wake up on fire. It burned a hole both in my sleeping-bag and my rug. Avebury seemed a very fiery place: the land's genitals indeed.

I was getting concerned at how tatty I was looking, longing to have clean hair. I washed my undies in the basins in the public toilets and when it was quiet, would have a quick wash of my smelly bits. I lay the washing to dry in the sun and took any chance to fill my water bottle. I carried a lot of water and water is very heavy. I collected post from the Post Office. What a different world it was over 30 years ago. No mobile phones, (the bit of modern technology I'd never be without now) no internet, no instant communication. There were just coin-in-the-slot phone boxes if you could find one which wasn't broken, and mail sent 'Poste Restante' to wait until you arrived. The man at the original Post Office in Avebury got to know me over the years as I called to collect my post. Bruce and I had always visited the wonderful Mr. Perry who had another little shop and painted views of Avebury on anything he could get his hands on, wooden spoons, bits of hardboard etc, selling them very cheap, and painting the whole of his kitchen the same way. Laughed at by local children, he had a notice saying 'Mr. Perry will answer questions about anything except what the stones were for'. When we did ask, he would say "If I told you then everyone would know". Long, long gone, and what a touristy place Avebury is now.

I had two long, beautiful days there, just being. I found space to do my practice, photographing the Frock on the solitary stone and making my exchanges of coloured disc to little plant. I slept by the same stone for 3 nights, the sun rising in my eyes, but eventually became anxious to start moving North: beginning to feel Avebury was 'heavy' and I needed to fly.

It was May Bank Holiday. I hitched to Swindon and booked my coaches to Derbyshire. In those days there was a grassy hill behind the bus station where I sat waiting a long while in the heat. Crowds were playing radios on the dry grass. I was people-watching as though I were completely outside their reality:

49

Jill with Clive, Fiona and Jason at the Arbor Low 'camp'

there were young girls in frilly ra-ra skirts and slightly older girls in black skirts split to their thighs, pushing prams. It is strange to visit Swindon now and find the bus station changed, the grassy hill – so vivid in my memory – completely gone, replaced by a windy shopping mall.

As I started my journey North everything seemed brilliantly and boldly coloured, razor sharp and beautiful – even Spaghetti Junction and electricity pylons. My first coach went to Cheltenham and the next to Chesterfield, from where I was going to embark on another pilgrimage. Once there I bought soft insoles for my shoes, asked some taxi-drivers the way to Matlock and began a walk which in my memory is one of the most vivid times of my life.

The air was sweet and light and everything seemed fresh and clean. I was coming into high moorland smelling of delicate flowers and here and there kept seeing beautiful chestnut horses. I was born in the Year of the Horse and felt at one with them. People in passing cars stared at me, I didn't know why. Maybe to them I looked strange, but I felt that I was the one who was normal, walking as our ancient ancestors had, and they were the strange ones, speeding along in their metal boxes.

As it drew into evening, I slipped through a hole in a wall by a forestry plantation and found a soft place to sleep. The moon shone through the trees and the air smelled gummily of pine. This night, as never before, I truly snuggled into the body of the Earth my Mother and was blissfully content and felt absolutely protected.

Next day I walked on, at last really rising – both up through Britain and physically climbing on this particular piece of land. My spirit was flying. Everything felt majestic; I was with the majesty of the land. There was heather growing here, reminding me of the distant Islands at the end of my journey. I noticed trees budding and flowering, learning when things happen in nature as never before, yet it all had a familiarity, as though I were remembering everything from past lives, or recalling ancestral memories buried deep in my DNA. All my life up to this point seemed to have been lived deep in muddy, murky waters and now at last I had broken free to burst out into the clear air and the bright sunlight.

Hot and tired I found a lovely cool tearoom where I refreshed myself with cups of the blessed drink, then rested in a churchyard until the hot air lost some of its intensity. It felt as though this were the Heart of England, even though it was the stomach of my journey. Indeed I began to worry that I was eating too much, never mind that I was burning off a colossal amount of calories each day. I felt that people with caravans were like snails carrying their homes on their backs but I was even more of a snail with my home really on my back, for my rucksack had become my home. In it I carried what by then had become all my worldly goods. Sometimes I longed to be even freer – to walk with only a long coat in which I would wrap myself at night: a coat with deep pockets holding just a length of string, a knife and a bent pin; that I should be able to find food from whatever surrounded me and live as my ancestors had done; but for the time being I pad-padded along in my little shoes with my home on my back. I kept myself covered from the sun but my face and arms were getting very brown. I wondered if my greasy, bleached hair with its growing-out roots would eventually clean itself, as they say it does, and had visions of Celtic peoples who put lime on their hair, turning it triple-coloured: black, red and yellow.

Walking down from the high moor I felt like a horse negotiating a steep descent, and eventually reached the stone circle of Arbor Low. Here the stones lie flat like a clock-face within a bank and ditch. Were they always like this or were they laid down when whatever was the Neolithic purpose of the place was over? I know of no other stone circle like this except at Achmore on the isle of Lewis. It doesn't seem they could have just fallen over, for they don't lie randomly but all point outwards, as though some faerie whirlwind had spun round in the centre and knocked them down. On one part of the bank there is a

51

The Frock at Castlerigg.

tumulus, built at a later date, and nearby a large mound, rather like a mini version of Silbury Hill near the Avebury circle.

That evening I did feel this place was the navel of the land, sucking everything in like a giant black hole, then transmuting and throwing it all out again, pure and clear and full of rainbows.

Lots of people were about, but as I walked through the circle they seemed to melt away and I went to the tumulus which was to become my resting place for a few nights. Here my Frock seemed wide- hipped and matronly as I carried out my exchanges, laying it on a central stone. There was a magnificent sunset with a great, deep red disk echoing the Tibetan colour of the one I was exchanging.

There was a caravan site nearby and later a group of children hung around, daring each other to talk to me, drawing straws as to who should speak first. They had thought I was a man, then thought I was half man, half woman – my hair looked like a woman but my face like a man - and I looked like a man from the back. They said they'd been told not to come to the stones at night for that's when the witches come out. 'Maybe I am the witch' I said. Maybe I was. Then they thought I was an old Druid. They were 11/12 years old. 'How old do you think I am?' I asked and they guessed 20/24. I was two months off 40. It was wonderful sleeping on the tumulus. Next day the children came back and said their parents didn't believe I existed. They seemed very excited by me, as though I were something out of a story and later I was invited to a picnic with them and their parents in the caravan. I described the mundane things of what I was doing, so they were re-assured I wasn't actually too much of a weirdo. The parents ended up calling me a faerie, but wanted to photograph me and I did come out in the photographs! Those pictures are the only ones I have of myself on that journey.

I moved away from the circle to do my Tibetan practice as there were so many people around. When I returned, the children were watching me walk across the field and said I looked like a monk or someone from the past. I was amazed, as I was just wearing what at that time were my ordinary clothes and wondered what I was becoming and what kind of energy I was giving out. I told the children I was moving on the next day and they were very disappointed and begged me to stay.

Getting up early I finished my exchanges, then stopped by their caravan to say goodbye. One of them gave me a painting and their addresses. When I returned to East Anglia I sent them pictures of my children and they wrote back and sent the photographs. They were called Clive, Fiona and Jason. Jason wrote to me several times. I still have the letters and have very fond memories of them all. Where are they now?

I got a lift to Bakewell with a farmer in a blue van. I had dreamed of the real Bakewell puddings for days: they are soft and luscious and so much nicer than the more common Bakewell tarts; but I phoned some people I knew and Dave said he was coming near, so gave me a lift back to theirs before I'd had a chance to buy a pudding.

The whole area felt extraordinary to me, because there was still so much that was real in a way which had already been lost in most places I knew. I got the impression of strong community life as it had always been, with revivals of old customs just for 'local people', not tourists: well dressings and football matches with dozens of people in streets and ditches. He showed me a place where young people camped on their own – his son was an excellent poacher, catching trout for breakfast. At their house I washed my hair and had a bath so deep I floated and Kath did my washing. Outside, the sky turned yellow and there was thunder and lightning. I had put on a lot of weight before I set out on the journey and was pleased to find I had lost half a stone, and was beginning to feel physically fit and strong. Kath was a potter – her work being of beautiful, magical wood nymphs, princesses in castles and mushrooms.

We went to a pub called 'Moon' and there was a power cut, so I was back in my ideal candle-lit world. A man came in who normally machine-milked his cows, and was now going to have to do it by hand. He had an awful lot of cows.

I slept on two armchairs pushed together and dreamed of a place I later realised was the Hebrides – more water than land. I was so happy and fulfilled on this part of the journey and recall it vividly.

Dave drove me back to Chesterfield, so once again I missed the Bakewell puddings. I booked a coach to Keswick and had a four hour wait. Feeling good to be clean again I sat writing near the famous crooked spire.

The next coach journeys were a long haul through Northern cities which all seemed to blend into one another. At times I felt very down, aware of how alone my future was going to be, how alone I was. At times I questioned what my journey was about, what awaited me at the end, how I would come back down from the heights and what on earth my future would hold. There were times I wondered whether I was meant to walk onto the Sleeping Beauty mountain and just die there. But suddenly we were free of the cities and crossing the Pennines, the spine of Britain. It changed everything and all became light and clear and majestic again. Lakes, mountains, and then the reddest sunset I had ever seen, going down between great blue mountains after being a vast orange line across the lakes.

I hated Keswick, finding it too touristy and middle class. Here there were very different reactions to me from those in previous places – shouts of 'It's a long way to Tipperary!' (whatever that was supposed to mean), and I got called a hippie.

I had difficulty finding the right road, but at last climbed the narrow, cool hill and before long was in Castlerigg stone circle: The Blue Heart of Britain. And it was so blue, with the brilliant white moon above. I was suddenly extremely emotional and stood for hours embracing a stone, holding a stone, loving a stone. I'd never felt like that before. It was like the love I had for my goat. The stones there are rounded and female and as I held on to one I was nearly crying, but found it so hard to cry in those days. This journey felt so massive, and I felt so tiny. It was an immense achievement to have got so far, yet I still had so far to go. I would panic as I reached each major place on my journey, wondering how I would move on and find my way to the next. I felt so little, surrounded by those huge blue mountains, so carried on hugging the smooth, motherly stone. Eventually I slipped into my sleeping bag and spent the night huddled against her, feeling I was now part of the circle.

In the morning cattle surrounded me, so I moved to the edge of the field but they followed and slobbered all over my sleeping bag and chewed my rucksack, then licked the grass from their wet nostrils and went away.

The day became unbearably hot. I stuck my head under a hawthorn hedge to protect myself from sunstroke. Everything got bluer and bluer, even the grass. After a while the shadow grew long enough to cover my whole body and I lay for hours listening to a skylark and watching a bee in the hawthorn. There were lots of visitors to the stones so I kept my distance. Sweat was pouring from my every pore and steaming from every scrap of skin. I was nearly out of water and wondered where I could get some. There were no houses nearby and I reckoned water from a beck would be full of sheep urine. My arms were burnt, my nose peeling. There was distant thunder and I wondered how I could catch rain. Then it rolled round bringing a vast storm right overhead. I covered myself with my plastic, but the rain somehow ran down my back and soaked my clothes and rug. I was scared of the lightning. I didn't know whether hedges, like trees, attracted it and worried that my sleeping bag had a metal zip.

It stopped as quickly as it had begun. The farmer came by and counted the cattle to check whether any had been struck by lightning and the tourists came back before I could change my clothes. Eventually I hung all the wet stuff on the hedge, but the air itself was still very damp.

The cattle returned, pestered me, and followed when I went into the circle. They chewed the stuff I'd laid on the hedge and just wouldn't leave me alone, though every so often they danced head to head round the stones in some strange bovine ritual. Their breath was vile, I suppose from the fermenting gases in their rumen. They didn't seem to bother anyone else – just me. So: I had wet clothes, no water and no food.

I was surprised how I could keep warm in a damp sleeping bag and clothes, how my body warmed the dampness which in turn wrapped me in a comforting warmth: but I realised this could only happen with natural fibres like wool, otherwise it might drain the warmth from me and I'd get hypothermia. I remembered how I'd read of the old Highlanders wrapping themselves in damp plaids for warmth as they slept.

The Frock with the Serpent Stone at Twelve Apostles.

Next morning I did my practice and exchanges and felt strong again. People began to stand behind the hedge to see what I was doing.

I walked back down to Keswick, which I still hated. People seemed so off-hand and there were notices like 'No Rucksacks Inside'. I bought some lovely postcards of faeries and goddesses, and some Kendal Mint Cake. At the bus station buffet I had breakfast: egg, salty fatty bacon, sausage, half a tomato and loads of grease for £1.50 - very expensive in those days. I was intrigued by the rest of the menu which included: T-bone steak, scampi, chips and peas; rainbow trout, chips and peas; gammon, pineapple, egg, chips and peas; and the children's menu which included 'Derwentwater Grill', and all this in a 'caff'.

I found a faerie glade beside the river and sat drinking fizzy Dandelion and Burdock, feeling it was mad that I had walked into town for 4 cups of tea and would sweat it all off again walking back up to the circle. There was very little fluid passing through my kidneys, it was all coming out in sweat. I had, of course, to carry everything with me: there was nowhere to leave anything.

Back at the stones I lay in bliss. My life for years had been so stressful; so busy, so full of anxiety and worry and responsibility and now I had the sweet luxury of being able to lie in the blue meadow grass with the skylark above, the haze all around, the warm breeze on my body and to turn lazily and see there in front of me a stone circle. And I could stay there as long as I liked. It was one of the most beautiful evenings of my life: the sky was intensely blue and it was absolutely still, with a purple haze on the hills and golden evening sunlight. Once again I felt I was being carried along on a wave of total inevitability.

Later that evening as I sat near the stones looking at a map, a crowd of drunks came and I was the object of their merriment for about 20 minutes. At first it was remarks about an 'Old English Sheepdog' and 'There's something the matter with that fellow', then they realised I was female and there was a lot of muttering that I couldn't hear. Why did so many people think this woman in long skirts was a man? Why did people think I was so strange? I was just sitting there looking at a map!

I went to sleep by a stone wall and had a strange, disturbed night with confused, muddled dreams, waking late feeling I had been somewhere out of my body in the night, sure I had woken once and seen full-size faerie folk dancing in a strange blue light in the centre of the circle. I got going quickly, bade farewell to the stones and headed down the hill past "dog roses, wild roses, English roses in blossom in Cumbrian hedgerows", white and purple crystals on garden walls and gateposts and "miniature megaliths, carefully erected", back to Keswick.

It was already getting hot quite early in the morning. I had to queue for ages for a coffee and cheese scone in the bus station buffet before having to gulp down the scalding drink in order to catch the 9.05am bus to Wigton. But it seemed the well-oiled machine which was carrying me on my journey was running to perfection. I took local buses – Wigton, Carlisle, Dumfries – local buses costing much more than National Express.

At 3.23 the thunder rolled round again and I felt the storms were following me. But I was in Scotland!

Chapter 4: Reaching Scotland and the Hebrides.

Only just, but in Scotland at last and suddenly it was as though I were past some 'great divide', some psychological barrier: everything now completely possible. These days I still find that when I go down to England, on the long hauls back up everything lightens once the border is crossed, as though I am returning to a finer reality with some terrible heaviness just falling away.

But this was the first time and I marvelled how 50 miles could make so much difference. I had just popped round a corner but into a totally different world. Even though I knew so little of Scotland or 'the Road to the Isles', things now started to fall into place much more easily, seeming more straightforward than in England. Setting off on this journey had been a great leap of faith, and an immensely scary one; now the last stages began to feel more real, and possible. I was on my line of light and being pulled unstoppably upwards.

When I got to Dumfries my heart was full of happiness and laughter. What a nice town, full of lovely, helpful people, so different from Keswick. I ambled around, getting my bearings, locating the bus station and Post Office, had tea and a roll and started to walk.

What a walk. What humid heat. Lincluden: months before I had done a performance of this journey with Keith Payne, and at one point, lying on the floor of a Suffolk barn on St. George's Day, had mouthed the romantic name of 'Lincluden'. Now I found it to be a vast, sprawling council house suburb of Dumfries, grey and boring with hardly a shop in sight: a flat industrial landscape. I walked a seemingly never-ending straight road, but came across a little corner by an old bridge and sat there, collecting my thoughts. This, then, was the Green Throat of Albion.

I reached the Twelve Apostles stone circle. Made of many huge, rough lumps of rock with big spaces in between and a hedge through the middle, it was quite over-looked, with little privacy, but there didn't seem to be many tourists; however. I decided to do my exchanges quickly in case anyone objected to my being there.

I'd not been there long before the electricity built up and – crash – thunder and huge drops of rain. I got the plastic together a lot better this time and only my coat got damp. I was learning. I lay there with the rain thudding down on my body, yet didn't get wet. It was a strange feeling.

Some bullocks came and nosed round me. Much nicer than those at Casterigg, they seemed to have heads and bodies like cows, but were male. It was still hot and the thunder rumbled on. How marvellously new this area was to me. I found it hard to imagine the circle as it must originally have been without the surrounding buildings or hedge. I decided to stay a couple of days, then walk back into Dumfries, noticing from the map other ancient sites in the area, including another stone circle I was determined to find. I knew I needed a pause to distil the experience of Castlerigg, which had been so pure, powerful and blue; almost too overpowering, almost a distraction from the clear sense of the whole journey.

But there, at Lincluden, in Scotland, I felt calm, serene and untroubled; almost 'ordinary'; with no extreme emotions of any kind. It was a form of relief. I was just there, though I expected things to build up the longer I stayed. I now needed to digest the experience of being somewhere I had never been before.

There had been hazy sun when it rained and I'd hoped for a rainbow as my reward for getting there, but there wasn't one. I'd not yet had a rainbow on my journey and thought maybe I should have to wait until reaching the brow. I felt this Green Throat required patience. Callanish seemed very far away, but it didn't seem to matter. I was truly in the moment, just absolutely in the place I was.

In Dumfries I had seen my first haggis. After decades of being vegetarian, I had gone back to eating meat when I met the Dzog Chen teachings. I learned that in eating meat with awareness I could place a good cause for the animal; that it was ok as long as it had not been killed for me and had passed through three 'hands' before it reached me. So, I rather rejoiced that I could eat haggis. I was very English, happily experiencing Scottishness for the first time. It is satisfying for me now to remember how I felt entering Scotland then, for it is part of why I am here now and cannot happily live anywhere else.

I watched the cattle, who had sniffed around me a bit. One was drinking another's urine as he was peeing! I had watched animals drinking rain and dew from grass, hedges and trees, realising that once we humans must have done the same.

Walking round the circle, I did some of my exchanges. The cattle followed me and it felt fantastic – a woman walking round a stone circle followed by a whole bunch of bovine males in an exotic circumnambulation of human and beast. However it was difficult to do much with them there, even though if I looked at them they'd jump away. I moved to the centre of the circle, near the hedge, sang one of my practices, and the cattle left.

The stones had seams of gold in them and standing on one was an amazing bird I didn't recognise. It had long legs and an enormously long, curved beak. Maybe it was a curlew.

My first impression of the site was of it being huge and spread out, but with a powerful energy spinning round. It felt very male - big and wide and craggy and solid. The more I was with it the better I felt yet wondered whether my initial feelings of balance had actually been rather negative, more a detached 'what did it all matter anyway'. Maybe it was just the massive change of place, environment and country. The grass was very green in the evening light. The sun began to set like a huge ball of orange flame in the misty sky. Just as I felt I should do some practice, the cattle returned and came right round behind me and there was also a lot of traffic, but in the late light I began to get the place sussed. There was a stone like a serpent's head pointing in to the centre. The green/gold clockwise spinning energy was the green, gold serpent coiled round the green throat of Albion, with a tail-like stone, round and pointed, sticking upwards. Eventually I did my purification practice and everything became strong and clear again. The places in the land were becoming even more powerfully the places in my body. I hadn't set out with any idea that this would happen, but realised it was what the journey was actually about. I was becoming the landscape.

The surrounding modern buildings and hedge melted away and I was just with the circle of stones as they had been since they were first erected. The energy seemed to enter at the tail, spin round to the head, then spiral into the centre. I didn't often have this sort of experience, so it was a powerful way of relating to the place. I presume it's the kind of energy which dowsers pick up. I liked the circle; I felt it was a good one.

I slept by the hedge in the middle of the circle. At 1am there was yet another storm. It woke me with vast flashes of lightning and forks which shot down, how near to me I wasn't sure. It circled round then seemed to be right above. There was one flash and explosion simultaneously over the circle just as there had been at Castlerigg. I huddled under my plastic and didn't get wet but got out of my sleeping bag because of the zip, remembering stories of golfers with irons getting electrocuted and wondered whether the circle of stones would be some form of protection. I lay under the plastic until about 2.30am, when it eased, then went into strong fragmented dreams which seemed to be flying off to someone else, as though my dream was becoming someone else's reality.

The cattle woke me before I was ready, shooting me violently from sleep to waking as though from a gun. I determined the next night I should find somewhere to sleep where I could merge from one state to the other more gently and at my own pace.

I was strangely down that morning. On days like this I seemed to drop out of the high energy of the journey and question what the point of it all was. I was living in two realities – one intensely charged, the other a kind of realistic over-view. For a while I wished I could step right out of it and have a day off, but knew I couldn't. What I was doing was so hard on many levels; not so much physically, but emotionally and psychologically. I was at a massive crossroads in my life, had walked away from everything, with no idea what my future held and was just living the journey and aiming for its ultimate goal: Lewis, Callanish, and the mountain at the Brow. I felt profoundly weary, wanting to relax, but there was to be no relaxing on that journey; maybe, I thought, no relaxing in my life ever again.

Once again a farmer came to count the cattle after the storm and I had a good chat with him. He was very pleasant and thought I might be someone who'd been sleeping out all night. I didn't say yes and I didn't say no, I just laughed. He said he'd never known weather like it, such heat, humidity and storms and I wondered whether it was me who was stirring something up. I discovered this was the parish of Holy Wood and there was an open shop nearby as well as a hotel. I was so longing for a cup of tea. At last came a cool breeze.

This was a Sunday, possibly June 6th. I did all I had to do at the circle, walked to the shop, bought a few things and asked for some water, then went up to Holy Wood church. It was constructed on the site of an old Abbey which had been pulled down in the Reformation and the tower was built from some of the old Abbey stones. People waved and smiled at me as they passed by on their way from the service. A man showed me round the church. "That used to be a balcony where the laird and his family used to sit", "Those are the collection boxes they used to pass round – didn't leave them out in those days", "That's the pewter plate they used to collect alms for the poor in", "Those windows are where the poor and sick waited outside, they weren't allowed in, and the alms were passed out to them". He was very proud of the place and its ancient history – "That old Druid circle down there was the beginning of Christianity round here". (I didn't understand that bit!)

I walked back down the road and sat on the grass under a huge tall tree. People stopped and talked to me; even a nosy Police car drove by. I thought I had better move from where I was drawing so much attention to myself, so went and sat by the river, knowing I couldn't go back to the circle as it was having such an unsettling effect on me, but still feeling I must take my time with Scotland and not just rush up to the Islands.

Children were swimming and riding horses in the water and picnicking in fields of buttercups and the skies rang out to their cries of "Oh, fucking hell" as they climbed bare-legged over barbed-wire fences. They talked of 'the Beastie' which made me wonder whether I should go to Loch Ness when I was higher up the land. I wondered where I could put my rubbish.

Another storm was threatening so I decided to try the Embassy Hotel, which had a bar, but they had no tea. Oh, how desperately I longed for a cup of tea! But it had to be cider and crisps. Three Scottish blokes came in and were all over me, buying me drinks until it got to the point where I thought I had better beat a hasty retreat, rain or no rain. I started to walk up the road, then hopped into a little glade in some trees, covered myself with the plastic and went off into a kind of half sleep, half trance state for about two hours. It was very nearly Full Moon and I thought the strange spaced out state I was in must be due to that.

I started to wonder where I should spend the night, wanting somewhere quiet where I could be alone to sort my head out, as I was getting so muddled and confused, needing to get clear before moving upwards on my journey. I was having quite a tough time there, the full moon blowing me apart. I thought maybe I would be completely mad by the time I reached Callanish. Maybe I was mad already. I seemed to have lost my confidence, lost my nerve. I really needed to cry, but couldn't cry any more, and just then really did need some time with a friend. That had been yet another storm and afterwards everything was fresh but still very damp.

I had found something marked 'fort' on the map, so decided to head there for the night. It was beautiful in the cool, wet evening and I was soon in lovely countryside. There were tree-lined roads like those of my childhood and good hedges which weren't mutilated as they were in East Anglia. There was a beautiful, soft, delicate perfume everywhere and wild roses in the hedgerows, all shades of pink and white. Columns of steam rose from plantations of trees on the hills as though the hot, damp earth were sweating.

Walking through a place called Terreagles I wondered what that meant - Earth of Eagles? Land of Eagles? I was very into eagles. I went up a steep track, half way up resting on a tree root. I felt that anywhere round there would be fine to spend the night, but knew I must make it to the fort. Up past a bunch of cattle, over a gate, up, up, past a rocky mound, on, on, higher and higher, another gate, up, up. I felt like an old Tibetan monk, was followed by a herd of heifers and huge rabbits running everywhere; yet another gate and then at last up to the rocky fort. It was high, bare rock, the highest point around.

This was the moment and the place I had waited for. It was so delicate and perfect it was beyond description. At last I felt absolutely clear after all the mental fog and confusion down near the circle. I wanted nothing, everything was perfect – as from the beginning, all perfected. I looked towards the

Hebrides and it was as though they were over the next hill and if I called out, people there would hear me, and they probably did.

I moved from the wind and lay in my dampness, and the dark misty night of the full moon cleared and I slept and slept.

In the hot morning everything dried and I knew such peace and contentment as I lay and burnt in the clear, clean sun. I thought I could lie there and die and no-one would know and the crows would come and peck out my eyes and eat my rotting flesh and that didn't seem at all a bad end. The sky was so blue, the clouds so white. There would be no more storms. I sat on the rock again, the breeze smelling of pine and felt at one with all the people who had ever sat there down through thousands of years.

There was silence apart from an occasional solitary cricket, then two demons from hell screamed across the sky leaving evil black smoke trails. But the peace returned and I stayed and stayed, my back burning in the sun; got washed and changed and suddenly felt someone coming close. I packed my things and prepared to leave, sitting on the highest rock. A man with a pack appeared. He was dressed in blue and white and was extremely tanned. We talked a while. He worked night shifts and went up there after work. What a place to go to after work, I thought. There was an awareness in his eyes which was comforting after most of the Scotsmen I'd met so far.

I left and walked back down the hill; a four mile walk to Dumfries, all exquisitely beautiful. I was offered a lift, but declined because the walk was so lovely. Why else was I there? My arm was burnt and I expected it to peel. I got to Dumfries and checked the P.O. for mail, but there wasn't any. I sat in a snack bar, drank endless tea, had a hamburger and chips and wrote cards to friends.

A man began to talk to me. When he was eleven, he flew 22 feet a yard off the ground: it was a miracle. I believed him. He used to go to a quarry and fly with a kite down to the ground on the wind. It was wonderful, he said.

Leaving, I sat on the grass by the bus station and wrote more cards to more friends, then had more tea, my body burning, my mind content. I decided to take another road that evening, to find the other stone circle, and walk back to Dumfries again the next day.

I walked about 5 miles in the still hot evening. It was no longer humid, there was a breeze and I was reasonably cool. I went down beautiful lanes of tall trees and past an ICI plastic works. I couldn't find the path which was the nearest way to the circle, so walked on and approached it from the back, so to speak. I was glad, as that way was so beautiful. I went up a narrow lane to a

63

church on top of a hill, where I paused under a huge tree. It looked very 18th century, like a lot of old William Stukeley engravings. The path was barely traceable but there were gates, and stones to step over walls where there should be if you were following the path. There were wonderful green rolling hills and gorse and sheep, and then I was at the circle. It was on a mound, with a kind of amphitheatre around it on two sides, overlooking the distant land, the sunset and sunrise: a faerie circle.

I did some good, strong, loud practice in the centre, then slept on a slope under two hawthorn trees. In a way it looked very Mediterranean, scrubby and dry, the hawthorns taking on the appearance of olive trees with their dry old trunks and lichen-covered branches. It was idyllic beyond words. I slept fitfully, and woke for the sunrise, the first I had properly watched on this journey; a golden burst over the far hills, then slept again and dreamed of being on a long journey.

When I fully woke it was hot again. I didn't feel like lingering and had the urge to be on my way, especially as there were now cattle around. I didn't know which gender, but was aware I'd not yet been surrounded by actual cows. Everything was just getting better and better. I took a few photos, as I'd probably never be there again, did some more practice, then sought with difficulty the way out which I hadn't been able to find on the way up, realising I would never have found the circle if I'd come that way the previous day.

As I walked I realised my left foot was hurting dreadfully. I didn't know whether it was sprained or had an infection or what. It felt like broken bones and made it quite difficult to walk. I started half-heartedly to hitch, and a woman offered me a lift. Very anti- the men in the housing office, "They think there's no more to life than what they're having for tea", she was trying to get evicted so she could be put in a nice council house down the road. She said she had two horses. For some reason, at this point I recalled that the previous day I had seen a girl mechanic in a garage and thought how great that was.

In Dumfries, I withdrew some money from my PO account, found I still had no mail and did some essential shopping. I sat and caught up with a lot of written stuff I had to get off to various people and a bird shat on my arm. I hoped it was lucky. I wondered if it was as hot in the Hebrides. I wondered if rain was waiting for me up there and felt I should like to dance naked in the rain.
As evening approached I set out for an old well I had seen marked on the map. My foot was in absolute agony and not just painful, but weak. I was hobbling and the other leg didn't seem to work either. I seemed to have no strength or energy to move my legs and it was as though they had forgotten how to walk. It was like trying to walk in a dream.

I reached a lay-by a distance away from where I wanted to turn off the road and walk down beside a line of trees. A man had driven one way, driven back and parked right where I wanted to turn off, so I sat and ate some oatcakes and wished he'd go away, not wanting to walk right by him and for him to see where I was going. I wondered what my muscles were lacking. Was it something in my diet? What should I eat to give myself strength? Was I lacking salt? What could I do about my foot? Could I wear a crepe bandage inside my little shoe? I needed new insoles anyway. I thought I would have a night in a B&B before moving on, to give my foot a rest, have a bath and wash my hair.

Eventually the bloke went and I found the route I wanted was actually signposted Public Footpath, the first I'd seen in Scotland. It had some nice stiles. I walked down to something called Crooks Pow. I couldn't see a well anywhere or even something marked on the map as Picts Knowe, but there were some lovely trees and I decided to stay there even though there were lots of biting insects.

There was a lot of water pouring into Crooks Pow, but I couldn't tell whether it was a spring or a drainage pipe. It seemed a bit odd that a spring should be in the middle of a stream.

I continued exploring and eventually found the well and it was worth searching for. It was really old with a circle of stones round it, near some sycamore, silver birch and hawthorn. The stones appeared to be for people to sit on in a circle round the well. It was a potent place, more than I had encountered thus far on the whole journey and I felt that this was the real green throat of Britain. I'd had to search so much to find it and here it was, full of presence and power and magic. I made my offerings, gave it a special gift and did my own magic. Three times the well gave a deep, guttural gurgle, and a load of bubbles came up from this throat. I felt there were faeries there.

What a place, what a night! That place was really the most purely magical place I had ever (have ever?) been. Shades of old, ancient, wise women sat there. I went to sleep at dusk but was woken at 11.55pm by the stealthy footsteps of something quite large and noisy walking around. I lay still, but then sat up and it darted away. At midnight a dark shape flew silently by: no wings flapping. There were tiny noises everywhere; little drips and crackles; little rustles of small animals. There had been insects like mosquitoes earlier which made no noise and now there was a high-pitched sound like speeded-up voices – were these really faeries? There were owls in the distance and cries of other night birds and a strange bark which came closer but was not a dog. A fox? I was excited to have found such a magic place and had many images in my head for pictures to create when the journey was over. The moon, not far

Jill's image of the old wise ones she felt to be sitting round the well near Dumfries

gone into waning, appeared sometimes with streaks of cloud over it. I watched it cross the sky and watched stars and planets move. I felt extraordinary.

A dense mist crept over everything and at last I slept and woke at sunrise to do a powerful practice by the well while half asleep. It was as though the old wise women sat on the stones and joined with me. The mist was thick and silent and the trees dripped. As the day lightened I slept again and woke at 8 in the sun. This night had been the high point of the whole journey.

I hobbled back to the main road and hitched to Dumfries: a lift from a woman again. There was still no post. I went to the Rainbow snack bar then sat by the river. It was cooler now. The Tourist Information Office gave me the address of a B&B – No. 3 Terreagles Street. Run by Miss Agnes Harper and only £3.50 a night. I had a shower and washed my hair and washed my clothes and hung them by the window to dry. I went out without my load and bought some scissors to cut my toenails. I had haggis and chips and was sure all the weight I had lost must have gone back on again, thinking I looked like a great brown Amazon except that I wasn't tall enough. I went back to the B&B, where there was quiet and peace and I could sleep in a bed. I can't better what I wrote at the time, so will quote it in full:

"And the clock ticks heavily and timelessly on the mantle-shelf, sounding like an old grandfather clock, ticking our lives away in the silence, and there are hand-embroidered antimacassars and floral cushions and floral curtains and floral lampshades and floral calendars and floral bone china and dogs on the mantle-shelf and little nick-nacks and leafy carpets. There's a spiral rug in front of the fireplace. There's silver in the corner cabinet and a tea trolley and old Victorian pots with flowers in and Constable prints on the wall and a sideboard and no porridge for breakfast, and old faded copper-plate notices on the bathroom walls and it's oh so still and quiet and watching and full of all the people who have ever been here. And the clock strikes twice at twenty to nine and the grandfather clock in the hall is silent and there are tea-cosies, and chairs that stand by the wall waiting to be sat on and misty mountains and Highland cattle on the wall and only half-a-dozen entries in the visitors book for 1982 and dark brown wardrobes and Izal toilet paper, at Miss Agnes Harper's at 3, Terreagles Street, Dumfries – and the breakfast alone was worth £3.50, and my clothes dried in the breeze and it is cool today and the room smells of my own bodily warmth and I must buy crepe bandage for my foot and repack my bag and it feels like the day I shall move on. It is all a strange dream, this journey". I felt clean and refreshed and clear as crystal.

As I walked towards the bus station, I was checked out by the police. It was quite friendly and I think I had my driving licence with me as ID. They ran me through their computer to see if I was wanted for anything or had been reported missing, though I didn't think anyone who was wanted or missing would have made themselves as obvious as I had. I now felt really impelled to move on up Scotland, had no clear idea of my route but decided to get a coach to Fort William and then decide on my next move.

'There were rows of Haggis hanging in butchers' shop windows... The Scottish sheep had long hair and they had not shorn the sheep in Scotland yet... There were water restrictions... They were making hay and silage in Dumfries while the sun shone... I saw a bull with a ring in his nose...There were lots of bulls in fields with cows and heifers – I thought I should have to watch where I slept...I saw the new 20p coin which I thought was tiny and would get confused with 5p's... girls in Scotland wore frilly mini-skirts that summer... the route was covered in mauve rhododendrons and the coach driver called me Wain...'

Arriving in Fort William I bought more maps, then walked a bit up Glen Nevis, at the foot of the great mountain. I had been driven past huge lochs and mountains and glens and it was all so new to me.

I didn't like Fort William. It felt like a terminus. For some reason I thought of Heathrow and how that had been built on (and destroyed) an ancient site. I felt poised on the edge of a precipice, almost being pushed off and wondered whether I would fly or crash to the bottom, or would the wind blow me hither and thither in a storm of confusion?

I walked to the end (beginning?) of the West Highland Way and along it a little way and was snapped at, chased by and had my back bitten by a strange, wild, little black pony, wondering whether it was a kelpie. I wanted to go higher so I could see the mountain. The energy of the area felt massive, explosive, and was shooting off in all directions. I sat under some trees and was plagued by what I kept describing as 'tiny flies' but of course, this was my first experience of the dreaded Highland Midge. I was completely covered and could hardly think for the plague of them.

It was 10.45pm and still light – my first experience also of the midsummer north Scotland nights which never get dark. I hid from the midges inside my sleeping bag although it was the hottest night of the journey, but slept and woke late and lay for a while watching the tall, thin trees waving in the wind, marvelling at the strength of the trunks bearing so much strain. The tops danced in wild patterns echoing my own confusion which had come upon me again. The midges were still around and I couldn't rest. The mountain, which had been clear the previous night with snow and ice still on its summit, was now hidden in dense cloud. I wanted to sit and contemplate, but there was no peace from the midges, so I walked back down past a cemetery which was on a mound surrounded by a moat, then into the town. My foot was very bad. I felt tired and hot. Thunder rolled round the mountain-tops reminding me it still followed my journey.
Sitting in the terminus buffet I intended to work out many alternative routes to the Isles, though the energy was so powerful and the Islands so close that I felt I could climb a mountain, flap my arms and just fly there. This area felt odd; a strange nowhere, yet with such power coming in from many different directions and sources. I wanted to sit quietly on my own by a vast loch surrounded by the majesty of the mountains, but all this was confusing me.

I wrote down times of buses and collected timetables, and words which had been romantic faerie- tale names of far-off, distant and impossible places were now but stops at the end of a bus-ride. It began to rain gently and I went to 'McTavish's Kitchen', had a beefburger and chips and the chips were like hot, raw potato. There were rhododendrons on the table and cotton tee-shirts for 1.99 and I wished I could find a cheap pair of socks. The confusion passed and my spirit sang and danced again. The clouds were rising from the mountains, making them look like volcanoes.

It was raining a bit. I walked back to the same spot and sat on a hill where I could see the mountain, but the midges were even worse, covering every scrap of my exposed flesh. I huddled, trying to protect myself by wrapping my hands in my towel. However, I did some strong practice, then walked on past a camp-site and restaurant, a shop and the YHA, and down to the river where I sat under my plastic beneath a hazel tree and spent hours poring over timetables and all my possibilities, paring them down and eliminating many. I couldn't sleep for hours. It rained all night, gently but continuously.

Next morning I returned to the town, crossing a field in bare feet. It was now quite cold. I was rising higher in the land and thinking of buying gloves. I walked three-and-a-half miles in an hour, which I thought good. My foot still hurt but was functioning better, and I seemed to have got back into the rhythm of walking again. I had a shower at the terminus and really indulged, washing my hair, some clothes, and all the dead midges off my body which was so bitten it looked as though I had measles. I had to carry the wet clothes in a plastic bag, hoping I would soon be able to find a handy hedge in a wind. My towel and my rug were wet, but I was clean.

At last I collected post which had been forwarded from Post Office to Post Office up the country and was covered in postmarks and bird shit. I had made up my mind to go to Skye and then decide whether to stay there a while or go straight on to Harris.

I reached Skye. I smelled the air of Skye on my breath, felt the change as I stood momentarily on its earth, felt its energy and presence and knew that this was not the time for Skye. I passed through it, saw its mountains and lochs and knew it wasn't fair to Skye to stop there, for I wouldn't rest, would be distracted, only waiting to move on. Another time, another lifetime maybe, I thought. The 'well- oiled machine' had brought me to the waiting-room for the Harris ferry, and it was to Harris I must go. The pull of the Outer Isles was undeniable, as though I were on some flow that wouldn't let me stop. I was only just realising there was no water between Lewis and Harris, that it was all one island, and knew I must arrive at some distance from the places which had called me, with time to adjust to such a different land before going to Callanish and the Sleeping Beauty mountain: the places which had pulled me up all the way from Cornwall.

As I waited for the ferry, already so much had changed. It was windy and the boat was late coming in. The waiting-room wasn't like anything there now; more like a shed on the pier. There seemed to be mainly local people waiting and lots of stuff to be loaded on board. I was shifting into yet another reality, but this seemed more real than any of the previous ones.

At last I was on my way to the Western Isles, spending most of the journey outside. Shafts of white and gold streamed down from the sun onto the sea, lighting it up. The horizon was knife-edged, the colour of the sea deep and dark. I had no idea what the Hebrides was like, imagining it having little villages with Post Offices, cafes and pubs – a bit like England. What an absolute revelation it was to arrive there. I had not imagined there were still places like this in Britain.

We pulled into Tarbert in the late evening light. It was like faerie-land to me. I walked up the hill and was overwhelmed by the sense that I had come home, not expecting to feel like that. I was not looking for a home in that sense, had this only as the goal at the end of my journey. It was an astonishing experience. I felt I belonged in this place which I had never been to before, had never seen anywhere like before and had not really even read much about. It is reassuring for me now to read things I wrote at the time, finding these thoughts and feelings aren't the imaginings of hind- sight, but what I genuinely felt in those first moments.

I was hoping to meet up with John Sharkey and Keith Payne at a place called Rodel at the southern tip of South Harris, so turned left and began to walk that way. I didn't go far that night, but found a little heather hollow off the road and snuggled down, sublimely content.

In the morning it seemed everything in my life had changed beyond words, a change I couldn't describe; I really was in a different world. I realised survival was now more of a challenge: not so easy to keep warm and dry and find food. There weren't lots of little villages with shops, but I was in paradise.
I walked to Rodel by the small east road, not wanting to rush, needing to adjust to the Hebrides. As when I sat on the old fort near Dumfries, I wanted for nothing. I sat by the sides of small lochans and their water gently slurped under the over-hanging rocks and as I walked the water in my bottle slurped in reply. I passed water covered in lilies, and reflected light danced and sparkled on it like diamonds. The black-face sheep were so delicate with their dainty thin black legs and fine faces and long straight wool. Unshorn, it was falling off some of them in huge fleecy chunks. Nowadays there are few pure black-face, they are mostly cross-bred (with, I think, Cheviots). When the black-face walked down the roads on their tiny hoofs it was as though they were teetering along in high heels with black tights on.

For all that most of Britain had had one of its wettest summers, the Islands had been extraordinarily dry. I can't now imagine many summer nights up here when one could sleep out as I did in 1982.

Getting to Finsbay, I rested a while and started to think about where I would stay that night. Though the sun still shone, the wind was cold. I noticed all the peat cuttings and how people had peat stacks outside their doors, like East Anglians had wood-piles, loving the fact that they used what was around them. From lunchtime I had walked 12 miles. My foot was complaining and I was really tired so decided to walk a little further then find somewhere to sleep. I could see other islands in the distance and wondered if they were the Uists.

Climbing up past a TV mast on a hill and along a little glen I found a beautiful flat bit on the side of a quite precipitous incline. I had a heavenly night. It was still light at 1am and full daylight at 3.24 with no real darkness in between. I watched the moon rise late down the end of the glen. There was no wind and I was warm.

I got going slowly next morning, drinking in this different world. I watched men carry driftwood in a barrow. I smelled at last the 'peat reek' blowing from chimneys and longed to sit by a peat fire. I find the smell exquisite, like a strange incense, oddly sweet yet pungent. It seems to evoke some primal memory within me and a strange yearning. The silence and stillness was breathtaking. Nowhere in England could you find such peace, as there is always the distant rumble of a motorway even on moorland. I got a sense of what most of our past must have been like, and how, before cars, most people walked everywhere and the place would have been full of people working and living outdoors.

I was getting hot as I walked. The 'little flies' were around again and I felt they had followed me to haunt and torment. The midge-bites from Fort William were bad, having flared up into great white lumps, the ones on my painful foot being especially awful. For the first time in my life I saw a cuckoo. I'd never seen one in England as they were always hidden in trees, but here I saw a strange long bird on an electricity cable, not knowing what it was until it cried "Cuckoo". There were yellow irises with long hard leaves which clacked

The Sleeping Beauty mountain from Ariavruach

together and houses with corrugated roofs painted with red oxide. Little did I know that a few years later I would embark on a decade of painting my own.

At one point I was at last crying at the beauty of everything. I walked past men cutting peat and had so many questions in my head, wondering how people there made a living and where the Harris Tweed was made: the questions people now ask me. I had never seen such colours in nature – the sky such pure blue, the sea deep turquoise, the grass so green, the heather purple and brownish- black, the sheep and gulls intensely white, the horizon clean cut with the dark blue islands clear in the distance. The sun was hot and happily I lay in it, writing "What is the sun for but to lie in. Walk in the cold and rain but lie in the sun".

I got to Rodel. It wasn't the English-type village I had imagined, but a great old church on a high rock, an ancient Dun overlooking it, a few houses and, down near the sea, round the back of the church, an old hotel. I walked on a built up path to a place called Strond which had a Post Office. This was tiny and the lady opposite only opened up when someone wanted to use it. She told me there was a shop at Leverburgh and gave me a bottle of water. I walked round to the hotel and found B&B was £8, which was beyond my means, so climbed up to the dun, finding what seemed to be a bed ready prepared for me by the faeries. I lay in it in peace and joy and slept and woke in my little nest and realised there really was no darkness – dusk to dawn with no black in between.

When I woke it was hot and close but I walked three miles along the coast road to Leverburgh with a song in my heart. Everyone I passed greeted me and I felt their lives were about living. An old couple were building a peat stack, there was a lot of building work going on, a trench being dug, lots of coils of alkathene about – could they only now be going onto piped water, I wondered. Yellow irises everywhere but no trees. I saw what looked like a whole fleece, but it was a dead sheep, its skull lying nearby, bleached clean. I saw two rams with massive curled horns, their voices gurgling deep and soft and gentle compared to the plaintive cries of the ewes and lambs.

I got to Leverburgh, made enquiries about buses, bought another map and food for 3 days, sat and ate some, and it grew quite cold. I walked back to Rodel by the main road which was barely wider than the C road, my load twice as heavy with all the food. The silence was only broken by an occasional bleat, the trickle of a stream and the rattle of a car on a cattle grid, its sound echoing back from the hills. Down near the sea was the sound of waves crashing against rocks and the low throb of a rare boat. The roads seemed very new as though it couldn't have been long since they travelled from village to village by boat.

A man staggered along the road towards me: "Hello, how do you like the Hebrides? You look like something from East of Suez (?) and you're a young girl! Do you want a dram of whisky?" he asked, pulling a huge bottle from his pocket. I declined, passed the time of day, laughed and walked on. It began to rain gently, an odd drop falling on my cheek like a tear.

I reckoned that as I'd walked about 7 miles all together, I deserved some tea, so went to the hotel. They took me past the silver-service dining room and up to a strange little tea-room like a conservatory, which had plain chairs and tables. It was lovely, with ivy growing up trellis and plants in pots and a wonderful white ship's figure-head of a woman in the corner, looking like the statue of a goddess. The toilets were Victorian with Victorian wash-basins and soap-on-a-rope which looked just as old. There was a rope handrail with kind of macramé covering the knob. It was as though nothing had changed for a hundred years and I wished I could stay there. I had a pot of tea and some biscuits, never mind the cost. It still rained outside. A young man who had been on the coach and ferry, who looked like a local lad returning from college, was working in the hotel as a plumber, mending a lavatory.

The rain eased. I walked to the church, then back to the Dun.

I met up with Keith Payne and John Sharkey and travelled around with them for the next couple of days, visiting places which would take me years to re-discover when I came to live on Lewis. There were some exquisite moments: a walk along a pristine beach to an old chapel, the sea pale turquoise over pure white sand, darker blue over seaweed; the sun and wind on my face, burning me as I walked along the edge of the sea, the water hissing and caressing my bare feet. My toes sunk into the sand which had fine lines on it where little waves had left surf edges like veins. In every direction the only signs of civilisation were a solitary stone wall, the ruined chapel on the headland, the soft ridges of old lazy beds, a piece of driftwood and a single piece of polystyrene.

My bare footprints in the pure sand followed the boot-prints of the two men walking ahead of me.

Another day we spent a long time in the St Clements church at Rodel. On one side of the tower there is a beautiful Sheela-na-gig. She is holding something in her arms and there is a rectangular shape in one corner. I was told she was a woman who had just given birth to a seal – a selkie? To me it looks as though she is sitting in front of a Blackhouse, and I think of her as a protective spirit looking out to sea and guarding the fishermen. Inside the church I climbed the tower, and everything seemed to be spinning with a massive energy wheeling round and round. Outside I climbed over a wall and felt the presence of a bunch of old cackling hags sitting there laughing at me; not in a malicious way,

Standstill on the Sleeping Beauty Mountain

but like old wise women laughing at my naivete, and how much I had yet to learn. They were like the hags round the well near Dumfries.

The day came when we headed north and I would be seeing the Mountain and the Stones for the first time. En route we stopped at Clach Macleod on the west coast of Harris. This is a single standing stone which seems to rise up as though about to fly free of the land which holds it. For me that day it was a green and golden goddess/ spirit of the land – welcoming and telling me I belonged on these Islands and must indeed live there at some time in the future.

On the way up, we stopped on the road, not far into Lewis and I saw the Sleeping Beauty Mountain quite close, etched clear against the skyline. I was overcome with emotion. Like a dream she had called me north; stronger and stronger she had pulled me up my line of light. Now I had reached my goal and was looking at her in actual physical reality.

On we went to Callanish, the landscape of Lewis very different from the mountains of Harris: high, flat, overlooking the land for miles towards the distant horizon. Clear and pure, this was a landscape I felt very comfortable with. At Callanish we went to their old camping place and met up with Lynne. It was a beautiful spot to the north of the Callanish village, high, overlooking village, Stones and Mountain. It was a small walled enclosure which had been

74

used as a bothy and had enough room for a few tents. At that time there was a kind of raised fireplace which could be cooked on, with a rough chimney up the rock-face which formed one side of the site. Over the years, I returned many, many times to camp there, but it became gradually spoilt by other campers, and then local people built a shed in it and nowadays the whole area is fenced off, the bothy full of rubbish and the land used by cows who have churned up the ground with their feet. But in 1982 it was like a little piece of heaven.

My first visit to the main Callanish circle was overwhelming. The stones were like strangers then, tall and extraordinary, but over the decades have become so familiar, like ancient beings themselves, allowing access to the ancestral spirits of those who erected them and their creation ancestors.

Many seem to hold images of people and animals, like totemic representatives of ancient tribes. Whenever I go to them I find new things I've not seen before. They have become like friends, and I feel welcomed and honoured and privileged that I have been able to touch them once more. But that first year it was a new and stunning experience, as was the whole landscape.

With Lynne, we continued to visit many more sites on Lewis, as John and Keith carried on with their book. I had no map of Lewis and again no idea where we went, taking years to re-discover these places. One I have still not found: a man rowed us out somewhere in his boat and we spent a day on something like an island. Lynne cooked lunch, and we each read, wrote, drew, whatever, and I knew Lewis would inevitably be my home, but it was a deep, sad knowing for I would be alone – and how was I to endure a life of such aloneness in this incredibly powerful place? I wanted to stay there for ever, to see it at all times of year, and knew when I left how much I would miss the light nights when the sun never really goes.

We visited the Claitair hotel on the road to South Lochs, where I was later to live. It had a lovely room then, with soft, sofa-like seats and here I enjoyed my first whisky, a drink I'd never liked before. The place went through many changes in the following decades, but I will never forget the welcoming and joyful place it was on that, my first visit.

They took me to meet Annie Macleod. When the group of them first visited Callanish in 1980/81, she had been living in the last inhabited black-house in Callanish, probably the last in the whole of Lewis. They had thatched her roof and all of them spent a lot of time with her, hearing many of the 'old yarns'. But by 1982 she had been moved to the council scheme Druim nan Curracag, just down the road. The hill between her old home and the new was called 'Peewit Hill' as there were always many around in those days. I think of her as an old lady, but when I first met her she was only about the age I am now. I'm sad I never saw her in her old house, which had a chimney, not an open hearth in the middle of the floor like a true black-house. One evening we all went to visit her and the conversation went on and on. Eventually we thought we had better leave as it must be getting late, thinking it was about 10.30 pm. It was 2.30 in the morning!

As it got closer to the Solstice, more and more people gathered to be part of our group, including Monica and some women friends of hers. When the Solstice eve and dawn came, many of us gathered at the Stones to stand in silence as the sun rose. It was not as it is now with people coming from far and wide, camping, some years in collections of living wagons, drinking, drumming, sometimes shouting and making a bit of a mess of the place. In the early '80s few people came, just perhaps some photographers driving up before sunrise if it looked like being a good one.

I had not yet made my final 'exchanges' at the Brow of my journey. I decided not to do this at the main circle, but at a smaller one nearby, known as 'Circle III', which I still visit whenever I can and dearly love. It has a very different energy to the main circle. Perhaps there I felt more connected to my line of light and the rest of my journey, spending a lot of time there that year. One night I slept in the circle, and early that morning dreamed I was on something which looked like a Mediterranean coast, high, with hills on either side, a turquoise ocean before me and a ring of islands out to sea.

Below me was a walled Cretan Labyrinth and out from this walked 13 women in gold dresses with pots on their heads, pots shaped like the stones of the main Callanish circle.

Some days later we went to the beach at Bosta on Great Bernera. The others went to look at the rocks on the beach while I walked up a kind of glen above it. I turned round, and to my amazement saw the place of my dream. Where the labyrinth had been was a cemetery. When I joined the others again they were excited, sure that this was where the Callanish stones had come from, being the same kind of rock, full of 'black crystal'. My dream seemed an affirmation of that. I think Annie had told them to go there, though she didn't say why. Nowadays archaeologists claim the stones came from a 'quarry' not far from Callanish, but I will always believe they came from Bosta (where an Iron Age village has been found, taken to Callanish by boat through Loch Roag, which was probably a river then, as the sea level was lower. Bosta will always be a sacred site to me, and in 1982 it was yet one more over-powering place to take in.

The day came when we knew we must walk in pilgrimage on the Sleeping Beauty. We drove down the Eisken road to start the walk near her feet. Keith came as our guide, as he'd explored her three times previously, and 'could never resist a beautiful woman', but soon after we set off we seemed to split up into separate groups and individuals. At one point the wind seemed to take me and carry me up one of her knees along a route I can't these days work out. Monica and her friends stopped after a while, feeling they didn't want to trample on her body, but I felt it was the ultimate pilgrimage and that my feet were caressing her. It was a wild, windy day up there, walking across her wide throat to her chin, her nose –where eagles had nested – and on to her Brow. Lynne had got there first, standing with her great red poncho flapping in the wind as though she were a giant firebird.

I lay on that Brow and all my journeys came together as one: the body of the land I had travelled from the toe-tip in Cornwall, the body of the Mountain I had just walked, and my own body. All one. I had the land in me. I had the Mountain in me. And I was in them. This was the culmination of my journey, this greatest journey of my life. I placed a stone from the journey on a cairn. I placed my brow on her brow.

We left, and returned to the camp, the memory seared into me for the rest of my life.

Chapter 5: Coming Down (Or 'The Long Winter of Death and Rebirth')

I had reached such heights, experienced such perfection, and lived a time of such extreme emotions. What next? How was I going to go back? How was I going to go down? For it would be down. Most of the others left after the Solstice, but Lynne and I stayed a while, visiting more places with John and Keith, but felt in the way, that we should go and leave the men to their work. There are few decisions in my life I actually regret, but leaving when we did is one of them. It wasn't the right time, yet it had to come sometime and maybe there never would have been a right time. 'Going down' had to be faced somehow, and lived through.

We set off to stay briefly with Sandra and Andy Bell, who were by then living in Newcastle. As I sat on the ferry, I felt crazy to be leaving – what on earth was I doing? – but I'd promised to return for the Faerie Faire at Cadder's Hill in Norfolk, and was keeping my word.

I learned a lot from Lynne about how to hitch up and down the land, and after a brief stop in Newcastle we got to the Faire, where I found I wasn't needed after all. But, for the first time ever, we did a performance together, about Ariadne's thread. I felt I didn't belong anywhere any more, so, desperate to try and recapture something lost, I persuaded Lynne to do a mad hitch back up to Lewis, but when we arrived, everything had changed: John had broken his arm and was no longer on the Island and everything was wrong. I did discover, though, that my love for the Island remained.

We all hurried off and I hitched back to Newcastle on my own. There I wrote a story about my journey and bought a drawing pad and some pastels to get down on paper some of the teeming imagery in my head.

Some days later I got a lift back to Norfolk and was dropped at the gate of what had once been my home, the home I had left a couple of months before: a couple of months which felt like a million lifetimes. Saffron was there on her own, as Bruce and Tiffany were away on the South Coast at some sculpture park. She was confused by my return – had I come back or not?

How do you 'come down'? My whole realm of experience had totally changed. I was going through enormous upheavals, needing time to get some sort of grasp on what I had done; to understand and reflect on it and try to work out where on earth I went from there. I began phoning friends and arranged to meet

Julia cut my hair off

several of them in a pub 20 miles away. Another friend, Jennifer Perry, had a caravan she wasn't using in a field, so I phoned her and she said I could stay in it for a while. At Brentwood Farm I slipped back into the 'Mum' role, doing the washing up, phoning a neighbour to say she didn't need to come round to milk the goat as I was there, and thought 'What am I doing?'. There was just one goat now - Gina, as my beloved Sarny Sou had died on the very day I walked the Sleeping Beauty, as though the mountain had needed some sort of sacrifice. They had buried her in the garden – and I suppose some aspect of me with her. Bruce phoned Saffron and I spoke to him, telling him I was going to stay in the caravan and he said "We've been getting on better without you anyway". So, that was it. I had left. No options. I really was on my own. My Morrie van was there so I drove off to the pub with the rucksack I'd been travelling with, but not much else.

I was in a deep state of shock on many levels. Staying in a caravan was the most 'indoors' I'd been for months. This one had electricity and running water, but I had virtually nothing. In a way this was a great freedom: all my life I'd been tied down by possessions; things I thought I needed to prove I existed and to give me some sort of identity. Now I just had what was in my bag. This was it. What was I going to do with my life? I had left everything that was to do with my performance work, and even that didn't feel very 'me' any more. I still wanted to perform, but what? And with whom? Who was I?

The first week or so I couldn't sleep in the caravan; visiting people and crashing on their floors, it taking a huge amount of courage to be on my own. I had spent all those weeks on my own out on the land, but hadn't then been alone, had been on the journey, with the land I had become. But now there was just me. I looked in the mirror and saw my raw self, with no illusions, and a new life had to start from there.

Writing this 35 years later, I remember very little of those first few months on a day to day basis. I have no proper writings, no diaries, so just recall fragments, and little of that is about actually being in the caravan, though I can remember evenings when I opened up the drawing pad, stared at the white paper, then closed it again, afraid of making any mark, afraid of not being able to create the vibrant images inside my head. Eventually I did manage some, and those early drawings, though tentative and pale, have a wonderful energy and life in them.

My life, though, had lost its shape. For years everything had been journeys: the performances, the journeys round sacred sites and terrestrial zodiacs, one round all the Alfred Watkins sites in his 'Old Straight Track' book, a walk of the Ridgeway Path, visiting ancient sites for Equinoxes and Solstices and Celtic fire festivals...then this greatest journey of them all from Cornwall to the Hebrides. Now there seemed no form, no shape to anything and I was in complete turmoil on every conceivable level, trying to make sense of so many issues in my life.

But things did happen in those months. There was a retreat in a field in North Norfolk with the Master, Namkhai Norbu, which I helped organise, the Dzog Chen practice being the one thing which gave some form and sense to my life. There were more Albion Fairs: at one I did some 'Fire and Water Sisters' performances with Sandra, which were quite profound with deep exchanges of energy. At another I was roped in to a 'Magic Ox' performance, playing the part of the Black Hen which eats the Grain of Wheat in the Taliesin story. With Keith I repeated the performance of the journey up the land which we had done earlier that year; it felt like a lifetime ago. I did a Dzog Chen type performance with Keith too; one where we sat on the tops of huge thin poles, high in the air, in the dark. I was in a state then where I knew no fear, not really caring what happened to me. I have no photographs, no record of any of these things, but occasionally will meet someone who saw them, especially the one on the pole.

At one fair Bruce did a huge performance with all the 'props' and sacred objects we had used together and I felt he had 'stolen' my language, stolen all the ways I'd had of expressing my deepest spiritual experiences, twisting them and turning them into something quite different. It was as though yet more of my self had been torn from me, and all those objects which had been sacred to me were being defiled.

At another fair, walking across a field I stopped to talk with Sylvia, who'd been an acquaintance for years. As we parted she said "It's so good to actually meet you at last", and I realised how, in all my years with Bruce, where he just talked endlessly at people all the time, it had cut me off from them.

Now I was out there, pure, naked, available for anyone to find, and got to know a lot of people, started to make real friends, and began to move among circles of women.

A few times Tiffany and Saffron came to visit me in the caravan, but I couldn't convey my turmoil to them, and they couldn't convey theirs to me. There was no way they could have had a home there with me and I would have offered them even less as a mother than I had before.

I was very restless and couldn't stay in one place for long. I took easily to hitching and reached all my destinations quickly. It was straightforward in those days: at the beginning of a motorway, or a slip road leading onto one, you would find long lines of people waiting. There was an informal queuing system, which some drivers respected, while others didn't, picking up a woman or someone looking more respectable, even if they were at the back of the queue. However, most of my hitching was on routes where there weren't many others going the same way.

I learned a kind of attitude – to stand facing the traffic, looking positive and friendly, leaning into the hitch somehow, picking a spot where the driver could actually stop. They would drop me at roundabouts or motorway service stations if they were going on in a different direction, it being important to avoid motorways which just branched off, as I'd then get stuck somewhere where lifts were impossible. On smaller roads, if lifts were slow coming, I learned to take anything, even for just a mile, as it got the energy of the journey going and lifts would then come more easily. Often I visualised a person leaving their house in a good mood, so when they saw me they would feel generous and stop. Sometimes people would say "I never usually come this way; I don't know why I did today".

It was a different world then, with many different vehicles: old, new, vans, trucks, much more variety than now. Laws were brought in during the Thatcher era which not only pretty well ended hitching on motorways, but meant most vehicles became similar, with no longer the rich patchwork of drivers there was. Some of the best lifts were with long-distance lorry drivers. They would call up my next lift on their CB radio, pull over, another truck would stop and away I'd go with them. I tried to learn their radio terminology: hitchers were 'seat warmers', but I've forgotten most of it now. I did tend to avoid the 'commercial traveller' type – a solitary man with a suit on a hanger in the back of his car: there was something a bit dodgy about them. I was 40 by now, but most drivers thought I was 18, asking what my parents thought of what I was doing. Some thought I was Canadian or Australian, never mind my London accent, as they couldn't imagine an Englishwoman doing what I was.

I never had any trouble. Sometimes, travelling through the night, I would feel the energy change and decide that would be my last lift of the day. I would get out and instead of hitching again, sleep under a motorway flyover until it got light. I learned to manage conversations which began "Aren't you scared doing this". Giving the impression of being afraid made one vulnerable; confidence seemed to be a protection. There were ways of steering conversations back to something else.

Maybe my years of market and social research interviewing had taught me some tricks.

So how did I survive – sleeping out with no tent through the winter, sometimes in wind, sometimes in frost and snow, sometimes in rain? The main thing was learning how to dress. It was layer upon layer upon layer, with everything overlapping over my middle: I had a big thing about keeping my kidneys warm. Starting from the inside, I wore two pairs of knickers – first, little ones, then a long woollen vest of my grandmother's, tucked into a big pair. Long-johns went up high over the vest, then long tee-shirts and thin jumpers tucked into loose trousers and a long, thick jumper over them; everything secure so it couldn't ride up and with no gap in the middle. Polo necks keeping the draught from blowing down; two pairs of socks; a long coat, hat, scarf and gloves. I still wear coats with hoods, tied tight to my neck by a scarf. I always carried the plastic to wrap myself in if it rained. I had no idea what I looked like and didn't really care.

I loved lying there under the sky, and if it was windy but dry would position my rucksack to shelter me from the wind. By then I had borrowed a down sleeping-bag, which made a lot of difference, and had a rug or blanket. The best sleeping–bags are the 'mummy' type with a hood. It is more important to have warmth under you than on top as the earth is cold under your body and drains the warmth from you. If I had any newspaper or cardboard it would go under me, but I usually managed without, lying foetally on my side, with the least amount of body or vital organs in contact with the ground, tucking my hands in my armpits or between my thighs. I once saw a picture of an Australian Aboriginal woman from when they were still living in the bush. She was naked, on her knees, tucked up very tight. It was captioned 'Woman preparing to sleep without fire'. I tried it once in a churchyard, though I had clothes on, and it did work: just your lower legs are in contact with the earth.

In the frost or occasional snow (though I wasn't ever out when it actually snowed on me) I mentally wrapped myself in the cold with my warm self inside. I would be aware of the cold but wouldn't let it get into me: a visualisation which became a form of practice. Recently, the old rule about keeping your head warm because a quarter of your body heat escapes through it, has been proven an old wives' tale, but it's safer to still believe it. Keep your head warm with no draughts down your neck, or up your sleeves. I never came to any harm or got ill and always had some food, like lumps of cheese and oatcakes. Nowadays I carry those thick oaty bars which are packed with calories.

There you are – now you can all do it!

The hour before dawn is the coldest, but even on the darkest, coldest, wettest morning, the sun does always rise, it does always get light and you can see again, get up and get on your way. I always felt safe in the arms of my Mother the Earth, and that is a very real experience, not something idly fanciful.

At the retreat I had become friendly with a woman called Erin, and persuaded her to hitch up to Lewis with me at the end of September. I was desperate to be back there, to somehow ground the craziness I was feeling in England. I was extremely enthusiastic and just swept people along with my ideas, though she did say en route that she was asking herself what on earth she was doing, hitching all that way with someone she hardly knew.

After visiting Lynne in Wales for a few days I hitched to Erin in London and we set off for the Islands. It took us 27 hours from Clapham to the Firth of Forth and the next day we were at Ullapool, waiting for the ferry. Erin was a magical, psychic person and on our way there the driver of our lift stopped to do some business. Erin got out, crossed the road and came back, not only with several four-leaved clovers, but a five-leaved one as well. "I just knew they were there" she said. She'd never been there before.

Autumn on Lewis can be like winter and my memory of that trip is that it was much more dark and wintry than it probably was. But it was typical Lewis weather – a lot of wind and a lot of rain. We had borrowed a tent as there would be no sleeping out without one at that time of year in the Islands. I had the down sleeping-bag, but otherwise pretty well what I'd taken before, though I did have some more substantial shoes this time. It was very, very good for me to be back. There was no doubt that this place felt like home, where I belonged, though I had no idea when or how I would ever move there. We camped in the same place to the north of the village. We visited Annie and her sister Ishbel, sitting by their fires drinking tea, and I spent time at Circle III as well as the main circle, re- finding my deep sense of peace there.

I was so into being outdoors all the time that I was rather imposing it on Erin, which annoyed her a bit. She wanted to go to the National Mod on Skye, so we hitched down to Harris and did stay in a B&B in Tarbert. On Skye we camped one night in a gale in the foothills of the Cuillins and our dome tent went crescent shaped in the wind. I dreamed of harpies nesting in mountain-tops, screeching as they flew around. We found a good place to camp in Portree for a couple of nights and went to some of the Mod. Erin was a singer and musician, so wanted to hear the Gaelic. (We had thought of going to a church service in Callanish, to hear the chanting, but feeling we might not be welcome, just listened outside.) At the Mod I was fascinated by the puirt a beul, or mouth music, which must have been used when musical instruments were banned by the church. People the world over seem to have some form of making music by mouth. It can sound instrumental and is quite extraordinary.

Our journey having been a pretty vibrant experience, we hitched back, Erin to London and I to East Anglia, soon back in the caravan at Kirby Cane. By now I had spent all my savings, had no income, no work and had to sign on for the first time in my life. I had no idea what I could do to earn a living, but at least wasn't having to pay rent.

The fragments of writing I have from the time I entered that winter show extreme levels of psychological and spiritual turmoil. There are exercise books where I have written from the back to the front, others where I have written different details in different books about the same events. Some I can't date or in any way relate to now. Some are of incredibly enlightened vision whereas others are like the writings of a madwoman, but I wasn't mad. I was working hard to try and sort out what everything might mean. As I've said, the Dzog Chen teachings kept me sane. I began to feel that what I was living through was some kind of shamanic shattering of every atom of my old being and a slow re-building of them into a new me.

I survived by giving it shape. I created a new journey and gave myself purpose and a physicality to the shamanic journey. I felt, as I always do, that I was going down, down, deep into the earth to reach the deepest place at midwinter; to slowly rise and come out into the light of a new reality in the spring; hopefully reborn. I intended to shape it by going to either a well, a spring, or a long barrow for each full and dark moon throughout the winter. I was back on a journey.

Having already been to Lewis in late September, I felt I must in reality, as well as symbolically, enter the earth at Samhain at the end of October (the Celtic New Year). Since then I have always tried to do the same: to physically enter a long barrow, chambered cairn, cave or something similar as my spiritual self goes deep into the earth for winter. It is a kind of hibernation and I wonder whether this is something we all experience at some level. I have met many women who share this sense of slowing down, both physically and mentally; of their daily reality becoming more still, meditative and silent as they approach the Winter Solstice – that pause at the swing of the pendulum, the pause between breaths.

As a species, when we moved into Europe and were on the fringes of the Ice Age, we must have tucked ourselves away somehow, even as hunter-gatherers; keeping warm with some stocks of fuel and food, slowing down our metabolism as we reached the depth of winter. I believe we still are those Ice Age humans and this is why many people feel so wrong in the modern world as the Christmas period approaches. As we slow down our society demands that we speed up, being busier than at any other time of year, rushing about like crazy when we need to just stop.

So, in that extreme winter of 1982/83 I needed to go into the earth. I hitched with a young friend (Jonathan) to Waylands Smithy, the place where I used to have my birthday parties. As a Neolithic long barrow high on the Ridgeway path, it is smaller inside than West Kennet, but has a main chamber, two smaller side chambers, and a long earthen mound stretching back from it. There are huge stones at the front and, as at Kennet, a passage to the chambers.

Jonathan went off to find food and while on my own I spiritually entered the earth. As I sat in the centre chamber I seemed to become an ancient woman who had once been there. I heard the sound of a huge stone being dragged across the front of the chamber so she was in complete darkness to have oracular visions. After a few days, they would move the stone away and she would tell them of the things she had seen and her interpretation of them.

Jonathan came back with Guinness and warm pies. We slept in the chamber. In the morning I emerged exhausted as though I had truly been that ancient oracle. My spiritual self continued her journey deep into the winter earth while my physical self visited the Uffington White Horse, the Blowing Stone, an earthwork nearby and slept another night in a barn. We walked through lanes of beautiful autumn hedgerows then hitched back to East Anglia.

85

So, I was in the earth for winter; going down, down, down, my atoms disintegrating into their most fundamental parts. I survived by observing it, letting it happen and trying to understand what was going on. As I went deeper I spent powerful times with my young friend Julia and with Lynne – trying to understand the universe, the nature of reality and how to attain clarity; being somehow of all time and of no time; trying to understand all that had ever been and all that will ever be and what it's all for and what I was, what my purpose was and what was the purpose of my relationships with others. It exhausted me; sacred places exhausted me; it was as though people, places and the universe drained me completely, as though I was giving all of my self in order to receive understanding. I hadn't learnt to ground anything, to observe without being carried along in the whirlwind of it all. I was hanging on for dear life to all my fragmenting atoms so they were still there to be reconstructed; hanging on to my sanity yet living such a visionary time, making connections and seeing far beyond the mundane. Everything was symbolic, everything had vast esoteric meaning. I was close to understanding the meaning of everything!

November 9th '82: I began to change my image. I started to wear black, wanting clear outlines with no extraneous flappy bits. Julia wanted to cut my hair off. I still had the white-blonde witchy hair I had used for my performances but had let it grow out and what grew out seemed greying but darkish. I was afraid of looking like an old woman and knew I could never again have long dark hair as I did when I was young. Then Julia just cut all the blonde off. So there I was, 40 years old with the mind of a teenager and short, straggly, greying hair; overweight and chunky, virtually living on Guinness and crisps. I had no idea what this new identity was.

I was very interested in people's reactions. Some didn't even notice, whereas others were completely freaked out. One man said I looked like a school-marm and should be wearing a twin-set and pearls. Women tended to like it because I was re-claiming my self, forging a new identity and finding the real me. It showed how people really saw me: the ones who didn't notice saw my true essence, so the hair was irrelevant, whereas the ones who couldn't handle it saw only an image. It interests me now, too, because as I write at around 75, I have vivid, longish hennaed hair.

Underneath the henna it is white/grey/a little still brown. If I cut it all off, many people wouldn't recognise me, for my hair has once again become my identity. I presume I would look older. It would be interesting to see whether there would be any people who didn't notice.
In all the years of being married everything I spoke of was as the experience of "we". It was a massive shift in reclaiming my self to start saying "I", for these new experiences were mine alone.

I went down to Cardiff to see Ian McDonald, with whom I had pic-nicked in Wiltshire on my journey up the land. He was into Egyptology and I had a powerful time there, surrounded by Egyptian goddesses. I pored over a book – An Illustrated Encyclopaedia of Traditional Symbols by J.C.Cooper (who is a woman) which provided me with all sorts of esoteric connections between things and everything was spinning again. I hitched back along the M4 in torrential rain in a car that drove at 90mph, leaving it to go to West Kennet for the November Dark Moon.

I went first to the Swallowhead Spring, which was dry for the winter, and 'became' the spring and the hole it flowed from, knowing the experience of being them through hundreds of thousands of years; then walked through mud and icy water to the long barrow. Long barrows had become my houses now, my homes, the places where I belonged. They were the wombs of the earth and I was the earth and they were my own womb and I was the child in my own womb, waiting to be reborn. The wind raged outside as though I were in a cave on a shore and outside was the sea.

The water dripped all night and the cold was a tingle in my body. It was so dark that when my eyes were shut it seemed like they were open and when they were open, it seemed like they were shut.

In the morning I once again sensed the ancient people chanting, the circle of elders, people in the side chambers, a line of light going from the circle to the outside. Later, in the courtyard at the front, I burned things from my journeys, and some of my old, dead, dry, blonde hair; burned incense for the elements and Tibet and gave the place small stones from other sacred sites. I slept another night, this time in a side-chamber, in the womb of the universe, a child joined by an umbilical cord to a placenta embedded in one of the giant stones. I began to write powerful poems, distilling the essence of my wild writings into a few clear, pure lines.

Back in East Anglia I saw an image of Glastonbury Tor on the inside walls of Barsham Church and was off, hitching down to be with the Tor and Chalice Well for the December Full Moon. I visualised Glastonbury and in no time was there in physical reality, walking its streets at night, then up the long 'spine' of the Tor, perceiving it for the first time as the body of a great woman with a deep cave within her. At the top the light of the full moon was brilliant. I became one with the light, one with the moon. I was the light. I was the moon. I disappeared, dissolved, as though I was dying: a shamanic death.

I spent the night in the tower on the Tor, in the wind and cold, bat-like creatures fluttering high in the tower. Next day I sat with the blood water of Chalice Well, then went to visit people in Street and began to lay plans.

I was becoming familiar with the strength of women together, women living the cycles and power of seasons, sun, moon and growth...and soon it was

December 12/13 and I went to Greenham Common and we encircled the base and were all one energy and all one power and it flowed round the circle and we sang the song of the Mountain, and for me the Mountain was the Sleeping Beauty on Lewis. I'd never been part of anything like that before; the organisation, the forming of support groups and the training for non-violent direct action as much as the actual event itself. I was becoming part of a powerful Sisterhood.

Staying for the second day we blocked a gate, and I had my first experience of confrontation with the police. At last I was free to take part in this kind of action and it didn't matter if I was arrested. I wasn't, but it changed me. I never lived at the camp, but visited for a few days several times after that. I was totally in awe of the women who lived there for months, years, in appalling conditions, being horrendously treated by the police. And in awe of people in other actions at that time who were arrested and imprisoned over and over again for what they believed in. I went back to the caravan in the field at Kirby Cane and that became my cave. I sat with the light and electric fire on, but was in the spiritual dark, so deep was I going. I was the earth and I was the Mountain and I was other people. I was boundless.

On the December dark moon there was a partial solar eclipse and I was so deep in my cave I didn't need to go anywhere.

A wonderful woman: Jan Dungey, much younger than I, but at that time much more mature, began running women's workshops in Norwich and I went to some of them, journeying on guided visualisations and gaining more insight into my woman-self. These workshops were attended by all sorts of women and were very empowering, helping us to understand what it was to be a woman and realise our creative potential. Jan was one of the greatest influences on my life at that time, maybe helping me to ground all the wildness I was going through. I think the re-integration of my atoms into a new self began around then.

Winter Solstice 1982: I had planned many things, thought I should go to Newgrange in Ireland, but in the end went to London. For Solstice sunrise I sat high on the Parliament Hill tumulus, sensing the place as it had been long before the city was there. It was perfectly still with frost and frozen dead leaves crackling under-foot. Nature waited. I waited. I sat so still a squirrel ran up my back. A flight of birds rose up right round me.
The year turned and I was on the way up.

There is so far to travel from the depth of winter to the height of summer, so the turn from my depths to whatever level of clarity and enlightenment I might reach was also a long journey. But something did turn. I did begin to move towards some new sort of self, some putting together of all those smashed

88

atoms into a new sense of me, a new being, a new life completely. As the turn began

I was wide open, formless, part of everyone and everything with no protection. Other people's power invaded me, used me, strove to control me and I fought to keep myself separate from their psychic battles raging inside this vast empty space which was me. I had wild ecstatic nights in the woods at Kirby Cane, in some sort of shamanic trance, thinking that a few hundred years before I would have been burned as a witch.

The 'Greenham factor' was a powerful awakening for many women, understanding for the first time the power of women working together. I gained strength as I spent time with groups of them. I began to think it was my task to heal the earth and help all humanity understand everything that I was beginning to see. A few years later, as I became aware of some dubious aspects of the New Age movement, I became shocked at what I might have been feeding my energy into and pulled it all back into myself. Since then I have worked in much more subtle and quiet ways, though ones that are no less powerful; but back in 1982/83 a sense of destiny and purpose was vital to my coming back together into this new self.

I suddenly had a beautiful, spontaneous Christmas with my 3 children at Kevin's place in London. After all those years of worrying myself sick for months trying to organise Christmases which ticked all the boxes, here was something totally unplanned which is still one of my happiest Christmas memories. Our Christmas dinner was a take-away curry bought from a local Asian shop round the corner: open on Christmas Day.

Although, in my spiritual celebrations of the year it is the Solstice which is the turning point, I still like to celebrate Christmas as a cultural time when everything does stop and people are together with their families celebrating something far more ancient than Christianity. I hated the fact that my inability to cope had made me a rotten mother over the previous few years, and now I wanted my children to know the new me and share in all I was learning, but you can't just impose your own stuff on people, especially young ones who are struggling to understand their own realities.

Full Moon, December 30. I returned to Norfolk and a powerful lunar eclipse was spent on Covehithe beach with a group of women. Strongly linked to the other 30,000 Greenham women and the ebb and flow of the moon and tides, it hadn't seemed necessary to go far from home, realising there were powerful sacred places nearby.

On the Dark Moon of January 14 1983 I sat in my van eating a Chinese takeaway with Lynne. We had a drink in a pub, talking of powerful stuff, then I returned alone to the caravan and slept, feeling some sort of control was returning.

Jan Dungey, Lynne and I went to Glastonbury and held a three-day workshop for women (Spinners of Fate), guiding them on a journey - firstly in the landscape, then within their own bodies and finally a labyrinth walk which let them realise that all three are the same. In a guided visualisation which Jan led, I experienced my re-birth as a wise old woman.

Full Moon, January 28th Having now got hitching down to a fine art I returned to Lewis to be at Callanish and Brighde's Well at Melbost Borve for Imbolc. I still had the down sleeping-bag and had borrowed a tent which was little more than a child's play tent.

The journey was really easy, everything falling into place: Kirby Cane in Suffolk to Ullapool in NW Scotland in 26 hours. For once I listed all my lifts: 1) To Gillingham roundabout with a friend; 2) With a man who was reading a book about Dunwich – to Norwich; 3) A red Volvo with CB to Blue Star services on the A1 near Worksop; 4) with a Scots trucker who lived in Peterborough and was born in 1942 (so was I) to Crawford, south of Glasgow. He chased after his mate 5) in a Hotpoint truck not carrying much, who took me on to the Stirling road past Glasgow; 6) a Scot in a hired truck who had come from Norwich after crashing his own lorry (Norfolk Line, which was a franchise). He was a potato trucker and very restless and hyped-up after his accident. At 2.30am he dropped me at a lorry park where I sat in a cafe for hours until the drivers started to get up; 7) next day, a truck to Inverness with a nice guy who made me a cup of tea; 8) with a man in a car with a child in a car-seat in the back – to Bewlay; 9) with a young man who said "I'll take you to Ullapool if you make it worth my while". I laughed and said "No thanks" so he took me to the outskirts of the Muir of Ord; 10) with a nice oldish man in a yellow parcels van, who started to teach me Gaelic – to somewhere there was a shop; 11) with a man who'd driven from London and whose son lived in California – to a new junction at Garve; 12) with a guy in a green sweater in a Range Rover – to Ullapool. He was a bit like landed gentry and made cracks about the 'darkies' driving the English out of England. He had a nose like Lynne's and I was tempted to ask if he was a Sinclair (her heritage).

I didn't comment on people's outrageous attitudes, just listened, as I used to when I was a market research interviewer, not getting into arguments with them. It seems cowardly, but I just tried to keep things calm and when I didn't respond they usually dropped the subject. Sometimes I talked about my life, and what I was doing, and some people were really pleased to have met me. They were in safe jobs with mortgages but had dreams of one day just taking off from it all. Meeting someone who was actually doing it somehow comforted them; re-assuring them it was possible. Meeting me kept their dreams alive.

I sat and waited for the Stornoway ferry in the Ullapool fisherman's mission. This has long-since closed, but then it was another of my 'best caffs in Britain'. You could sit there for ages in the warm, steamy air with a mug of tea, listening to all the fishermen and local people who were living what I called real lives.

I was a bit concerned about my appearance by then. The blonde hair was gone, leaving the short horrid grey and I had put on even more weight over the winter. I must have eaten more than Guinness and crisps, and a lot of it was comfort eating as I made my shamanic journey through hell. I don't put on weight in a lovely voluptuous way, but become thick and shapeless and chunky with legs like tree-trunks. Maybe I put on weight to keep myself warm. The ferry arrived and I crossed once more to the Isles. In those days it was a boat called the Suilven, much lower in the water than the ones which have replaced it. The Suilven felt more like a local boat, built for 'local people' rather than tourists. I used to feel I was already on the island once I was on it. There weren't a lot of passengers that time but a small group called me over and bought me rather a lot of Cognac, not something I normally drink. This was the only time in my life so far that I received verbal abuse from a Scotsman for being English. He was another passenger who, hearing my accent, came over and gave forth, but was told to shut it by my companions.

Arriving in Stornoway I was given a bed for the night by the people I had joined. On these unplanned journeys, sometimes things just turned up when I needed them. So, I was in the Hebrides again, in the winter again. I was certainly learning the truth about Hebridean weather, under no illusions from my first dry summer visit. Every time I arrived I wrote that I had come home, that it was normal to be there and I didn't feel in any way remote from all the people I knew. Distance meant nothing; the Islands became somewhere I popped up to as though just going to the shops.

Next morning I caught a bus north to Ness, an area new to me, although I was probably driven up that way in '82 without really knowing where I was. Melbost Borve was a place I had never been to before and getting there under my own steam helped me get to know the area. I had the well marked on my map - Tobar Bhrigdhe or St. Bridget's Well. Nearby are the ruins of a little chapel also dedicated to her. I called at a nearby house. The lady there looked deep into my eyes, gripped my arm and showed me where the well and the ruins were. She seemed to care deeply and be very pleased that someone was visiting them.

It was a beautiful afternoon so I put the tent up beside a wall, overlooking a bay where two rivers run down to the sea. I went to sit in peace by the well which in those days was fenced off in a little enclosure with a gate, then went to the chapel ruins where I'm sure I heard a church bell ringing, though they don't have church bells on Lewis. I heard the voice of a woman singing a lullaby on the wind, and thought maybe it was a selkie. The ruins were less over-grown than they are now, as though it had been kept clean. It seemed to have been built with stones from the shore, rounded by the tides of centuries. It is hard to see now whether my memories are correct. I walked down to the beach, the big, smooth stones making a haunting noise as the sea-water swept over them and they were sucked back by the under-tow of the receding wave.

As the dark of evening came, a wind blew up and turned into a raging gale. The tent poles fell down, the pegs came out and I found myself simply lying in the bag of the inner tent which was weighed down by my rucksack. The fly-sheet blew off and I bundled it up inside the bag.

Every so often there was horizontal hail storming in the wind, building up on the orange tent; however, this was the full moon and for much of the time the sky was clear, lit by the brilliance of the moonlight. In the night, I crept out, trusting the tent was weighed down enough not to blow away. I went to the well again and sat there in the raging storm, finding peace coming from its waters and a gentle calm within myself. I gave the well gifts from other sacred places and drank some of its own clear, pure water, then went and lay in the small oval of the womb-like chapel ruin, the storm roaring above.

Back in the tent I lay listening to the wild ocean thundering on nearby rocks, the crash of the waves reverberating through the earth. I was so content to be there, to have made the journey, to have come to the well and to be in the right place. It was a pure experience of being, with no teeming thoughts streaming through my brain as they usually did.

In the morning (a Saturday) it was no longer clear, but dull with just the wild wind and snow-covered land. It took ages to pack up the tent and as I set off I struggled to walk, but got back to the main road and went south to the Ballantrushal area. People spoke to me and asked how I'd got on and said I was 'hardy'. I had been told that somewhere out on the moors was a stone which was a Neolithic carving of the Sleeping Beauty Mountain and wanted to find it. As I walked it was hard to keep on the road for the strength of the wind. I passed a shop, managed to buy some supplies, then went to the Trushal Stone which is, I think, the tallest standing stone in Europe, certainly in Scotland. I spotted what looked like an abandoned barn and wondered whether I could stay in it for a bit of shelter. I called at a house nearby and some men there said the owner lived on the other side of the Island and that it would probably be alright but not to say they said so. They invited me in, gave me a large dram, a cup of tea, some cheese on biscuits and 2 Jaffa cakes. I went to the barn, lay out my sleeping-bag and wrote postcards until the dark came. Outside, the wind still raged. I slept for a long time, having strange and vivid dreams.

In the morning my eyes were swollen and I thought I looked like a whale. The wind had dropped and outside there was thick snow. I felt apprehensive of my search for the carved stone, wondering whether I would find it. It was Sunday, but I didn't know then how strictly the Sabbath was kept on Lewis. It was a gloriously sunny day, and clouds in the distance had snow falling from them and sometimes snow would fall on me. I trudged all over the moor, marvelling at the colour of the peat and the old heather. I wished the sheep would lead me to the stone, but couldn't find it, no matter how hard I tried. I thought maybe I was not meant to find it, that maybe it was secret. It seemed the day was about the beauty of Lewis and my getting to know and love it more. I walked for miles, awed and astonished by the landscape, until it turned to dusk and I returned to the barn. I tried to write postcards by candle-light, but the candle guttered in the wind and I gave up and slept fitfully.

Next day I hitched to Stornoway and tea, then caught a bus to Callanish and stayed with Ishbel. The first evening there was a power cut and we sat by the light of the peat fire and an oil lamp. It was lovely to have a bed to sleep in and real meals. For a couple of days I went again and again to the main circle and to Circle III, spending hours with them in a kind of trance. I had visions of being the Old Hag dying and giving birth to myself as the maiden of spring. From the chamber in the centre of the main circle I physically emerged from the earth and the winter. Rain washed much of the snow away, but in the centre of Circle III there was a little left in the shape of the British Isles and I was amazed. The low winter sun shone on the brow of the Sleeping Beauty Mountain. I felt very alone, seeing that my future in the Islands was just going to be me, and I had to face that and be strong in that truth. It was wonderful to walk in the still air, in such silence, everything white and blue and sparkling like diamonds and I wished I could walk without leaving footprints. Steam rose from the loch making it look like spring.

I went to see Annie and spent a long time with her as she sat at her mother's spinning wheel twisting knitting wool for a neighbour. Being with these older women made me remember those of my childhood and wonder for the first time about my own female ancestors – that lineage going back through thousands of years – and how little I knew of it. As Annie fed me, the electricity came back on. I walked to Circle III again and watched the moon rise. I found myself singing soft love songs which just came into my head, I didn't know from where.

Back at Annie's she told me she had been afraid of the dark since her mother died when she (Annie) was 13, but walked me up Peewit Hill, guiding me by torchlight as I returned to Ishbel's. I felt so secure in Callanish with these elderly ladies. On the news I heard there had been storms and floods down south and felt apprehensive about my return. I think this was more than about the weather, though: I had come through the winter and survived; I had come through the darkest depths of disintegration and re-assembling; I had come back to Lewis and emerged. But it was only a beginning, and now I had to make something of my new life, and that was terrifying. Now I had become free and fled the cage anything was possible, and the fear was that with anything possible, what might happen was nothing. My greatest fear was nothing.

Looking back from the ferry, the receding island was dark brown with an 'icing' of white like a wedding cake. The return was easy -Ullapool to Inverness; a short lift out onto the main road, a sleep without the tent – "a lovely frost" was my only recorded remark. Darlington; the M62 turn-off; Doncaster; Worksop; Norwich; a little way round the ring-road; Poringland – then the bus to Bungay and a walk to Kirby cane.

Here I found that my own home was waiting for me as Jenny Perry wanted her caravan back. I had borrowed £60 and bought one of my own and it had been delivered to a far corner of the same field. This felt like the first home which was truly mine and I moved my few paltry possessions into it. As it had no electricity or running water I still used the Perry's house for the toilet and washing facilities. It had a Calor gas ring and I learned to live by candle-light and fetch water in a 5-gallon container which had once held apple juice. I put a notice on the door which said 'Beware of low-flying tea- bags'. The days were growing, spring was coming, I was living the rhythms of dark and light.

I was now facing the cold harsh reality of my new life. Not only could I not see which path to travel but there didn't even seem to be any paths to choose from. The future was like a vast, virgin meadow as far as the eye could see – with no landmarks.

I remember days in that caravan, writing powerful poems and really looking at myself. From very early childhood I'd had little self-esteem, had felt that everything 'wrong' with me was my fault, wanting to be like other people, yet at the same time wanting to be 'different' in interesting ways. I had never liked myself, always feeling a failure as a person. Now I began to see that younger self in a whole new light; saw all those previous failures as my strengths. They were what made me me; advantages, not weaknesses. Maybe for the first time I began to love myself, re- connecting with my 13-year old self. At 13 I had rejected my grandparents dreary suburban plans and determined to go for the life I wanted, which was to go into the theatre, be an actress and have the life I imagined went with it. I had such dreams then. I wanted to be well-known and respected for what I did, standing on stages and being applauded – loved maybe. I now saw that 13-year old as someone to whom I had a responsibility, a duty to make her dreams come true. She is still some sort of standard I measure my life by, feeling I owe her something, cannot die having failed her.

I had started to write more constructively, condensing experience into a few words, rather than my previous endless ramblings. I did more of my tentative pastel drawings as it felt important to create some visual record of my experience and understanding of the places I had been with. I exhibited the 'Awakening' drawings in a Norwich cafe: the journey of the 'Frock'. I developed my story about it, focussing on what were the most important aspects while it was happening, writing it in the third person, needing to share what I had experienced with others.

Jan Dungey got the use of some premises in Norwich which became a Women's House, and organised a wonderful exhibition called 'Arting About'. It opened my eyes to the art that a lot of women make in their own homes, not just stuff which evolves from art school training. I was given a space under some stairs which I turned into a cave, sitting like the old oracle of Waylands Smithy with writings of my winter journey pinned to the walls.

Although I felt that journey was over, I went to the West Kennet long barrow for the February full moon and, standing on top of the barrow, threw my winter to the winds. The rain was sharp and stinging and I was ecstatic, filled with the strength of the barrow, the earth, and the coming spring. I was barefoot, my feet cold in the Wiltshire mud, stones cutting them, the wind wetting my coat and making me smell of wet wool, rain dripping from my hair. I walked in the mud to the Swallowhead Spring, which was flowing now, the whole River Kennet full. With my muddy dress, wet hair and face in the wind and rain I was a child again. I drank from the Spring, its pure clarity in my mouth, and gave the Spring water from many places on my journey. I walked on the stones of the riverbed and laughed as my feet sunk into the grey chalk Wiltshire mud.

Now in my wellies and wet coat, a scarf round my head, I walked to the Sanctuary, a basket of sacred objects in my arms, singing 'The river is flowing, flowing and growing, the river is flowing back to the sea. Mother Earth carry me, your child I will always be; Mother Earth carry me back to the sea.' I walked in spirals round the concrete markers of the Sanctuary and with objects from my journey, connected all the points on it into a web. It felt like a Dreaming Path which I had re-awoken. I lay down in the rain and wind and felt I had just been born.

I visited Mr. Perry. He put his hands on my arms, guided me and felt like one of the old wise ones. I felt raw and new and he seemed to understand.

I returned to East Anglia, feeling full of a power and strength which astonished me. All around me people were ill, physically, mentally and psychologically, but at last I was well and didn't get sick from all the lying in the wind and rain.

95

Jan Dungey, and others from her performance group, The Company of Imagination, got their own caravans and moved into the field around me. I was rather resentful, having enjoyed peace and solitude in the corner of the field by the wood, the pheasants sounding like rusty hinges, the wood-peckers rattling away. The neighbours, who hadn't noticed me being there, didn't like what now seemed to be an encampment, and by the Autumn we all had to leave.

I went to more actions at Greenham, especially a big Easter one, where I left my sleeping-bag while driving some women to a safe house, only to get back and find it had been taken. Hitching down there a man asked me 'What's so precious about life anyway?' which led me to wondering how would the beauty of the earth, even with no life on it, be appreciated if there was no-one there to observe it, and that maybe there is only life on this earth, and surely that is precious and we have a responsibility not to destroy it. I went to actions at Lakenheath, where there was a mixed peace camp, meeting lots of new people and strengthening friendships with old ones.

In the meantime, Jan's company gathered performers together and we set off on journeys round East Anglian villages doing theatre pieces. It was called Signs of Life and there were a men's group, a women's group and a mixed group: I was in the mixed one. We camped on the village greens and our group travelled with a horse and waggon owned by a woman called Nick who lived in Dunwich, the village which had once been a great city but had gradually slipped into the sea, leaving only a few houses and a pub. The pony was called Polly, a Welsh cob. I usually slept outside, often under the waggon, which was actually a flat-bed trolley. It was good to be performing again and I put a lot of creative ideas into the writing of our show.

Jan told me of another journey she'd heard about – the Walk For Life – a peace walk from Faslane in Scotland to Greenham Common, and suggested I go on it. I got information about it from the organisers, but people were to gather again at Callanish for the 1983 Summer Solstice, and I thought I must be there. I began to devise my own journey – I would go to Callanish, then up to Orkney, which was calling me strongly, then down through Neolithic sites in Scotland and England to join the Walk further down the country.

I had already slept many nights outside my caravan, in the soft leaves under the trees in the corner of the field in Kirby cane. The summer was coming. It was time to get on the road. Another journey was beginning.

Chapter 6: Summer Journey 1983

When I first heard of The Walk For Life, my initial concept for my own journey was to begin it in Orkney, believing then (and recent discoveries seem to confirm this) that those islands had once been the Neolithic seat of ancient knowledge. From that starting point I planned to travel down through important Neolithic sites in Scotland to meet 'The Walk' in Glasgow, and go with them all the way to Greenham. I would veer off any time we neared an ancient site so that my journey and theirs entwined like a spiral/helix, linking the wisdom of the ancients with the modern nuclear; in my mind feeding positive energy from the past to counteract the negativity of the present.

In East Anglia the spring and early summer seemed exceptionally lush, green and tall, giving me a sense of claustrophobia and I longed for the wild wind and bare rocks of the Islands. I tied up a few loose ends and signed off, having very little money. I was hoping to borrow £100 from an older woman friend I had worked with when I was an interviewer, and that would have to last me for weeks. How times change: I remember in 1960 going to the South of France on holiday with two friends, taking £10 with me – and coming back with some of it!

At last I left once more for the Isle of Lewis. Hitching was so much a part of my life by then that I thought - even if I had money for fares I would still hitch because I enjoyed it so much. I loved setting off with just an ultimate destination and no real deadline and seeing by what route the lifts took me; loved sleeping out and being with wherever I was, and having that sureness that I would get there. This time it took me 10 hours from Norwich to Hamilton services just south of Glasgow. It was quicker than if I had driven myself, for then I would have needed many rests.

I felt clear as crystal; calm and strong without any extreme emotions. The journey felt like a meditation; completely different from the previous year. I felt different too.

Sleeping in long grass near the service station, I woke early, covered in huge black slugs which reminded me of leeches. The truckers were already on the move so I got up hurriedly and started to hitch. It was harder and slower now and the lifts were shorter. I wanted to partially retrace my '82 journey and go to the Outer isles via Skye and Tarbert, then walk up to Lewis from Harris, passing the Sleeping Beauty on the way.

Travelling through Fort William, I still hated it, then got a last lift from Fort Augustus to Uig on Skye, where I waited again for the ferry to the Outer isles. That lift had been interesting. He was a diver who inspected oil rigs, and had just been on a course to do with fractures in steel and how you test for them by their magnetism, with iron filings showing the polarity. He'd first moved there to live with a group of friends as monks, blending Christianity and Taoism. I began to feel as though I were on some kind of retreat.

From the ferry I watched birds fly on air currents, watched their shapes and patterns of movement and seemed to enter into the being of bird. I watched every muscle movement as they balanced on the air, the flick which turned their flight, the movement of eye and beak as they searched for food and plunged down for it. I entered the knowing of bird.

Reaching Harris once more I sat on the damp grass in the indescribable silence. There were few birds, but there was a breeze, the grey rock – and midges! I was there again, in the summer again; what more could I want?

Walking up from Tarbert, I turned the other way from the previous year. Going at walking pace I watched the Sleeping Beauty gradually emerge from the hills as I slowly moved north. She wasn't like a hill or mountain, but a sleeping giant, lying alive and full of presence. I could almost feel her breathe and stir as though she might shake herself, rise up and walk the earth again as she maybe did in the Dreamtime. It would not have surprised me if she had.

The sun shone on her yet all the other hills were dark, and for a long while only she was light, shining in the sun, then her head went into shadow and finally the whole of her. I wanted to sit and watch her for days, weeks, years. Getting to where I could see her best (somewhere near Ariavruach), and having walked nearly 20 miles I went off the road and found a place where I could sleep and not be seen and lay there watching her as she filled my horizon, then slept.

Next day was a hot Hebridean Sabbath. Silence: a few birds, a few sheep, a few passing-place signs rattling in the wind. I walked on towards Callanish and eventually a nice old man from Bernera "his face destroyed by the whisky", gave me a lift and said call by if ever I was over his way and he'd give me a cup of tea. I had come back, healed, free and full of joy.

I met up with some of the others who had been there the year before. Everything was different. It was the 4th summer that some of them had been there and they seemed to feel it was all over for them, that something was dead; but for me it was only just beginning and growing strong. My relationship with the stones and the Island was deepening and I felt completely at one with the place.

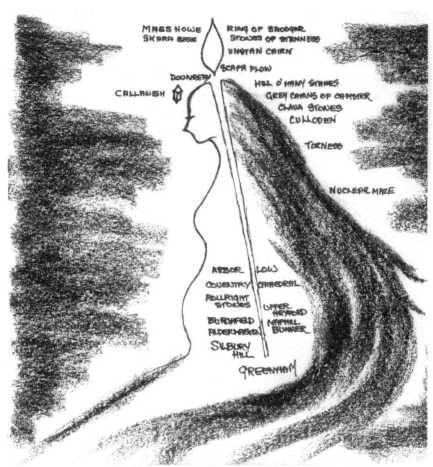

My plan of the summer '83 journey

At the Solstice sunrise it was very misty. Two drunk men from the Black Isle thought I was the Cailleach and were a bit spooked, but they came up to our camp later and made us laugh.

Everyone was going their own way, off to different lives. Lynne and I went to see Annie and asked her about many things – including rainbow trout. A bit later she disappeared to a passing grocery van and soon we were presented with a wonderful dinner – of rainbow trout!

Lynne set off down the islands to find a carved stone she'd heard of and I went to the beautiful beach of Bosta, where I still believe the Callanish stones may have come from. I slept on the beach, listening to the sound of the waves, which were like the earth and the sea breathing; and became one with the

99

sound. I thought I would have the next morning alone there, but suddenly there was a whole school of children having their sports day on the beach!

I returned to Callanish and Lynne came back too, her journey not having worked out. We sat in the stones for the full moon. The river was in spate and the loch full of salmon. A man walked up from the water and through the stones with a salmon in each hand, dripping moonlight.

Lynne left. It had been a strange time, full of deep sadness which I had to overcome. I felt the others were abandoning the place and that I must not, for it was maybe my responsibility now. I thought the deep emotional pain which I sometimes experienced in myself was really the pain of the earth; a pain at the loss of something of which humankind had once been a part – living from it, giving to it and understanding that relationship; that this had now been abandoned by people of the modern world and the earth hurt because of that loss. I felt I must bring more and more people to Lewis, to the Mountain, to the Stones, so this place would no longer feel abandoned.

I imagined the journeys I was making, linking place to place, were bringing back a little of that lost connection between human and earth, that the right human caring is needed for the whole to function properly and that maybe I could heal a little by the path of my walking. I was slowly coming to terms with my aloneness, though sometimes longing for friends, feeling a desolate emptiness left by old loves gone; longing for a companion to walk with me who would share the ordinariness of each day. Sometimes I felt this companion was nearby, waiting in readiness until I had fully come to terms with being alone.

I left Lewis, knowing I would return and was not really leaving. I sat on the ferry with a boat-load of soldiers who had been training for the Falklands: so many different realities sharing the same space.
Reaching Ullapool, this time I turned left and headed north, to round the north-west 'corner' of Scotland on my way to Orkney. To begin with I walked, taking my time, feeling joyful to be adventuring again. After a while though I was given a lift by a blue car painted with stars, moons and suns, driven by a German guy who looked like a little gnome. He didn't have good English and I have no German, but we seemed able to communicate. He asked my profession and I said 'an artist', but he thought I said 'anarchist' and it seemed to stick. We laughed a lot and kept looking words up in a dictionary.

The north-west coast is very like the Islands, but felt different. The mainland coast is joined to the rest of Scotland, and there is always somewhere else to travel on to, whereas the Islands are complete unto themselves and there is nowhere else to go. They are the destination, the end of each journey rather than a dead-end; a place to feel complete and fulfilled and no longer restless.

It was quiet up on the north-west, a road not much travelled it seemed. At one point there was no more road and we had to go on a tiny ferry across a loch, which rather annoyed the little German. That night I didn't sleep in his car, but down the slope of a cliff smelling of seaweed. He thought I was a bit odd. We carried on along the top of Scotland to John o' Groats. I wanted to experience Orkney alone, so was relieved when the little gnome decided not to come with me. I so enjoyed being 'on the road' and wondered whether soon I would take to it on a permanent basis. Lynne said she reckoned the next time she saw me I would be with a horse and cart, but I thought I would rather just walk and use my magic thumb.

The north-east of Scotland was very different from the north-west: rather flat and featureless. I took the little passenger ferry from John o' Groats to South Ronaldsay. There was a bus from the ferry to the main island but I didn't feel ready to move on yet. I wanted to ground myself on Orkney, so let the bus go, thinking I would get the next one in the morning, wondering whether I was further north than I had ever been, unsure whether the places I went to in south Norway had been higher.

There wasn't anywhere very nice to sleep, but I was so used to sleeping anywhere it didn't seem to matter. I hid down on some rocks among the rattling leaves of yellow irises. It was windy and cold, but I was so excited to be there I didn't mind. I had no tent, but had the down sleeping bag and the plastic to keep me warm. Keith Payne had left his cloak with me to take back to East Anglia, so even though it was heavy it gave me extra warmth. It was some kind of tweed and his dog had died on it in the winter of '81. That wasn't morbid, but somehow deeply spiritual and the cloak became a good companion and rather like a little house.

I had £1 cash left for the bus and only a little money in the Post Office Savings Bank, so thought I should have to find work to pay my way. Somehow food happened: the German had fed me; Annie Macleod had sent me off with boiled eggs...

I slept in the cold wind, sublimely happy, feeling I was living as never before, simply being. I giggled myself to sleep with the stupidity and total sense of it all, feeling I was sane and the rest of the world mad. It was very wet under me, but I was dry and warm and slept with the roar of the ocean.

Next morning I got the bus. There were great concrete blocks everywhere and relics of two World Wars. I had already passed the nuclear power station Dounreay on the way to John O'Groats and as we passed Scapa Flow it seemed my journey had begun; a strange interweaving of places of war and nuclear threat with the ancient sacred sites and great Neolithic structures I intended to find. I was curious about Orkney, so different from Lewis, rounded and soft yet without hills. I had no feelings for it in the way I had for the Hebrides.

Reaching Kirkwall, I got a bit of money from the PO, had tea and bought a map. I went to the Museum and was fascinated to discover that the previous year there had been an exhibition about the Tomb of the Eagles, whose owner had excavated it himself as he couldn't get archaeologists interested. He found human skulls and bones buried with those of Sea Eagles and kept all his finds in boxes in a shed. Later I bought a book about it but still didn't know exactly where it was, and it wasn't until 2003 that I returned with my youngest son, only to discover it was not far from where I had slept that night on South Ronaldsay! Now there is a small, informal and friendly museum nearby, run by the family of the man who excavated it.

I got directions from Kirkwall and began to walk. My load was heavy and I didn't feel like walking, but the traffic didn't stop for me, though eventually I got a few lifts to Maes Howe, a magnificent chambered cairn. It looked like a round, soft, pregnant belly and I wanted to run my hands over it, though it did also remind me of a space ship. There was a locked gate so I went to a nearby building and asked if I could go into it. A girl with a torch showed me inside and rattled off her 'spiel'. It wasn't as I would have wished, would have loved to have time in there on my own with a candle, but at least I had some experience of it. Silent and powerful and even better than I expected, its structure and massive stones made me wonder how on earth those ancient people managed to build such things – how lift such weights and position them so precisely?

Very tired I didn't feel like moving on, so waited until the girl had gone and then went round the back of the cairn. It was so womb-like, so comforting to be near, like a physical manifestation of Mother Earth. I thought then that tumuli, round barrows and round cairns were built as symbols of the earth and a dead person would be laid foetally inside them, ready to be reborn into another dimension – a symbol of life, not a memorial to death.

My face was getting very weather-beaten and I wanted to age like an old gipsy woman. I became deeply aware of the fiery molten core of the earth bubbling away beneath me, and that the earth we stand on is but a thin skin, like the skin on my face.

Orkney seemed fertile and green, reminding me of South England rather than Scotland, formed from a very different rock from that of Lewis.
There had been many black birds on my journey that day. One even dived at me as I walked along the road. Two dead ones had their black wings spread along the roadside. I found a black feather and put it in the pocket of Keith's cloak.

Nearby were some sheep which pestered me a bit; maybe hand-reared they didn't behave like most sheep I'd met. I found a spot out of the wind and huddled down to sleep. I felt drained but slept a warm, deep, healing sleep, cuddling up to the place as though it were my mother.

Early in the morning it began to rain and I wrapped myself in my plastic and the rain washed off the mud of the night before. I was surprised at how much I loved Maes Howe and how healed and comforted I felt being close to it. I felt oddly connected to Ireland and wondered when I should go there. I dubbined my shoes, washed my face, cleaned my teeth and when the rain eased, packed up and walked to a nearby restaurant. I was wearing a pink sparkly jumper under my coat and it seemed oddly ridiculous. I had hot chocolate and a scone and welcomed the chance to be indoors for a while.

When I was ready to leave it was still raining. A nice lady gave me a lift and I soon got to the Stones of Stenness, spending a long while there until the stones sang to me. It seemed a place of deep male voices. I walked to the circle of Brodgar and stood in the shelter of a stone, watching a man fish in the grey water nearby. It was a grey day, wet and misty. I didn't feel the old magic in the land of Orkney as I did in the Hebrides, but found magic in some of the people I met who seemed exceptionally alive. I went into the circle and the rain stopped. I felt like the old woman of the moors and wondered whether I would one day live all the time like this, though it would be good to have a bit of shelter and a fire. A stone sang to me and I sang with it. The grey mist drew closer.

After a long while I went into the deep ditch outside the circle and made my place for the night. I took off my shoes, socks and trousers and, having no watch, had no idea of the time. It felt strange being in Orkney and I wondered whether, when I left, it would be as though I had never been. The grass was long and the undergrowth lush. I had bought Orkney cheese, and it was very good, like real cheese should be.

I slept a good, warm night again, though there was a lot of condensation on the inside of my plastic. It really was a good little home. My trousers and socks had dried a bit and I put them back on before the first tourists arrived, many of them being German. They thought I was a bird-watcher; well, perhaps I was, for I did watch them closely, and listened to the magical sound of the snipe, a bird I'd never heard before I first went to Lewis. The sky cleared and just a few fluffy clouds scudded across the sky. I spent more time with the thin, angular stones which were so unlike the sarsens of England or the sinuous patterned Lewisian gneiss of Callanish.

The grey had lifted and the colours become sharp and bright and rich: brown heather, vivid green and yellow vegetation and a deep blue sky. There was a drying wind, which was good because my load was even heavier for being so wet. I walked round the stones barefoot and the peat of the circle rang under my feet. I wondered whether we would ever return to a time when the sound and movement of people would link earth with sky and make the whole vibrate and hum as one being.

I had been drawn to Skara Brae for a long time, feeling sure there had been a community of wise women living in this Neolithic village by the sea, their stone houses linked by passageways, the whole thing surrounded by midden. It is possible that midden wasn't just discarded rubbish, but somehow sacred, for in other sites in Britain huge mounds of it were used for carefully placed burials. It was just my own feeling that it was a women's community, but I had read a theory that the measurements and geometry used to lay out stone circles and henge monuments were held by people at Skara Brae who then travelled to sites throughout Britain and were fed and housed as they oversaw the constructions.

Not many Neolithic villages have been discovered, certainly not as intact as this one. Because of the nature of the Orkney stone, which splits into thin slabs, and the lack of wood, everything was constructed from it: not only actual buildings, but furniture – beds, display shelves, central fireplaces and boxes in which fish and sea-food would possibly have been kept alive until needed. Seeing all this makes their lives very close and real, not different from ours. One of the buildings seems to have been a pottery and is shaped like a woman/goddess with the firing being done in the womb area.

The village was abandoned very suddenly, seemingly in a violent storm (some have even suggested a tsunami) and the whole thing was completely buried in sand for thousands of years, only beginning to be exposed in the 20th century. I felt I had come on a pilgrimage to this place to honour those ancient ancestors. In 1983, although you couldn't walk about inside the houses, it was all more or less as it had emerged, with only a small hut housing a couple of warders who took ticket money. Now it is a major tourist site with a huge visitor centre and replica village which you file through with all the tourists from the dozens of coaches which turn up continuously. I'm glad I went there before all that.

To begin with I just wanted to be nearby. I walked on the firm sand with its line of jellyfish left by the tide and more dead birds everywhere. I sat and watched the tide go out, rocks emerging from the turquoise water. What a privilege it was to have time to do that. I felt I could sit there for eternity watching the Atlantic waves roll in and break on the shore. I could feel the tide turn, I was so part of the ebb, part of the flow. A young rat walked past me, not noticing I was there. Rats didn't seem unpleasant beside the sea, were just another kind of animal and I thought the villagers probably ate them if they had been there that long ago.

This journey did seem to be a form of retreat and I was at peace after the torments of the winter. I walked in Orkney's rolling green and noticed how square the few grey, angular houses were.

Everything felt very clean. By the roadside were an abundance of fat red clover heads and I picked a few and ate them and they filled my stomach. I phoned my friend and she agreed to lend me the £100, though actually most of it would be used to pay bills back in East Anglia.

I felt very close to the ancient ones who must have sat in that bay and watched the ebb and flow of the tide as I now did, and watched the moon and stars in the dark nights.

A mist began to roll in from the sea, which had turned grey with the threat of rain. I saw a stone hut further round the bay and wondered if I could shelter there. I had only a handful of sultanas, two teeny packets of sugar and some garlic, but was content just to be there, watching the tides, waiting until I felt the time was right for me to go to the ancient village. I marvelled at the dry-stone walling in the hut and wondered even more at the Neolithic corbelled roof of Maes Howe: such incredible skills passed down through ages. With the light nights and the grey days, it was hard to tell when day turned to night or back to day again. I listened as the tide rose to full, crashing on the rocks below and smelled the smoke of a driftwood fire.

My dreams were vivid and I thought I was still working a lot out in my sleep. It was good to have a bit more space. I changed my clothes and saw my familiar body emerging at last from what had been the unfamiliar mountainous flesh and flab of the previous few months. My muscles were returning and I was happy to walk and not eat much, though knew I mustn't get weak. There was a shop 2 miles away, but I only had £2 and would have to spend 70p of that to get into Skara Brae. However, after sitting to watch the tide and collecting tiny pearlised shells from the beach, I went and bought a few oatcakes, a pear, a banana – and a new pen! I am so pleased now that I carried on writing. I cannot remember the detail of those days and the writing brings it all back and I live it again.

At last I went in to Skara Brae, paying my 70p and spending 40p on postcards. The lady was very friendly and told me some theories about the place. They had a little museum in their hut, but much of the stuff which had been found there was in Edinburgh. I sat by the houses and drew one of them, feeling close to the lineage of women who had lived and worked there. It wouldn't have been an isolated community; there would have been many people around and also much passing traffic from the sea, as boats travelled from Scandinavia, round and down to Ireland and even further south. The Northern and Western isles, and islands like St. Kilda, would have been convenient stopping-off points as they island- and coast-hopped. Whale bones were used for rafters and they thatched the roofs or covered them in skins. There seemed to have been doors which locked. What were they locking out – or in? Maybe they locked out the wind and the sand.

As I sat there in the cold a Thames TV crew turned up which was a bit distracting. The custodians asked me in for a cup of tea and a Penguin biscuit. What a treat. They had noticed me around the previous day but no-one seemed to mind my sleeping in the stone hut.

I talked to the friendly TV crew as they packed up. As they were about to leave they called me over for sandwiches and a beer, then gave me a whole bag of food which was now an embarrassment to them. They'd thought they would be out in the wilds, but had found a pub for lunch. That morning they'd asked the place where they were staying to provide them with a packed lunch and couldn't go back with it uneaten – so gave it to me: brown bread chicken sandwiches, white bread ham sandwiches, a packet of shortbread, a tomato, an apple and 3 cans of Kestrel lager. The series of programmes was called 'Treasure Trove' and this particular episode was called 'Signs of Life' – the very name of the journey round village greens I had not long ago been part of in East Anglia. I felt the universe was looking after me. The custodians offered me hot water, saying that if I'd had a Thermos, they would have filled it for me. I was quite overcome by island kindness - a Londoner wasn't used to this. I returned to the little stone hut and gleefully consumed some sandwiches – there was enough to last me 2-3 days.

The next day, after noticing more dead birds on the shore – some huge and black, some black and white – and a breakfast of 3 sandwiches and a can of lager, I left Skara Brae. The food was heavy to carry and one of my shoes was beginning to split. They were the best shoes I'd ever had to walk in, but I had no spares and wondered what I should do. I washed some knickers and hoped they'd dry. It was a warm day with enough of a wind to cool me. A tiny local Post Office didn't do the Savings Bank, so I would have no more money until I reached Stromness. Patches of sun moved across the hills, changing their colour. They were making silage – tractors with trailers full of green grass packed tight - then spreading good honest muck on the land. I passed one field of cattle with a huge male in it. He seemed to be castrated, yet was very bull-like. He charged towards me, snorting and roaring and pawing the ground with his great hooves, bucking and rearing like something in a cartoon. I'd never been so glad to have a fence between me and an animal.

The lush land seemed to be very pure with little evidence of weed-killers on the rich soil, which was abundant with buttercups, daisies, poppies and much else. Young calves were with their mothers and with many of them there was a bull. It began to rain again. A lift took me to Unstan chambered cairn which was still, strong and powerful, yet its whole roof was now a concrete structure with skylights. How completely black it would originally have been in there; a place for dark retreat, a place for the living to sit with the dead. Once more I felt like an old woman whose houses these cairns were. I recall this one being in someone's garden and I had to knock on their door for the key – I hope that memory is correct.

I had to walk on in the rain, sheltering in ruined houses when it got too bad. I walked a lot that day and sweated as I carried my heavy load. Eventually I got a lift to Stromness, which reminded me of a Cornish fishing village, smelling of sea and ships: a smell I likened to that of small boats – stagnant, salty and pungent. I started asking for work, but must have looked too much like an old peasant woman, as I didn't get any, and I wished I could be a bit smarter. I got a little more money from the PO, so was able to sit in a cafe which had children playing a juke-box as I wrote postcards and planned artworks.

Moving on, I walked in the rain to the 'Standing Stones Hotel' where I sat a while in the bar with one sock wet from my leaky shoe, then walked on again. The cars passed fast on the straight, wet road until I was given a lift by a young Londoner in a 'hideously overloaded' van. He'd lived in Orkney for 2 years and said the local people hated English incomers and thought the place was becoming a last resort for down-and-outs. As we neared Kirkwall he was going to drop me behind a garage, but remembered a camp-site and took me there. I hadn't told him I didn't have a tent as I thought that might have sounded just too weird.

There was no-one on duty in the office, so I went to a far corner and made up my little plastic sleeping place and the rain meant there weren't people about to see me. It rained heavily all night, but I was reasonably sheltered and warm with hardly any leaks – I was getting it down to a fine art by now. The worn-out grass was covered in bright orange netting.

The rain stopped, the wind blew and it seemed like morning so I got up, went into the block, had a hot shower and washed my hair, which was bliss. It was a warm, dry space to sort out all my stuff and prepare to go out in the wind. There was no warden when I left, so I got away with a night on a camp-site for the cost of a 20p shower. I didn't feel guilty for not paying just to lie on the ground wrapped in plastic.

Feeling really good as I left, I had no idea of the time, though knew it was early. The bus to the ferry was at 8.50am. I walked into Kirkwall which was asleep, almost dead, with only the milkman loading his vehicle. I asked him the time: It was 6am. It had been light for hours, yet still the town slept. The wind blew but it was a clear day with blue sky. I was reminded of American towns in films, with things creaking and clanking in the wind and a solitary cat. I thought of the film 'On The Beach' and wondered what the earth would be like after The Bomb. Would the wind still blow, would the sun still shine? Would it still all go on with no life? I remembered the man's question – "What's so precious about life?" as he drove me to Greenham.

Sitting in front of the Cathedral I ate my last 2 chicken sandwiches, wary that the ham ones might have gone off, and watched the town come alive. At first there was silence, then a few people walked their dogs; a few cars, then a lot more. A pipe band gathered and went off in a bus. I watched a man sit in a car talking through open windows to a woman whose car was pointing in the other direction, it seeming like a strange lovers tryst. At 8 o'clock I found an open cafe and had some welcome tea. The town was fully awake now.

Catching the bus back to South Ronaldsay I crossed concrete bridges with dead hulks of ships rising from the sea as monuments to war, then got the little passenger ferry back to John o'Groats. I had kept dry all that wet night and most of my time on Orkney, but sat outside on the ferry and got soaked! However, there seemed a difference between the insidious wet of rain and the sharp, sudden showering of the Atlantic waves. I sat next to a man who was standing, and his oilskins poured water all over my trousers. However, it was a glorious journey, as I rode the great turquoise mountains which had rainbows in their wind-blown surf. People were being sick, but it had no effect on me. I felt I was of the sea and the wind and thought of the Skara Brae villagers and wondered whether they travelled down by sea in leather boats to the farthest corners of Britain.

Reaching John o'Groats the salt dried white on my face and my wet things dried in the wind. Though my socks were damp they weren't foul and my body was clean. My shoes smelled only of wet leather and Keith's cloak smelled of wet tweed: good country smells. Back there on the mainland, I sat admiring the use of old oil-drums for litter bins, loving things being re-used. The skipper of the ferry had chucked a bag of rubbish into the sea and I'd nearly screamed at him "the sea is not a dump". It's why the beaches were littered with plastic and the dead birds were entangled in old ropes. I felt so strongly that we shouldn't be making things we cannot get rid of, that we cannot bury nuclear waste in oil-drums in the sea, cannot fill mountains with death.

Looking at my maps I decided that because of the nature of my journey, I had to go back to Dounreay. I stood on a corner hitching for a long time until I got a lift for 3 miles (I needed to go about 30), then waited by a church for literally hours in the wind and rain and nothing would stop for me. I said to myself that if another 25 cars went by and didn't stop, I would turn round and hitch the other way. Dounreay seemed to be putting out a powerful negative energy which was keeping me away. I couldn't face walking 30 miles to a nuclear reactor, but felt I should somehow connect with it. I felt that if I overcame the negativity from Dounreay, this would have a positive effect in the macrocosm; that defeating its energy was my task. As soon as I thought this a bus with PRIVATE on the front stopped for me. The driver was on his way to the start of his working journey and gave me a lift 20 miles, though he shouldn't have done.

He dropped me at Thurso where I had tea and got lots of leaflets about Dounreay and postcards of it floodlit and looking beautiful. They glorified the place locally because it brought work but I thought "Just you wait until there's a leak!" It was already too late to be shown round and I wondered whether I would be 'vetted', and rejected. I realised I'd have to spend yet another night out in the rain. I was already so wet – my bum wet, my feet wet and itchy, and I was aching to hang my wet socks in a drying wind.

I walked out of the town, which was touristy and so different from the Islands. Once I was on a clear road an old guy stopped for me. He was appalled when I said I was going to Dounreay: "You don't want to go there. I was at Hiroshima after it went off. I had to go in and clear it all up. You don't know until you see it". He was a doctor. It was hard for me to explain what I was doing and why it was important for me to go there. He lived round the Kyle of Tongue and told me of all the ancient sites and rocks with cup and ring marks in that area, and of places to camp, hostels etc. He knew a friend of mine – a geologist turned archaeologist who had written about that area and had taught my son Kevin at Uni. He gave me his address and phone number and said he had a book with places he'd like to visit, and asked me if I was fey.

It seemed all he had told me of was part of another journey, all too much to take on just then. I felt that my journey was following on from the Signs of Life and was feeling the Walk For Life pulling me strongly towards it. The old man dropped me off right opposite the floodlit power plant and I went round behind a concrete hut by some old rusting farm equipment in a field of sheep. During a gap in the rain I tried to dry my wet things.

The night was very wet and I didn't get the plastic right this time. I didn't know what I was lying on either. I had extricated an old windscreen but there was some kind of metal grid under a load of chickweed and I wondered whether it was an air-vent from Dounreay. I slept well, though. I felt different back on the mainland, as though I had 'come down', as though being in the islands was another reality, taking me into a very fine state, and again I wondered what it would be like to actually live in the Hebrides.

The sun came out when I woke, though all my stuff was still wet and heavy to carry. I walked to the nuclear power station with my pack, looking like a tramp, but was allowed into the exhibition.

Detectors on the door counted everyone in. I did learn quite a few things about how nuclear power works, but the whole thing was such an obvious PR job it made me laugh out loud. It was heavily promoting Sizewell B (in East Anglia) which was yet to be built and against which there was a lot of protest. One exhibit was a kind of Victorian glass which used Uranium in its making and it said Queen Victoria would have had to have sat surrounded by her 100-piece tea-set for 1,000 years before she got any more radiation than the normal background kind. There was a newspaper called 'Atom News' with housewives and farmers saying how wonderful Dounreay was.

It was a Sunday, but they still did tours, so I went with another 6 people and 2 guides. I had to have a pass and put on a white coat 'to keep your clothes clean'. There was a lot more information about nuclear reaction and how they closed the reactor down if anything went wrong. We went through a radiation check. They apologised for the fact that it wasn't working properly as it was new and would take a while to settle down and told us not to worry if it went off! We went through airlocks into a low-pressure area (so if anything happens the air goes inwards). At one point I looked through a window which was filled with a yellow liquid (zinc chloride?)which makes 6 foot look like 2'6" and enables you to see round corners. I was thinking how unnecessary it all was anyway, that we don't need electricity, and that was before the digital age and everyone had home computers, mobile phones and endless gadgets which need to be constantly charged.

In the entrance hall was a stone sculpture commemorating the opening of the reactor. It had Pictish animals and fish carved on it and a design of the reactor core using a Pictish symbol and Celtic knot to symbolise the molecule. It was supposed to link the ancient to the modern.

My head was reeling as I left, walking past cows and sheep grazing outside – another PR exercise. I was thinking a lot about ancient people and all the knowledge their society had, which most people now refuse to give them credit for. I thought of all the ancient sites which they had left behind and wondered whether they had actually been for something scientific and not the 'ritual' or 'fertility' explanations archaeologists gave them. I had always thought the avenues leading into the Avebury circles were like some sort of particle accelerator. What will future people make of the remains of our present world when the context has gone? Even now, sinuous green trackways snake across the country and what explanation would be put on them if there was no knowledge of railways or Beeching? Ritual pathways?

Returning to a leisure centre in Thurso I sat and wrote postcards. I thought a lot about my daughters and how, because I'd had to go out to work, I felt cheated of their babyhoods and childhoods, which had gone so fast. For over a year I had longed for another child, one I could be with all the time. I wanted to be with my daughters and wondered how the life I now had could allow me to see more of them. Already I was living as The Old Hag, yet my body was still ripe, still wanting to be enjoyed.

I got an amazing lift from two men. The people in that area sounded more like those from Orkney than what an Englishwoman thought of as 'Scottish'. They talked of burials discovered, of cists and stalls discovered. They talked of a man found perfectly preserved (the older man had seen it) in the peat, or moss, as though he'd lain down there yesterday, and when the archaeologists came to look at it in the evening it had all gone in a puff, like an old fungus, into thin air and turned to nothing.

They talked of another man from the time of the Rebellion who was found perfectly preserved in his uniform, of skeletons found sitting up, and of how short life is – you reach maturity and then you're in your grave. What little time we have here – all we do is reproduce – and then they talked of things I couldn't hear.

Another cafe, more tea, more writing – and then Bowie came on the jukebox. If I waited long enough in cafes and leisure centres Bowie would always come on the jukebox and it was like my cue. You've waited, you've heard him – it's time to go.

Chapter 7: Going down again.

The lifts down the top of the north-east Scottish coast were easy: a couple returning to Inverness with a large 9-month old dog which had earlier chewed up a friend's hat, then a water-bailiff with a German Shepherd in the back who was returning very fast to Wick for his 2 days home a month.

He dropped me almost exactly where I wanted to be and I was relieved that the green of the far north had given way again to wild moor, heather and stones, and although there were acres of peat being dug mechanically it felt like 'my country'. I no longer had OS maps of where I was, just a map of Britain and a book of ancient sites by Janet and Colin Bord.

I had come to 'The Hill o' Many Stanes', which are rows and rows of standing stones. They are only 1-2 foot high, not like the huge megaliths of Carnac in Brittany, but were immensely impressive. One theory is that they were used to make observations of the moon. I wondered over what period of time – years, centuries, millennia - it would have taken the dedication of generations, with all the knowledge passed on orally. I realised I had not seen the moon since it was full, when it had changed the weather and brought the rain.

As soon as I got there I had the urge to walk up and down every row of stones, and visualised lines of people walking the stones together, fanning out as the rows do. The wind had dropped to a breeze as though it had returned to the cave in which it lived. I felt like the old woman of the caves who could never escape them: even in Dounreay the place behind the 6-foot thick windows, where the rods go when they come out of the 'mortuary' (or was it straight from their 6-month cooling, I couldn't remember) was called 'The Cave'. Uranium, Neptunium, Plutonium – names firstly of gods, then planets, now elements which can create power, death and ultimate destruction. Like gods.

I lay overlooking the sea and couldn't believe the beauty and stillness of where I was. I heard the buzzing of a bee, a curlew, a snipe and a skylark. I felt I could stay there for ever, even though grey clouds rolled overhead. I knew that one day I should have to live by the sea, by water, by moorland and stone, and wondered where. The future was so unknown. I was filled with a gentle ecstasy at being alive and wanting for nothing in that moment. The earth is so beautiful and I felt desperately that it must not be destroyed by the actions of civilisation. Destruction felt so imminent in those days. At that time sudden total nuclear annihilation felt close, rather than the current gradual, relentless crawl of global warming.

As I paced each stone row and the distant horizon appeared, each seemed aligned with some notch or hill on the next rise. Did people walk a different row each month, each year, each lifetime, observing some cycle or pattern?

I walked back along the road into a field of sheep. It sloped down to the sea and I sheltered beneath a rock. I tried to dry my wet things in what wind there was, hoping it wouldn't rain again and wondered why my pack was so heavy, as I had so little in it. The gorse was thick and rich yellow with blossom. I drank another Kestrel lager, read more about nuclear reactors and fell asleep loving the sweet earth. My heart was full.

The night was dry, the sky quite dark, and a boat with its lights on moved along the horizon. I woke, initially a bit negative, wondering how I would obtain the few things I wanted for my future, afraid of a future which was so hard to imagine, but then berated myself, for I was alive and the world still existed, so why was that not enough? By now it was July 4th.

I was heading for the Grey Cairns of Camster – a group of chambered cairns 5 miles up a turning off the main road. It was a grey day and I felt grey. There was no reply at a house where I tried to leave my pack while I walked there, but a nice lady in a yellow car drove me all the way. A powerful experience at the cairns, which stood alone on the wild moor, has stayed with me ever since. This seemed the time simply to discover the place; that I should return in some future winter to spend a night there. There was no key, no locked doors; you could just go in and crawl along deep passages to get far inside. It was like entering birth canals and as you crawled out, being reborn.

One was round with yet another skylight, and felt 'heavy'. A few German tourists arrived, but soon left. I had no food that day and it didn't seem to matter, and I had no idea of the time. The place was strong and I felt physically weak, as though an enormous burden had been placed on me and I was dealing with something without knowing what it was. The cold wind blew right through me, yet the place felt strangely familiar, as though nothing much had changed in 5000 years and I had been there before in some ancient lifetime, part of what went on there. In this life I had once been known as 'Little Miss Chambered Cairn', then 'Old Mother Long Barrow' and now it seemed I had become 'Old Mother Chambered Cairn'. I was the cold wind, the black sky, the dark heather, the grey stone, the black peat which sinks and bounces under your feet as you walk; the grey stillness of the stone mounds and the silence within them.

I had never known so 'dark' a place, never known somewhere so much of the dead, and of the magic which I felt when reading ancient Celtic tales, yet this was a darkness from long before the Celts. I felt ravens circling around me, yet there were none in physical reality.

113

Compelled to leave after a while, I made my way back to the main road. A short car journey was a long 5 miles to walk with few cars passing, so I walked and walked amongst the wild moors knowing if I just kept on I would eventually get there, but get where? On and on the road stretched ahead of me, some relentless force I couldn't resist pulling me down towards England, even though the idea of leaving these high places filled me with panic. I felt grief at leaving the Highlands and Islands, yet was caught up in the energy of my onward journey almost against my will.

It was hot as I walked. The road was sheltered and there were midges. The silence hung heavily though a few birds tweeted in flight and a distant lamb bleated. It was still grey and people drove past on that strange road and did not give me a lift. It was becoming a wearisome journey and I didn't want it to be like that. I wondered at my urgency, my almost desperate need to get away from that road. Black skies rolled round me but it didn't rain. It felt as though some awful unknown thing had happened that day which I somehow carried with me. The landscape was physically like the Islands yet this dark energy made it very different. I passed new peat cuttings with people's names on them as a slow tractor and trailer went by carrying a good, black load of them. A man drove and a woman sat on the trailer like something from the past. As I walked on, though still wild, it gradually became greener, and after some miles I could see the ocean ahead, yet the road stretched on so straight. The whole day was like a strange dream and everything felt unreal.

Two drunk men stopped and said it was only a mile to the main road. My back hurt and my feet were sore. A bit later I passed the same men in a house, and they called me in for a dram but I didn't go as they weren't the kind of people I wanted to be with just then. Eventually I made it to the main road, having no idea of the time. I rested a while watching men with good dogs herd sheep.

Returning to the main road I felt I had just come back from faerie land - real faerie-land. The people I had passed seemed otherworldly, not of normal reality. I had been to an oddly magical place and thought maybe if I tried to find it again it would be gone.

Walking on to Lybster I bought a little food and ate some outside the shop, for I was almost fainting from all the walking on an empty stomach. It was a holiday and 5pm anyway, so the Post Office was closed. I walked down the village to find somewhere to pee and get some water, pondering what strange machines we are – in one end and out the other. The sun came out and the clouds rolled back and it became really hot. I took off loads of clothes and it seemed that things were changing.

I stood and stood with my thumb out until someone stopped. The first lift was a man who was born in Stornoway – his family had the last croft in Point or somewhere, but my Lewis geography wasn't yet good enough for me to know where he was talking about. He took me 8 miles. The sun shone again. A van stopped. The driver asked me if I spoke English. People giving lifts still seemed to think women hitching must be foreign. He said his name was William and he must have a sleep soon and find somewhere to stop and eat, then he had to drive to Edinburgh.

I sat in the welcome shade of his van while he slept in a field. He'd only got married 2 days before and the celebrations had been exhausting. He told me he ran the Lyth Arts Centre and I realised I had picked up its literature in a Tourist Information Office as something about it had caught my eye. He was an interesting man, the same age as me, but born the following year. We drove on a while, then stopped and he took me to supper. It was odd to suddenly have a meal when I thought I'd had all my food for the day, but it was a good one. I had been so out of touch with the art world that, talking with him, a different part of me came alive again making me feel I should keep in touch with the arts and not completely lose that part of myself. He knew Andrew Logan and had been to the first Alternative Miss World. He knew of my soon-to-be-ex-husband and it was strange, on this very different journey, to be talking of the performance work I'd been doing not all that long before. I thought I should soon need to find places to exhibit and do new performances, and this place seemed a possibility.

As we talked on, it emerged that he knew other friends of mine and had been to Chelsea School of Art with one of them, who he described as a chancer who was out for anything he could get. I found it interesting to hear this perspective on someone I now knew from an earlier time in their life. What a small world it suddenly seemed. I talked of wanting to live in the Hebrides and he spoke of his experience of living in small Scottish villages, though he was born in Thurso and known as 'Angus' when at Chelsea. He said I would end up as the old crone of Callanish, cackling away...

I became indecisive about whether to stop off at Inverness or go all the way to Edinburgh. I kept phoning a friend there with whom I hoped to stay, but there was no reply, so Inverness it was, Edinburgh maybe being too big a step south on my journey.

William put me on the right road, so I wasn't abandoned in a darkening town (as it was then). The weather was hot and close and I was hot and thirsty, so drank nearly all my water. I had a kind of claustrophobia of towns and cities and wondered whether I was actually claustrophobic of civilisation. I didn't like touristy areas and was shocked at how everything was aimed at people with cars and how society no longer seemed to allow for the possibility of walking. Along desolate roads I would see signs saying 'In case of fire, phone such and such a number' and wondered where I would find a phone – this being long before mobiles. The assumption being that everyone would be driving.

As I walked thirstily on with my heavy load it grew dark. The landscape changed to fields and something vaguely approaching moorland. I went inside a Forestry Commission plantation which warned of felling. I stripped nearly all my clothes off, which was a relief, and lay in my sleeping-bag on the softness of pine needles and bits of broken branches among the gentle smell of old wood. The still-wet sleeping-bag cooled my sweating body, but I knew I must hide my face for fear of midges.

It was a good night. I woke cold in the morning, but the cold was welcome. I lay a long while afraid to emerge for the midges, but it was ok when I eventually nosed my way out. It was good to change my clothes, putting on a damp but clean t-shirt. But then I had to beat a quick retreat, for there was the sound of approaching chain-saws. The old pine trees were covered in lichen and I told them they would make fine poles and hoped the bark would be used for something good.

I walked to the Culloden tourist centre, passing the memorial cairn and graves of those slaughtered in the battle. This place had just cropped up on my double helix journey as I continued to entwine ancient sites with memorials to war and nuclear danger. There was a walkway with stones to mark where the clans had stood. It was all neatly tended, but so many were buried unidentified in 'mixed clans' graves. In 1983 it all seemed so far removed from what had actually happened there. Close battle, fought man to man, men raising their arms to let their weapons fall on other men; one man firing on another. I wondered, as ever, what it was that made them do it. So, there was I, not feeling very English, but as one with the men who had walked all night, tired and hungry, only to be massacred.

Now it was full of gawping tourists and I wondered if they had any sense of what it had been like then. Did people still long for man-on-man battles, now that thousands of miles away one finger pushes a button and it's all done by computer: the missiles fly off and everything is killed.

I paused by the Well of the Dead.

The tourist centre appalled me, for you had to pay 90p to go in and everything was inside, including the toilets. There were no litter bins as everyone came in their cars, bringing their own food and taking the remnants away. There was no tea. It was shut. I was so enraged I crossed the road and had a shit among some trees, but still needed somewhere to dump my rubbish, always having to carry it everywhere until I found a bin. I began to have some understanding of those who deliberately drop litter, as it is the only gesture of protest they can make. They have no voice in the society in which they live.

On my way to the Clava Cairns I waved to some giggling children, spoke to the man of the house as he left for work, and was able to leave my pack by their front door. I walked down the steep hill, the places on this journey pulling me to them, out of my own control. The journey was creating itself.

It seemed an unusual place for there to be cairns, low down in a river valley with fields rising up and away on either side, rather than sited in a high prominent position as most are; but the energy of the place hit me like a sledge-hammer and I became part of its power. Everything was still and warm and as though there were a strange garden of trees surrounding these ancient mounds with their stone circles. I entered one and its energy spun round me, almost more than I could bear. The whole place felt like pure energy, mine and its flowing as one, in and out of each other, like a living being. There was such mass in the great grey stones and I felt it was so much better to leave them as they are, roofs collapsed, rather than covering them in concrete with skylights on top.

I went to the second, then to the third and sat a long while, mindless, just me and the mass of the stones. The energy was very different from the Grey Cairns of Camster, and I sat by one huge stone until other visitors arrived. I could easily have stayed there much longer, sensing the place had much to teach me, but would not reveal its teachings too easily unless it learned to trust.

Walking back, I collected my pack and returned to the tourist centre, which was now open. I told the woman I couldn't afford to go in, but wanted to buy some postcards and she said 'Go in and get your postcards then', so I did – and went to the toilet. I had a drink from a tap and regretted not taking my water bottle with me. Outside I sat on the mowed lawn full of daisies. All around me the tourists got out of their cars, vans and coaches, and sat and ate their plentiful picnics. I had no food but once again it didn't seem to matter – I'd had a meal the previous night. I wondered whether to go back into Inverness or carry on down the A9 with no money and nothing to drink. I watched the tourists, some of them hardly able to walk and thought that people who go everywhere in cars are forgetting how to move their own bodies. People seemed to be getting separated from everything real, living in their centrally heated houses and driving everywhere in metal boxes. I felt I was becoming part of a race apart.

Deciding to go south I walked to the A9. I was very tired. The lifts were slow to begin with, but then came more quickly. One man gave me a cup of orange juice which was very welcome. I could have got lifts to London, Carlisle or Glasgow, but had managed to contact my friend David in Edinburgh and

117

decided to visit him as he was soon going to the USA for a year. I didn't want to leave Scotland too soon, needing to make my leaving more gentle. By the time I reached Edinburgh I already felt very far south and people told me there was a heat-wave in England.

I stayed a night at David's house, had a bath and slept with no clothes on. When I dreamt, I dreamed of home and for the first time 'home' was my caravan in the field at Kirby Cane. What a treat it was to feel clean again. I rose early as it was light for hours, drank coffee, sorted my stuff and re-packed my bag, looked at maps and marvelled at all there is to see in Britain.

I went to a Post office in Edinburgh and then David drove me to the A1 and I got a lift all the way to Newcastle with a nice trucker who didn't talk much but with whom I felt very comfortable. It was very hot and I'd had little to eat and sometimes felt faint. The land was covered by a heavy heat haze, the grain in the fields growing full, though still green. I went off into a state of powerful fantasy at one point and then another truck drove into the side of us and damaged a £500 tyre on the £45,000 combine harvester we were carrying.

Dropped in hot Newcastle I walked over Town Moor to where Sandra and Andy Bell were living and there on the front lawn was a mass of ladies sewing a 600ft length of walling for a Peace Maze and before long I too was involved. It was a wonderful rest being there, living in the moment and forgetting the past and future. They wanted me to stay, but I felt I must finish what I had set out to do. I phoned my friend, Freda, and she sent me the rest of the money I was borrowing, but said not to pay her back!! I marvelled at the friends I had, the fantastic people I knew, all the love there is in the world, yet wondered why all that love still couldn't overcome war.

I did stay a few days. I sewed the maze. I went to some exhibitions, including one of holograms at the Spectro Arts Centre, which included Andrew Logan's 'Goddess of the Void'. I walked the hot Newcastle streets. I washed my clothes and mended things and sent stuff back home to myself, so I didn't have to carry so much. I read The Tibetan Book of the Dead as though it were a thriller which I couldn't put down, glued to each page. It all seemed familiar, made sense of everything, making me feel that what I had done in long barrows and chambered cairns lifetimes before was to ease the recently dead through the stages which happen just after death. My old job, so to speak. Andy Bell lent me The Tain, the story of Cuchulain. I ate lovely food, went out and had a chocolate binge and worried about getting fat again.

I painted the Sleeping Beauty Mountain on one of the maze walls and she seemed to take on a life of her own. Powder paint and glue was an interesting medium. I had deep conversations with Sandra and worried about a debate the government was having about bringing back hanging. I did more painting and wrote poems on the maze, stating that if you hurt women you hurt the Earth, because they are one. I drew Callanish, Glastonbury and Britain on it with wonderful colours and symbols and foetuses and felt these were the best paintings I had ever done. I had conversations with all kinds of people and understood how they are in the world and how they view others. I felt I was working through a lot of karma from past lives.

I knew that soon I must move on because it would be too easy to stay. I had got used to being with people and become a little afraid of being on my own again. Setting off with Sandra and two of her friends we sped down the A1 to jolly music. Once on the road I no longer had any negative feelings about leaving, but all day had a sense of unreality and distance from all I did, as though I were in a dream. We got to Richmond, which had a strong military presence because of the Catterick Camp and RAF bases nearby.

We painted children's faces to promote the opening of a Co-op travel agency: moons and stars for little girls, lightning flashes for young boys. I got paid £15. Sandra and I spent our lunch money on beer and fish and chips, did more face-painting and left at 3.30pm. I bought some milk, which we stood in the centre of Richmond and drank, this becoming a ritual 'Milk of Human Kindness', the energy of which we sent out to heal those who make war. We tried to send some to Margaret Thatcher, but she felt strongly resistant. We painted a Peace Dove in milk on the pavements of Richmond.

We drove to Scotch Corner and they left me, Sandra having bought me some blue shoes from the Oxfam shop as an early birthday present. The lifts were swift and soon I left the A1(M) and got one to Derby, knowing now that I must go to Arbor Low. The man thanked me for my company. I waited a little for the right lifts, summoning them up. This was one of the occasions where people told me they didn't know why they had come that way, it had just suddenly seemed the thing to do. One guy who was a Jehovah's Witness picked me up, thinking I was a lad, and said he wouldn't have if he had known I was a woman, and then a man took me all the way to Arbor Low, even though he didn't really know where it was, driving all around the little Derbyshire lanes to find it.

Then I was there again, walking to the stones. I had dreaded how I might feel, returning to this potent place of my previous summer's journey, so much having changed since, but it was fine. I had moved far on in my state of being and Arbor Low always moves me on a stage further. I revelled in the soft shape of the place and felt the furriness of the grass. I walked to the bank and sat and lay a long while, there seeming no difference between being there in physical reality and travelling there in my meditations. Reality was a dream and a projection of my own mind.

119

I slept in the ditch. There seemed to be six people with rucksacks in the stones at one point and the night was filled with strange noises and the presence of hosts of beings from other realms. In the morning I lay on the centre stone and gave it some gifts from this journey, feeling I was at the centre of everything: the centre of Britain but also the centre of the whole world. I found the place unbelievably beautiful.

On that quiet, hot, humid summer Sunday I left Arbor Low and walked the Derbyshire lanes. The lifts were easy: families and couples and an old guy wearing a wig who took me to Bakewell, where I paused a while and at last had a Pudding, but couldn't find any postcards of Arbor Low. As a kind of 'Postal Art' piece I was sending cards from each major site on the journey to a friend, Karen With, in East Anglia. I sat, sweating, drinking hot mugs of tea in a cafe which wouldn't serve people without shirts and reserved the right to refuse people smoking at the counter. (This was long before any smoking bans).

I headed for Chesterfield with another lift from someone who found themselves where they shouldn't be, not knowing why, then had a fast lift to the M1. On the way we passed many horses and I wondered whether I had been born in the Year of the Horse because I had once been a horse, and pondered on all sorts of lives I may have had – 2,000 years ago...4,000 years ago...10,000 years ago...The lift took me all the way to the old Coventry Cathedral which was bombed in the 2nd world war and left as it was.

I walked into the Cathedral – and there was The Walk For Life. They had travelled a long way from Faslane, like a river flowing down the land, as I too had done on my own journey, and now the two rivers had come together and were about to entwine. I had joined the Walk For Life.

Chapter 8: The Walk For Life.

The Walk For Life had started many weeks before at the Faslane Peace Camp in Scotland and gathered momentum, and people, as they walked. They had begun as a close-knit group but, as others joined, a problem arose for some of the original core group in assimilating those who came towards the end.

I had journeyed on my own in an intense relationship with place and, although I had been in touch with the Walk before it began, was apprehensive about joining. Would I be accepted? Would it be easy for me to suddenly be with a large company of strangers on a journey which was no longer my own? I had to make this remain part of mine and keep it alive until it was complete. It was strange to walk into the ruins of the old, bombed cathedral with a cool breeze blowing through it, wondering what would happen next. I met two people I already knew and that was some comfort.

By that time I was in an extraordinary state, having reached this point on my long journey over the previous year; in my healing of a lot of deep emotional pain and in finding a purpose to my new life; in the development of my Tibetan practice and now this summer journey which had been like an intense retreat. I was using written language quite strangely, with very odd grammar, a bit like Yoda in Star Wars, and knew that somehow I had to change key.

It was a beautiful experience encountering the energy of their journey and they seemed to be lovely people. There was a calm peace around and I too felt calm and at peace. There were photos of Hiroshima, and that night there was a vigil. The moon shone: the previous night at Arbor Low I had at last seen the moon for the first time since it was full at Callanish. I sat on the Cathedral steps as candles burned, the lights reflecting in the new cathedral, and saw again the great coloured window and huge sculpture of St.Michael killing the Devil. In front of this is an area of grass where twice in the past, Bruce and I had done ritual performances. They had been powerful and I wondered whether some energy from them had brought me back to this place; part of a then unknown journey which led me to this part of my new life. A drink of milk was passed round and I drew more milk doves on the stones of the cathedral. The candle-wax wept tears down the steps.

All night masses of birds swooped around with sharp, shrieking, demonic cries, while others chattered shrilly: I didn't know what either kind were. A mist gathered and a clock-face floated in the darkness, though I couldn't read the

121

time. At last there was silence and a cat walked through, ignoring the burning candles: just another night for a cat.

In a cafe, women were weaving a tapestry. An old man slept on a bench. A solitary blue balloon with a white dove on it blew in the breeze. The stone was still warm to the feet after the long hot day.

Young people slept on stone where once bombs fell. Woven grass wafted in the breeze. The city was light and quiet; sleeping. The sleeping did not resemble the dead of Hiroshima.

At sunrise a Buddhist lady chanted and drummed and the vigil ended with a powerful circle of about 60 people. I felt I was doing something very new which might not be easy and that 6 months before I couldn't have done it at all. I didn't speak with many people that first day, was having to push myself hard on a social level and was finding it tough. I wove wool from Lewis into the tapestry, and some fleece from the ground where I slept in front of the Sleeping Beauty Mountain, and wove in a black feather from Orkney and tied on a shell from the shore at Skara Brae.

Walking with them was different. They walked fast. I walked bare-foot some of the way and got blisters, wearing out the soles of my feet like shoes. My bag was carried in a bus, so it was good to be without it, but I walked not noticing the land I was passing through and all my energy was drained. We walked 10 miles and at the end I was tired and hungry, but I was on The Walk For Life.

People embraced and held each other, but no-one held me. No-one even touched me though I was screaming inside for physical contact, so I set myself the task of talking to one new person each day. There were women with babies and small children and the Walk people shared in looking after the children and in helping the mothers.

The Walk took over and I found it difficult to write. I felt apart from people a lot of the time, though I got to know a few, and found it hard to get involved in communal activities, even the cooking. I have very few clear memories now, just recall fragments, in particular leaving the Walk to visit nearby ancient sites and taking people with me, keeping up my own journey alongside The Walk. At one point we neared the Rollright stones and I set off to them, at last being with the land in my own way. Soon others came and joined me and we slept in the stones. Next day we made corn dollies and hung them on the fence of the bunker nearby which we believed to be a Regional Seat of Government. As we watched, a man in a bowler hat emerged with a brief-case.

We'd had a stop at Stratford-upon-Avon, which had meant so much to me in my teens, and I recalled a time when I was 16, sleeping on the concrete outside

The Walk for Life bus.

the theatre as I queued to see Laurence Olivier in, I think, Coriolanus. I visited the theatre museum, feeling a deep nostalgia for my teenage self and her dreams of a life ahead.

We came to a place called Naphill, which had been given to The National Trust, but they were allowing the heart of it to be gouged out to build a nuclear bunker. There were notice-boards describing how beautiful it would all look when the work was done and they'd covered it over with grass and trees. I've never had much trust in the National Trust since then. That night I slept on beech mast under tall trees which were now dark green at the height of summer, beside this great gash in the flesh of the earth. It caused me deep psychological, emotional and physical pain to experience that wound in the earth. I had become the earth and it was like a wound in me. I slept with my head beside a little beech sapling 8 inches high and wondered whether it would have the chance to grow 60ft tall.

The next day, after a lot of discussion, some of us decided to go down inside the great hole. We found an unguarded gate and climbed over some barbed wire. I tore my trousers. We passed a single tall red poppy. The wound was a giant building site deep in the earth. We went down a rickety ladder and across rough loose planking...down...along...down...along. A policeman stood watching and dared not stop us as it was too dangerous; all he could do was warn us. We went so deep, so far down into the earth, then sat on steel rods and sang. More people joined us: some were afraid and left, some were really afraid but stayed. We wrote statements to the press. The policeman said we

123

would have no food or water but someone from the Walk came down and brought some, and toilet paper, pens and candles. We got a light from the policeman, who was actually quite supportive.

Some people went up and others came down. They brought crayons and wrote on the chalk walls. One played a flute. Many sang as they came down and the way the place affected the sound was otherworldly, magical and powerful. We had plastic to lie on and others came with blankets and clothing, and then we slept, down there so deep in the body of the earth our mother.

In the morning they threatened us with hoses and many left. On top, television crews came and interviewed those who had gone up. In the end there were 5 of us left, including one who had diabetes and had to go out to get his insulin, but came back. We decided to stay a full 24 hours. The workers came and one threw us a can of orange and another turned on the water which the police had turned off. The police said they couldn't forcibly remove us but would not allow us any more food and water. It was so hot in the sun, deep down in the ancient white chalk of the earth. I wondered how many millions of years it was since it had been laid down and how many millions of years since the sun last shone on it. Now they were filling it with concrete and steel and would close it over so it could no longer see the sun. It all seemed ridiculous: the place would not survive a direct hit by a nuclear bomb, the water and air would be contaminated and it would become a gigantic tomb.
The way they had gouged the land out had left giant pillars standing, so it resembled some bizarre cathedral to war. Already moss was growing on the pillars, showing the strength and persistence of life. It made me think of Grimes Graves, the Neolithic chalk mines in Norfolk, and how those people had dug deep into the earth with just antler picks. They, though, were aware it was their Mother's body and left offerings to her, but it made me wonder whether that was the beginning of human industry leading us to where we are now.

All day the work continued and there was so much noise compared to the stillness of night. We moved a bit when a crane-driver asked us to, and he thanked us.

After 24 hours, we left. It was very hard climbing out and our legs hurt for days after. The men watched us with no animosity, just curiosity. The police wanted no trouble and drove us to the gate. When we got out, the media had gone and we arrived unceremoniously to find the few people who had waited for us – including someone with a skirt for me to change into as my bare bum was showing through my torn trousers and I wore no knickers.

We were hot, smelly and dirty but knew we had touched something far deeper than anything any of us had previously known, and we were empowered by it.

124

Now I was settling in among people, I became very emotionally dependant on them. I still got very tired, moving at a pace that was not my own. Each day was unpredictable, and each was like a lifetime.

We stopped at military bases. I wrote a poem and we painted it on a sheet and gave it to one base and I read it to what I hoped was an American officer. We went to Aldermaston, it being my first time there. In my teens I had wanted desperately to go on the Aldermaston marches but my grandmother would never have let me.

By now I had been with the Walk for 3 weeks.

We got to the Orange Gate at Greenham and held a circle which was huge by then. I felt humble in the presence of those who had walked all the way from Faslane, for I had not. I met some friends: Sandra was there with a group from the North East; others had made their own journey from East Anglia. There was Sylvia Isaacs and her daughter Jessica with their waggon and pony, Bracken, and Mandy Fry who I had met at a Lakenheath action earlier in the year, with her daughter Zillah. I settled in a quiet place by the fence near Sylvia's waggon, for over by the Walk it was noisy with music, generators and rubbish. Crickets chirped where we were. A green helicopter hovered above. Sylvia washed nappies. Two policemen walked past inside the fence - I smiled at them and they smiled back. I felt at home with the East Anglians.

In the evening The Walk went off to float candles on the nearby river, but I chose to sit by the fence and burn candles there: the last I had taken on my journey. I put a white feather in the fence. The police kept driving by, watching me and my candle, shining headlights and torches on me, keeping me under observation. A black beetle came out from the base, in a straight line towards me, and I felt it had escaped and found its freedom. The moment came when it was 38 years since that bomb had exploded on people as they went about their ordinary lives and I seemed to live through that moment with its blinding flash of annihilation. I wanted there to be no more wars, and thought if each of us could deal with our own anger then at last there would be none.

People hung their washing on the fence to dry and I picked up litter. I had seen the colours of the earth change in 3 months and by now it was a soft yellowish-brown. Ripe wheat still stood, barley straw was a rich yellow-gold and the hay was good and green. The land was parched but the harvest was fine. Leaves on trees were dark now, the grass brown and seed-headed; bracken was still tall and green, horse chestnut cases fat and hazelnuts nearly ripe. Blackberries were rich and succulent. The earth was bountiful. I wished we would not destroy it.

125

Jill tying poppies on the fence of the supposed Regional Seat of Government near the Rollright Stones

My summer journey was over and I set off back to East Anglia. For over a year I had been making a film with Bruce celebrating the turning seasons at Avebury. The final piece was to be about Lammas and a group of people from many different parts of my life gathered for a ritual ceremony on the top of Silbury Hill. It was potent, and as I came to the end dark clouds gathered and produced a violent hailstorm. In August. A few of us slept on Silbury that night and I felt I became the land of Albion even more deeply: my journey from Orkney down to Wiltshire now also held within me.

The film was funded by the Arts Council of Great Britain, but because Bruce and I had split up, was never completed, which I deeply regret. Bruce would have produced electronic music for the sound- track and I had intended to write a sequence of poems and record them for it. The reels of Super-8 film are now in a tin on top of my wardrobe, needing to be digitised and edited.

I returned to my caravan in the field at Kirby Cane, and not long after walked the Ridgeway Path in Wiltshire with Saffron. It was lovely sharing it with her, the ancient trackway now becoming quite familiar to me. It was easier this time than when I had done it with Bruce some years earlier, as several taps had been installed, so you didn't have to leave the Path or carry heavy gallons of water with you.

Again it was strange and difficult to 'come down' from the Islands and the north of Britain and this time to disentangle myself from the weeks spent in the

126

particular energy of The Walk. Hard to get back into some idea of what I was going to do with my life.

I had become friendly with one group of people from the Walk, and met up with them at times to discuss peace actions. Most of them were much more active in this than I was (and younger), but I did get involved in a few events with them. One day we did a 'reclaiming' of the London Stone; once an important ancient stone in the heart of the City of London. Now it hides behind a metal grill in the front wall of what was the Bank of China. I did a lot of research about it and we made speeches on city pavements to passing bankers.

Eventually a large gathering of people from The Walk was held, to discuss what everyone wanted to do next. As with many such things, there was a feeling of family or community, of wanting to continue doing things together and to not all go our separate ways. Many wanted to do 'Peace Theatre', and as I sat listening to them I realised that here was a perfect situation for travelling The Gipsy Switch journey, which I had wanted to do for so long – to travel round the country for a year, celebrating the zodiac as we passed through every area of the land, to move round the land as the sun moved through the zodiac in the heavens – and to perform theatre pieces wherever we went.

I proposed it to the meeting, it caught the imagination of quite a few, and the decision was made to go ahead with the plan. We would initially head for Arbor Low, which was the 'hub' of the 'wheel' of the Gipsy Switch circle, from there make for Appleby Fair in Cumbria (Gemini) where all the travelling people gather for a week in June, then set off round the country to finish the journey back at Appleby the following year. Some people decided to buy a double-decker bus as a base in which everything could be carried, and possibly even be converted into a pull-out stage and travelling theatre, people camping around it at night.

Chapter 9: The Long Preparation for 'The Switch'

While this initial planning was getting off the ground, life went on.

One weekend I hitched down to South West Wales to take part in a pagan gathering with people I had met through Monica Sjoo, and through various pagan magazines which were produced in the early '80s, such as Pipes of P.A.N. (Pagans Against Nukes) and Wood and Water. During the subsequent decade I wrote many articles for these magazines, and some of my work was used on their covers, and this was the way in which I became known at that time. Some years later there was another important journal – the magazine of women's spirituality, From the Flames. These were of their era and have all now ceased publication. There has been nothing to replace them and they leave a huge gap.

During that weekend I began to suspect I might be pregnant. I had tried unsuccessfully several times in 1982 and, as someone who had easily conceived my first 3 children, was shocked when these pregnancies failed. I was only 39/40 and at that time didn't realise how quickly a woman's fertility drops off after her mid-30s. This book isn't about those brief relationships, they are a different story. But no, it wasn't a 'virgin birth, then' as some men have remarked when I haven't gone into details!

A few weeks after this a small group of people from The Walk decided to go back to the Naphill bunker, feeling we had not been there long enough previously. We met up, waited for the right moment, then went down again into this great monument to war, thinking we would be able to heal some of the negative energy being put into the ancient hill. This time we were not tolerated as well as previously, though we did chat to some of the workers (employed by Taylor Woodrow). They just wanted the work, and any issues they had were only about their pay. I felt I needed to know that vast, deep hole in the earth really well so that, if needed, I could return to it on a shamanic journey, and its cathedral-like presence is still held within me now.

We were there a few days, and when we decided to emerge, were arrested and charged with 'obstructing a police officer in the course of his duty' though I have no idea how we did that. Several months later we appeared in court, where a nervous policeman read out statements which we were supposed to have made, but which were all identical. We said our pieces, making a fool of the whole situation, were fined £15 each and bound over to keep the peace or something for two years. Many people I knew at that time were involved in actions (one was Snowball), getting arrested, not paying fines and being imprisoned as a further form of protest. By that time I was well into my precious pregnancy and didn't feel like going to prison, so a friend paid the fine for me. Thank you.

After the occupation I went to an event in London and got stranded, unable to get back to East Anglia. I arrived late at Julia's, and discovered I was bleeding. It wasn't bright red blood like a miscarriage, more like menstrual blood, but completely freaked me out. I had felt sure this pregnancy was at last going to stay and couldn't believe what was happening, feeling I was going mad. The next day I managed to hitch back to Kirby Cane where, though still feeling pregnant, I continued to intermittently bleed. Eventually I went to a (woman) doctor who examined me and said I had been pregnant but had probably had what they called a 'missed abortion' and, if I went home it would all come away at the weekend.

Very, very luckily, an old friend was waiting for me outside in the car park and whisked me off to his place where he and his partner told me vehemently "You are not going to lose this baby!"

After a few days I had to return to my caravan, as a large group had gathered to camp in the field for a meeting, partly to discuss the Gipsy Switch and partly to plan a midwinter event at Lakenheath with a walk to Sizewell. Among the people there were Mandy Fry and her then partner Bernie Chandler. They were a kind of support group for the Lakenheath peace camp, living nearby with their house being used as a retreat for people needing a break from the camp. Learning of my condition they took me back to their place and looked after me. I lay and rested and had the extraordinary experience of a golden yellow light surrounding my struggling womb. I knew people were sending me healing and have never before nor since been in such intense receipt of specifically directed love.

When I stood up and walked around it felt as though my whole abdomen was about to fall on the floor, but towards the end of my stay Mandy and Bernie took me to see a friend of theirs – Jess – who was a practitioner of some form of healing. (I didn't know much about these things). She massaged my feet and as she did so, asked me a lot of very pertinent questions. I can't remember any of them now, they were so in the moment, but they were things no-one had ever asked me, things I had never even thought of asking myself. Quite crossly she said "You're not in your body. Get back in your body: how can you expect a baby to stay in there if you're not in it yourself?!" I understood what she meant and re-reading a lot I had written on my summer journey can see I wasn't at all grounded but just spirit flying around all over the place.

Peace walkers performing a mummers play during a stop at Worlingworth en rou te to Snape Maltings yesterday

Local newspaper coverage of the group of performers on their way to Sizewell. From left to right - unknown, Richard Ford, unknown, Jill, Mike Andrews.

Another friend, Sylvia, drove me back to Kirby Cane. I walked across the grass to the caravan, and everything changed. I lay on my bed and met my son properly for the first time, knowing without doubt he was a boy. I was grounded. I was back in my body. I stopped bleeding.

I went back to the doctor and at 11 weeks, to satisfy her, had a scan, and was told "It's got a heart- beat, and a head – some of them don't". The baby was about two inches long by then. It was the only scan of a baby I ever had.

Not long after this I went to another action at Greenham and walked right round the base, with my baby now feeling safe inside. Tired but grateful, I gave enormous thanks to the earth and all the amazing friends I had at that time.

The Tibetan master Norbu was holding a retreat in Devon, so I went to that, re-connecting with my Dzog Chen community friends. The teachings by then were a very deep part of me and I realised I was receiving direct transmission, entering the state of the master and receiving the teachings by becoming part of his experience of them.

Walking along a dark Devon lane late one evening I said to my baby "Tell me who you are. What is your name?" After Devon I did a personal retreat with Julia at a friend's house in Norfolk, and when we had finished sat waiting for a lift. I thumbed through a book and a name jumped out at me – Taliesin – and I knew this was my baby's name. At that time I knew nothing of the legend of Cerridwen or of the historical bard Taliesin, but when I started to research them was stunned to realise that, when I had been roped into the Magic Ox performance months before, I had played the part of Cerridwen in her manifestation as a black hen chasing the boy Gwion through a sequence of shape-shifts. (He had been stirring a magical potion she was brewing for her son Afaddu, and had sucked his finger when the hot liquid splashed on him, giving him all the wisdom in the brew.) Gwion turned himself into a grain of wheat on the threshing floor, Cerridwen/black hen gobbled him up and became pregnant with him, carrying him for nine months and giving birth to him as Taliesin.

Now I was pregnant with Taliesin.

Back in Kirby Cane the neighbours didn't like there being so many caravans in the field. The others had tried all sorts of wheezes, such as planting Jerusalem artichokes and claiming we were 'seasonal agricultural workers', but it had no effect and we would have to leave. I was quite annoyed, as it had been ok when I was in the field on my own, but with several caravans there, especially Jan's huge showman's waggon, it was more than the locals could bear.

Sandra and Andy Bell still had their house in Ditchingham. Their current tenants, the theatre group Forkbeard Fantasy, were leaving to move to Devon, so Sandra and Andy asked if I would like to move in while I was pregnant and having the baby. Hearing this, the 'core group' of the proposed Gipsy Switch journey decided they'd all move in as well, so we could be together.

Over the Christmas/New Year of '83/'84 there was a big gathering at Lakenheath. A large group built a semi-underground dwelling and held a fast. Being pregnant, I thought I must eat and rather than be in the smoky underground, stayed in a tipi on a very windy hill feeling I and my baby needed fresh air. Over several days the tipi gradually went very lop-sided, but stayed up. We then walked to Sizewell, protesting against the building of Sizewell B, and performed a lovely theatre piece at stopping places en route.

After this the core group moved to Ditchingham, where I had a room to myself. People visited and many came and went. Gradually, the number planning to come on the Gipsy Switch dwindled as they realised the commitment of going on the road for a year. A few decided they wouldn't travel all the time but just come and go, especially to join in the theatre pieces.

It seemed that the main group had become: myself and my baby; Richard Ford, who had studied drama at Loughborough and been one of the instigators and long-term members of the Lakenheath Families Against The Bomb peace camp and, more than any of the others, understood what the Gipsy Switch was really about and the importance of doing it; Mike Andrews, red-haired, keen on gardening, vegetable-growing and self-sufficiency who wanted to become a story-teller; Ros Hudis, a small, quiet girl, very interested in theatre and an excellent performer, especially of mime; Tony Heales, extremely tall, interested in theatre and performing, a maker of costumes and a juggler, and Fenella, who knew more about horses than anyone else, but not about driving, travelling and living out with them. The group was now called Square Wheel Theatre.

The people who had bought a bus discovered that those who had sold it to them didn't actually own it, so that plan fell through. As we had been told the journey was that of gipsies travelling round a cycle of horse fairs, surely we should be travelling with horses, so we decided to do just that.

In the process of getting divorced I knew I would get some money from my share of the house, so for the first and only time in my life I borrowed quite a lot. Most of the others were much younger than I and several seemed to come into inheritances around that time.

I started to look for horses and was told of one, Daisy, who sounded ideal. When I went to see her I took someone with me who I thought knew about horses, and decided to buy her. She was a good strong-looking coloured pony trained to pull, and I persuaded Jerry Perry to let me put her in his field at Kirby Cane. Not long after, Fenella turned up, went to see Daisy and discovered she had laminitis. This is a serious leg complaint brought on by over-feeding and too-rich grass, so it seemed impossible to travel with her. Fenella confined her to a pig-sty, which Jerry thought was cruel, though it was the right thing to do, and tried to treat her. One day she and Tony took her on a long walk and she nearly collapsed. A lot of money wasted and back to the drawing-board yet again.

For Imbolc I set off hitching to Avebury, pausing in London to visit Jonathan Harvey and Rita Harris who ran the Acme Gallery where Bruce and I had previously had two major exhibitions. Lynne had suggested I go out to Ayers Rock/Uluru in Australia to have my baby and I had decided to apply for an ACGB Performers Training Bursary to get there. I had written a good application, stating that I wished to observe Aboriginal ceremonies as a way of developing my own landscape-related performance, and needed people in the art world to give me references saying why they thought I was worthy of the bursary. The other person I asked was Jasia Reichardt.

As I hitched to London, my lift dropped me at a railway station and I had no idea where I was. It only had one platform and a line going in one direction. I asked a man on the platform which way it was going and he backed away from me in horror as I had actually spoken to him! Later, in the carriage, he looked absolutely terrified of being alone with me. Later, walking a road near the Tower of London, I asked another man for directions and he too recoiled in shock. A human had spoken to another human! That's cities for you.

At Avebury I slept once more in the West Kennet long barrow, then walked to my beloved Swallowhead Spring at dawn. How different it was in those days. Now it seems to be dry all year, the hole where the water poured out in danger of collapse and the river itself dry and overgrown.

People do still visit it, and there are many offerings and a shrine built round it, but in the '80s it was untouched and clear, dry during the winter and flowing again at Imbolc. Visiting the Ridgeway Cafe I sat and listened to the truckers banter. I was still doing it all, but with my son snug within me, I was no longer alone.

I was successful in my ACGB application and awarded my bursary. I got my Australian visa and a lot of information from a midwife friend as to what to do in certain emergency birth situations. I think one was – if the umbilical cord is round the baby's neck, stand on your head, push the baby back in again and untangle the cord with your fingers – or something like that. But I developed misgivings and decided to postpone the trip. There were many reasons, but a big one was feeling that it was an imposition for a white Englishwoman to go to sacred Aboriginal lands for something as powerful as birth: as though I wanted to take the magic from their land. It felt wrong.

For Beltane a group of us found a beautiful place not far from the house, where we awaited the dawn, and I realised not only ancient sites are sacred and powerful. The summer was coming.

I was speaking with Nick, who lived at Dunwich, about my Daisy problem and learned she had decided to sell her pony Polly and flat-bed trolley. It was these we had travelled with on the Signs of Life: the trolley I had slept under. It was meant to be. Polly was a Welsh cob, dark brown in colour, feisty but well-behaved, so I bought her. To begin with Nick lent me the trolley and I bought it at a later date. It was brought over and put in the front garden of Sandra and Andy's house. Mike Andrews bought a pony, Rosie, and got himself a little two-wheeled trolley. Fenella got a large horse called George and was going to get something called a totter's waggon. Ros decided not to travel with us all the time, but to join us now and again, cycle along with us and be in the theatre pieces. She worked hard at promoting and publicising the journey and found places for us to stay when we needed to park up for longer than over-night roadside stops. Richard was going to come too, hoping to get a horse and waggon somewhere along the journey. Other people would visit as and when they could. It was all going to be much smaller than originally planned.

The time of my baby's birth grew closer. We went to a wood and cut hazel to make benders on our trolleys. Mike had a canvas tarpaulin to cover his and I had a blue plastic one. All this was in the front garden which was beginning to look a mess. Around that time a lot of things seemed to be decided without my having much say in the matter.

Once I had decided not to go to Uluru I told my doctor I wanted a home birth. I'd had Kevin and Tiffany in hospital, not feeling in control during their births, having to lie down, the babies taken away to a nursery as soon as they were born, so I didn't see them again until the following morning, and this affected me so profoundly I still haven't really got over it. Saffron was born at home with a midwife who thought I was mad not having any painkillers. It was lovely sitting around the day I was in labour, with the midwife and Chinese nurse eating fish and chips for lunch and the latter talking of how her grandfather grew opium poppies in his window-box, and with Tiffany, Kevin and his friend Chima playing downstairs. But when it came to transition I still gave myself up to the midwife and lay down when she told me to. After Saffron was born I was rushed to have the placenta, as a man in a van came round at 4pm to collect them and we didn't want to miss him. But when it was all over and the midwife and nurse left, my baby was my responsibility right from the start. Now, however, I was older (I think I was called an aged multi-gravida or something), nearly 42. The doctor didn't like the idea of home birth and tried to do deals with me. If she 'allowed' me one would I agree to go to hospital if the baby was more than 2 weeks overdue? She said she wasn't bothered about me, but didn't like losing babies. She tried to scare me with stories of cerebral palsy and I felt I was being blackmailed. The midwife came to inspect my room and when I said I didn't want any pain relief said "Well, we'll have it in the next room just in case" and I wondered whether, in the throes of labour, I would have the strength to fight all this off. I said I didn't want symptometrin, which closes the cervix quickly after the birth and is supposed to stop you haemorrhaging to death (which can happen), but means you have to cut the cord before it has stopped pulsing and give birth to the placenta pretty fast.

At the pagan gathering in Wales I had met Eveon Gaines, who lived in the tipi village at Talley Valley. She was the valley midwife, had done loads of births, and suggested I go down there to have my baby, and this began to feel right: to be in a natural place, not a building, and in control of what was happening to me and my child.

I think I was about eight and a half months pregnant by now. Around this time there was an Albion Fair where our group performed an enactment of the journey we were about to make. There was much excitement about a book which suggested there was another zodiac sign – Arachne the spider – making 13 signs in all. This meant the dates of all the other signs were jiggled around so it fitted in somewhere between Taurus and Gemini. My baby was due to be an Arachne baby. The Greenham women did many actions involving the weaving of webs, and the power and magic of the web was very strong just then. I made myself a wonderful black, white, green, purple and silver costume and became Arachne, the spiderwoman, and sat resplendent with my huge belly in the centre of a circle, while all the other zodiac signs wove a web around me. We had evolved the story of the journey through powerful guided visualisations during the months before, and our performance at the fair was a magical enactment of what we hoped our journey would be.

Richard offered to drive me to Talley Valley as the time of the birth drew near. By now I had an old car which I had bought from Mike who had inherited it from his grandfather. We set off, but after a few miles, the car broke down and we were stranded, not far from Mandy and Bernie's place at Icklingham. They came and picked us up and over a few cups of tea, made some big decisions. They had been about to go off to Devon for a weekend Alan Stivell concert. Mandy had been doing active childbirth training and decided that she and her two-year-old daughter Zillah would take me to Talley and be with me until the baby was born. Bernie would go to the Alan Stivell and then come on to Wales. Richard would sort out my car. (When he got back to it, it started and the problem resolved itself: very strange).

So, Mandy, Zillah and I set off for Wales. We went across country, avoiding motorways, and found ourselves passing Kilpeck church with its famed Sheela-na-gig, which I had never seen before. I began to sense Taliesin controlling the journey and things evolving as he wanted them to. When night came we found a wonderful spot beside a river where we just slept out, Mandy never having done this before. My memories, lying curled up on the earth with my arms round my belly are as if I were sleeping with my son already in my arms.

The next day we drove on to Talley, where we found people had given up their tipis both for me and Mandy and Zillah and we were made very welcome. I was in a beautiful spot deep in the Valley, surrounded by running water and lots of trees. My baby was due on the dark moon.

Monica and her son Leif came down to the valley to be near us for the birth, but had to leave before Taliesin was actually born. On the day of the dark moon there was to be a partial eclipse of the sun and the Valley people built a huge bonfire with a labyrinth or spiral around it. Eveon was a great ceremonialist, and at one moment of crescendo Monica, Eveon and I walked the spiral naked and stood with our bellies pressed together, my great child-filled one in the centre as though it magnificently belonged to all three of us.

But my son didn't want to be born on the dark moon, so many more days passed and I got very fit and brown walking up and down the valley. There was a young raven around the tipi and sometimes it would come right to the door as though visiting. Another friend, Aida Birch, who is like a little Neolithic faerie woman with incredible eyes, who was working as a district nurse at the time, visited me as I waited and examined me. The baby did have a tendency to lie to one side, although his head was down and engaged.

There was a farm gate near the tipi which I often stood by. A pregnant mare, Luna, would come and stand on the other side and we faced one another, very still, in that same shared space of two beings about to give birth, in complete wordless understanding. The Valley people laid bets as to who would 'foal' first. It was Luna. She had a son. When we met after that we were just horse and woman and the shared space had gone.

After a couple of weeks I began to get concerned. Would he ever be born? He who initially seemed so difficult to hold in my womb now didn't want to leave it.

Near full moon Mandy, and Bernie who had now come down to the Valley, took me out for a drive, walk, anything to try to bring on labour. When we returned to the tipi I was quite upset to find that Eveon, without asking me, had rolled up the bottom of the tipi to air it and had moved all my stuff. I had made my nest in there and was distressed that it had been disturbed. I got things back to normal and hoped the upset might have given the baby a wake-up call to get a move on.

Next day I went for a long walk on my own with my baby, feeling he was reluctant to commit to a purely earthly existence, for I'd sense him flying off into the vastness of the universe quite a lot. Was he ready to be grounded? I re-assured him as much as I could. As we walked, a badge from a festival on the Isle of Skye lay on the path before us and it felt like an omen that we would one day live in the Hebrides.

That evening, back at the tipi, I began to have what felt like contractions. I hoped they wouldn't go away.

Next morning I felt pretty sure it was really beginning to happen. I walked up to Mandy's tipi to tell her and as I walked everything around me was still, and I knew the deep peace and strength of acknowledging that I took responsibility for whatever happened. I was so in tune with the pregnancy and the baby that I

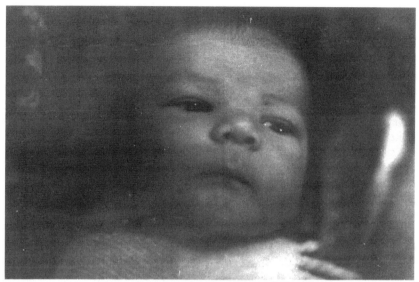

The newborn Taliesin (photo Bernard Chandler)

was totally confident all was well. Mandy had a car up the top and if there was any emergency we could get to hospital.

It was a long day. It was hard work and for a lot of the time I felt I was getting nowhere. Each contraction seemed to push him back up rather than out. I had hoped to squat, but my legs had no strength in them so I hung onto a rope hanging from the top of the tipi. I began to feel I wasn't a big, strong woman after all, and couldn't do it; but we realised my waters hadn't broken, so Eveon had a good look and watched the amniotic sac bulge out as I pushed and said she'd have to cut it on the next one. I was terrified the baby's head would be hurt, but trusted her to be careful. It all whooshed out over her dress and she said she would never wash it again. Aida had left us lots of disposable sheets which were useful for mopping it all up.

Soon after this, Taliesin was born. Mandy ended up being my 'birthing chair', her thighs under my thighs, taking all the force of the push. By then the tipi was encircled by women – all pushing. They had aching bellies the next day. They said the raven was sitting on top of the tipi, welcoming the bard Taliesin. It was full moon.

Eveon said his head came out the other way round from any babies she'd ever seen born, so I'm pretty sure he was 'face to pubis', which is possibly why the labour had been just one long horrible backache. It was very like the labour with my first son, Kevin, in hospital where they laid me on my side and explained nothing – and in fact, told me off for bruising his eyeball! My two daughters had popped out pretty effortlessly and I always found labour hard work rather than painful, the only real pain being when their heads were born, stretching my skin really tight and hurting, but I never tore or had to be cut. Well, here was Taliesin, and he was huge, looking more like a 3-month old than a newborn, apart from his puffy eyes. I lay there, amazed at his perfection. Because of my age I had been prepared for all sorts of things, but he was perfect.

All the women came in and filled the tipi, but after a while we realised the placenta wasn't coming, and I understood my one mistake – I hadn't kept on peeing while I could. I had a very full bladder which was stopping the placenta coming out and the placenta was stopping me being able to pee. Eveon didn't want to pull the umbilical cord as he had been over-due and the cord was 'old' and might have torn. My heart sank; after all this was I going to have to go to hospital?

But, like a ministering angel or faerie midwife, who should pop her head round the door-flap but Aida. She had come to visit thinking he must long ago have been born. We explained the problem. "Oh, I've got a catheter in my car" she said in her beautiful Welsh accent, so we all waited while she went up (quite a climb) and returned with the trusty instrument. She emptied my bladder and it half-filled a bucket. No wonder poor Taliesin had such a hard time getting out! Then I crouched over the (now empty) bucket and gave one last massive push – aided by all the women in the tipi – and out it came. The next day we buried it on the spot where he was born.

Wow. Fantastic. Hello, Taliesin, after this great long wait! When the greetings and palaver were over, at last he and I were alone for this first night. He still seemed to be part of some other, magical realm, still in touch with the vast expanse of the Universe. Most of the time he looked like a little Buddha; opening his vivid blue eyes wide, as though seeing realities I couldn't. In the night there were occasional strange sudden sounds and he would start and stare with those wide-open eyes, knowing realms I didn't. I began to share his experiences as I had done throughout the pregnancy, but had to pull myself up quickly and stop: he was his own separate person now, and to continue would be an invasion of his privacy, so I closed the door on that, and shut it off.

So here he was, my companion in life for the next 24 years, until he moved to Norwich and I returned to the Hebrides; still connected by letters, text messages, phone calls and a few visits a year by one of us to the other. I think he's my best friend really.

138

After a few days, Rik the Vic of the Valley (an actual ordained minister) did a naming ceremony for him by the Valley well and he became Taliesin Rainbow (part of the Rainbow tribe) and we were ready to set off on the return to East Anglia. I am so grateful to the people of Talley Valley for their caring and love. Although we have rarely returned, Rik always sends us Christmas cards and remembered when it was Talie's 21st birthday. Blessed and kind people. We visited Monica at her home near Fishguard and took Talie to St. Non's Well at St. Davids, where Monica dedicated him to the Great Mother, then on our way back stopped at Silbury Hill. I was able to climb over the fence and felt I had got my body back. We slept up there: I on my Mother's belly with my baby on mine.

When I got back to Ditchingham, things weren't really what I expected. I suppose, watching the little children and babies being somewhat communally looked after on the Walk, I had thought Talie would be the baby of The Gipsy Switch. It seems such a presumption now, but I thought they would have built the bender on my waggon while I was away; would have made a home for Talie and me to return to, but they hadn't. The others had used all the best hazel to build structures on the other trolleys and I was completely taken aback. Having just given birth and with a newborn to look after, I had to build my own bender on my trolley with what hazel was left, though Richard did give me a lot of help. The garden was in a terrible state with paint everywhere, and Fenella and Tony had banged huge nails into the living-room walls, on which to hang the harness and tack.

I was really shocked. These were all young people from middle-class homes. Would they have done such things to their parents' houses? They were young, and unthinking, and it made me realise I was almost a generation older than most of them, and that made a big difference. Andy Bell was furious when he found out about the nails. It wasn't just the damage to the walls; they were very expensive inner walls which had been installed to deal with the damp in the house, which had been almost a ruin when Sandra and Andy had bought it.

All the others moved out. Ros came round a lot to help me clean the place. We scrubbed the kitchen for days, with Talie propped up in the corner of a sofa. We also got the blame for things we weren't responsible for. The previous tenants had gone out one night, leaving wood to dry on the Aga. It began to smoulder and when they returned (luckily not to a burned-down house) the ceiling was blackened by smoke. They had also left lots of stuff behind: we piled it up in the front drive and I had to hire a skip to get it cleared away. It shows the strength of our friendship, that Andy and Sandra are still two of my dearest friends, although we rarely see each other these days.

Things I had put into communal spaces had disappeared, and some quite special books had gone from my room, even though I had asked that no-one but Richard use it while I was away. I was trying to practise non-attachment, but found all this very difficult. The tyres on my car had been worn down to the metal, even though a local man who knew me would have replaced them and let me pay when I returned. The police turned up not long after I got back, and even though I was the owner, were very kind, seeing that I had been away giving birth and not driving the car. I was so angry about it that I did tell them who had been responsible!

It was all suddenly very stressful and not what I had expected to come back to, but I had my babe. I tied him onto me and carried him around until, months later, I bought a wonderful baby-carrier called a 'Snugli'. At other times he slept in a Moses basket.

I was breast-feeding, which was quite an issue for me. When I had my first baby I had floods of milk, but stopped feeding him at 3 months as I was trying to get work, regretting it ever after. I intended to feed my daughters for at least 6 months each, but had no-one to give me advice about expressing milk, so, as I was working, if I missed two consecutive feeds my milk just dried up. This happened with both of them at 3 months. I felt I was being punished for not feeding Kevin for longer and this is why I was so emotional about the milk-yields of the goats. Being able to carry on feeding Talie was vitally important to me, and in fact I ended up doing it for two and three-quarter years.

I had been in a strange trance-like state at Talley Valley and now felt I had lost the 'self' which I had become over the previous few years journeying, and wanted to get back to being that person once more.

Talie put on weight at an incredible rate. At a week old he was 9lbs, so was possibly even heavier when born, as they usually lose a bit in the first week. He was so bonny and healthy and the joy of my life.

As I hadn't gone to Australia to give birth to him, but was still intending to go once the journey was established, I had to deal with a lot of bureaucracy getting him put on my passport and getting visas for both of us. I also had to spend time seeing my solicitor, sorting out all the business of the divorce. I didn't fight for anything, didn't even get my own valuation of the house, just wanted it all over as quickly and simply as possible.

The time was getting close to when we would have to vacate the Ditchingham house and we were nowhere near ready. The year was moving on and already way beyond the time of Appleby fair. Of the horses: Daisy had laminitis and couldn't work; there was my Polly, a real little goer, full of spirit; Fenella's George, a big, tall, dark gelding and Mike's Rosie who was still at the dealer's about 70 miles away. Of the waggons: mine was the large flat-bed trolley with four good pneumatic tyres – I think it was called an Ely Dray, and the Totter's

140

waggon, which we had bought from a traveller called Happy near Lakenheath. This was also a flat trolley with a seat at the front for the driver – a bit like the ones used by rag-and-bone men - and then there was the little two-wheeler of Mike's, which had odd- sized pneumatic tyres which were somewhat bald.

They had made a nice top for the Totter's waggon, and Tony and Fenella set off with George to collect Rosie, taking Polly along for the exercise (without asking me). When they got to the dealer's, George collapsed and for ever after we (especially me) were being threatened (not by experts) with the dire consequences of over-working our ponies – which we never did! They collected Rosie and when George had recovered, set off on the return, alternating George and Rosie in the shafts.

Richard had gone off on holiday to Morocco.

We next heard that both George and Rosie had developed sore shoulders, meaning neither could work for two weeks, so they stopped off at Mandy's. Mike heroically volunteered to go down and walk back with Polly, an exhausting trek. I was desperate to get on the road, but Ros and I were left alone to clean the house. I devised many plans, trying to solve all the problems, feeling that Tony and Fenella didn't really want to begin the journey at all, and one day they turned up with Mandy and said they weren't coming. Mike returned with Polly to discover we were now minus Tony, Fenella, George and the Totter's waggon.

The day finally came when we had to leave the house, with still only one horse, so we decided to move onto a grassy building plot nearby to give ourselves some breathing space. We got my waggon onto the road and Polly happily pulled it round the corner. As my bender was made from the flimsiest hazel, the top twisted to one side a bit en route. I tightened the strings which held them together but for ever after I would lie inside and gaze at its lopsidedness and wonder whether it was getting worse.

Mike had built a lovely little top on his, with a raised bed at the back and all sorts of hanging shelves and bells and things. It was a bit like Dr. Who's Tardis, seeming larger on the inside than out. The shafts were resting on boxes because a two-wheeler won't stand horizontal without a horse in them. We people-handed it to the pavement, but it was back-heavy and tipped back with the shafts pointing skywards, with no way to right it without the help of some wary neighbours who were called over from a Christening party. The next problem seemed to be that the shafts were too narrow for Polly. We just about managed to get her in for this short journey, but they squeezed her sides and would soon rub her sore on a longer drive: and Rosie was much bigger. As she pulled it round the corner it jangled and clanged and swayed and twisted on the bumpy ground and even placid Polly nearly freaked at all the noise. Big lesson:

don't have lovely bells hanging inside a horse-drawn waggon. The top twisted very badly. Another big lesson: you can't suspend heavy trays high up on a moving bender. I had taken some advice from Sylvia who hangs everything in bags.

We were quite jubilant to have got away from the house and managed to balance Mike's into the horizontal by laying a big red trunk which belonged to Richard on the shafts. Later in the evening we sat in it having a celebratory meal and drink, cosy with an oil-stove alight. Outside a wild storm raged. Mike climbed up onto the bed to get something, there was a strange sound and movement and the trolley tipped backwards again – with us in it. Miraculously, the oil-stove extinguished itself and seemed to find its own way outside and no-one was injured.

Mike's top was even more damaged now and I went to bed wondering whether Polly, in her metal shoes, tethered to a metal chain and half-shaft, would be safe from the lightening. (She was).

In the morning one old friend, Karen, came round, but she was the only one. I felt really abandoned by most of the people I had thought were friends in East Anglia over the previous few years. The vision I'd had months before was of a triumphant exit of a whole band of horses, waggons and gaily dressed performers, with all our friends out in the streets cheering us off; now the reality was two waggons, one horse and three bewildered people wondering what to do next.

Mike was very depressed, questioning everything. Not only did he have to completely rebuild his top and work out how to keep the waggon horizontal with no horse in the shafts, but had to solve the problem of the shafts being too narrow. Also, his wheels were different sizes, the tyres bald and one had a slow puncture. He had another axle and wheels he'd bought from a traveller, but they seemed rusted up. New tyres would cost £35 each and have to be specially ordered. What had we been doing for the previous six months to be so unprepared?

Having had the car for a few months, I was now letting it go. Ernie the mechanic was going to repair it with bits from a similar one so a friend could have it. It was quite an emotional wrench: now I had only the mobility of my own legs and Polly.

I felt I was now on a different kind of journey, but wasn't sure what that journey was. We'd left the house and entered a new life but I felt odd, sensing a lot of negative energy around us, yet feeling really positive myself. I was desperate to get on with The Gipsy Switch as I had given up everything else in my life to travel it. I felt even then that maybe Talie and I were meant to travel it by ourselves. Everything seemed to have changed. I had lost my new-found sense of identity and was very alone, with just my little son for company.

The next week or so passed filled with these mixed emotions. The weather was beautiful and at least it was an unpressurised time to get into a rhythm with Talie, who was now about 6 weeks old. We had lovely walks along tree-lined lanes, the skies reflecting in his clear blue eyes. I used to wake long before the others and make a fire in a 9-inch high tin of Mike's which had holes punched in it, like a miniature brazier. It was excellent for boiling water, so I made tea, soaked and rinsed nappies, hanging them to dry on the shafts, and washed up, soon learning not to let food dry on the plates the night before. It wasn't easy to cook a meal on this little fire, though. We got water from a friendly man up the road, using big red containers from a health-food shop. They would wedge into a bike which could then be pushed. I could do this with Ros, but not on my own carrying Talie. I carried him everywhere possible, believing that a young child should remain in close physical contact with its mother most of the time.

Mike bought loads of wood and built a new top for his waggon and made supports to stop it tipping back again. I found a man with a Land Rover and horse trailer and took Daisy to stay with a lovely woman called Helen in Suffolk. She had a false leg and over time she and Daisy, who also had leg problems, gained confidence in one another and established a wonderful relationship. We then brought Rosie back in the trailer. The police came by to see what we were doing and how long we would be there, but when I explained all our problems, they were fine.

Polly and Rosie quickly became bosom pals, though Rosie kept running round and round in circles, breaking chains, pulling out stakes and slipping collars. Ros and I did the bills, sorting out the household accounts from the months spent living communally, and working out who still owed what. One day Talie and I hitched off somewhere for the first time and I felt happier than I had done in a long time: just me and my feet and arms, with Talie on my front and a rucksack on my back, and felt that was how we should really be travelling.

But I was very happy in my little home on wheels. I had the lower part lined with my grandmother's old green front-room carpet and underfelt, a narrow mattress from my old caravan down one side which Talie and I managed to sleep on, a kind of 'chest of drawers' of suitcases containing our clothes and a box of books like a bedside table. Near the front I had a gas ring and cylinder and a wooden box of crockery and utensils. Right at the front was a metal box of 'sacred objects' for use in ritual and performance and this acted as a seat when I was driving the waggon. Then there were numerous bags of costumes, nappies and bedding, and bowls and buckets full of assorted miscellanea. A beautiful lace curtain, given to me at the time of Talie's birth, hung at the front at night; otherwise the front was open, and there were lengths of string acting as washing lines. When we came to load up to leave, I found I had to take a lot of extra food, water, communal things and Richard and Ros' belongings, which made my load (or rather, Polly's) much heavier than I had intended. Dear Sylvia, who was very supportive of what we were doing, had lent me a little wood- burning stove, but it didn't seem practical in a plastic covered waggon, so Mike had that and I had his oil-stove. My waggon felt very 'un-ethnic', but was what had evolved to make things possible, and I loved it.

Although I felt largely abandoned by my local friends, I still had a strong supportive network all over the country, and indeed the world, so once I allowed myself to expand my horizons away from the immediate locality, things didn't seem so bad, yet it was hard to deal with the negativity which was directed towards me by people who had originally been going to be part of the journey and their friends. This wasn't paranoia, but real stuff directed specifically at me. I didn't understand it, and to this day still don't.

Wednesday August 1st, 1984. I couldn't believe it was August already, and it didn't feel like Lammas. I thought of the many women gathering at Silbury Hill, wishing I could be with them, and wondered whether the coming full moon would make me feel more in tune.

This was the day we had decided to leave. A woman we knew, Sue Carpenter, came with her (proper) waggon and big horse Dobbin, and was going to travel the first part of the journey, and Andy Bell came to see us off. This was the first time we had got both Polly and Rosie into the shafts at the same time. Mike found Rosie fitted his shafts after all as she was taller than Polly. They both played up, knowing we were inexperienced and we felt they'd probably planned it for days while they stood around munching grass. We got them in eventually but I'd never harnessed-up before and it all seemed a muddle of lengths of leather and buckles and I wondered if I'd ever manage to do it on my own.

We set off quite fast in convoy. I was sitting, driving, and feeling quite confident. Rosie took a lot of persuading to go round the first corner, then we went up a hill and Polly really struggled, stretched out almost flat, but she was such a goer she made it. I knew she would get fitter as we went on, but definitely realised I would have to make our load much lighter. I also learned to get out and walk at her head when the going got too hard.

We were trotting. Mike's bike was on the back of his waggon and suddenly it fell off and dragged along the ground behind them – and Rosie bolted! Thank goodness my wonderful Polly didn't follow. We didn't know which way Rosie had gone and it was very frightening. We followed a trail of broken bits of Square Wheel Theatre signs and Mike's possessions. We went down a hill, which freaked me out as I didn't think Polly would be able to hold the waggon back (there were no brakes), but with Andy's help, she managed it. Then we saw Mike's waggon by the roadside, and Rosie was at last caught. She had run back to the field we'd been in and, not finding us there, turned round and set off again trying to find us. Mike's belongings were strewn everywhere; his new top was smashed, but miraculously, neither man nor horse were hurt and the actual trolley and harness weren't damaged.

Back we went to the building plot, completely shattered. I felt I had to totally re-assess my plans and was full of doubt; very clear as to what I wanted to do, but feeling this wasn't the way to go about it.

Over the next few days Sue and Mike took Rosie out on drives, and she became more settled and Mike more confident and happy. A few friends did come by, including Paul West the horse dealer, who gave Mike a lot of advice and re-covered Rosie's collar so it wouldn't make her shoulders sore again. We had quite a collection of collars, I having held on to Daisy's for sentimental reasons; and I had learned just how much one depends on the good condition of the harness, for, as long as the horse stays on its feet, it's the only thing which holds the waggon, especially going up hills.

Mike decided not to rebuild his top, at least for the time being, just to put his stuff on the trolley, cover it with the tarp and camp beside it. He left a lot of his possessions behind and I left some of mine at Sandra's, especially a large, heavy mirror I had thought we could use for theatrical preparations. I helped her paint her kitchen and things became easier between us. Everything has a reason.

So, as ready as we could ever be, we decided to set off again.

THE GIPSY SWITCH PLACES

GEMINI - Appleby (Cumbria)
CANCER - Durham
LEO - York
VIRGO - Lincoln
LIBRA - Cambridgeshire
SCORPIO - Essex
SAGITTARIUS - Kingston-upon-Thames
CAPRICORN - Wiltshire
AQUARIUS - Glastonbury
PISCES - Lampeter (West Wales)
ARIES - Anglesey
TAURUS - Ireland

Aries, Leo and Sagittarius are fire signs, Taurus, Virgo and Capricorn are earth, Gemini, Libra and Aquarius are air, Cancer, Scorpio and Pisces are water.

145

PART TWO

Chapter 10: The Gipsy Switch Begins. To Virgo.

It was August 6th when, finally, in a very anti-climactic way, we made our second attempt to set off. The date was fitting, as it was the anniversary of Hiroshima and the day The Walk For Life had ended the previous year. It was now Leo, and I had this new little human being as my companion.

We were still intending to aim for Arbor Low, and from there out to the circle of the Switch at whatever point we were near time-wise in the zodiac. I carried with me the twelve painted zodiac signs I had used in the Albion Fair performance several years before, intending to leave one in the appropriate part of the country as we travelled – creating a circle on the land.

There was no given route for the Switch; we were just going to make our own way as best we could, ensuring we were in the right part of the country for the appropriate zodiac sign and its time of year.

Ros travelled with us in the early days, cycling ahead to find places for us to stop each night. There were no mishaps this time and we travelled a few miles to our first high stop, surrounded by fields of rape seed, tall trees and hedges. For the first time I began to have fears I never had when walking and hitching with my rucksack. I worried about money and food and water and wood for fires. It was all such a big change and I hadn't yet adjusted to the difference from my years travelling alone, accountable to no-one but myself. This fragile, blue plastic covering to a flat-bed trolley was the only home I and my little boy had. Would I be able to get it all together each morning? Would I have a flat tyre? Everything was so much more complex, and I was now responsible for Polly as well as my son.

The next day started late but ok, though I was still not able to harness up on my own. We went wrong on our route and had to go miles out of our way, but Ros found us a good stopping place. At the end of each day we had to get water in the huge 5-gallon plastic containers. They were so heavy we didn't completely fill them, just got more whenever we could. Nothing at that point felt very spiritual; however, we slept to the sound of the wind in some aspens.

146

We decided not to do too many daily miles to begin with and over the next few days things got slowly more relaxed. I got very tired, walking with Polly most of the time rather than driving.

Sometimes Talie slept in his Moses basket, or just lay enjoying the motion of the waggon; at other times I carried him, which made him happy, but hard for me to walk and guide Polly.

There seemed so much to do each day. Always some part of the harness had to be mended, some stitching somewhere having broken. I was aware from the beginning how much younger the others were than I, and that they didn't realise how much I had to do with Talie, and how much of my time and attention he took. Each day there was lots to do before we set off. I had to do my washing, using different bowls for different things – one for clothes, another for dishes and another for Talie. I boiled water on the gas ring, and apart from drinking and food, all water had to be used several times – washing things which gradually were dirtier. That which washed the clothes had to wash something else; that which rinsed them had to be used for more washing or the washing up. Nothing must be wasted.

After a few days it was my 42nd birthday and Saffron came to join me for a few days and it was wonderful having my two youngest children travelling with me.

It all gradually got easier. I had to walk, keeping Polly from the ditch or the centre of the road or from bumping into Mike's waggon. Going up hills was scary: what if Polly couldn't get to the top? I still thought my load was too heavy and hoped the breeching wouldn't snap. Downhill was even worse as she had to hold back all the weight pushing against her, but she found her own pace, walking slowly, step by step, not allowing the whole thing to run away with her. Mike had the design for a kind of metal shoe which could be put on one wheel when going downhill as a kind of skid to slow the momentum, but we would have to find a blacksmith who could make them. For the time being when we went downhill Ros hung on to the back of my waggon, and then we waited at the bottom while she went back for her bike. She looked at the road signs for us, as both Mike and I were short-sighted. We realised we had to work out routes which didn't have any steep hills, so sometimes they meandered a lot when plotted on a map.

If policemen spoke to us they were very apologetic at having to do so. People often stopped to chat, really pleased to see us travelling with horses. A man who owned a field and used to do horse - ploughing gave us loads of advice and there was a lot of genuine nostalgia for the days when horses worked. Inexperienced as we were, we were actually doing it for real, as a way of life, and people appreciated that. There was still much practical knowledge around

My Harvest (photo Juliet Yelverton)

which we hoped to get hold of before it was completely lost. For example, a young lad whose father used to be a horseman, gave us tips, such as: when putting the collar on the horse,(it has to go on 'upside down') go as though to kiss them through it, then quickly put it on and turn it around.

I greatly missed going to the Islands that year, as they were already so much a part of me, but we were heading for the Bedford levels and already there was a sense of being high in an open landscape, which was a relief, as I didn't like being too enclosed.

These were lovely windy, gorgeous, late summer hazy days, but we were aware of the earth around us being full of chemicals. Travelling by small roads we saw much we weren't used to, such as huge piles of plastic containers full of fertilisers, pesticides and herbicides.

As the days went by our relationships with the horses got better and better and much more relaxed. We were surrounded on all sides by the rich harvest and I felt part of that harvest as I travelled through it with two of my children. Everything felt ripe and full, and I sensed the tiredness of the earth whose job was nearly done for another year, but wondered why we had to poison her to reap her riches. The sun shone hot late into the evenings and I fully felt part of the time of year.

On this part of the journey we stopped many evenings at places where there were people we knew, and at one I had a bath. We did, however, usually start off much later than we would have liked and, though getting better at it, I still needed help harnessing up. I was still very tired, though I often woke early and lay looking at Talie, so happy when he smiled at me.

On August 12, Richard and his partner Juliet arrived and we already had many adventures to tell them about. He was delighted by all that we'd overcome and already achieved, how calm we seemed and how well we seemed to be getting on. He'd been talking with the people who had decided not to come on the trip and they had led him to expect us to be in a terrible state.

One day we drove on into the dark after the red sun set and the orange moon rose, and stopped on the Peddar's way. Saffron built herself a little home under the waggon, just as I had done on Signs of Life. The next day, after a sluggish start, Polly took the lead, making a steady pace to Grimes Graves, the old Neolithic flint mines where we'd stopped on the Signs of Life, and John Lord and his family let us park up in their front garden. He was a brilliant flint knapper, re-creating perfect Neolithic implements, his son Will having now taken on the same craft. We stayed a few days, recovering from our exhaustion, mending and larding harness to keep it supple, and in trying to make the bender on my trolley a better shape, ended up making it worse. We were supposed to clean the harness every day and oil it once a week, as the grease and sweat from the horses would cause it to rot (and in the winter, so would the mud). We didn't have proper harness oil so used lard, which was horrible but good for the hands. You are supposed to undo all the buckles, but I didn't because I thought I'd not be able to put it all back together again.

I found England so beautiful. Apart from the harvest, everything was still green, and with rich red sunsets it was a joy to be alive. At last I was doing it and, hard as it was, it was real.

Mick Massey, a farrier, came and shod both horses. Polly was a dream, but Rosie quite difficult. We reckoned that, in future, Polly should stay near when

Rosie was being shod. He fitted riding shoes with filler, as driving shoes need to be tougher, and put one stud in Polly's back ones and on all four of Rosie's, to give them more grip and stop them slipping. He just used what he had in his bag and put them on cold and charged £15 each. I think that means each horse, not each shoe.

On the 15th, Bruce turned up quite suddenly, picked up Saffron and they rushed off without my being able to say a proper goodbye. I missed her terribly and was lonely when she'd gone, even though there were quite a few people around. I particularly valued having Juliet there, as she was a woman who'd had children. Later we set off but didn't go very far, stopping on a verge where people offered us water without our asking. Polly was happy with her new shoes and I felt more relaxed with what I was doing.

How different communication was before mobiles. We were employing the services of a Secretarial Agency, so all our post went to them, and when we stopped somewhere for a few days we let them know and they would forward it on, usually Poste Restante to a nearby Post Office. They took phone messages for us, so we called them whenever we could get to a phone, telling them where we were in case anyone wanted to find us, and they passed on messages and phone numbers.

As we left, I worried about some wrinkles on Polly's shoulders for if she got sores we wouldn't be able to move on until they were better, but she had quite saggy skin anyway and had lost some weight. I tried her in Daisy's collar as it was lighter and bigger and easier to cope with. However when we stopped for lunch we had a meeting which left me completely shattered. Mike just wanted to go on travelling all day long with no time for stops. He was impatient with the pace I was moving at, my pace of coping with both a baby and a horse. I didn't want to be driven on a treadmill, and suddenly was in despair, just when I thought things were getting better.

Next morning things were calmer and got we got off reasonably early. We went a bit off our route to a 'riverside pub' which sounded welcoming, but the publican told us to move on. We parked farther up the road and went back for a drink, but then he said they were shut! Later, we paused and I lay on the earth in the sun and felt myself become one with the land, reconnecting with that union I had created on my Awakening journey. I felt all the sites alive again in my body, with the land lying like a goddess in the sea and reaching out her hand to enfold us, drawing us caringly towards her red centre. Such moments were so precious, touching once more the deep reality of what we were doing beneath the mundane surface of things. We made a fair mileage that day, which pleased Mike, but I was totally exhausted towards the end. We were 'adopted' by an old boy who led us to a place where the horses went in a field with long grass.

Although we were still in Norfolk. We were in the fens and the landscape had changed. The earth was now black and growing vegetables.

In the morning, Polly was covered in ticks, which are great grey shiny things when they are full of blood; but they dropped off later. The old boy – Tom – came back with loads of useful advice. People seemed to emerge, pleased to see us on the road and wanting to help all they could; though Mike had been laughed at in a pub the previous evening for being 'old-fashioned'.

Now we were on a lot of straight, narrow roads, and traffic sped past with no care about their effect on us. A juggernaut roared past and the vacuum behind it sucked out all the staples holding one side of my blue tarp onto the waggon, so I had to staple it back. We kept going quite late and trotted instead of just walking, and Polly enjoyed that. The harvest all around us, we stopped at March and huge combine harvesters worked all night with strange lights shining on the corn. It felt like a rape of the sleeping grain, a rape of the earth more than it would have in the day, and was so far from the old ways of doing things which were about giving as well as taking. However, the stars came out and that was a comfort.

One day it was too hot by the time we were ready, so we decided to wait a day. I spent a lot of time under the waggon, trying to get some shade, and staring at the dragon which someone had painted on the back – she had a smile like the Mona Lisa. We had a big discussion and decided not to go to Arbor Low, but to the nearest part of the actual journey and start with the harvest sign, Virgo. It suddenly made everything exciting and imminent – we would soon be properly on the Gipsy Switch! That evening the sky was the most beautiful range of colours and I saw a shooting star.

Most of the people who now stopped to talk with us were travellers or gipsies who had settled in houses. We thought they might ridicule us, but they really appreciated people doing it, no matter how inexperienced – as long as we were living it and 'didn't have a house'. We always had an open fire, would collect wood as soon as we stopped and kept hot water going a lot of the time. We had a trivet made from 3 horseshoes on which to stand all my old pots and an enamel kettle I had bought in a Belgian flea-market years before, which was now battered and blackened by smoke.

Next morning I went into March and discovered there were complications with my passport and I'd have to go to Peterborough to sort it out. There was no news from my solicitor about my divorce or when I might get any money. It seemed I couldn't free myself from the complexities of modern life.

Mike was planning to go by himself on a trip to the Molesworth peace camp, and went ahead to practice travelling alone. Polly was in an awful state without Rosie, wanting to go like a bomb and sweating herself up. I slowed her down, but then she became temperamental, stopping and starting and going all over the road. It wasn't like her, and I wasn't all that good yet at driving or leading her. She kept making wide berths round donkeys and piles of earth and farm equipment by the roadside and, at one point went right off the road to avoid some white plastic. But we got past Whittlesey and both Richard and I had strong sensations of slipping back in time on a bit of old road.

A famous gipsy – Fred Walker ("in all the books") – came to visit and gave us lots of advice, especially to Mike about his Molesworth trip, letting him know of places to stop on the way. We had pulled up on a traditional stopping place and, at one point, a man called by asking if we were 'Bella Walker's lot'. They didn't seem to mind us being there, and a man gave us a bunch of carrots. Richard and Juliet found a quotation – 'Happiness lies along the road, not at the end of it', and I hoped our journey would be like that and vowed to try and make my life's journey so too.

I was still of two minds about going to Australia as I felt so content on this journey, for all its problems, and didn't really want to go off to the other side of the world and leave it. After all the business with my car tyres and the damage to Sandra's house I was also concerned about leaving Polly, the waggon and all my precious belongings in the care of others, and asked myself why I would risk my beautiful baby in great machines in the air when it was enough of a concern travelling with a horse. The others were encouraging me to go, though – wanting to be rid of me?

Mike went off to Molesworth.

I was getting behind with repairing and oiling the harness and grooming Polly, but managed to work on the harness by getting up very early. I now had an awl, so it was easier to make holes in the leather, but didn't yet have proper needles, though we did have special waxed thread. When it cooled from the intense heat we moved on, Polly again very erratic, wanting to trot through roads which were narrow with sheer, deep ditches on either side.

Leaving Juliet with the horses, at lunchtime Richard and I went ahead to Crowland and saw a harness-maker who told us which bits of ours were most vulnerable and dangerous if broken, and would need reinforcing. His premises were amazing: he made collars and harness by hand in the traditional way and got orders from all over the world. We bought needles and some bits of useful leather. Crowland had an old, steep bridge where 3 roads came together over 3 rivers and had once been the only crossing point.

We stopped on a plot owned by 'I.B.Blackbird' and were surrounded by lots of children who Juliet was very good with. At last I went to the Peterborough PO, collected my passport and took it to the passport office to have Talie's name added. There were no personal letters and I was quite upset, wondering whether everyone had forgotten me already. I sat in a cafe with Talie who was by now making little talking noises and really communicating. He was getting very strong, and I thought that soon I would have to carry him on my back as he was getting too big for the sling. I looked quickly into the cathedral, which had lozenges on the ceiling, an ancient symbol used in Neolithic times, if not even earlier.

Back at the plot the children did a lot with Polly, decorating her, plaiting her mane and riding her. One of them said he was born in a caravan. The neighbours were very friendly and one man gave us some beetroot. When we set off Polly was still behaving erratically, giving wide berths to plastic sacks in hedges and going so fast I feared she might bolt. We stopped at a lovely place with good grazing near a river which was so nice we decided to wait there until Mike returned, and I realised I wouldn't travel any more with the waggon until I returned from Australia.

26th August. It was the dark moon. We had been travelling through the harvest lands of England and I still hadn't got myself a sheaf of corn from a field edge, needing one to carry round the land for a year and use in ceremonies. I hadn't been walking among fields and trees enough and felt a bit 'dead', which was so different from my previous journeys. I kept thinking that when this one was over, I must walk another just with Talie and experimented with carrying him on my back, which worked, though I didn't like not seeing him as I walked.

As the moon began to wax, I moved out of my dark moon despondency and realised I was just very tired, that I'd had no rest since Talie was born, so stopped feeling guilty about not moving on or doing all my multitudinous chores. Pausing was a good time to experience Lincolnshire and the energy of Virgo. The flat land stretched away into the distance with its fields being intensively harvested; birds flew high and there was a feeling of space. Many people sold vegetables outside their houses and buying them was the nearest we could get to living from the land.

Down by the river there were tiny dragonflies as blue as my waggon and one stayed with me a whole afternoon. Richard said they were 'Dainty Ladies'. All across one field of burned stubble were white feathers: stark white on black ash for yards and yards. One evening there was a beautiful sunset, but stubble was being burned with flames an unnatural colour from all the chemicals on the crops. The fire looked like blood.

Eventually I got my sheaf of corn, gleaned from the edge of a field which had been harvested, and Juliet photographed me both holding it and Talie: a beautiful picture of me with my own harvest and that of the earth. I lay on that earth and wondered how we feel to her – are we like the soft touch of my son's little hand on my skin or are we like flies that crawl and aggravate, that sting, bite and poison? Will she rise up one day soon in annoyance and simply shake us off? I thought of how once the earth grew everything her children needed, but now the affluent half fills her with poison and force-feeds her to over-produce for them while the other half starves.

So this had been my Virgo of The Gipsy Switch: fields of force-fed earth being harvested at night by huge machines with strange lights, the corn glowing fluorescent blue-white in the moonlight; blood- red sunsets accompanied by the blood-red flames of chemically treated burning stubble; and fields piled high with enormous machine-made bales and huge barrels of chemicals.

When I left, the plan was that Mike, and Richard in my waggon, would continue north to Lincoln, to perform and celebrate Virgo there, then turn south onto the Gipsy Switch journey, to be in Cambridgeshire for Libra, maybe stopping at St.Ives, Huntingdon, then down through Essex to Saffron Walden where I hoped to meet up with them for Samhain (October 31st) and Scorpio, leaving the wooden Virgo and Libra signs with Richard to place where he thought fit. I was being propelled towards Australia by a momentum over which I had no control, like jumping off the top board at a swimming pool, no stopping and no turning back. I sorted out my waggon, packed some things to leave at Sandra and Andy's and a few to take with me.

After all the depression and worry I suddenly became excited at the prospect of being somewhere I would gain enormous strength and clarity and, hopefully, understanding. Much as I wanted to stay, I knew that going was what I must do. It was just the getting there which was the problem!

Mike came back from Molesworth in a wonderful glow, cooked a nice supper and it was a good evening. The stars were clear in the dark sky and there was a crescent moon which set early. I put Talie into disposable nappies for the first time and wondered where we would be in a week.

I felt that The Gipsy Switch journey was now alive. People were travelling it, energising it, and as long as some continued, it didn't really matter who, as long as they had the awareness of what they were doing. Others came and went; this time it was me who was leaving. We were coming up to Libra, the time of balance. They would be living the Autumn Equinox in the same moment I lived the Spring. I was encircling the Earth as they encircled the country. It intensified the whole thing and I felt I would still be on the Gipsy Switch: a bigger, even more powerful part of it.

154

The last day of August came and Richard drove me to Norwich to get the cash I needed from an advance on my divorce settlement. I made a will – primarily so people who had lent me money would get it back if I died, and there would be someone to look after Talie if I died and he didn't. Richard was very patient, as this took ages. He drove me to Sandra and Andy's where I helped her hem curtains and stayed the night.

The next day I did some laundry and helped Sandra polish the kitchen floor. I didn't have a rucksack but Karen With came round and lent me hers. It was a tiny red one and I could carry less in it than I now bring back from a shopping trip to Stornoway. I was going with so little, and it all seemed so last minute and almost spontaneous.

Chapter 11: Australia and Libra

September 2nd: I woke Sandra with a cup of tea and she drove me to the coach for London. On the way down through East Anglia I watched the green of late summer England, having just come from the dry, golden fields of the just-been-harvested. I drank in that green, thinking it would be gone when I returned, feeling a deep part of this land we were passing through. The day was bright and calm. It was the beginning of something very new – Talie and I off on an adventure together, and he was brilliant.

It was hot at Victoria.

I spent several days in London visiting friends, being given many good luck charms, as people realised how scared I was of the flights and what an enormous thing I was doing with this new tiny person. I had prepared so little for this trip, and it was only when I reached London that I went to a travel agent advertised in the back pages of Time Out to get my ticket.
We were flying Garuda. (This appalled Australians once we arrived, as they couldn't believe the wings hadn't fallen off!). As we were going to Darwin, where Lynne was to meet us, we would have an overnight stop in Bali. I was advised to book overnight accommodation, but it was too late so I planned to spend the night sitting in the airport. I got travel insurance, traveller's cheques and some Australian and US dollars, unsure of the exchange rates. How money has changed since those days, when I was shocked at a 50p tube ticket and a £6 taxi fare across London.

I didn't even have a sleeping-bag with me, needing something compact and light, so bought a thin one with a reflective lining which nowadays I use as a groundsheet. It was odd to still be using my married name, but I was still married and that was the name on my passport. Everything continued to feel more and more unreal, like a dream out of my control.

All my London friends were so kind and I finally stayed with Erin and her daughter Rachael. She was very patient with me. Although I was at least ten years older than her, I was like a young girl in my nervousness, and she became like a mother figure to me.

September 5th: A taxi called for me at 5.30 and took me to Victoria, from where I had a coach ticket to Gatwick. Wandering round the airport with little idea where to go, I somehow managed to find the right places. At one point as I sat waiting an old man said I shouldn't be taking so young a baby on such a long flight, which was the last thing I wanted to hear as it was what I was thinking myself. I had waited so long for him, what was I doing, taking him on a plane?

At the baggage check I met an Australian girl returning home after working as a nanny. She was going to Darwin too, so we agreed to do the Bali stopover together as she wasn't booked in anywhere either. All I had with me was Karen's little red rucksack with a few clothes and my knitting in it, the tiny thin sleeping-bag, Talie and his blankets in the rush Moses basket and a blue cotton bag holding my few most personal possessions. I'm not sure I even had a coat. The girl, Sue, had loads of luggage, and as I had so little asked if she could put some of hers through on my baggage allowance, and even though I had a slight wariness, I agreed. She seemed like a gift from the universe – a nanny to be with me as some sort of company and support.

Although I was terrified of flying, I had chosen to do it, so just had to get on with it. We had one stop at Rome and then an 11-hour flight to Bangkok and this really got to me. I know it's taking off and landing which are the most dangerous, but couldn't believe a plane could stay in the air for 11 hours without stopping. I couldn't sleep: if I lay down, all I could feel was the air flowing and buffeting under us. I felt I was keeping the plane in the air by my own will-power, and if I slept it would simply drop like a stone.

Talie was wonderful. When we first boarded, he was put in a cot and the hostesses all crowded round, adoring him. He was radiant, with his huge vivid blue eyes, and I really understood what charm was – a kind of magical energy which was beyond just being cute. Now he gazed at me with his big, trusting eyes and I nearly cried. What was I doing? I had to get myself into a state of not thinking negatively, not really thinking anything, just having an empty mind in a pure state of being.

Then it was the next day; a day of endless takings off and landings. The food was wonderful, but all the sitting was making my legs swell - I don't think they'd invented flight socks in those days. The times on the ground were such a relief, and sometimes I slept then.

At Jakarta we had to change planes. I wasn't used to tropical atmospheres and found I could hardly breathe in the humidity. Here I went through a customs check. My knitting was in the rucksack and the official didn't know what the needles were and thought they were some kind of weapon, but it was all ok in the end. The next flight took us to Denpesar, Bali.

Well, so much for naive plans! I had imagined the airport would be like Gatwick or Heathrow, but this was just a big, panelled hall with seats round the edge. Some workmen told us ours had been the last flight of the day and the airport was to be locked up for the night. We thought maybe we could be locked in, but a security guard came along and said we could stay in his office where there was hot water to make tea. It sounded a bit dodgy, but there were two of us, and we decided to follow his directions. This was the only time in my life where I have been near anywhere equatorial, where the night comes down like a curtain quite early in the evening. I was so used to long twilights and late summer evenings, but this was almost like someone switching the light off.

We searched. We thought we had found the bloke's office, but he wasn't there and what we found was something like a police station with a lot of men on duty. They weren't very friendly but agreed to let us stay, taking our passports and putting us in a corridor on the way to the toilets. There was one narrow, slatted, wooden bench, which I couldn't sleep on with Talie, so Sue had that and Talie and I slept on the floor. There was a drain nearby and lots of mosquitoes which bit us, and I hoped we wouldn't get malaria. The men watched TV all night and didn't disturb us. So much for cups of tea!

And that was my night in Bali.

Early in the morning the men turfed us out, telling us the airport was now open and returning our passports. Back in the big hall we finally got tea. On the counter were open tins of Nestles condensed milk to put in it, which I thought hilarious, but any tea was welcome. The sunlight streamed in and I felt happy sitting there waiting for the last flight of our journey. The worst was over and this would be a last easy hop, and I was excited about getting to Australia.

When we landed in Darwin we had to wait for ages on the plane until they came and fumigate us. I said goodbye to Sue and seemed to be the last one to go through customs. They were very suspicious of me. They didn't exactly unpick the seams of the rucksack, which I had heard of them doing, but went through absolutely everything I had. Eveon had given me a lucky nutmeg and I had small bags of dill and fennel seeds for teas to help keep my milk flowing. They were most suspicious of these, presumably thinking they were illegal drugs, but I hadn't realised you can't take plant matter into Australia, and they were seized by the quarantine department. I said I must have them back, explaining why, and gave them the address where I would be staying and, sure enough, a few weeks later they arrived in little plastic bags with their Latin names on. They didn't seem to mind some henna and almonds I also had with me.

At last I was through, and outside the airport we met Lynne, who had become worried when I didn't appear, wondering whether I'd missed the flight. Lynne was very tall. After I'd been with her a while I stopped noticing, but seeing her again after a long time I was very aware of her height and felt small beside her.

She'd put on weight too. When I'd known her in England she'd had very little money, walking across London looking for work, and had got quite thin. She'd booked us into a hotel where I had a shower; then we went out and had supper and ices and talked and talked and talked. It was humid here too and took me ages to sleep: I was tired, but full of excitement at being on the other side of the earth. Talie slept like a log. It felt right being there: I had done it and it seemed like the only place to be. I was calm and relaxed and happy in a way I hadn't been for months; the real me again, back in touch with what my life was about. Lynne was part of that world, that life, which is why it was so good being with her again.

The next morning we went shopping, then got a bus to Alice Springs. I had no words for the sense of perfection I felt travelling through the bush, seeing huge ant-hills which looked like standing stones. On the journey Lynne was like a tour guide, telling me about the land, about everything we saw, about Australian politics, and so much else. I drank it all in but didn't say much: indeed what could I say? I don't think I said much of any significance in all the time I was there – it all going in to be made sense of later.

We arrived in Alice at 7am and had breakfast. Years before Lynne had worked with Aborigines. She'd been thrown out of where she was teaching and sent to teach them almost as a punishment, but she learned from them and it was they who told her to come to Britain to find her own Dreaming. In Alice she explained the terrible state the People were in, having had their land and their way of life of maybe 60,000 years taken from them in such a short while. Now there was a problem with alcoholism and young people sniffing petrol, and you would often see them lying around in dried-up river beds.

On another bus we headed for Uluru, where Lynne was working at one of the motels still open right near the Rock. The new 'tourist city' of Yulara had been completed but not yet properly open to the public. There had been a camp-site near the Rock, but it had been closed after the Lindy Chamberlain incident, when it was thought her baby had been taken by a dingo. However, she had been arrested and accused of murdering her child. Lynne said the Aborigines knew it had been a dingo because something had happened to anger the spirit of the Dingo Dreaming. This did make me doubly sure I wouldn't leave Talie lying around alone anywhere.

Lynne was living with one of the rangers, Hilary, who was away at the time, so we would be staying in the ranger's house, right near the Rock. The Aboriginal women used to come and sit with Lynne and Hilary on their veranda as Hilary had been initiated into the local Pitjitjinjara tribe and spoke their language. They didn't come while she was away.

There was a community shop nearby, run for the local Aboriginal community. Most of them still lived in 'humpies' round about the area. These were like benders covered in tarpaulins and made me think of my waggon back home. They still travelled their Dreaming paths, carrying their sacred objects, but now did it in pick-up trucks. When they had punctures they mended them by heating up a kind of gum they got from spinifex grass. None of them actually lived in the bush as they used to, though they still collected 'bush tucker' when it was in season. However, when asked about it, many of the women said they didn't bother any more as "we have flour from the shop now". I was sad one day when I saw an old man in the shop. He was a tribal elder wearing a red head-band and was looking in the freezer cabinet for fish and chips.

Talie had a bit of a cry on the last part of our journey, and when we got to Yulara the driver wouldn't let us stay on the bus, but Lynne got one of the rangers to give us a lift. It was about 18km, and we were there at last. The house was amazing to me after the life I'd been living for years – air conditioning, all mod-cons, even a washing machine. I questioned myself for staying in a house like that while the Aborigines camped in make-shift humpies, some of which were indeed made of blue plastic, like my waggon.

That first evening the sun set red on the far side of the Rock, which became a black shape against the red, gold and dark blue sky. Later the night became wild and windy, which wasn't what I had expected in the Red Desert. There was a lot of rain and the wind blew things against the house, but at dawn there was a double rainbow. Taliesin Rainbow Smith was working his wonders. I began to think that it was more he who had brought me to Australia, rather than I him. He had been greeted by Aborigines and I thought maybe he would get the Dreaming, not I.

We rested the next day and he slept a lot. It was good to be so near the Rock, to watch its changing colours, to be near the Aboriginal people, and I was filled with awe and respect. I had questioned why I had gone, but once there knew why: to focus and put everything in perspective and find balance – the balance of Libra. The Rock was like a great mother and I felt I could stay beside her for ever: she was so strong and big and I was already filled with that strength.

After the rain the rock was purple all day and the wind blew like the wind of the Hebrides. We slowly recovered from our journey, not so much jet-lagged as having come from one reality to another in a very short space of time. Being with Lynne reinforced my sense of what I was doing in life, for she understood and supported me, whereas I felt so unsupported in Britain.

As Lynne was working, once we were rested Talie and I set off for our first walk to the Rock. Spring was a perfect time to be there; not too hot and with the snakes not yet out. I love snakes, love to hold and feel the muscles of them,

Taliesin, Jill and Lynne Wood at Uluru

but feared poisonous ones which might shoot out and bite me as I walked by. When we passed one of the men's sacred places I felt I shouldn't even look at it, should avert my eyes. Around that time the Aborigines were trying to claim back their sacred sites from tourism and were trying to stop planes and helicopters flying over the Rock, some even landing on it.

After a while we came to a cave which it was ok to enter and climbed up and sat in its shade. I looked out over the ancient landscape as people had done for tens of thousands of years and could sense all that time stretching back, the land changing only in subtle ways, being looked after by people who were of it and part of it and who understood it on every level. I thought the teachings I would receive there would be very subtle and that to relate to the Rock powerfully would not be disrespectful to her guardians. I knew I must be very careful in everything I did.

The stone of the Rock seemed like flesh, flesh of the earth, mucous membrane, its colour constantly changing. Holding that ancientness within me assured me that, on my return, I would relate differently to the sacred sites of Britain, and have a deeper sense of their age too. I noticed though, how even out there in that desert so much had already changed, with aircraft streaking high in the endless sky, sudden sounds of vehicles on unseen roads, even the air being full of invisible waves: electrical, radio, microwaves, beams from satellites – and that was in 1984.
The Rock is the top of a mountain in a sea of wonderful rich red sand. The flowers and plants were subtle pastel colours, as though already bleached by

the power of the sun; the only bright colours being the yellow balls of paddy melons and the blossom of the wattle. When the first few white people ventured out into the centre of Australia they took camels with them as the only viable way of travelling, and the saddles were stuffed with the melon plant. When the saddles split or were abandoned, the seeds fell out and the plants have spread everywhere.

I talked quietly to the Rock while Talie lay on his rainbow blanket gazing up at the faded paintings on the roof. The people had gone who had once had this cave as part of their Dreaming, but it was still tended by other tribes.
Not far away was a place called the 'Little Rock' which has natural upright stones looking like standing people, so we paused there a while before walking back. I had to be careful not to let any direct sunlight fall on Talie, and a few days later, bought him a little sun-hat. The sky was a rich deep blue and so clear it was maybe one of the last clean air-spaces on earth. It seemed as though there was more sky reaching farther from earth than the British sky I was used to, even in the Hebrides.

The moon rose yellow and huge on the horizon. Talie got very excited and tried to fly to it.

When it was dark I found myself under a strange and unfamiliar sky. Although I don't know the constellations as seen from Britain that well, it's a night sky which is part of some deep place within me, and in Australia it was unsettlingly different. There seemed fewer stars, even in that clear sky and I felt that in all my lifetimes I had never been in the Southern Hemisphere before.

The next time I walked to the Rock with Talie I found a lovely place with waterfalls which Lynne had told me about and we lay by it a long while. It was totally still and almost soundless apart from the occasional bird. The energy flowed into both of us and I felt I was being taught things on a very deep level. I didn't need people to teach me in words; the place itself was teaching me, as though I were tuning myself into a transmission from everything around me. I just had to absorb it and the understanding would come later, but I had to be careful not to get 'spaced-out' and overwhelmed, so had to keep grounded.

I was quite bothered by the sand-flies, understanding why Australians wear those hats with dangling corks, but decided I'd better not use fly-repellent on my skin as it said 'toxic' on the label and if Talie touched me and then put his hands in his mouth he might get poisoned.

We walked back as it got cooler, and it began to rain as the sun shone and there was another rainbow, and later a heavy downpour with black clouds over the Rock, followed by a strange night. There was a lot of noise from the Aboriginal camp and Talie was very restless, thrashing about so I couldn't

162

sleep. The moon was very bright and I was up at first light, tired, and saw grey/brown clouds like smoke casting strange shadows on the Rock.

Later that day heavy dark clouds formed, followed by the most incredible storm with lightning, thunder and torrential rain. The clouds were wonderful, darkening the Rock which then almost totally disappeared into mist. When it cleared, the Rock was dark grey, silver and purple, its deep lines and contours etched more clearly than ever, shifting later into dark reddish-purple and silver-grey. The wind blew and lashed the trees. We were having all forms of weather and I wondered whether before long we might even have snow and hail! It was an amazing spectacle – a performance of nature showing her strength. It cleaned me, and I felt fresh and strong again.

Afterwards I walked outside and the air was rich with the smell of the desert: a smell of perfumed wood, or newly sharpened pencils. The wet red sand and water on my feet made a walk to the shop worthwhile, even though I found it shut. There was another strong and vivid rainbow, though only its bottom ends were on the horizon with the rest hidden by a huge cloud. What a day! I had been reading that rainbows are the rainbow serpent coming out because he's offended and I hoped it wasn't us who were offending him.

Although I wrote a few letters to people back home I gradually became less able to write and my diaries became little more than brief notes. However, my memories are still vivid and all I have forgotten is the order in which things happened, which doesn't really matter now.

Some other friends of Lynne's came to stay as well, so we had quite a houseful, but it did mean there were more people to help look after Talie. I often walked to the community shop, changing my traveller's cheques and meeting the Aborigines. The women always wanted to know where Talie's father was and when I said "A long way away" they asked if I meant Alice Springs.

Some days I would walk on my own (with Talie) to different parts of the Rock; on others we would go with Lynne and her friends. On one walk right round the Rock we stopped at a place where there were some aboriginal women and children, an older woman showing a younger one some painted symbols and teaching her about them. Young boys were jumping from high on the rock into a deep and beautiful pool. The older woman came over to us and we chatted to her about bush tucker and she seemed to be treating us as friends, but after a while one of our group asked if it was ok to take a photo of the boys jumping into the water. She said yes, but soon after got up and walked away.

The energy had changed and in her mind we had been relegated to tourists.

However, one day I was in the house on my own with Talie when there was a banging on the door and there stood two excited older Aborigines. They didn't have much English, but kept saying "get billie". I went to the kitchen and got a saucepan as there was no billie-can. They took me out to a tree on which the fruit had just ripened, and picked a lot, filling my saucepan as well as their own. They were still keeping their eye on the bush tucker. These fruits were nearly all a big stone, wrinkled like a brain, with a thin layer of quite firm flesh on the outside. They were called quandong and I recently looked them up, finding they are true Australian fruits which grow in very arid areas. The men of the tribes round the Rock considered the flesh to be a substitute for meat, though the gathering and preparation was women's business. They also had medicinal uses. More recently they have begun to be cultivated by a growing 'Bush Food' industry. I brought a few of the stones back with me and still have one or two.

As I've said, the top of the Rock is sacred and should not be climbed except by Aborigines who do it just by their hands and feet as part of an initiation rite after attaining a high level of teaching, but there was (is there still?) a horrible chain fixed to metal stakes driven into the body of the Rock, up which tourists hauled themselves, quite a lot dying in the process. Unfortunately the shop sold tourist gifts saying 'I conquered the Rock'. One day one of Lynne's friends decided to climb it. I felt quite shocked, but don't recall any of us criticising him. He came back with an eagle feather which prompted him to tell us the story of Jumping Mouse, a traditional Native American tale which has been re-written by many authors as a children's story. The now-adult Talie has recently given me this brief resume of it:

"A brave little mouse plucks up courage to leave his tribe of mice in their home under the roots of a tree, to explore the world beyond, despite its danger of The Spots (eagles) who haunt the skies looking for tasty morsels. Along the way he meets a frog who teaches him to jump high enough to see the Blue Mountains. He then meets Forgetful Wolf and a sick Buffalo, each of whom can only be cured by the donations of Jumping Mouse's eyes. All three then help him in his quest to reach the Blue Mountains where he discovers his destiny. Blind, he reaches the mountain where they leave him alone. There are lots of eagles. One of them eats him and his spirit enters the eagle and he becomes the eagle and can see again."

It seems to be a story of attaining enlightenment. Talie suggests it is about the transmigration of souls and says that in Celtic legends birds eat people to take their spirits to other realms.

One day we drove to the tourist spot where you can watch the spectacular sunset on the Rock. It's that brilliant shining red/orange which you see on all the postcards. It was wonderful to see it in reality.

Another time we hired a car for a trip to Katajuta (the Olga's), which means 'many heads'. This is a completely different kind of rock which has been wind-eroded into shapes that really are like many heads. How ancient these rocks are and how long it must have taken for the wind to erode the original rock into these extraordinary shapes.

It was getting dark when we arrived and found a place to camp. We slept out without tents – in fact we slept in 'swags'. I'd never seen one before or really known what they were: big, heavy, kind of sleeping-bags that you roll out. I was a bit nervous of snakes and poisonous spiders creeping in during the night, but it was all fine. After sleeping in a house it was such a relief to be outside again, this time cool and fresh under the southern stars.

The next day we explored the area, including the 'Caves of the Mice Women' which is a valley with a long row of vulva-like caves high up on the rock. Nearby is a hill which looks like a man lying on his side. The story is that he had raped the mice women and they attacked him and I think, killed him,

and he has his hand to his head where he was hit. Another valley was aligned to the rising moon. It was all pretty awesome.

Back at Uluru we decided to spend the Equinox night in one of the caves which was no longer part of a Dreaming. Although still sacred, we didn't feel we were defiling anything by being there. It was the cave I often visited when I walked on my own with Talie and it had become special to me, so it was powerful to spend the night somewhere we felt accepted. We woke to a beautiful dawn with a crescent moon sharp in the clear, deep sky. At the moment of Equinox I felt joined to people all over the earth, connected to the women at Greenham, sensing many voices chanting, and felt close to The Gipsy Switch as they celebrated the Autumn Equinox in Britain. It was the Libra moment of balance: Spring in the South, Autumn in the North, and I marvelled at the Earth and the seasons which manifest on different parts of her throughout the year.

Information continued to pour into me and I couldn't process it while it was happening. There was the daily life of being with my growing baby in such a different landscape under such a different sky; then there was the physical pain of being where people had lived in a way that worked perfectly for such an astonishing length of time until so very recently, when white people - us - had come and destroyed that whole way of life almost in an instant; destroying the people, even shooting them like vermin, destroying the land and bringing in cattle which fouled the water holes. It really hurt me. I felt responsible; it was so recent, like a still-open wound, with everything on some level in shock.

One day I did write: I wrote of walking on the red sand which was hot beneath my feet and between my toes. I was aware of the place where there was the experience of heat, the place where skin and sand met and became one; the layer where neither was either, the sensation of both being shared by both. There were gnarled, dead trees burnt black like a landscape after a nuclear holocaust, yet all around grew the new - grey, green, cream, white and bleached pastel; lilac flowers on a grey bush. The earth was an old woman, a red mother, a living animal shedding her skin.

On that day I seemed able to spirit-fly, to be above the Rock and look down on her, huge and red, like a squatting goddess with the plain all around her. I knew I mustn't try to draw her. Some sort of mapping inside me was beginning as had happened with the landscape of Britain – the land in me and me in the land. Once we were all like that – the Aborigines had been, and many still are, but those for whom the stories have become - just stories, are lost; lost to a culture of 60,000 years. And we did that.

I could hear the wind on top of the Rock. In a cave there were some carvings which weren't at first apparent but appeared slowly as though emerging from her skin. They had a familiarity, reminding me of things in Britain. I was being taught things I had perhaps always known, but had forgotten, only now becoming conscious of them again. A potent day.

Dead branches lay across my path like old bones bleached in the sun. We usually saw the 'willie wagtails' at the Ininti Pool, but that day it was a crow. I thought 'where is the bird?', heard a noise and it came and sat in a tree above us, black like a small raven.

Our time at the Rock was nearing its end. I continued to go to a different part every day, to deepen my relationship with each place, to drink in as much of the experience as possible. One day there were incredible clouds and the Rock turned silver as though it were made of ice. We walked to the

Ininti pool (where we had seen the boys jumping) and a double rainbow guided us. I asked for rain because I wanted to see it hit the pool, as drops falling into the water looked like cup and ring marks. We sat in the cave with the carvings as black clouds gathered, followed by thunder and lightning.

Walking on a bit we sheltered under a little rock where a plant like heather grew. On the way back there was yet another double rainbow. At the house we sat on the veranda and watched the storm turn into a thickly rich sunset. The night was disturbed and huge cockroaches fell from the ceiling near the place we were sleeping.

Oct 3rd.The time of leaving grew closer. I went with Talie to the Ininti pool for the last time. The day was clear and hot and extraordinarily still and quiet. I could hear every insect move, every little animal scuttle away from the path. I lay a long time in the shade of a tree the colour of the earth with my little son sleeping beside me, and in the silence could hear a sound like a million mosquitoes: was it the sound of the edge of the universe? Or the Rock singing? The shadow of the Rock lengthened as we sat beside the pool.

Lynne had given me a long necklace of Ininti beads, strung by Aborigine women. They are dark red seeds a bit like kidney beans. The women drill holes in them and traditionally strung them on twisted human hair, but these were on wool. I dipped them into the pool so I would always have some of that water with me. I have used them in many rituals since then, re-strung them on Hebridean wool when the moth destroyed the original, and they were last used in a ceremony at Callanish when we scattered Lynne's ashes there in 2013.

The moon was in the sky all day and night, appearing different from how we see it in Britain, sitting like a dome on a flat bottom. When it was crescent it lay on its back with two upright horns.

As I neared the time of leaving my mind started to get busy and only then did I realise how still it had been for the past month. I had been in a pure state of being, living in the moment, absorbing everything, aware. I realised what a gift that had been, a state of contemplation which was how I should always be, but now all the usual worries came flooding back – all the everyday things about packing and the journeys ahead; the fear of my flight home and concern as to whether my waggon would be alright when I returned. I'd had letters from both Richard and Juliet telling me what they had been doing in Lincolnshire and how they were now passing through Cambridgeshire (Libra), but nothing about my home. I began to torment myself that I hadn't done all I should have at the Rock, yet what I had experienced was much more than anything I had planned and I was enriched beyond my dreams.

We were leaving to spend time in Adelaide and Sydney – and I dreaded that. I feared cities would wipe away this experience and thought I should go straight back home to process it all, yet this was a once in a lifetime trip. I doubted I would ever return.

Oct 6th. Our last walk to the Rock. We sat in the 'Equinox' cave, gazing at the paintings on the walls. It didn't feel like the last time I would be there, didn't feel as though I were leaving. I felt I belonged there and would return, even if only in spirit. Maybe the Rock is part of me now, so I never did fully leave.
Oct 7th. My last visit to the community store. The Aborigine women were singing at their camp. It sounded strange and uncanny. One of them sang round

167

the house we were staying in and Lynne said we were being 'sung back', so who knows. I've always felt that Talie would return one day.

With Lynne we got a bus to Alice and stayed in a hostel. Talie cried in the dormitory so we were put in a separate room. Good onya Tal! Next day we wandered round the town where I became a bit dazed and confused, dithering about spending my last bits of money on small gifts for people back home, but feeling I wanted to buy things while still in the Northern Territory, and 'in the country'.

An exhibition of Aboriginal art disturbed me, as once-sacred spiritual imagery had been turned into artworks to be bought and collected by white people whose ancestors had stolen the land from the People and destroyed their way of life. We saw work by women in a group called Ernabella Arts who create traditional designs in batik on silk. The work is very beautiful, and much later Lynne bought me a length and sent it to me in England. It's important for these people to be part of schemes enabling them to earn a living, but it seems to be exploiting their traditions and spirituality.

We hired a 'mini-moke': a tiny vehicle with open sides. I had to hire it as Lynne had only recently got her driving licence and in Australia there was a probationary stage after your test before you got a full licence, and she couldn't hire on that. I drove down the main street of Alice to meet her and when I did she was 'having kittens'. In Britain drivers on the main street have right of way, but in Australia no-one does, so I had sailed along quite regardless of what might have shot out at me from side streets. She did most of the driving once we left Alice.

Heading out in the tiny vehicle on the dirt roads in the Australian heat with my little son I felt very vulnerable. What if we broke down? There was very little passing traffic. I tried not to panic and we didn't have any disasters. It was strange in the desert which covers thousands of miles to suddenly come upon an area of rivers and lakes and huge rocky gorges with trees and wildlife. We walked through Standley Chasm which has narrow, steep sides and was utterly different from all the surrounding land, and reached a campsite at Ormiston Gorge where there was too much water to walk any further. I can't now remember whether we took a tent or if there was a kind of shelter to sleep in, but there was a toilet and washing block and special places to have 'barbies'.

It was incredibly hot and I had an uncomfortable night, which was unusual for me sleeping outdoors. We walked down to the gorge and sat there a long while and with Talie I found my way across rocks to the other side of the river. Walking with bare feet, the sand was so hot it was making me feel sick and really burning me. The trees leaned over the river and the reflections of the water made shifting patterns on their white bark. I tried to photograph them but

168

it didn't work – they were quite magical and didn't want to be captured on film. After lunch at the camp we climbed a hill where there was no path and sat looking at a mountain known as 'The Sleeping Lubra' (Mount Sonder)which is in the form of an old hag-like woman. We got back to the camp at sunset. The climbing had been precarious, but Talie was totally trusting, sleeping as I carried him.

Next day we got up while it was still dark and drove to where we could see the Lubra while the full moon was still in the sky, then back to Alice in time to return the mini-moke and catch the 8.15am bus to Adelaide. There was a lot of room on the bus and Talie was wonderful. It is unbelievable that the journey from Alice to Adelaide only took 24 hours, but we seemed to get there early the next morning. We went down the Stuart Highway and my memory of the road is that most of it wasn't

made up, just red dirt. We stopped for lunch somewhere which looked like an old town in a Wild West movie, and later had a stop at Coober Pedy, which is unlike anywhere else in the world. It is an opal mine, and because they started mining long before there was air-conditioning, they built a whole town underground, where it was cooler. There is a church and everything a town would need. Nowadays it is a tourist attraction, but I presume the mining is still going on and I was deeply affected by it, as I am distressed by all mining, especially that of crystals, precious stones and minerals. I feel their place is in the earth where they were formed and it is wrong to tear them out and move them to other places all over the world.

A lot of opals and jewellery were for sale. The fire-opals were stunning, their multi-colours moving as you looked at them. For all that I have just written, I fell in love with them as though I were bewitched, and yearned to own one. It was a bit like the pull of the ring in the Lord of the Rings. I didn't buy one of course – resisting their enchantment.

All the coaches had 'roo bars' and in the night we saw kangaroos leaping across the road. One hit the front of our coach near the entrance and slightly damaged it. I don't know if it was killed as the driver didn't stop. Just another night, just another Roo.

Reaching Adelaide we stayed with Lynne's cousin and spent days going round exhibitions, art galleries and book shops as well as meeting Lynne's friends, one of whom made stunning brightly coloured painted clothes. We all posed for photos in them and she made a little jacket for Talie. My memories of Adelaide are of sun, lightness and brightness.

After a few days we caught another bus to Sydney. There was a strike on and the very old bus was extremely full. We passed through fruit-growing lands but

169

I found myself homesick for the outback, where I had felt so comfortable even though awed by it. One morning we breakfasted in Canberra, but I remember nothing about it, not realising until I read my notes that I had ever been there.

I wasn't happy in Sydney. My impression was of big, looming old buildings and general darkness, and I felt quite lost, not wanting to spend 10 days there, just wanting to go home. Suddenly I was exhausted, everything catching up with me. Lynne borrowed a car and we drove to Eden, which I remember as being a national park. We arrived in the dark after a marathon drive and found a campsite. It was windy and there was snow on the mountains. Talie suddenly seemed to have a cold and kept waking up and Lynne got fed up with his crying, so I went and spent the night in the car and everything was fine. There was a lovely dawn and we heard kookaburras and saw kangaroos. We drove right down to the rocky coast, where waves crashed high, as in the Hebrides. Lynne said this was the most south-east point of Australia and the next place south was the Antarctic.

It took all day to drive back. Talie was ok but snotty. I now felt as though my spirit was already in England and my body desperate to follow. I recall little of those days, but we went to a beach and there are sunny photos of both Talie and I looking fat from all the Australian dairy produce. By this time I was incapable of writing, though I had a mountain of words in my soul, ready to set down once I had time to put it all in perspective. I never did write it but all that experience became
assimilated into my very being and I understood much more deeply my relationship with Britain. Perhaps it's all still beyond words. One thing I did write seemed to be a message I got 'on the wind' at Uluru:

"You know when they have entered your land because you know the sense of your land and you know the sense of them, and you know the sense of the two coming together. You know the touch of the two coming together and the change it makes".

The day came for our return. I was terrified of the flight, but had to get on with it. It took a long time to leave Australia as the first leg was to Melbourne, and I wondered when I would ever be on my way home. It was a different route this time with more stops and shorter distances between them, which I preferred. Melbourne, Bali, Abu Dhabi, Bahrain, Istanbul, Zagreb, Linz, Frankfurt, London. I think we went over Russia at one point, but at last we were over Europe, then down through the cloud, landing in a grey, wet London. I remember a big lift in the airport. I remember a cold, windy underpass where I waited for a coach into the city centre and somehow I was at Erin's again. I had massive jet-lag and slept for about 36 hours, and so did Talie.

Chapter 12: Scorpio – Essex

In London for a few days I spent some time with Kevin; then got a taxi to Victoria coach station which was unbelievably crowded as a strike was only just over, and somehow managed to get one to Bungay in Suffolk.

Soon I was back at Sandra and Andy Bell's, back in the English countryside, everything changing, realities shifting, the pace slowing down. I met a few other friends, some of whom wanted to know about my trip on a spiritual level, but I had no words for it yet. I don't know if there ever have been words for that experience, which had seemed to be not of words but a different way of being. I met and had a lovely time with Tiffany and Saffron, thinking Tiffany more beautiful than ever and Saffron's room amazing – she was already developing her ability to turn any space into something magical.

In Norwich I bought my own rucksack. This felt significant – as though I were taking control of important aspects of my life.

I packed up all the things I had left at the Bells, got a lift to Norwich, a coach to Cambridge, a taxi to Saffron Walden Common, and there they were – the two waggons, the two ponies, just as we had planned all that time ago, our two separate strands of the journey coming back together into one. I hadn't known what to expect, what state my only home would be in – wondering if I would still have a home; prepared for anything but everything seemed fine.

They were parked beside the Saffron Walden Maze where, a few years earlier, I had held a saffron picnic for Saffron's 10th birthday. A huge crowd had turned up, dressed in yellow, to walk the labyrinth and feast on yellow food and drink. Now I was here with the green and gold of English autumn, back from the spring in the red desert, back with my waggon and Polly, back on the Gipsy Switch.

I thought of walking the path of the labyrinth in the darkness of midnight, for it was October 31st, Samhain in the old Celtic calendar and the night which gave birth to their New Year – the night when the ancestors walk the earth again and the doors between realities are open. Instead I burned an Australian candle all night, making the link back round the earth to where I had come from, and walked the maze at dawn. They call it a maze, but it is a labyrinth – a single path wound in a long convoluted pattern, this one having four 'corners' with a mound in each. It was grey and misty and I felt I was walking the foldings of

171

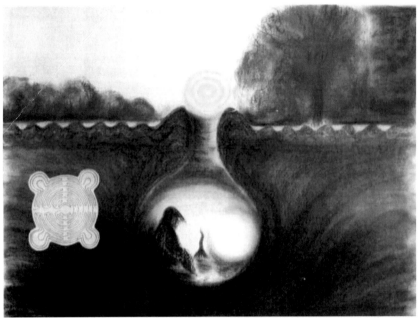

My image of the Crone beneath the Saffron Walden Maze

my own brain, twisty-turny, this way and that, entering the reality of labyrinth. The path was a silver-grey line in the moonlight, each mound powerful and dark, a world of its own, a secure island surrounded by a spiritual sea and the twisting lines of the path.

In the centre, I 'sensed' that below, in a deep circular hollow cave with a tunnel up to the surface like the neck of a bottle, sat an old woman on a bench, huddled over a fire. She threw shells onto a midden heap and wore necklaces of beads. I had gone into the earth for winter, the Hag of Winter reigned and I was hag again.

The winds were cold. England's autumn was turning to winter.

It was strange for Richard, for he had been looking after Polly and the waggon for 2 months and it had become his home. Now I was back and it was my home again and awkward that I had to turn him out into a tent, but that had been the arrangement and it was no use my feeling guilty. He had looked after the waggon beautifully and everything was fine with very little missing. My lovely lace curtain over the front entrance had gone, though. At some point Richard had been away and some other people had a bit of a fire in the waggon and the curtain had burnt. My washing line and the folded plastic at the front were all different, as the blue had dripped molten plastic everywhere. They'd had to pull the whole tarp forward and re-staple it.

Richard had cut a window at the back because when it was windy the whole thing had filled like a balloon and Polly couldn't pull it; and had put the bed on the other side to how it had been. Before I noticed this all my things were back in, too late to change it even though I realised we would now be sleeping roadside rather than kerb-side and would be more vulnerable to passing traffic.

Mice had eaten great chunks out of my beautiful black, white, green, silver and purple 'Arachne' costume. My sheaf of corn had been near it and attracted them.

Astonishingly, the others were rehearsing a show to perform a few days later in the Village Hall and an old people's home, and what else was it but Jumping Mouse – the Native American tale I had been told at Uluru. That circle connecting us round the earth had been very real.

The few days' pause while they rehearsed allowed me to settle back in, to be back in England and the journey. I had to buy things for Talie and start him on solids. I bought Milupa dried baby food which I could just mix with boiled water. There were many varieties: some savoury, some sweet. He loved them and ate them for years afterwards. I don't think they are available any more. In Australia I'd been eating their rich dairy produce and it had enriched my own milk, so Talie was pretty chubby and well-prepared for winter. I had lots of woollies and cuddly blankets for him.

One night the wind blew right through the waggon as though it were a tunnel and I feared it would blow to bits. It was also pretty cold, so I went to some charity shops and bought several heavy bed covers which I hung like curtains over the entrance, fixed one up at the back with safety pins, and pulled some excess carpet up to shelter our heads. I hung my grandfather's old moth-eaten green travel rug on the walls. I had grown up with this and now it created a moss-like cave for us. Cosy and warm, it felt like home, and I was the Hag in her cave for winter.

I had the paraffin stove as a heater and boiled water and cooked on it, but we were entering a very middle-class part of the country where I doubted there would be many outlets selling paraffin. I also had the gas ring and hoped I could get fuel for that too.

Richard and I had long talks about all that had happened while I was away. When I had left them on the Bedford levels, they had headed for Lincoln – the actual Virgo of the journey. They got to within 15 miles of it, to a village called Sudbrook, but found Polly had a sore under her girth, so had to stop and rest her while it healed. You can try to harden horses' skin with surgical spirit (or even urine) but sometimes they just get sore, and Polly did have quite a load to pull. They managed to find a 15-acre field of mushrooms where they were able to stay, so decided that was near enough to Lincoln and would be the Virgo place. They performed 'The Golden Box and Other Stories' in the Village hall. The audience brought food and they had a harvest celebration. Richard placed the Virgo sign in a tree in the field and painted Virgo on a huge cloth we had tied to the back of the waggon. It had the circle of the journey marked on it and as we got to each place we painted on the appropriate zodiac sign.

When Polly was better they turned south, at last on the Gipsy Switch route.

For the Equinox they had stopped at a place called Holy Well, so from there we had linked in our circle of light round the earth. The place they chose for Libra was Bourne in Cambridgeshire. Many of the 'places' on the journey were whole counties, so there was much serendipity about where one actually travelled and the places which emerged to become significant. Bourne boasted the only parish church with a maze in it, under the tower, and they walked it and placed the Libra sign in a churchyard yew tree. They moved on south to Molesworth where they knew a lot of people, and then to St. Ives in Huntingdon. They were joined by Ros and also by Tony. Mike made jam from hedgerow fruit on a wood fire, they began to plan their next performance and headed for Saffron Walden, Essex and Scorpio.

We were parked up under a tall and beautiful golden-leaved beech tree. On the Sunday a crowd of women organic gardeners visited with their children, did their own ceremony in the centre of the labyrinth, sang songs of the earth and stood in a circle of empowerment holding one another. I then walked the labyrinth with them as I burned elemental incenses. In the centre I blew my conch, the air spiralling through the huge shell. I carried water round the windings of the mound and poured it into Talie's abalone shell, which has the colours of the Rainbow Serpent within it. I dipped the Ininti beads in the water, joining north with south. The water flowed through the holes in the shell onto our Scorpio sign.

At the great beech tree, 3 women kneeled, their heads nestling into the roots. Mike climbed onto their backs, up the tree, and hung the sign in the branches. His hair the colour of the leaves, he looked like the spirit of the tree. They placed a crystal in the tree roots and planted a circle of crocuses for Saffron Walden – but mainly for Caroline, for it was she they had come to remember. A young woman from the Walk For Life – a vibrant person full of glowing energy, she had a baby daughter, one of several children born at that time who seemed to be a new tribe of enlightened beings. I wonder where they all are now. She was in a relationship with a man from Talley Valley (where Talie

174

was born) and was moving to live with him there. Something happened to the vehicle and they pulled over. I don't remember the full story, but I think she got out, was hit by another vehicle and killed. It is terrible how in just a brief moment a young life can be snuffed out and the lives of others changed for ever.

One evening we went to supper with some people called the Ogles. Mrs Ogle was translating the poems of Taliesin (from Old Welsh) and revealed a few of the legend's mysteries. She said the shape-shifting sequence where Cerridwen chases Gwion after he has tasted the essence of all knowledge was a shamanic journey round the realm of the elements.

We had been given permission to camp next to the maze for only a week, and it couldn't be extended, but were invited by the Friends school to stay in their grounds a few days. It was good to handle Polly again as we moved the waggons. I had feared I might have forgotten how to do it all and wondered whether Polly would be ok with me, but Richard had got her standing very well and going into the shafts even better than before and she was just as good with me. We parked by what I thought was a hazel tree and sometimes its leaves blew into the waggon.

Ros left, which was disappointing as I needed the company of women. We did storytelling in the Friends school and I read some passages from 'Touch The Earth' – a book of North American Indian sayings. These children were already into Peace and the concept of a living Mother Earth, so it all went well. The girls were entranced by Talie who behaved perfectly. We were treated to food and hot drinks in the staff room.

It was getting damp, misty and very November-ish, the days much shorter as we prepared to leave Saffron Walden, and it was almost afternoon by the time we left, watched by lots of interested children. After successfully harnessing up I walked leading Polly, the roads busy as though we were already nearing London. We parked up on a big green corner and I rejoiced at how such things still existed: remnants of the days when everyone travelled as we now were.

The moon rose orange, getting brighter as it rose higher, then a thick mist descended and there was stillness. A wind blew in the night and I wondered what the exposed plains of Salisbury would be like.

The next day was damp and rainy but I was up early, so happy to be on the road again. Although Talie and I were ready to go by 10am, Mike was working on his waggon and Richard got up late, so we didn't get off until 12.30, but managed 9 miles with no stop. I walked most of the way and Talie either sat propped up in his cot or slept. A few times I carried him and he enjoyed watching the world go by.

175

We now had skids for going down hills and I used mine once. It was an open metal box which one wheel of the waggon rolled into so it skidded downhill on the metal. It made a terrible noise as it screeched on the grit of the road and you had to pour water to cool it down – quite a feat when you were also holding the reins. At the bottom of the hill you had to persuade the horse to take a couple of steps backwards so you could pull it away from the tyre, all steaming, and hang it up again. When not in use it was chained underneath the waggon, dangling and clanging as we went along. It was the only means of braking we had, but made such a difference and it was no longer so scary going downhill. Over time the bottoms would wear thin and we would have to find a blacksmith to replace them. We still had to plan routes which had as few hills as possible though,snaking our way along the path of our journey.

8 November. We reached the premises of horse dealers John and Vanessa Goode. They were full of admiration at the fitness and health of our ponies, though they seemed surprised and I wondered what some of our so-called friends had been saying behind our backs.

We put our ponies in their paddock and parked our waggons. They gave us supper and we talked a lot about buying a horse for Richard so he could travel with us properly. He already had his eye on one and I said I would lend him the money for it when my divorce came through. There was more talk of horses and waggons and all sorts of combinations of which horse would pull which waggon...plan A...plan B...

I enjoyed being stopped somewhere I felt I could relax. I had loads to catch up with and this seemed an ideal place to do it. Both Mike and Richard went off - Mike to return the borrowed stove to Sylvia and collect one of his own. He had built a new top to his waggon with a chimney in it. There was a caravan I could use to lay out Polly's harness and clean and oil and mend it. When it got dark I wrote letters until 2am.

The next day was peaceful, just me and Talie alone, overlooking the paddock. Our ponies were completely covered in mud and I wondered how we would ever clean them, but they were enjoying being off their tethers. The Goodes' horses were all inside and had to be rugged up if they went out. They looked over their stable doors in envy as they watched Polly and Rosie running around free. I walked down to Haverhill to post my letters and do some shopping. Talie was getting heavy and I realised I would soon have to find some other way of carrying him. I was given a lift back up the hill by some Americans.

I had a lot of suitcases in the waggon and everything in them was muddled. There were some things I could get rid of and others I could leave somewhere if I could find the right place. I wanted to start sorting it all out, but the work on the harness seemed more important. In the evening I had one of the rather uncanny experiences I sometimes had with Talie. He was propped up on a sofa and I gave him a book to look at. I thought he would just play about with it as an object, but he knew exactly what it was and wanted to turn the pages like an older person, only his baby hands wouldn't do what he wanted them to and he got very frustrated. He wanted to read and made 'book-reading' noises. (He was now nearly 5 months old).

A thick fog cleared slowly, the sun coming through beautifully. Richard returned and was going to travel with Mike's waggon for the first time and we had to clean all the mud off the ponies with curry combs, so it was late when we set off – with a jar of Vanessa's damson jam to feed us when we stopped. It was tough going for the ponies at first, and we wondered whether they were getting enough to eat, but when we got to level roads, we made a good pace and got to Great Yeldham as the light began to fade, found a little triangle by a phone and post-box and put the horses in a playing field. I was pretty exhausted, but Richard cooked a nice meal. We too had to eat well! I slept wonderfully as ever, in deep, rich contentment.

We woke to a glorious golden English autumn morning. It was a lovely place: a man had offered us water as soon as we arrived, rather than one of us having to go and ask; there were 'old boys' standing by the church chatting in the morning light and I had a talk with a lady delivering the parish magazine. We took things slowly as it was such a wonderful day and got off calmly. I felt so good – as though things were as right as they had ever been or ever could be and I was fulfilling the purpose of the journey.

But how quickly things can change: while I was away a lot of stopping places had been set up and this part of the journey seemed to be between groups of people some of us knew. I didn't know the people we now stopped with – they were the women and children who had come to the maze and they had been around a lot while I was away. Just as we had got back into the flow of being on the road we had to stop again and I couldn't understand why and suddenly felt overwhelmed and trapped.

The set-up there seemed strange, almost like a harem, with one man who was treated like a guru and loads of his wives and children and I didn't like the energy of it at all. I didn't know what they were into and felt wary, needing to psychically protect myself, for fear they would get into me and suck out all my energy. I really didn't like being there, wanting desperately to get away, the only good thing being that Talie could have the company of children for a while. I just wanted to be in the waggon on my own, sorting out my belongings, but they seemed to think that very odd. When I did spend time in the house I felt uncomfortable and awkward.

Sylvia Scarlett holding Talie with friends, and Mike Andrews, beside my waggon.

It didn't help that Richard had made plans to completely strip my waggon down and rebuild it once we got there! They had workshops, but nowhere to put it under cover, nowhere to put our possessions and nowhere for us to live, so I said, no, thank you very much, I'll stay in it as it is– I've only just got back on the journey and I'll do a bit of work on it to make it more waterproof and sort out the window at the back so it doesn't leak.

I found myself getting angry with Richard, at his and others way of treating me at times, as though I were a stupid child or an imbecile with no mind of my own. There continued to be a lot of criticism of me – that the waggon was too big for Polly, never mind it was the one she had always pulled – and really, anything I could be criticised for I was. Richard would talk down at me in front of others in a way I was really beginning to resent. He was much younger than I, and so were the others. I was 42 with a whole life behind me which I had survived in hard circumstances and I'd already reared 3 children before Talie in very tough physical conditions. It was a great shock after Australia where I had been treated with respect and acknowledged for who and what I was.

We stayed there over a week. I was able to sort out my suitcases and get the place back into being our proper home. It rained the whole time and the ground outside turned into a sea of mud. We went into Braintree for some shopping, buying lots of healthfoods and dividing them between the two waggons. I did some washing in a manky laundrette, but it came out still muddy. I usually dried washing on the shafts of the waggon, but it was impossible in the rain.

Much of the inside of the waggon was soaking wet, so I made a big flap of the blue plastic which could be tied down to go right over the back, and big flaps at the front which would pull across completely and tie closed. Juliet had arrived, and she and Richard did help me with this and one day Juliet looked after Talie for hours, and I was very grateful for that. Talie had become fractious, as though the energy of the place was affecting him too, or maybe he was just picking up on my feelings. He would often try to 'talk' to me, to explain things, and once again get frustrated because his little mouth hadn't learned to say the words yet.

There was a patch of 'roof' which was leaking where the tarp had rubbed away on the hazel and I patched it with an Ayers Rock carrier bag which had a cartoon kangaroo on it, and that seemed to work. I wondered whether the rain which could no longer get in would fall on Uluru instead.

Mike came back from his stove swap with Sylvia and her youngest daughter and another friend. Their company made life seem more normal. The 'guru' returned and I was disturbed by the way the women kow-towed to him and ran around waiting on him hand and foot. I didn't understand it and still felt incredibly uncomfortable when I was in the house with them. The whole situation seemed to drain my energy, leaving me totally exhausted and not able to do much at all.

I took a few days off and went to London. The 'guru' gave me a lift – obviously with no interest in adding me to his harem, but questioning me about a friend of mine who he was fascinated by. She was a pretty powerful feminist and I thought she'd probably eat him alive if he tried to involve her in his set-up. I was grateful for the lift though. What a strange fellow. Meeting up with a lot of friends in London I got a better sense of my self back, and went to the opening of an exhibition by Andrew Logan, who creates sculptures and jewellery from broken mirrors. He's one of the loveliest people I've ever met and seems to find the best in everyone and in every place he visits. I dressed Talie in the fluorescent painted jacket he'd been given in Adelaide.

I got a train back to Braintree and the others met me at the station. I returned to a wonderful bundle of letters from friends and one from Saffron, so altogether felt somewhat happier.

I found out Juliet was pregnant and there were all sorts of emotional issues around her relationship with Richard, so maybe that explained why his behaviour had been so extreme at times. He and I spent a long time talking about it, which was helpful, and for once I felt that being older enabled me to bestow a little wisdom. Juliet was about to go off for 2 months to Eritrea, accompanying a wheat shipment from Molesworth, and Richard was in an emotional state about that, never mind a lot of other issues.

The continuous dark and wet didn't help the general sense of depression. I started to have disturbing dreams, some about nuclear disasters but others about people threatening me, and my daughters going off to live in Majorca. Talie seemed disturbed and so did the younger children in the house, so I wondered what was really going on.

November 20. At last the stop there was coming to an end and I started to feel better at the prospect of getting on the road again. The sun shone and we came out of the grey. Talie was fascinated by the sun shining on my hair and jumper, and the soft patterns of leaves moving outside made delicate shadows in the waggon. I longed for this weather to continue. I felt more relaxed with the people in the house, but maybe that was because we would soon be leaving.

It was 3pm when we drove off, the women and children accompanying us for a while, and though we only went a mile we were on our way. We stopped on a little green and some gamekeepers told us we must move early the next day. It was a warm night and the sound of the wind in the trees was comforting. Mike had gone again, so it was still just me and Richard.

The next morning was beautiful with that pale, bright, winter light of a sun which is well into the day but low in the sky. Polly behaved strangely when I was putting her in the shafts, it taking 3 attempts. She kept charging about, caught the breeching and snapped 2 chapes which I had to replace with baler twine. Maybe they had been just about to break anyway and she had saved us from some terrible disaster. Animals can sense these things and it was actually quite a downhill day.

It rained heavily and I felt sorry for the poor wet horses but completely connected to the time of year in all its aspects. There was so much green – both of the grass and the new blades of winter crops in the fields. Where the rich, dark earth had been ploughed it had sensual, fleshy, shining, vaginal surfaces. Mother Earth was beginning to lie still and hold her breath for the long, dark winter – the not-so-barren Hag holding the seeds of life as they slept in her womb.

That night the horses kept pulling out their tethers and walking off down the road, the chains dragging and rattling past. Because of Talie I couldn't go after them but Richard coped heroically and a farmer later let us put them in a field. I cooked supper.

I slept a deep and beautiful sleep until about 4.30am when a horrendous wind blew up. We were on a hill and it blew diagonally into the front of my waggon. I stood, hanging on to one side of it, willing the whole thing not to snap, holding my fragile home against the immense power of the wildness.

When it subsided I fixed the front flap and managed to sleep again. Talie never stirred nor wanted a feed and hardly even wanted one in the morning. As a Gemini he was an air person and I wondered where his spirit had been off to and what he had been up to while all this was going on.

Near morning it worsened, though I was able to move and feed the horses and watch the sun rise looking like the moon, but the wind was freaking me out and I was shocked at my reaction. I couldn't eat breakfast, make tea or do anything but be paralysed with panic. Richard fixed the front flap so I was tied in while he got some hay for the horses. We both began to feel that it was caused by ill-thoughts directed towards us, and I was distressed by my inability to protect myself against negativity or successfully deal with it.

As we brought the horses over I felt calmer. I travelled with the front closed against the wind and rain, and felt there was nothing I would rather be doing, nowhere else I would rather be. I wasn't afraid of wind when I was just out in it, part of it, but feared the damage it might do to my home. That night we found a grassy corner by a letter-box and I backed into the wind, so we were more sheltered, but I still sensed some strange battle of the winds going on – or maybe it was of the wild wind witches.
We called at 2 garages which had no paraffin, the lack of which was becoming a problem as the stove was my only means of heating. Talie wouldn't sleep, so I had to carry him, walking with Polly and trying to keep up with Richard. One day we discovered we'd gone the wrong way, had to turn back and in the end only made about 2 miles progress. Once that had happened I did feel I'd shaken some of the negativity off, but that we really must pull our socks up.

Another day began beautifully but turned to rain. We searched for pony nuts, calling at two places which were shut before finding some – but still no paraffin. I had 3 bags of rubbish, but couldn't find any bins. This was a day of much stopping and starting: Rosie's girth broke and Richard had to tie it up with string and Polly was very thirsty and kept stopping to drink from puddles. But the countryside we were passing through was glorious and in spite of all the difficulties I was filled with great joy, feeling this was really how to live, was how people had moved through the land even in comparatively recent times, before the invention of motor transport, and their moving was part of the land they moved through and part of the changing seasons.

I kept hearing a strange noise and when we next stopped found the old khaki rucksack which I had travelled with on all my previous journeys, which had been stuffed roughly inside the front of the waggon, had gone. It had been with me through such huge changes in my life, had once been all I had in the world, and now seemed to have been taken as some sort of sacrifice. The evening became beautiful, and we stopped at a place called Ford End, high on a great slope. I backed into the wind again. At sunset the sky was rainbow coloured and a sharp crescent moon followed the sun's leaving.

The next day was Mike's birthday and we wondered whether he would return, but he didn't, so we found a phone box and left a message for him with the Secretarial Service. Ford End had no Post Office or paraffin but did have a rubbish bin. It stayed beautiful and we went through Pleshey and came upon Castle Mound, rising like yet another dark pregnant belly from the earth and surrounded by a circle of silver water.

We passed a tethered horse by the wayside, then a woman sitting by a caravan, then behind that a horse-drawn waggon with a man and his sons by a fire. We stopped for a chat. He was very friendly and told us the routes they took year after year – "My father and his father before him and my sons after me", and it seemed in that moment that here in England the old dreaming paths were still being travelled and lived. Richard asked him about farriers and he said there was a man who always came to him but he didn't know how we could get in touch with him – "I see him driving by here sometimes – he's got a van with a lot of letters down the side". He told us of a good place to stop. It wasn't on the route we had planned, but we took his advice – and passing through a village came to a shop selling paraffin. I felt a bit wobbly. We hadn't mentioned our need for it, but had we gone the way we'd intended would have missed that shop. I guess he was Romany and there was a touch of faerie about that encounter.

Next dawn there were incredible red patterns across the sky. The faerie traveller man came to visit and had a long chat with Richard, giving him lots of advice, and said he'd buy my trolley if ever I wanted to sell it. It was very windy again, but we were sheltered down by a stream. I walked into a nearby village (High Easter). I had been using the khaki rucksack on my back to carry shopping and it had balanced the weight of Talie on my front, but now, having to carry bags in my hands and with him so heavy, it was hard work. The man in the real old village shop said "Did you see that sky this morning – it'll be a wild day". I bought sandwiches for my lunch for I often forgot to eat in the middle of the day, which was maybe why I felt so tired and weak much of the time.

It was getting dark as we looked for somewhere to stop. All the roads were ditched and banked with no wide verges but, as so often happened, at the last moment there was a perfect place. I cooked a stew. Richard usually came into my waggon to eat supper and often for breakfast as well. We had some good chats, which were important, as otherwise we'd have been two isolated people travelling in our own little worlds.

Looking at the map of Britain and all the places we had to get to I wondered how on earth we would get across London with the waggons. We had to get to Kingston-on-Thames while we were in Sagittarius and then to Wiltshire for Capricorn. We planned to go to Stonehenge and although I don't like the place much, it was what the others wanted. We had to get to Glastonbury in Somerset for Aquarius and then right over to Lampeter in West Wales for Pisces. At the rate we were going it all felt impossible, yet to be in the right place at the right time was the whole point of the journey.

The next day continued changeable but warm and I didn't wear a coat. It was up-hill a lot and hard work for the horses but they made a good pace. The last mile was interminable, but we made it to a place in a beautiful setting where we were going to stay with the band CrAss, who were all much older than I would have expected. We knew them through Bernie Chandler who I think occasionally played with them. They were really friendly and I felt completely relaxed with them. They gave us a lovely supper and I had a bath!

While there I was able to do a lot of work on the harness, oiling it and even roughly repairing the chapes. I did a lot of washing, but the dye came out of some trousers and everything turned a muddy blue colour.

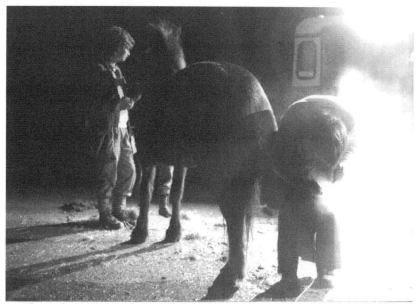

The craftsman farrier shoeing Polly whilst we stayed with the punk band 'CrAss'

Mike returned and once again there was endless talk of horses and waggons and which would go with what. Mike was going to have the totter's waggon, as his original one wasn't up to it any more, and was going to work on it when we got to our next stop. However, as soon as he was with other people Richard would start talking down at me again. Here though, the CrAss people were more mature and could see what was going on. Once more I was endlessly criticised, yet nothing practical was suggested as to how we might solve the problem of Polly pulling a big waggon. But who said it was a problem? I never felt Polly found it too difficult. She was a tough, strong little goer. Again I wondered why there was all this negative talk behind our backs with so much of it directed at me. It was starting to grind me down.

One day I was able to leave Talie (who had a lovely time) and walk down to the village alone. I needed to get away from men and all the talk of horses which went round and round in circles and got nowhere. I was beginning to dislike the company of men, needing the presence and support of women and often wished I could travel the Gipsy Switch on my own with Talie. All the negativity was disturbing what I felt to be the purpose of us doing it – to heal and tend a Dreaming path in the land.

I was getting anxious about quite ordinary things like shopping and continuously having to find paraffin and bottled gas, frightened of being without them and worried about the difficulties in liaising with my solicitor who was trying to finalise my divorce. I realised the money I was going to receive would never be enough to buy Talie and me a house, and I was having to face the final letting go of Brentwood Farm, which had been my beloved home and overseen such huge changes in my life. The documents came and I signed them with a heavy heart. Bruce's father had died, leaving him enough to buy me out, otherwise it would have had to be sold.

One glorious warm day I had a lovely walk to the Post Office – maybe 3 miles there and back with Talie done up in the front of my coat so his little head stuck out like a kangaroo joey. I talked to him a lot and he laughed.

Later a farrier came round. He was so different from the last one I'd seen, regarding it as a craft and himself as a craftsman. He made each shoe on the spot from strip steel and everyone came out to watch him for two and a half hours. It was like an elemental performance. I took a few photographs, for the visual images were fantastic. He worked at the back of his van with an anvil and proper fire. It got dark and was raining so we lit him with a tungsten lamp. Everything looked black and white and then there would suddenly be the brilliant red of the hot shoe, and when he put it on the wet hoof there were great clouds of white steam and smoke. He charged £20 each, which seemed really cheap.

184

Mike had come back with rotten flu and all the people in the house had colds so I hoped I wouldn't catch anything and felt it was what comes of living in houses with all that warmth. Richard went off with one of the men from the house to pick up the totters waggon. We were due to head through London for Kingston-on-Thames but still hadn't managed to contact the people there who we hoped to stay with. I had hoped Ros would join us or maybe go ahead and do our admin, set up a gig and publicise it, but we heard from her that she wouldn't be coming.

I had started to write quarterly articles about the journey for the magazine Pipes of P.A.N, and wrote another instalment here, thinking how little I was now writing, querying the need for words, as though they were an obstruction to pure experience, to that absolute clarity which is beyond words, yet it seemed important to share our experience with others. I am glad now that I wrote what little I did, and it's astonishing how many people read those articles and followed what we were doing.

Richard returned, having taken the totter's waggon to our next stop. He had been driving around all day yet hadn't even thought to get pony nuts or paraffin and I was really pissed off with him. That evening we sat around poring over maps and planning our route through London. I phoned Saffron, and wished so much that I could see my daughters more often. Richard left again, this time to see the Goodes, some other friends and his parents, but I felt cut off from my own family.

Eventually Mike was well enough and we set off, accompanied by some of the household. How kind and nice CrAss were and what a lovely energy there was in their house.

It was by now early December and we had been in Sagittarius for some days. I hoped we would get to Kingston-on-Thames before the archer's time was over.

Chapter 13: Sagittarius, Kingston-on-Thames.

We reached the place where the totter's waggon was waiting for us. In the absolute flatness of endless Essex fields there was suddenly a raised area which was owned by Ray and Joan. Ray was an Irish traveller who had just had a colostomy or something. He owned this 3 or 4 acres – his junk yard, his caravan, his garden, his trees and a lake. It was just what I needed, parking up under a huge, tall yew tree. It had been an old rectory site and there were many other yews around, meaning we must be careful with the horses as yew is so poisonous. As I sat in Ray and Joan's caravan having a cuppa, Phil from the crAss house turned up with two bales of hay and a gallon of paraffin and wouldn't take any money for them. I was overwhelmed by how wonderful some people are and it was a relief to have my anxieties understood, with something useful being done to allay them, rather than the endless destructive criticism.

I felt a cold coming on and had a strange night, shifting realities under the yew.

My cold got worse – my skin all 'creepy' as though I had flu, but I got up because I had to, having a morning cuppa with Joan and Ray. I didn't secure the front flap of the waggon and a cat got in and drank two pints of milk and ate a third of a loaf of bread. I should have known better after my time with the Talley Valley cats which could get at almost everything

I drove down to Ongar in Ray's pick-up, finding it difficult to get back into driving a vehicle after being with a horse so long. I was now quite ill and walked around in the rain in a daze, trying to keep Talie from getting wet. I got a few things, but couldn't carry very much so drove back; then left Talie with Joan to go out with Ray to get pony nuts, still having to drive because he was disqualified. The place was shut; the gears on the pick-up got increasingly difficult and finally jammed. I had to drive all the way back in first.

My flu got worse and I lay in the waggon with a temperature, dreading the night and following day, but Mike cooked a supper with masses of cayenne, and something shifted. I went to bed at 7.45pm, and waking at midnight thought it was dawn. I went into other realms under that yew tree, as though I were going deep into the earth and hibernating each night. Next morning my flu was over – a miracle cure: I suppose we were by then pretty fit and healthy. The day was lovely and Mike worked on the new waggon. I felt all I had learned in Australia was beginning to meld into my understanding of being

The waggons parked up under the yew tree at Ray and Joan's place in Essex

here in this winter Britain. Things were making more sense and everything was connecting into a comprehensible whole.

Unfortunately Mike had left the big bags of food under a tarp on his old waggon and Ray and Joan's cats and dogs completely ravaged them. More lessons learned. Ray had one dog he kept tied up on a chain which he said was a man-killer!

There was little light in my waggon under the great tree and it seemed more and more as though I were under the ground, deep below the tree roots; like a little shrew gathering my stores around me in preparation for my long winter sleep. We were getting close to midwinter and I worked on a 'Hag' show for Kingston-on-Thames, showing her nurturing aspect as well as her winter darkness, feeling we should reclaim the King Stone for her. Eventually we did get some pony nuts and Mike and Richard worked on the totters waggon by floodlight in the pouring rain.

After that the ground was very boggy. I'd left my boots outside and the insides were soaked. Why was I doing such stupid things? We set off on a big shopping trip, but everywhere Ray told us to go became a wild goose chase – or rather, a wild gas chase. Mine had now run out, and although we managed to get Calor butane for Mike, mine was Shell propane and no-one sold it.

187

Later that day Ray started to talk about his magical powers and I understood everything he was saying. I'd never heard anyone talk quite like he did, explaining the state he went into when willing something to happen. It sounded like really hard work!

Outside the sky was rainbow-coloured as the sun set and the brilliant near-full moon reflected among the dark shadows of trees in the lake. Later there was a frost. I told myself not to despair and wished life went on longer so we could put to use all we learned, and wished our bodies didn't grow old so quickly and let us down.

Next day I walked across the fields to a phone and heard I was at last divorced and a free woman. Walking down a path from the churchyard I blended deeply into that area of Britain, absorbing it into my self. The days were so short, and as we walked back across the ploughed fields of that flat land the sun set deep red on one horizon as the full moon rose on the other. They looked at each other and the energy flowed between them as they acknowledged each other's power – and Talie and I were there in the middle, receiving it, and that extraordinary moment has stayed with me to this day.

On that full moon the waggon was light all night, but more than that, I had the sense of not being covered, as though I were lying bare under her brilliant white, having it pour over me like a physical substance, with her energy flowing through me. Outside everything was painted silver-white by the moonlight, like some form of insubstantial snow. More and more I felt in the yew tree, part of the yew tree, becoming the yew tree, as though she had taken me into her cave and enfolded me in her dark green-ness. She so embodied that time of year; her living 'leaves' holding death, yet I had been told that in past times Gipsies ate the red flesh of the berries after removing the seeds, for the flesh brought life though the seeds death. Life in death, death in life. Like winter.

I recalled my previous times in long barrows and felt there was work being done. Everything was beginning to stand still again as we moved towards the pause of midwinter.

What a powerful time it was on that slight rise above the flat Essex land. Talie was entering a new stage of development, using his hands to explore what they could do; going for things – no longer content just to look. I sewed reflectors on the back of the waggon and crudely nailed others on the sides. It was better than nothing. On a clear, cold day I heated water hot enough for washing on a grotty bonfire. Richard made a structure for hanging Ros's bike on the back of my waggon – two bits of wood which stuck out at an angle and poked through the spokes and somehow held it secure. At sunset we took Rosie for a trial run in Mike's new waggon and she was fine. The top he had built on it was very funny, looking like a little mobile chapel, as though he were an evangelist priest travelling round the Wild West.

I was apprehensive about leaving and heading for London. Polly was raring to go and I wondered whether it would be hard to control her. Sometimes both ponies charged around on their tethers, rearing and leaping about. There was a lot of hunting in the area and maybe they could hear that, longing to go off on the chase – but there again, it could have been the full moon. At one point in the stillness I heard a strange rhythmic roaring and thought "That's either a dragon or a hot-air balloon". Sadly it was the latter but even so it was exciting to see one passing quite low overhead.

December 10. The day we were to leave. I was up early, watching the sun rise blood-red quite late as we were now so close to midwinter; the gently frosty, misty, yet clear mornings being so beautiful. Talie was settled and asleep and ready to leave by 10am, but the men were long-winded and I had to sit knitting while we waited for them, but at last we were off with fond farewells from Ray and Joan; past the man-eating dog and away in quite a controlled manner with the waggons swaying and swinging down the bumpy track.

We walked on in the beautiful December white, bright sunshine – our last look at the countryside for a while maybe, and it did us proud. I had been surprised at how late the leaves had stayed on the trees, but even the golden were gone now, leaving just black fingers trailing the sky and the dark depths of them in hedges. That day I was acutely aware of the presence of the spirits of many trees, but from that point on it seemed we would have to breathe carbon monoxide. I changed Talie's nappy as we went under the M25, Richard leading Polly.

We got to Chigwell Row, tired and happy, stopping on a parking place by the edge of Epping Forest where it said 'No Overnight Parking'. The forest keepers came along and got a bit heavy, but their boss arrived and allowed us to stay as long as we were off by 8am. A friendly man gave us half a bale of hay and there was no problem getting water, but both horses were tired after 2 weeks of not working.

I was up at 5.45am to an otherworldly misty forest morning, the moonlight having shone into the waggon all night. It was hard finding the horses in the mist – or even Richard in his tent, which I had to do by calling. I rushed Talie and was ready to leave by 8, but again the men weren't and we didn't leave until 9.

I tired quickly that day, feeling weak with no strength. I felt very alone with the two young men, more alone than had I actually been on my own, when I would have been doing it all at my and Talie's own pace. I carried him as it felt safer,

189

and we fixed cycle lamps on the backs of the waggons to make them more visible in the fog.

We had a lunch break and tethered the horses on some grass out of sight. When I went to give them water I found Polly wandering around a bus stop, with no sign of her chain or its collar; then saw Rosie roaming free, trailing her tether. I found both stakes but we couldn't find Polly's chain. There was no way that could have happened without someone doing it deliberately. I was really pissed off as it was a good chain with proper fittings and later cost me £15 to replace, which was a lot of money in those days – but how lucky we were not to have lost the horses! We never again tethered them where we couldn't see them unless it was somewhere very secure.

Setting off, we came to a cattle grid where it was impossible to get the horses across. We had nothing we could lay on it for them to walk on, and there was nowhere at the sides they could cross, so we had to retrace our steps and find another route. Time was getting on, but we passed a school and all the children ran to the railings in excitement and disbelief, and that made our day.

The fog was beautifully Dickensian and we made it to Stoke Newington. Under cover of the fog and coming darkness we were largely unnoticed on the common, only the occasional surprised dog- walker knowing we were there. I sat under drips from condensing mist and there were slippery London Plane leaves on the grass. It was extraordinary to be in London.

Mike used to live in that area and was excited to be back. Lots of his friends came round and he went off with them. Some people came by and talked for ages to Richard in the other waggon. Only when they had gone did he come and tell me they were from 'Horse and Bamboo', a theatre company which travelled with horses and carts, even to the Hebrides. I would have loved to meet them, thinking they might have heard of me from my Community and Performance Art days and we might have had mutual friends and acquaintances. I was upset that Richard hadn't bothered to call me over. Anyway, it was good to be out of Essex. Although beautiful it had seemed to go on for ever.

In the morning the police paid a token visit, but all was fine. Mike took me to an ironmonger to buy a new chain and clasp for Polly's tether and some plastic tubing to cover it where it went round her neck. She was temporarily on a rope but I would need to put the chain together as soon as I could. We found a City Farm for hay and pony nuts.

The waggons crossing Tower Bridge. Mike Andrews in foreground (photo Richard Ford)

So, we were all set for the centre of London. It felt such an important thing to be doing, a real statement that it was still possible, that all which goes on in the modern world doesn't matter if you can take it on as we were doing. It was fascinating to sense the size and shape of the city as we walked right across it.

In the early stages I realised I was following a personal Dreaming Path. Not only did we enter London by the route I had taken a few years earlier when, weekend by weekend, I made my great leaving of the place of generations of my ancestors; but the route touched many places which had been focal points in my life. What we were doing seemed enormous. It wasn't just 2 horses, 2 waggons, 3 adults and a baby moving through the streets, but a huge reclaiming, a making of our own law, for there was nothing really that anyone could argue with. We were in a kind of timeless bubble in the midst of the modern world and there was massive power in that. We reclaimed a right, a natural order of things. In a way it was a political action, a triumph: the conquering horses returning.

It was almost like magic, but it was intense and concentrated and drained our energy. We crossed Tower Bridge and were much photographed by tourists, even though traditionally, anciently maybe, the travelling people would have crossed London Bridge. I carried Talie and led Polly, who was quite nervous and didn't want to be far from Rosie. It would have been impossible without Richard.

We reached Clapham Common. I had just started to settle when a man cycled by and told us we shouldn't really stop on the common, but to go over near a visiting circus (but not to say he'd told us to!). We did. I was having a difficult time with Talie that evening, trying to feed and settle and calm him down for he was really upset, apparently in pain or discomfort. In the midst of all this Mike told me we had to move yet again: the GLC didn't allow animals in circuses and the circus people were worried that it would be thought we were part of them. A man had been heavy with Mike and threatened him and he over-reacted. I felt it might have helped if I had spoken to the man and got him to be a bit more reasonable, but Mike just told me to move. Right now. Richard wasn't there and I couldn't find the sledge-hammer in the dark. Some bloke had turned up to see us and at first Mike said there would be help, but when I asked for it was told I had nothing much to pack up anyway, not half as much as he. No, I only had a screaming child to look after and wasn't even allowed to wait until Richard came back. I told Mike he was being cruel and he said I was pretty self- centred. This sent me into a deep state of shock, as I realised Mike simply didn't acknowledge he was travelling with Talie and all that entailed, and if he wouldn't make necessary concessions I really would have to leave and do it on my own, at our own pace. I knew I could, but wanted us to do it together, feeling an intense sense of failure at being unable to communicate with these young men. I should be teaching them how to treat women, and I wasn't, because I felt too emotionally vulnerable and would rather run away from the whole situation. Later, when Richard was back Mike said he wasn't enjoying it all as he thought he should be and I never did any work when we stopped and it was always he who had to get the water and hay for the horses. I wanted to explain that I had Talie to feed and settle after he'd been so good all day, but thought if I said that I'd be told I shouldn't be doing the journey at all, so kept quiet. I went to bed completely devastated. My memory now is of it being one of the worst times of my whole life. It had been a fantastic day and then it all just blew apart.

December 13. Talie was 6 months old. I woke still in a terrible state of shock, but was calm about getting up and ready, and we were off by 10.30. No-one had bothered us at the place we'd finally ended up. We only had 5 miles to go but it took nearly all the short day. We tried a road across Wimbledon Common which looked passable on the A-Z, but came to a locked gate and had to turn back. My feet were agonisingly blistered. The last part of the journey was through a private estate, past a private school with little clean white-socked girls being collected by car. More than one of them walked past us with faces screwed up in distaste saying "Pooh, they smell". What a contrast to the spontaneous excitement of the children in Hackney.

We got to Kingston-on-Thames and the community in Crescent Road who had invited us to stay. Des Kay, who had actually asked us, had promised that in this area of polo ponies there would be plenty of stabling available for the horses, but nothing had been arranged so we had to put them in the back garden. I had a bath and washed my hair and decided to stay in the house as I felt it would be weird to live out in the waggon in a London street in that kind of neighbourhood. I feared if people heard Talie crying they would call Social Services.

The problem of the horses became a major issue. There seemed nowhere for them to go and looking for somewhere was taking all our time and energy. Everything which seemed possible eventually fell through, being too far from the house. The horses would have to be walked there and then visited twice a day to be fed and watered. They were making a mess of the garden with their hooves and, although some of the people were happy with it, the rest were getting quite fed up, and the whole situation was very distressing.

Richard and I had worked out a really good performance, rather like a mummer's play, which we had wanted to do in the Market Place, but the energy for it just disappeared. It seemed that in this Sagittarius of our journey (Sagittarius being either an archer on a horse or a centaur) all our energy was going into concern for our horses. In a strange twist to the Christian Christmas story, there was no room for our ponies in the stables. However, the Sagittarian horse-link seemed potent. It was all crescents – the crescents of horseshoes and the archer's bow; Crescent Road in an area full of horses, and there was even a crescent moon.

Moving round this great Zodiac on the land of Britain, there seemed to be local terrestrial zodiacs in several 'segments' of our journey, and there was one here in the Kingston area, proposed by Mary Caine. Having just returned from Australia and been so close to the Aboriginal Dreaming paths, I could feel the living energy and life-force of these Kingston figures as though they were real, living and quite visceral beings, flexing their powerful muscles.

The great event of our time in Kingston was a visit from Mary Caine herself. She lived nearby and was a wonderful woman. To be in her presence, in the zodiac she discovered, in one of the zodiac areas of our own journey, and to hear her talk, was a great inspiration. I felt lifted into another reality, as though I were receiving direct transmission from a great master, taken into her way of seeing, her way of perceiving landscape and everything about it as living mythology. It was the closest thing to the Aborigines and their way of seeing that I had experienced, and I felt the great zodiac figures as part of our own ancient Dreamings, our hunter-gatherer fore-mothers and fathers having tended and celebrated them as the Aborigines do their ancient but still living Dreamtime ancestors. I grasped the reality of this in Mary's presence and realised how we have a living mythology in place legends which are the

Sagittarian Mike with flaming disc at the King Stone ceremony, Kingston-upon-Thames

remnants of our Dreaming stories. What a wonderful teacher, a true inspiration. Thank you Mary.

Having abandoned any hope of doing our Mummer's performance, we rose near dawn and walked into town to visit the King Stone, on which many (Saxon?) kings of England were crowned. The morning was beautifully clear and as we walked from Crescent Road, the white crescent moon sharp in the blue sky before us. I wore my glorious Arachne dress and carried a sprig of yew from the tree I'd been parked under at Ray and Joan's. In the Beth-Luis-Nion Celtic tree alphabet calendar, Yew is the waning midwinter tree, mistletoe being the actual point of midwinter and silver fir the point where the year begins to wax again. All that winter long I lived the energy of the Old Yew Mother, she with the power both to kill and nurture; and the depth of the shamanic death journey – destruction and enlightenment in one.

The streets were thronged with Christmas shoppers and Salvation Army carols and we felt we were adding the pagan touch, celebrating what was there before

194

Christianity. We went first to a church where there was an old Mary chapel and near there on a green grassy patch had the feeling this might have been the original site of the King Stone, for we knew it had been moved from its ancient position. We held the wooden Sagittarius sign and lit a big red candle flare and carried them through the streets to the stone.

This became the Sagittarius celebration of our journey. We each walked round the stone, focussing on whatever we wished for ourselves and the world. We realised that we three adults were all fire signs – me a Leo, Richard an Aries and Mike the Sagittarian. We poured lighter fuel on the wooden sign so it burned while not actually damaging the sign, a bit like brandy on a Christmas cake. Mike carried it round and placed it on the stone, honouring it once again, then gave a baptism of fire to Richard, echoing his role as the zodiac traveller in our performance at the Albion fair all those months before, and to Talie, who continued to have a sequence of elemental baptisms.

With yellow wool I tied some Yew onto the railings which surrounded the stone. I lit a red candle and placed before the stone an amethyst which Sagittarian Lynne had lent me. Richard placed another crystal. We felt tuned into the place and the time and the stone, hopefully creating a little bit of balance and harmony in this crazy world: a small moment, but maybe moving greater things in the macrocosm. We extinguished the torch which remained as a Sagittarian arrow to fire into the new year at Solstice, removed the crystals and walked back to Crescent Road feeling our time in Kingston was fulfilled, and later in the day the sky turned black and produced a colossal, vibrant double rainbow.

Des took me to a Calor dealer and I bought a new cylinder for my gas ring, leaving the Shell one at the house in case they could change it for themselves one day. The sacred and the mundane wove together into the reality we lived. As Richard and Mike had both been away quite a lot, it seemed to be my turn, so I went off for a few days to see friends and family.

We had placed the Sagittarius sign in the garden at Crescent Road, so Richard and Mike moved on while I was away and Richard phoned to say they had decided to go to Greenham Common as there was one gate where it was ok for men to go. I was thrilled as I'd felt it to be an important place on our journey, but hadn't wanted to push the idea too hard. Now the men had come up with the idea themselves. We were going to use Sandra as a telephone contact so I would know where to find them when I went back.

In Norwich I went to my solicitor and got the rest of the money from my divorce. I met up with my daughters, went to Ditchingham, and Bungay where I saw the bank sub-manager as I was paying in rather more than I usually did, and visited a few friends. I wrote loads of cheques to all the people who had lent me money, then set off back as I wanted to be in the waggon for the Winter Solstice.

What a saga of a journey it turned out to be. I left Ditchingham at 11am but my first bus to Norwich was half an hour late so I missed the coach to London and had to wait hours for the next one. I then got another from London to Reading but by then it was early evening. I called Sandra, but there was no reply. I kept phoning and phoning and still there was no reply. I didn't know where to head for, wondering what Richard would do, as he would have to keep finding phone boxes as they travelled. I discovered there was a bus to Burghfield where I knew they had been heading, had fish and chips, made loads more fruitless phone calls, got the Burghfield bus, but somehow got off at the wrong stop.

I was cold and so was Talie. I think I even phoned the police to see if they'd seen any horses and waggons, but they hadn't. I got a taxi and drove around all over the place, the driver getting more and more annoyed, but we couldn't find them. He eventually dropped us at a pub, where they let me use the phone and at last I got through to Sandra, but she said Richard had phoned Saffron with the information! At last I got directions and they were somewhere quite different from where I had expected. I called the cab firm again and they found another driver as I think the other one refused to come out to us again. It was now well after midnight – but we found them – parked up on a wonderfully wide verge. Never had the waggons looked so welcome. Richard was asleep in mine with candles burning, as he'd given up any thought that I would arrive. I felt awful having to turf him out but had to sleep somewhere with Talie and he went and slept in Mike's.

It felt as though this place was in some elusive Berkshire triangle, or somewhere hidden by the pixies, but we were back and it was nearly Solstice. Winter Solstice 1984. I wasn't sure at all where we were. It was a strange place that I would ever after have to search for on a map. I woke before dawn on the clearest day imaginable, called Richard and we stood to watch the beautiful sunrise. What a day it was – peaceful, calm and completely clear in absolute perfection. We seemed at last to be a proper group, together in what we were doing, rather than the disparate individuals we had been for so long.

Later in the day Richard went to Reading and got lost on the way back. I really did think we might be in faerie-land, certainly some place slightly out of sync with normal reality.

I went shopping, walking with my little boy, sharing with him the land, the black winter trees, the dark mouldering earth, the sharp clear sky and the birds which were staying with us through the dark and cold and weren't migrating to warmer climes. We walked beside cold, sparkling running water until a woman gave us a lift. We shopped and walked back. The colours of the cloudless sky were subtle and rainbow-hued. We passed a still lake surrounded by the silhouettes of dark trees and watched the sun go down golden. I was poignantly aware of the whole of this shortest day and its shape, following the sun from rising to setting as it travelled its low midwinter arc. What a beautiful day among so many which had been dull and wet. What a gift. Time stopped and I felt a sense of absolute bliss.

Mike and I cooked different bits of a celebratory Solstice supper and ate it in Mike's waggon: men, a male child and me the only woman. We were a close group in that moment and that was so rare. We exchanged Solstice gifts, reclaiming what has now become a Christmas ritual to its rightful day.

Later we went outside under the dark sky and the canopy of the starry zodiac. Mike lit the arrow end we'd brought from the King Stone ceremony. Richard, (the traveller from the summer performance) wearing the crown of the old year (the band from his Christmas cake)was blindfolded, turned around to disorientate him, and then fired the arrow – so this was the dying king firing the arrow of continuing life into the new year. We left it stuck in the earth where it had fallen, and the 'crown' was passed to Talie – the new young king. The arrow of the Sagittarian archer had been fired into the Capricorn of the new year.

There was a heavy frost in the night. The condensation on the inside of my waggon froze to a thin sheet of ice which cracked when I lit the stove. The water in my saucepan froze. We had to be careful with the horses when it was frosty. When there was snow they could push it aside and eat the grass underneath, but if they ate frosty grass they might get colic, or something worse. Mike left for Norfolk to collect a new stove.

As we set off it began to rain quite heavily. Mike had cycled to a railway station so we had to call there to pick up the bike. Before long a woman offered us a place for the night, but qualified it with remarks such as "You aren't CNDers are you?" and "We are fox-hunting people", so it wasn't a likely stop and was too soon anyway. Eventually we found a place by the Forestry and the horses had heather to eat. Earlier, another woman had given us a bale of hay. People's generosity really did restore one's faith in human nature.
It got much warmer and we had a cosy night. I could hear the wind in the trees but it didn't seem to touch us. The Solstice and Dark Moon had passed and the year had turned. We hadn't made it, as originally planned, to Stonehenge for Solstice, nor even to Greenham Common, but our Berkshire verge had been perfect and now we headed for Greenham anyway and maybe still to Sonehenge as our Wiltshire Capricorn place.

Chapter 14: Capricorn, Wiltshire.

December 23rd. Richard and I were both ready early so we set off in good time. It was warm and people were friendly. We got milk from a milkman on his rounds and filled our water containers in readiness for being at Greenham, the Goddess now taking control of our journey.

Once again I felt I was on a Dreaming Path, and one very relevant to the time we were in. We had gone by Aldermaston, which we had passed on the Walk For Life, now doing something even more powerful in our movement through the land.

We reached Greenham. I had wanted to pull in to the place where the Star March had stopped when we met them at the end of the Walk For Life, but Richard wanted to go to Orange Gate, which in the past had been a 'mixed' gate for both men and women, but had now, like the rest, become for women only. At first we were greeted warmly by the women there as they thought we were going round all the gates, but it became a problem when they realised we wanted to stay.

So in the end we moved to the Star March place. Richard was like a petulant little boy, quite put out that he wasn't wanted. He had been at Greenham in the early days when it was mixed, and had been inspired by it to start the peace camp at Lakenheath. I felt that I too might have been regarded negatively by the women for travelling with men. On the way there Richard had been cursing and swearing at Rosie, though he had curbed it as we approached the base.

I was so starved of the company of women that I wanted to go straight to them but Richard kept me talking about all his problems for hours and I felt I was putting all the energy into him which should have been directed towards the base, healing it and ridding it of nuclear weapons.

After a marathon journey Mike came back with his new stove. He'd been apprehensive of being at Greenham; not of the women but the base itself, and decided to pretend it just wasn't there. I did sit round a fire with women that evening, drinking whisky while they sang, and not having any supper.

December 24th. I felt pretty lonely, missing my other children. Although I don't celebrate Christmas as such, it is what has evolved from the ancient tribal midwinter gathering and so often the family is the tribe. That year I didn't feel part of any tribe. I wasn't with the Greenham women and I wasn't with my family. I felt I was standing alone outside of everything.

We three talked in the morning. It was good when we were together, but there was so much we didn't say. How isolated from each other we really were.

I felt physically filthy and untogether but walked to the local shop where I was very pleasantly treated. I kept trying to phone my daughters but the line was continually engaged or there was no reply, making me feel even more shut out. There was an incredible wind, but the sky was bright and later it became calmer. I contemplated walking right round the base, remembering when I had walked it pregnant with Talie, but left it too late. The energy there was so heavy and potent. It was where two worlds met, like two realities crashing head-on, and where there was real magic, those women being truly capable of creating change. Looking back decades later it is wonderful to realise that the magic did work – the base and the missiles went and Greenham became a Common again.

On the fence there was a rainbow serpent and things from Suffolk and I wondered whether anyone I knew had done it. I went to the fire at Orange Gate and sat with the women there. A Welsh girl read to us from the Mabinogion as she understood who Taliesin was/is. She knew Bedd Taliesin which she said was the birthplace of the bard. I later found it was (also?) his burial place. There is a village called Taliesin there, between Aberystwyth and Machynlleth. Talie was passed around the women, which both he and they enjoyed.

I felt so good in their company, though I was incredulous at the harshness of what they were doing. I felt my own life was quite cushy in comparison, but perhaps I shouldn't have underestimated the challenge of what I was doing myself. I felt drained, as if I had no energy to give the women or the place. Instead it was I who needed to receive strength from them and to recharge my own batteries.

Richard went home for Christmas. Mike lit his new stove and it was good to see smoke rising from his waggon. He said that night he dreamed of Aboriginal women at Greenham building gates of power from light.

Christmas Day. A night where I was unusually cold and had neck-ache, but managed to keep Talie warm. The heavy frost of morning turned to rain – how very changeable it all was. As we were about to leave a woman gave us half a Christmas cake, some apples and an orange. Many people would stop by and give the women food and sometimes they had too much. It was a treat I really appreciated.

The rain lashed like ice as we went round the top of Greenham Common. I walked it as a kind of pilgrimage, moving my own Dreaming Path, especially the bit near Blue Gate as I remembered being there for the great December encircling of the base, and the strength those days had given me. I got upset

199

though, for now Mike was shouting and swearing at Rosie, and I was embarrassed when we met women walking the other way. His energy seemed no different from that inside the base and I hoped Talie would grow up differently from that.

I drove a lot of the way and sitting on the waggon was frozen as we travelled through cold, wet, empty streets with everyone indoors. We had received so much friendship, encouragement and gifts in the time leading up to Christmas, but now it was here people were enclosed in their own worlds. However, we found good wide verges, the rain stopped, the sky cleared and there was a beautiful new crescent moon. I cycled through the delicious countryside to phone Saffron and arrange a Christmas-time with my family and we decided to all meet up at Kevin's in London. I cooked supper and Mike made stuffing. We had a Christmas pudding and it ended up a nice Christmas evening.

Boxing Day. I woke to an incredibly thick white frost under a clear blue sky and a golden sunrise from behind the surrounding hills. The frost didn't thaw for ages, in some places not at all, so all morning the horses couldn't graze and we had no hay. It seemed ridiculous that we had found good grass and now they couldn't eat it.

When we set off it was glorious but very cold and the first day I wore gloves, though I still only wore jumpers and no coat. The roads were very slippery and I wondered what we would do when we met icy hills. It was breathlessly still with that magical, watery, midwintery light expressing so powerfully the pause of the year – nature herself holding her breath. The tight buds on the trees, so full of life, waiting to burst forth with the energy of Spring, embodied the sleeping night of the year, pregnant in their own way.

It began to get late and dark and we had found no verges. Mike went to ask a very upper-crust guy for hay, explaining our plight, and he let us go in one of his fields as long as we would be off the next day. It was great for the horses at last to have good grass and hay. The man told us not to leave rubbish or abuse the place.

The timings of our comings and goings were going to be a bit daunting. I planned to leave the next day hoping Richard would come back in time for them to move, then I'd get back the following day in time for Mike to go off and Richard and I to travel on. I hoped it would all work out. It snowed. It was very wet in the waggon – a combination of leaks and condensation – but WE WERE IN WILTSHIRE.

I got up early and was away by 8am. The snow had mostly gone on our field but the nearby ridge was white, echoing the chalk beneath. It was lovely to drink in the energy of Wiltshire as I fed and moved the horses, feeling sure I'd had many past lifetimes in that area. I hitched a lift easily to Hungerford and caught a very full bus with people standing, got to Victoria and was at Kevin's by 12.30. Tiffany was there for about an hour, so for a while I was with all four of my children and felt a bit despondent when she left. It wasn't a very Christmassy day, though we ate chocolates and drank sherry and they gave us a children's version of the Taliesin story by Robert Nye. In the end we didn't go to bed until 2am.

I was awake at 5 and left by 6.30am. There were lighted flares at the end of the underground platform which I thought strange. Mike had phoned the previous day to say Richard had been so late back they hadn't been able to move on and had to stay in the man's field another day. It was odd to retrace my steps but I was glad I hadn't missed a day travelling in Wiltshire.

It was very foggy and I slipped in and out of different realities as we travelled. Talie slept nearly all the way back to Hungerford on a bus which this time only had 3 other people in it. I found a taxi firm who invited me to wait in the warm until the driver came. The fare was only £2 and I was back with the waggons by 10.15am.

Mike then left for his family Christmas. I was elated being in Wiltshire and we were soon off. 'Housekeeping' was getting a bit lax. I seemed to have lost my hoof-pick and the harness badly needed to be cleaned and oiled: I was just bundling it up any old how under the waggon, wrapping it in an old blanket, but even that was wet and frozen, as was my front hanging.

In the distance the chalk ridges covered in snow were like white serpents. The day's travelling was really good, though the horses tended to slip on the ice a bit; trying to avoid hills meant we mostly walked on the main road. We did take one detour through some beautiful landscape and saw a mill, but the road was icy and we were glad to make it safely back onto the A road, where we immediately found a wide verge and a man gave us £5 for hay. I was tired but euphoric. I cooked some slushy lentils and Richard said they smelled like roast turkey.

Early next morning there was a banging on the side of my waggon. I wondered if someone was going to tell us to move on, but it was a man and his daughter who had stopped by in their car. He was a flat-cap, green-wellie type. "Do you want a bale of hay?" he asked. "Yes, please". "Do you want a sack of potatoes?" "Goodness, yes please". "Do you want some eggs?", handing over a dozen in his flat cap. Lesson: don't judge people by appearances! A bit later a woman gave us half a bucket of pony nuts.

On a fine, dry morning with just a bit of wind, we went into Burbage to find a shop though it was a long way off our route. I'd already cycled to the nearest village and found it was shopless. I was getting fed up around this time because I seemed to be buying all the food. We had split the original communal lot, but I never got any which was in Mike's, though they both came into mine, took stuff out and ate it. Mike had eaten the mincemeat, and all the dried fruit had disappeared. I had to buy my own food and hide it away, yet was also buying all the communal stuff. Things like this were becoming an issue for me.

Several people spontaneously and separately told us to go a different way from the one we had planned and to stop at a picnic spot in a forest, so somehow it just seemed we weren't going to Stonehenge any more but were going to Avebury. It was what I had wanted anyway, but again wouldn't have pushed the idea with the men. I find Stonehenge male and patriarchal, as though constructed by a much later invading people, whereas for me the Avebury area has a strong female energy. We had headed for Stonehenge as that was what we planned when we first got out the maps months before, but as we hadn't got there for Solstice, it now seemed pointless, and we were heading for Avebury without really having to make much of a decision. The Goddess moves in mysterious ways! The route was becoming more and more powerful, as though we were guided by some force beyond us. We stopped at the picnic site which once again had no litter bins.

The nights around that time were strange. Talie was restless, disturbing my sleep and dream patterns. I did a Tibetan practice in a dream, which was a first, and that helped. I felt close to many of my women friends, picking up on their energy.

It got much warmer, yet there were still patches of snow in the morning. The beautiful twigs with their bursting buds held on to the old wizened fruit of the previous autumn, and dripped diamond-like drops of water. That day I asked the earth for some of her strength and it seemed to come.

There was a one-in-seven down-hill on our route and we approached it calmly. Rosie was fine without a skid shoe (Mike not having yet got one made for the wheels of his new waggon). Richard kept her close to the kerb in case he needed to go into it or up onto it to brake, but it was a good test of Rosie's strength that she had no problems. Polly wanted to race to catch Rosie up, making it hard for me to pour water in the skid to cool it while holding her back. It just wasn't on to trot down a steep hill in a skid shoe, Polly!

We passed through Marlborough, where I had so often stopped while hitching to Avebury. We bought cakes, mince pies and jam from Edith's cafe, which was another of my great caffs of Britain. It became very misty and we walked on through swirling cloud. I was keen to get to the end of the Ridgeway Path but both Rosie and Richard were tired so we stopped at West Overton beside a beautiful bit of the River Kennet where we sat for a while on that calm British

The waggons parked up on the Ridgeway path near the Ridgeway Café and the Sanctuary.

winter evening. These were the gems of the journey, part of a reality outside the mundane one of roads.

The next morning was so warm it was too hot in the waggon with the heater on. Mike returned, and was pleased we were going to Avebury rather than Stonehenge. After about a mile and a half we parked up on the Ridgeway opposite the Sanctuary, and I enjoyed approaching Avebury in yet another way. We had a cuppa in the Ridgeway Café, with chips and apple pie and custard. Yummy.

Richard and I walked down to Avebury and round the stones. By now it was dark and I felt I belonged there, almost as though I lived there. Over the previous decade, I had introduced so many people to this place, as though it was what I was for. Although we had slept on Silbury Hill just after Talie was born, this was his first time in the stones.

When we came to the largest stones I had a totally shattering experience: for about 30 seconds I was totally joined with someone from my past, as though our essential spirits beyond any incarnations were as one being. I could hardly bear it and yet it was perfection. We seemed to be completely merged with a golden light round our heads. I'd never experienced anything like that before, gasped, and leant against a stone as though winded. Then it was gone and the loss was vast and there was a grief at that loss beyond description, as though everything in me had completely drained out.

We walked on, and I entered a double reality; still knowing who and where I was, yet the great stones seeming to grow even taller as though I were in some huge temple filled with a dark, brownish-golden light. I felt small and contained in this giant place before walking a processional way with the presence of many other people. I never took drugs and wasn't even fasting. It was as though, living and travelling as we were: outdoors, part of everything around us, part of past, present and future, the veils between realities became very thin. Once this was how everyone lived. How much we have lost.

We returned to the waggons, had supper and went to bed. The New Year which people in houses were celebrating had no meaning for us. Ours had been the Solstice.

January 1st 1985. Talie's restless nights had resulted in a new tooth. Top front left. (He already had some bottom ones).The night had been cold and I thought I heard snow – tiny hard things falling on our roof like faeries clog-dancing, but maybe it was just the sound of frost forming. It was a calm, clear morning with a rainbow sky and in that pure dawn we went to the Sanctuary for the golden sunrise. I stood on the central concrete stump, which would once have been a great wooden pillar, and looked back over the previous few years of my life with all its pain, and the initiation which had brought me to what seemed like a calm state of being. The previous day I had been awed by all I did not know, and could never know, and by all that those circles of stone must have been for, far beyond the realms of the earthly.

This was the first day I wore long-johns and a thick woolly vest.

We had tried to contact Capricorn Ros, hoping she might join us for the Capricorn of our journey, but couldn't find her anywhere. We walked from the Sanctuary to West Kennet, not by the road but by paths across fields. We entered the ancient long barrow, the womb of the Old Hag Mother of Winter and the deep peace of her ancient, nurturing body. The floor was strewn with rosemary, from someone else's Solstice rites. It was so good to be there, but I felt I would never again sleep in her; that those powerful nights had been a stage on my path which were no longer necessary.

We walked up to the Swallowhead Spring. A strong wind was blowing but down by the spring it was completely sheltered. The spring was flowing from the little 'cave' in the cliff and the clear, pure water was bubbling up through the earth. We placed our Capricorn sign above the spring and I lit a beeswax candle which burned with barely a flicker. To me Capricorn's energy is that of a gentle, warm, brown goat. My mother was a Capricorn, and although I have

The Capricorn disc at the Swallowhead Spring.

no memory of her, that morning at the spring made me feel closer to her, as though being in her sign brought me some sense of her energy. Down there it was earthy and protected and we found a hollow tree beside the river and 'posted' the wooden sign deep down inside it.

We walked back along the path to Avebury, Mike 'wearing' Talie under his coat. We sent Ros a birthday card and returned to the waggons. It was so cold under the bright moon.

Next day we breakfasted in the cafe and had a 'business meeting', writing each other cheques for thousands of pounds and receipts for debts settled and IOUs for those not. Money seemed quite meaningless, just numbers on bits of paper. However, I was worrying about how I was going to live in the future; a future which seemed completely unknown and impossible to visualise. In the moment, though, I looked at the waggon, parked beside those familiar tumuli high on the Ridgeway Path, and thought "I'm so lucky".

The morning was cold and dry with a slight wind which dried my front hanging a bit. Richard saw us back onto the road and then left. We didn't know when we'd see him again. Part of the cheque- writing had been my lending him money for a horse, so maybe when we next met up he would be with his own waggon. We drove up the road beside the Avenue to the shop and P.O. at Avebury, then down the other road to Beckhampton and on towards Devizes. Surrounded by tumuli, long barrows, earthworks on tops of hills and the beautiful wild, rolling landscape, I breathed the ancientness of that land and I was that land.

The days were now beginning to grow, each one a few miraculous minutes longer, giving us precious extra travelling time.

Next day when I woke, the inside of my blue world was a myriad of tiny diamonds – or stars – a cosmos within my home. It was a lovely morning in every way: cold and clear, Talie happy and going to sleep as we were ready to set off. Polly went into the shafts like a dream even on the edge of the road – and then suddenly Mike's trace hook broke and he couldn't mend it without a drill bit he'd have to get from Devizes, which was still 5 miles away. The traces are the leathers or chains which join the horse's collar to the waggon and actually pull it, The trace hook is where the trace joins the waggon.

It was terrible! At the very moment we were about to leave after everything had gone so perfectly, having to un-harness and stop was unbearable. It was like stopping the countdown on a launch-pad at 10 seconds or having your lover walk away just before the moment of orgasm. It took a long time to come down from the adrenalin rush and take in the fact that we wouldn't be moving that day. I oiled my harness and sat in the winter sunshine with Talie and had a walk up the nearest tumulus.

When Mike came back I fetched water from an amazing old man up the road. He had about 30 chickens in a small back garden run that I would have worried about having 6 in.

My hoof-pick had re-appeared. I hadn't really thought it was lost. I slept cosy and untroubled, hoping we'd move on the next day.

It was a cold and windy day and I had to drive a lot as I couldn't keep up when walking. We were surrounded by a lot of military stuff, feeling they were taking over all our sacred sites. At Devizes we found bins for our rubbish, and later Mike bought hay and got calf food instead of pony nuts and then didn't want to feed it to the horses as it had growth promoter in it. There were lots of hills but both horses had masses of energy: how fit they were, in really tip-top condition. I didn't even bother with the skid shoe a lot of the time as Polly seemed so strong. At one point Mike decided to trot a hill and to keep up Polly cantered! I hadn't thought horses could canter in the shafts, but it was fine. Polly trotted to keep up with Rosie's walk and cantered to keep up with her trot. At Potterne I managed to buy 2 gallons of paraffin.

Mike had a radio and on another glorious morning he said it had been the coldest night of the winter and there was snow in places like Kent and East Anglia. As we were near a little river I washed my hair, myself, and a few clothes. It was good to use what was around us and it felt so precious to be near water. I hung the wet clothes on the shafts, but they froze instantly.

Travelling fast up and down little hills kept us warm. The rolling countryside began to feel like Somerset, so we surely couldn't be far off. We found a good place at 3pm so decided to stop: it was good getting off early, stopping early and not getting too tired. I sat in the waggon with the front open and gave Talie his lunch as we watched the sun set over a fantastic view, halfway up/down a hillside. I'd got our drinking water the previous day from a woman with one eye and wondered if she were a faerie.

It was midday before we got off, our energy somehow having slowed. We had to push the waggons backwards before we could go forward and a man came and helped. A part of me was getting tired and worn out, but I didn't know which part. I was getting happier and more together and yet in some ways more pressurised. It got warmer very suddenly and all the frost disappeared. I had enjoyed walking on the hard, frozen ground in my shoes instead of living in my wellies, but now it was all muddy again.

There were wonderful views: Coombe Hill with an earthwork – possibly Bratton Castle, and a white chalk horse carved on the hillside; the whole sky full of hang-gliders as though we were in some magical land with strange flying creatures in the air. Mike's radio said all points east were totally snowbound, even bits of the M4, yet there was nothing where we were, as though a patch of fine weather hovered over us.

There was one slippery hill which Polly could only just manage, and there followed a long stretch with nowhere to even pause, with heavy skies and night's darkness coming. We came to a cross-roads with wide verges which we pulled onto, got un-harnessed, unloaded and Mike went to get water. Talie had been crying for the last bit and I'd had to carry him so there was no way I could move once we'd stopped. We were opposite a garden centre and the owner got very irate and threatened to call the police, which we wouldn't have minded as police understand that if your horses are tired and you have no lights, you can't be on the road in the dark. I think there was some acknowledgement that you were allowed to stop one night somewhere as long as you were off next day. I went in, carrying Talie, and tried to speak to the man, but he would only send out his poor, embarrassed minion. When he did eventually appear he was shaking with that uncontrollable red-faced rage some people get into. I explained to the minion that we wouldn't cause any bother, told him what we were doing – travelling the Gipsy Switch, doing theatre, raising money for Oxfam, and that it was impossible for us to move on any further that day.

We stayed and had no problems, nor police visits, but it wasn't very relaxed. It was such a rare thing for us to be treated with hostility; almost everywhere we went we were welcomed, or at least tolerated. I told Mike he could go on ahead if he was really worried, but he said Polly would be awful without Rosie and I wouldn't be able to cope with her, which was probably true, so he stayed. He was really afraid of being set upon and attacked.

We were up in the dark, waiting for the light so we could get off. There were men building and burning a bonfire next to us but they were very friendly. The sunrise was beautiful and it was fantastic being off so early. I was glad we had stopped there as there was no other possible stopping-place until Frome, which was miles away. We crossed the border into Somerset and the signposts began to say Glastonbury. At one point it snowed a little, the flakes coming from nowhere. The sky was blue and the sun shone and it was as though the snow came from our thoughts, dancing like shining faeries in the sunlight. At midday we had a lunch stop at a cafe with attentive and kind people and actually read some newspapers.

Later we parked up on a narrow verge and put the horses on the other side of the road on a wider one. We were very near traffic and the waggon wobbled every time something went past. We were travelling on main roads now as they got gritted. Mike went off for a bit and I watched the sunset. A farmer and his daughter came by. She was worried about our ponies and he said we should put them in his field which was right next to us. He was concerned about the waggons, so said put them in too. The girl wanted a pony ride and I said when Mike came back or next morning. At first, when he realised I'd got a baby in the back he said half-jokingly "You're a cruel woman", but I got Talie out and when he saw how well and happy he was he was amazed, saying he was the fattest baby in the world - but I pointed out that half of it was his woollies. When Mike returned we pushed the waggons into the field. It was down quite a slope and mine started to run away, but we managed to stop it before any damage was done. It was hard work but I felt happy when I saw Polly and Rosie free in a field after all the time they had been tethered.

It was sheltered down there and I could hardly hear the traffic. Mike went to see the farmer and get water and came back with a pint of milk and half a dozen free-range eggs. What a complete opposite to the previous day. I felt sad

'The fattest baby in the world?'

for the man in the garden centre and thought there must be so little happiness in his life. I was now as content as I had been in summer, when I lay down to sleep on the earth in the arms of the Great Mother.

It was a cold night and when morning came it began to snow properly, it having at last caught up with us. Under a dark sky the snow blew fiercely in the wind and the road soon covered and it seemed foolish to move on. Mike spoke to the farmer's wife and she said "stay as long as you like". It was a secure place to get snowed in and a miracle to be there.

I looked forward to a day of peace reading and writing, but there was rumour of a lift to 'town'. So I went down to the house, thinking it would be a quick trip for supplies and I'd have the rest of the day to myself, but I had to wait an hour for the farmer, having a good chat with his wife, who made remarks about Glastonbury feeling 'different' and 'strange'. By the time we got off in the Land Rover it was too late to get to the village shop so I went round with them as they fed their cattle and broke the ice on the troughs (he pronounced it 'trow'), they in one case having to carry water from trough to trough where the pipes were frozen. It was a fascinating experience and made me realise how hard farmers have to work looking after animals in the winter. I met two nice goats there in Capricorn.

In the end I got to the shop and had to rush round. They didn't have much I wanted but I did get a gallon of paraffin. I got back as it was getting dark. It had been a wonderful day and the farmer's daughter had her pony ride.

209

It was the warmest night we'd had for ages and my nose didn't freeze and neither did the (used) teabags. The red sun rose on a beautiful day with a clear blue sky, turning to gold and then white through the still low heavy streaks of snow cloud: white, white, everywhere white, with blue shadows on the snow and black, black trees and bushes.

We made ready. The farmer's daughter rode Polly again, and the farmer's wife came with some milk to see us off, and told us that ten years previously they'd had the last two working shire horses in the county. She saw we might have difficulty getting up the slope to the road, so got two lads to push us, and we certainly needed it. Rosie was struggling and there was no way Polly would have pulled our waggon out on her own, but with their help we got out and on our way.

For a while it wasn't even a day for coats. There was a paradise of streaming mists dripping from trees and catching the sunlight and I found myself going off into a strange reverie. It was something to do with the magic of the snow and the mists and the black and white colours. We went through Shepton Mallet and when it was too late to go any further and we stopped on a nice corner near water. It was beautiful outside with a gold setting sun, but a cold white mist crept across the fields. Mike went off on the bike to suss out the route for the next day as we had to head off the main road onto the snowy side ones to find our way to Patrick's White Field at Butleigh.

Looking at the map I realised we were at Steanbow Bridge which was the tip of the hoof of the Sagittarius figure in the mighty Glastonbury zodiac, so we had unknowingly stopped there with our horses as our first touch of it. The sky cleared and it was very cold. I recalled it being in a Butleigh pub that Nick had first said we could borrow Polly and the waggon for Signs Of Life in 1983 and now here I was owning them both and travelling with them to stop a while in Butleigh.

Mike came back with frozen trousers and bootlaces and we wondered how we lived so untroubled by the cold. By now at night I had the sleeping-bag inside the bedclothes, as Talie always seemed to end up with all the blankets. We were parked under high power electric cables which crackled continuously; my plastic tarp – and my head - being constantly bombarded by highly charged particles.

January 10th. I woke with aching lungs, a sore throat and toothache! We had faith that the low freezing fog would lift as the sky above was beautifully clear. The countryside was stunning and I felt it was so special to come to it in that stark black and whiteness.

Rosie seemed shatteringly slow-moving and I thought we would never get off the main road but eventually we came to the turn-off and went along the back roads where there were wet patches in the middle to give the horses a sure footing, dear Polly concentrating hard on each hoofstep.

It got snowier and snowier: down a lane, through a gate, across a field to park under some willow trees – and this was to be our home for several weeks. The plan was to stay there throughout much of Aquarius, then head off in time to get to Lampeter in West Wales for Pisces. Richard was going to get his horse and waggon together at last and would join us from then on.

Chapter 15: Aquarius, Glastonbury

Suddenly everything was different. From nomad to settler, the whole feel of life changed. The cold makes you tired but clears your head and my clarity and vision were honed to a fine edge as we stopped in the centre of the great Glastonbury zodiac; the huge landscape figures lying around us in a massive circle. My sense of their reality, which had been powerful enough in the '70s, was on a different level of awareness now and it was extraordinary to be staying there in the heart of them.

Throughout the journey I had been doing silent contemplation and Tibetan practices whenever I could as well as my own work on a shamanic level. Now it seemed the time for a deep and powerful retreat, where a combination of the Tibetan, the Australian, the pagan traditions of Britain, the tribal origins within myself, the residues of past lives and this place in which I now found myself, would come together into another phase of my initiation, opening more doorways into an ancient remembering.

I found myself inventing my own practices. A great number of people at that time were working on many levels to shift consciousness in the people of power, to change their way of seeing and understanding, in the hope of some sanity, some peace, some end both to war and the exploitation of the resources of the earth. It all seemed possible. There seemed hope. We were trying to 'Save the Earth'.

Sadly, several years later I became suspicious of many aspects of the New Age movement. I had been working with powerful energies for some time and was suddenly unsure of what I'd actually been feeding it all into, so withdrew myself from those networks and began quietly, but no less powerfully, to work on my own. But back in 1985 I was very much a part of the Peace Movement as well as working on my own spiritual development.

I walked across the field to meet Patrick, who owned it. He had named himself after the field – Patrick Whitefield: a very special person who lived by his beliefs. He usually lived in a tipi in the field but was wintering in a caravan near the house – the Dove workshops. We were parked quite a way from the house and walking to it across the field was almost an assault course, especially for me carrying Talie: across streams, over fences, through other fences, over stiles...I realised it wouldn't even be easy to get water and dump rubbish. In the stillness and silence of the field of willow and sheep no-one need know we were there. It was up to me to move out into the world and make contact.

Mike cooked red cabbage and there was no sound of vehicles. At first I indulged slightly in just being and in being still, sorting the waggon and unloading things which didn't usually get unloaded to give us more space.

Next day we walked in to Glastonbury (3-4 miles) with me carrying a back-pack full of dirty washing. It was foggy and freezing and the roads were slippery, so I was glad we had arrived the previous day. Glastonbury felt such a focal place. Already Mike belonged more than I, as he had been there recently doing a sacred dance course. A woman gave us a lift and at last we were actually in the town.

To begin with the washing machines in the laundrette wouldn't work, then I put the coins in the wrong one, but eventually it was ok and the drier kept working without money so things balanced out. It all felt rushed and there was certainly no time for a leisurely browse around bookshops, which I was aching for. I didn't see the Tor, as it had retreated into the Mists of Avalon, nor was there time to visit the Chalice Well, but I was intensely aware of being close to them.

As we returned, frost of beautiful patterns formed on my hair, on whiskers on Talie's hat and where my breath fell on my clothes. It was so cold the air itself seemed to freeze. It was hard getting a lift until a man who knew us picked us up, but then his van broke down. Just as we stood again at the roadside a woman who had seen us set off came looking for us and took us all the way back. I had phoned Caryne of Gog Theatre who were based at the Assembly Rooms and arranged to see them on the following Monday to discuss dates for us doing a performance there.

And so the days began to pass. Although it was cold, there were sudden temperature changes and ice would turn to water, but then just as quickly freeze again. I went to the Butleigh shop, where the people were really nice and happy to receive our post. They had lots of wholefoods as there were so many 'alternatives' around. Mike got hay and went off for pony nuts and gas. I knew I'd have to find paraffin soon as I was burning more of it as well as candles while we were stationary and spending more time in the waggon. I put Talie back in 'proper' nappies instead of disposable ones and revelled in having time to read and write long letters and in starting to knit again. The moon's crescent was shrinking fast and I watched her go with sadness, almost dreading the dark nights with no moonlight.

Now we weren't moving and I wasn't walking with Polly the cold seemed to have got deep into my core, but the beauty of the days warmed my spirit. Talie was very happy. One day I muttered to him that I wanted a new coat and wished I hadn't left my other one in East Anglia. Later that day I hitched into Glastonbury and got a lift from the first car. I had a lovely talk with the woman driver who was very interested in what we were doing. On parting she said "I hope you won't be insulted, but my daughter's got a duffel coat hanging doing nothing, would you like it"?!! That day I saw the Tor for the first time, lying like a maiden sleeping, veiled in white, waiting for Bride's Day, and with Talie I went to the Well which was wonderfully peaceful and strong. Icicles hung at the sides of the waterfall and the blood-like water flowed endlessly, steaming from the warm body of the earth. I was full of a blissful joy and we got back to the waggon just as dusk was coming.

I went looking for the woman with the coat, but couldn't find her.

The days sped by and there was much to do. So much for a quiet retreat! I went to the Gog Theatre office, which was a hive of activity, and received a great welcome. (I'd made contact with them when Lynne, Jan Dungey and I did the 3-day workshop in early '83.) Although it was all a bit speedy, chaotic and hard to pin down details I excitedly chose a couple of potential dates for our performance in the Assembly Rooms. There seemed so much potential around Glastonbury, but I wondered how you turned it into anything concrete. When I later lived there I found this was a general problem: lots of people with ideas, some airy-fairy, some realistic, but very few with the practicality to bring them to fruition. Things flower and die quickly and those which do become established and persist are rare.

I had a drink with Tom in the pub where everyone gathered in those days and encountered the notorious matriarch-hating Anthony Roberts, who had written extremely abusive letters to many women I knew. He didn't seem to mind me, though. I went back to Tom and Caryne's in Street for a while where Talie enjoyed the company of other children, then Tom took us back to the waggons and we finalised the performance date with Mike, it now becoming a priority to really get the show together.

I developed strange concepts of time which weren't in tune with other peoples' and decided that, while I lived in the world where others had time and clocks, I'd maybe have to get a watch.

I had a possible lead to follow towards my potential coat, but walking in the snow was becoming an enormous effort. I had to be careful not to fall while carrying Talie and was having to look at the ground all the time and not at the wonders around me.

Mike briefly let the horses off their tethers, having to be careful, as Patrick had planted young trees in the field; yet when they were tethered their hooves damaged the precious natural ancient meadow.

Mike went off to things like sacred dance workshops on his bike and was getting to know people and having a good social life, whereas I was rather stuck in the waggon on my own. I was still in a state of winter hibernation really, although beginning to emerge; still huddled away in the protective body of the Great Mother, drawing on my own inner resources, with a state of still contemplation within me; but the daily external chores were a struggle.

Whenever I could I would sit by the Chalice Well, feeling nurtured by her. The white Tor lay so pure and virgin I felt I could not walk upon her body until Bride's Day was passed, when maybe the white would go and she would be green again.

It seemed to be getting even colder and I tried to hang up more things to keep it out, there still being winds even in this sheltered spot. One day large soft flakes of snow fell and lay thickly and there was no edge between land and sky and even the dark marks of trees and buildings faded into indistinguishable softness.

I wanted to make some new costumes, as they had been such a powerful expression of my creativity in my Performance days, so planned to make two for our forthcoming show – one white and one red.

At a meeting with Mike we started to write the show, evolving it as a good balance between his ideas and mine. He had once sat beside the Well and had a vision of going down to a land beneath where he met three women. To me these must be aspects of the Goddess. The show was going to be partly a child's fairy-tale quest, but would hopefully also convey something of the Goddess in a year's circular journey, as the Hero sought the magical water from the Well at the World's End. There was to be a bit of enlightenment involved as he finally came back to the place where he had begun, only to find the well had been there all the time, but now he could see it.

 Around the time of Imbolc it was important to do something about wells and their healing powers, so I felt I should contact some women's groups to organise a celebration.

One day, on a water-gathering trip, I saw a farrier shoeing horses at the Dove. He tried to sell me a lurcher pup, saying that all gipsies should have one. He was taking the piss and I didn't like him at all. I had enough to do coping with a baby, let alone a dog, and anyway I wasn't a gipsy and wasn't pretending to be one! Apparently, though, he was coming to do our horses at 9.30am the following Wednesday. He wouldn't come to where we were, so we would have to walk them round the roads to the Dove so he could shoe them on a bit of hard standing.

I now had the phone number of the lady with the coat, so called her, found where her house was and went round, meeting her husband and mother-in-law for coffee and a chat. She was concerned that in the waggon Talie wouldn't have anywhere to learn to crawl. She taught dyslexic children and many of them had missed the crawling stage. I felt sure that not crawling wouldn't cause dyslexia, but possibly the factor causing it also manifested the 'symptom' of not crawling, and children who are going to crawl do it whatever. Tiffany had learned to stand up with no support on a wobbly bed. I hoped that when the Spring came there would be the good earth for Talie to crawl on, and anyway, he was often on floors in other people's houses. (He did crawl and isn't dyslexic).

She gave me the magnificent coat – what a joy that was – and a pair of shoes. Her mother-in-law gave me some mittens: what generosity there is in the world!

It got warmer and slowly the snow began to disappear.

Two girls often rode Polly and Rosie, which was important as the horses weren't getting much exercise and we needed them to be fit when we eventually left.

January 21st. Dark Moon. The night was very dark and it rained and rained and rained. I woke to a world of no more white, a world of green and brown and very much mud, and the rain went on and on and on. I felt the dark moon had been the true Imbolc, the turning of energy, the shedding of the veil. There was a sadness in me, for a kind of magic had gone; the snow had been beautiful even though difficult and tiring to walk on. Now it was mud, mud, mud in the strange twilight time before Spring; a time of waiting, like a coiled spring waiting to burst into life.

A big event was the final arrival of my new Snugli baby carrier. It had become increasingly difficult for me to cope either with my home-made one which had to be tied onto me by someone else, or a silly little Mothercare thing I'd bought which was already too small for him. The Snugli was an incredible miracle of sewn engineering made of thick, dark blue corduroy. It was very strong with lots of zips, I could wear him either on my front or my back, and it could change shape and carry him until he was quite a big toddler. And I could put it on by myself.

I did a layout for the leaflet advertising our show and Tom took me to a printer in Wells to get the leaflets done and I was pleased with how they looked. The writer Geoffrey Ashe came in and seemed to have some kind of feud going on with Tom. I became aware of how, in Glastonbury, energies polarised and brought about conflicts which seemed nothing to do with the place itself.

One day, walking from Street to Glastonbury alongside Wearyall Hill I saw a hawthorn tree with mistletoe growing on it. It was the first time I'd ever seen this and it made me so excited I was lifted out of a bit of a down mood I'd been in.

I sorted out more practicalities about the forthcoming performance and bought fabric for costumes, which meant I'd have to find a sewing machine and somewhere to sew them.

With Caryne I went to a women's Peace meeting – the first they'd had for a year, but it all seemed rather negative, saying Greenham had 'had it', which wasn't at all what I had felt when we were there. Speaking like that felt like a betrayal of those women living in cold mud, being evicted every few days, physically and verbally abused by the police, just because these middle-class women in their cosy homes weren't getting such a powerful high from it any more. I had much to say, but didn't, which was just as much a betrayal, but I felt on the outside of a local clique.

On the Wednesday we rushed the horses round the still-icy roads to the Dove. We were on time, but waited three-quarters of an hour for the farrier, only to be told he'd been and gone. Mike was very annoyed and we decided to find someone different as this guy obviously wasn't taking us seriously. We had to walk all the way back, but it was nice to have been out so early.

In preparation for the show we got out Richard's trunk and my bags of costumes, some of which were going mouldy. I hung them on trees to air and cleared a big space inside the waggon. I had a rising sense of elation to be standing high in the zodiac centre looking at the now-green still-sleeping body of the great mother, and was full of the power of the place and that particular time of year.

The energy had really changed: the year was growing and there was a breath of the coming Spring. There was a thin sliver of a new crescent moon in the clear sky. It, too, was growing.

It was always lovely to get post. We heard that Ros was going to come over to do the show with us, and I got a letter from Tiffany, which meant an awful lot to me.

Sue, of Gog Theatre, said I could use her sewing machine, took me round to her house and I got on with cutting out the fabric for the costumes. In the past I had made them on a shop-window dummy which, although it was a funny shape, made it easier to create costumes if they hung on some kind of body. Now I was going to have to do without one. I cut out the white fabric, pinned and sewed it by hand, deciding to do the red one on the machine. The white costume was very simple, too simple perhaps and I never did the magical embroidery on it which I had planned, indeed the magic seemed to have gone out of my costume-making. In my performance days they had been part of my real magic, but these were just costumes and didn't work on that level. I was disappointed. A lot of people came to the house and I found it strange to sew in front of them, as my costume-making had always been a very private thing, no-one else seeing them until they were complete.

Later Mike came in for a chat, which was good as I'd not seen him for a week. He'd done some successful story-telling and was getting his own gigs together, wanting now to be a one-man story- teller.

I carried on with the red costume, which was made from unbleached fabric which I wanted to tie- and sew-dye. I had the house to myself this time. When I got back I found Mike had taken my water, so had to go and get some more, then found he'd taken the cooking oil, the tomato puree and goodness knows what else. It really was getting me down how much he was taking from me – candles, matches, toilet paper and endless other things - especially as he had more money than I did. He would just come into my waggon, help himself, and never replace or return anything. I would never have dreamed of going into his to take things from him.

He had told me of two women I should meet – Lorye Keats Hopper and Phillipa Bowers – and at last I met Lorye and we discussed having an Imbolc sweat lodge, as she was into North American Indian medicine-wheel work. She lived in a caravan nearby and I found her a very interesting woman.

Around this time I developed awful toothache. It was a bottom one at the back and all the glands in my neck had swollen terribly. I also had a hole in a top back one, so could now eat hardly anything.

Everything was changing: Richard would be coming soon, and Ros; there was the coming Imbolc weekend and then our show, and not long after we would be preparing to leave. It suddenly felt quite rushed. My whole tooth, jaw and throat was really bad and I was experimenting with various homeopathic remedies.

The elements were having a powerful effect on me, which was probably somewhat due to my being slightly ill from the abscess, but I was completely in contact, in a living, vibrant way, with the place, the zodiac figures, the Tor and everything which surrounded me. I had a wonderful walk, noticing everything about the trees, right down to each little twig. They were giving out a powerful energy as the life-force of the new Spring began to flow again, little buds growing on elder which always seemed to be the first. I was collecting twigs from trees of the Beth-Luis-Nion calendar to use in our show. I had discussed this with Patrick as he was concerned about my taking from living trees, but I said I always explained to the tree why I wanted a little bit of it, how it would be used and asked permission. I still do this and find they usually give willingly, but if they don't you always know and then you don't take. I watched the winter birds, and the Tor going in and out of the mist.

Talie's hair suddenly went all curly.

I carried on feeling strangely ill, my whole mouth and neck swollen, so hitched into Glastonbury and made an appointment with a dentist.
We were getting concerned about how we were going to get into Wales, having heard you couldn't cross the Severn Bridge (the original one) with horses and waggons. Some notorious people from Talley Valley had once come across from the Welsh side on the foot/cycle path having camped nearby overnight and set off at dawn; but going from the English side you couldn't do that as you would initially encounter the tolls and be unable to sneak onto the bridge. This meant we would have to go right up to Gloucester and cross the river there. I was worrying about time as we needed to reach Lampeter in West Wales while it was still Pisces. I phoned the police to ask if we could have special permission and at first thought the man was going to say yes, but the answer was no. Gloucester it would have to be then.

On the way back to Butleigh I passed Richard with Michael O'Connell and arranged to meet him next day at the dentists. So, Richard was back, with a waggon he'd bought from a traveller near Lakenheath, and soon his horse would be arriving. It had been called Hercules, but Richard wanted to re-name him Atlantis. I thought he was more of a Henry or Harry, but it wasn't my business.

I took some homeopathic remedies which gave me quite a blast and initially made me feel even worse. In the waggon Richard had left some lovely clothes for Talie – a present from Mandy Fry.

January 31st. Imbolc Eve. I woke next morning and all the pain and inflammation had gone, affirming the genuine efficacy of homeopathy. Walking a lot of the way to town I was hot and sweaty, but everything was as beautiful as ever and I came across an alder for my tree collection. Immediately after this I got a lift so it seemed that finding the alder was why I'd had to walk so far.

Juliet and Richard met me at the dentist and looked after Talie while the man pulled my tooth out. There was a great abscess like a pea on the bottom of it, so I didn't take it home for the faeries. I thought I would have to pay, but wasn't charged.

We sat for a while in the Glastonbury Experience cafe, it feeling good to have Juliet around, then went to the Chalice Well. With Richard we re-enacted part of the performance from the Thorpe Fair the previous summer. The Aquarius/Imbolc time was for opening the eyes of enlightenment and waking the senses by bathing with the sacred water of the well. I took Richard on an initiatory journey through the garden and trust he emerged from the darkness and opened his eyes.

Afterwards there was a flow of energy which at last carried me up the Tor. Talie fell asleep as soon as we started to ascend and I felt him shift into another realm: Taliesin, the Merlin of Britain, returning a-while to Avalon. The climb was physically hard, but often the wind just blew me up, buffeting me, so I had to take great care with my steps and not be blown off. There at last, on the great mass of her body, I felt her energy pulsating beneath us. She was truly awake now. At the top the shelter of the tower held complete stillness while the wind raged all around. Although I always imagine the Tor bare, as it once must have been, the tower did not offend me as much as it did some women, who saw it as a phallic symbol of patriarchal dominance.

Sitting there I felt part of the magical, timeless realm of Avalon in a new way, and walking back down her dark green body, had the vision of all these mountain women, creation ancestresses, rising up again and walking the earth, crushing cities and civilisations under their great feet.

As I descended Talie was still asleep in my arms in the raging wind. Taliesin the wise and ancient was having his 'Air' baptism. As we reached the bottom of the Tor he woke.

February 1st. Imbolc. We had another go at walking the horses round to the Dove for an appointment with the farrier, but after waiting an hour, he never turned up. Obviously he regarded us as a joke and was just messing us about. How unprofessional though, with not much regard for the horses, who needed to be shod.

We walked them back and at last Phillipa Bowers turned up with 3 friends, so it was hard to fit them all into the waggon. I had so wanted to meet Phillipa as she made beautiful goddess sculptures and figurines. Three of them knew of me from my previous life, which by then felt like a past life, and it was comforting to meet people who, in a way, knew who I really was. (It still is!)

Patrick didn't want the horses in the field any more, as they were causing too much damage and had got at some of the saplings. Mike found another field where we could put them for £5 each a week. I was going to be occupied the next day, but Mike reckoned he could manage to take them both.

February 2nd. Candlemas. Although I now celebrate Imbolc and Brighde's Day on the 1st, this year we were celebrating it on the 2nd. I woke while it was still dark and sat with a pale blue candle and incense as it got light. I broke my fast with a drop of water hanging like a jewel from a hawthorn twig.

I met up with Lorye and we walked across fields to the Gog and Magog trees, which are ancient oaks and probably the last of an avenue leading to the Tor. I had never been to them before and it seemed right I should meet them on this special day. It was a long, hard climb above the town, across stiles and muddy fields. At first, only the top of the Tor was in mist, but then it completely disappeared and the whiteness descended further as we walked, until we were just in a tiny circle of visibility which walked with us and shifted everything into a deeply magical reality.

It was wonderful to be taken by someone who loved the trees, especially to Magog, the old woman. I would never have found my way alone by that route, which was timeless, spaceless, with no sense of normal reality – in the realm of faerie almost. Then we were upon them. The old gnarled woman stood to greet us, her many faces watching and waiting as they have been for centuries, her 'body' fluid and female. Moving round, from another angle her facial features became quite vulva-like. A small stream flowed past her roots and her great still-living branches rose like ancient hair. The other tree, the male, seemed quieter, more tree-like, with a less distinct face, in repose, as though still in winter sleep.

We trudged on across the fields to Chalice Well. The experience had been so intense I wondered whether it could be sustained, but it grew into something strong and focussed and beautiful. Other women came to join us round the well and we were 7 women and the boy-child. I took him from his Snugli and held him so he faced inwards and was part of our circle. He 'talked' a lot and it was felt that he had given a lot to what was going on. We placed candles round the well. I placed a beeswax one from Avebury and a rainbow one for Talie. I placed my Ininti beads, a carved yew talisman, a Venus figurine, a 'teardrop' stone from Iona which Lynne had given me and we burned incense. One of Phillipa's statues which had been to Greenham stood behind us holding a candle. I carried a piece of paper soaked with some of Talie's birth-blood and amniotic fluid and a bottle of water from Brighde's Well on Lewis.

We opened the Well lid and each threw in things, some in thanksgiving, and spoke whatever words felt right. Lorye suggested we threw in negative energies and drew out positive ones. When we felt it was done we exchanged the remains of the candles and left. I had laid some costumes behind us and they were wet with the faerie mist.

221

Phillipa gave me a lift back. She had tried several times before to get to the Well, but been prevented, so this had been her first time, on such an appropriate day. On the way back we stopped to pick up someone hitching – and it was Ros! She had been to the Well, sure she would meet us there, but left just before we arrived. It felt so good to have her with us again – and I felt I had known Phillipa for ever.

Things began to hot up as we moved towards the performance date. One day we borrowed Patrick's van and went wooding in Park Wood, in preparation for the sweat lodge. I drove it: a lovely little Morrie like the two I had once owned and loved. In this one you turned the ignition on with a wooden stick. It took a long time and when we got the wood back to the field it still had to be carried to where Patrick wanted us to have the sweat.

I kept phoning to make sure when we could use the Assembly Rooms for rehearsals, only to find it had been double-booked and we would have few chances to rehearse there before the show. It was a big blow meaning we would have to find somewhere else and felt like another case of people not taking us seriously.

We asked Chris Black, who owned a place called Higher Rockes, both whether Ros could stay there and if we could use a room to rehearse, and he kindly agreed to both. I slowly got on with sewing the dye resist for my red costume, tightly sewing and tying patterns which would remain pale when I put it in the red dye. Very late, Richard arrived with his great horse, having driven from Suffolk. We had to tell him that next day he would have to take Atlantis to the field with the other horses.

On the day of the Full Moon I went again to Chalice Well, almost overcome by the power and strength of the time of year, the month, the place we were at. I felt both exhausted and exhilarated, as though my physical reality were ceasing to exist, and it was hard to keep the normal level of human life together at all.

I got back to where they were preparing the sweat lodge and having trouble lighting the fire. I put my Leo energy into it and it lit. Patrick offered to look after Talie while I did the sweat, but I felt incredibly exhausted and in the end didn't do it, feeling I just wanted to sit in contemplation by myself in the waggon. I didn't do any formal practice but just focussed on the Tibetan lineage and teachings.

They had a good sweat, though it wasn't very hot, and after that it seemed impossible to go to the Assembly Rooms for one of the few chances we had to rehearse. We had arranged to meet Ros there, but in those days before mobile phones, had no way of letting her know, so she was very fed up when we didn't arrive. She couldn't get back to the waggons and had to stay in a B&B, spending the last of her money.

The next day she came with me to visit the horses. When the others went they used the bike, as it was a long way to walk, but I couldn't do that with Talie, so it was hard for me to do my 'turn' at feeding them. Atlantis was a fine fellow, but the three horses had already established a pecking order and there was no doubt as to who was boss lady – Polly (the smallest). Oh, my wild black mare! It was good being with Ros and I wished she were around more.

We had a good rehearsal at the Assembly Rooms after fish and chips and waiting for a children's dance session to end. Richard would be Jack, the king's son, going off to find The Well at the World's End. Mike would be the king and the storyteller. Ros would play the piano and I would be the three women who were the three aspects of the goddess: young girl, mother and hag. Richard carried Talie, who fell about laughing at my acting. Actually I wasn't very happy with what I was doing – it was too corny and obvious; stereotypes rather than archetypes, but it was a good rehearsal.

Ros and Richard stayed at Chris Black's and heard of the Molesworth Peace Camp evictions (which were pretty violently carried out by the police). Ros had been living there all winter and was shocked and disorientated by the evictions happening while she was away. From then on her mind was more at Molesworth than Glastonbury, but she stuck with us, bless her.

The days grew wetter and muddier and more and more dark and dismal, but in the waggon I managed to both henna my hair and cold dye the red costume. Once this dried I had to carefully unpick all the sewing and tying I'd done for the resist. I was disappointed with it as the colour was too pale and the patterns too subtle: too late I realised I should have used more dye. So, two new costumes which were a disappointment, neither of them anything like the ones I used to make.

On the 9th we had a final rehearsal in Glastonbury after a lift from a taxi driver and waiting for a jumble sale in the Assembly Rooms to be over. We built the basic structures for the show: a hazel bender for the well, a green Spring mound for Brighde, a garden, a picnic of plenty and field for the harvest mother, and a cave for the Crone. Tom set all the lights for us.

February 10th – Show Day! Talie had been developing a cough and wasn't very well, needing lots of cuddling and I wondered how I would get ready, but had a really deep talk with him which seemed to help. Down at the Assembly Rooms we got the rest of it set up. We made an egg-shaped space in the centre with an archway entrance. The audience sat in this and the performance took place all around the edges of the room, moving from 'set' to 'set'. I put lots of my own sacred and magical objects into the space and surrounded the room with a circle of the 'Beth-Luis-Nion' trees. Mike put his medicine-wheel stones around. The room was quite dark with just the performance areas lit. Charlie of the Assembly Rooms cafe gave us free food for the day and Monica and Phillipa came and looked after Talie.

It was Sunday lunch in the cafe and it seemed the whole of Glastonbury's alternative society ate there and then came to our show: loads of people, loads of children – and their dogs.

At the beginning I cast a circle with Tibetan colours and British incenses. The show was quite magical at times. We got the audience to bring candles and near the end they made an avenue of light for a phoenix to fly down and finally take Jack to enlightenment and the Well at the World's End.

So - the story: The king is sick and his land is sick also. The only cure for them both is water from the Well at the World's End. Jack goes off on a quest for it, sits to rest and shares his food with a raven who tells him he is sitting by the entrance. He spirals down and down and meets the Maiden, sad and alone. He asks her help and after staying the night his senses start to awaken and Spring begins. She gives him a gift for her sister and one for himself. He moves on to the Mother and the summer harvest. He stays a night. His senses waken more. She gives him a gift for her sister and one for himself. He moves on to the Crone and winter. He is forced to enter the darkness of his own fears and to bring out the light. He is awakened even more. She gives him a gift and calls the phoenix who takes him to the Well where he meets the silent one who is like Brighde but somehow different. She gives him the water. He returns to his father's land, which is now riddled with pollution, radiation and people's lack of care for one another. His elemental gifts from the women overcome these and he goes to his father and gives him the water. Land and King are cured.

It took ages to pack up. Monica and I went back to Phillipa's chapel at Wookey Hole. It was a cold evening and Talie was quite ill. It was lovely to be with Monica and Phillipa, who tucked us up with a hot water bottle. It was a cosy night and Talie had his best sleep in ages and woke quite late, certainly not worse and perhaps slightly better. It had been the coldest night on record so I was glad we hadn't been in the waggon.

Back at the waggons I found Richard had spent all day getting his horse to our field and harnessing up so he could take his waggon to Higher Rockes to work on it and get in a bit of driving practise. I was very aware of how behind we were and worried how we would get to Lampeter for Pisces. We had set ourselves the 21st of February as the date to set off, but I wondered how we'd ever get away or even get anywhere as it was already the 11th. Finally getting out of the field, Richard hit the gate and injured his leg quite badly.

The next day he was in a bad state of shock and it would be ages before he could even start to work on his waggon and I was sure he'd never be done before we were due to leave. Realising there was nothing more I could do in Glastonbury, I got a bus to Bristol, met Monica, and we hitched to London in two lifts. It felt good to get away and on the road. Mike had gone away too.

It was a strange and emotional few days. I stayed with some friends and felt awkward with them, yet met others who inspired me and clarified things. I went up to Norfolk, desperate to see my daughters, saw Saffron briefly, but Tiffany said it was too short notice. When I tried to see Saffron for longer she too said it was not enough notice. I was devastated and felt I was being denied access to them. I did see Kevin in London, though.

Monica said that when the Journey was over I could stay at hers for a few months if I wanted to. That was a really big thing for me as I had no idea what on earth I was going to do at the end: where we would go, where we would live? I had an exhibition about the Gipsy Switch organised for London in the October, so there wouldn't be much time at the end of the Journey to get to Wales, and I wondered how I would do it, and what I was going to do with Polly and the waggon.

I knew that back in Somerset there were so many decisions to be made, realising it was only I who was concerned about being in the right place at the right zodiac time. We should have been on the road already and I was seriously thinking I might have to complete the Journey on my own, and beginning to contemplate what that would involve in practical terms.

I got a coach back from London. It was a 'Rapide', where a hostess served drinks and food and there was a film on. Whatever next, I thought. There was England's beautiful countryside outside the windows and people were watching a film! It was strange to pass in a few hours through land which had just taken us weeks to travel.

At Bristol I was suddenly back in a different reality, as though I'd just come out of a black hole, felt great again, got a bus to Wells, phoned Phillipa and was taken to Wookey Hole where I had supper and went to bed in her basement.

She drove me to Glastonbury in the morning. It was really warm, felt like Spring and stayed light really late. I had the energy to move on and was preparing myself to do so; I certainly didn't intend to stay there much longer. It was wonderful to be back and Talie's eyes lit up in recognition and happiness as we got back into the waggon.

The next day was warm and glorious, really productive and I had a great sense of achievement. I opened the front of the waggon and moved my cases to a new position, making them more accessible. It felt like spring cleaning. Now the days were longer they seemed to go more slowly and it was possible to get more done. I had a talk with Richard, making it clear that I just had to get on the road and on with the Journey. He was still dithering about everything, but I think while I was there he pretty well made up his mind not to come.

I was flowing with the year. Fearing it might already be Pisces I wedged the Aquarius sign in a tree next to my waggon. It felt ok with the tree and that I should put it there rather than in Glastonbury itself. A few years later I was told the tree was growing round the sign, taking it into itself, so it was becoming part of the tree and there was now no way it could be removed.

The days were often misty to begin with, later becoming sunny, warm and light with the mist far off in the distance, and I was revelling in the growth of everything. I watched buds open on twigs, new shoots burst up from the bulbs beneath the ground and there was such strength in it all. I got so much done in those long days, sorting out the stuff in my cases, chucking out what I could and thinking I would ask Phillipa if I could leave a bag with her.

I called on Richard who had definitely decided not to continue on the journey. In the immediate it was a relief, but in the long-term I found it sad and depressing, though I could now perhaps be more sure and self-contained about what I was doing. I was afraid of what Mike would say when he returned, of Richard's reasons for not coming; and of his not coming. I was dreading the next part of the journey. We would have to go up the Mendip Hills (very high and steep) and on to find somewhere to cross the Severn. I hoped that once we got into Wales it would maybe be flatter, with mainly rivers and the coast to follow.

It was so welcome to see the lunar crescent in the clear sky once more, though the nights in the waggon were still filled with the energy of the dark moon, and I woke after weird nights of seemingly not sleeping, yet having strange, disturbed memories from my childhood.

Mike came back and we set off early to get the horses, met Richard, picked up Anna, one of the girls who was looking after them and walked them to a farm near Lower Rockes where a new farrier shod them. There was no problem with this one. Tiny and wiry, he used to be a jockey and was very different from one's image of a big muscular blacksmith. Richard didn't get Atlantis done, but got a lot of advice. His shoes would have to be specially made and be very expensive. His feet were the size of dinner plates and just then Richard couldn't even lift them up to clean them. Atlantis made Polly and even Rosie look quite tiny and Polly's feet looked almost ridiculous by comparison. A lot of people were telling Richard that Atlantis was too tall, that he should have something the size of Rosie (fourteen and a half hands) but a bit heavier. With a tall horse the angle of draught is wrong and it's as if the horse is pulling the waggon up off the ground all the time.

Once again I got a hint of the horrible stuff which was still being said about me behind my back. Richard had said quite nastily that although Polly may seem to be alright now, she'd be ruined by the end of the journey and her legs would get something called 'splints', so I asked this farrier and he had a good feel of her legs and said there was nothing wrong with them and anyway horses like her didn't get things like that because they were bred to the work. Only thoroughbreds got that sort of thing. After the journey was over I realised that all this talk was a manifestation of jealousy from people who weren't doing it themselves, but still wondered why they had turned against me specifically in such a relentless way.

Richard drove us to Glastonbury. Mike and I sat in the Avalot cafe and began a tentative discussion. I didn't know why it was so difficult to talk and say the things we needed to. We decided to carry on with the journey together, but that there must somehow be more communication between us.

Mike said he resented always having to get the big water containers full and get the hay etc, and that I never seemed to show any gratitude. I attempted to explain that I had a child to look after and so some things were physically impossible for me: on my own I would do things in a completely different way. I felt that when people expect you to fall over yourself with gratitude all the time, especially when you know they resent having to do things, it rather freezes your natural expression of thanks. I think I've learned to work better with that problem in the years since. I hope so.

He said he didn't mind showing me how to do things but wouldn't do them for me. I therefore had to work out how I was going to make roller brakes (to stop the waggon rolling back if the horse stops when going up-hill) and something called a whipple tree. I didn't know what that was or what it was for, possibly to harness two horses to one waggon to get up steep hills. I returned, wondering how on earth I was going to do all that, and why we hadn't discussed it at the beginning of our time there and made a start on it weeks before.

I was pretty depressed about everything, though I carried on doing a lot in the waggon. Mike went about as though he were silently fuming with anger, so I wondered again what on earth I was doing and why, as a woman, I seemed to have no strength to assert myself and was letting a young man the age of my eldest son have such power over me.

Preparing to leave Glastonbury: Jill, Polly, Taliesin with Lorye Keats Hopper and her son.

By now it was the 28th and I woke in the depths of despair, totally drained of everything. Talie was teething again with sore gums and was very restless. I just wanted to go off on my own with him, but hitched into Glastonbury and met Lorye after buying a lot of maps, and we went up Chalice Hill where I had never been before. She did a wonderful ceremony for healing a split pot, the split in ourselves and between each other and the hurt of the earth. I buried the pot and its healing contents under a great oak tree. Everything felt better and we had tea.

Back at the waggons Patrick showed us some routes to get us past Bristol. I was very tired with a bad cough. Talie was in pain with his teeth and cried every time I coughed. I went to bed because there didn't seem any point in doing anything else.

Chapter 16: Pisces, Lampeter.

March 1st. St. David's Day. I couldn't believe it was already March and we were still in Glastonbury when we should have been in Wales. I did a lot of last-minute chores, paid £2.25 to have my post sent on, sterilised the water containers and got rid of all my rubbish.

Phillipa and Anne came to say goodbye and she took a bag of my stuff to look after. By now most of my remaining possessions were in bin bags and boxes in other peoples' lofts right round the country. We brought the horses back to our field.

Next day was a long and protracted preparation to leave. People came to visit us, I visited a few people and Mike and Richard went off to get stuff. But at last we harnessed up and, though it was late, at least we set off. Young Anna, who had loved looking after the horses, was upset that we were going. She gave Mike and me presents, which was really moving. Mine was a little pottery mouse which I kept throughout the journey and many subsequent moves, including to and from the Hebrides. A few days previously Lorye had given Talie a little wooden Welsh dragon and me a tiny metal horse.

At last we were on the road again, just me and Mike after the long and powerful pause on the Isle of Avalon. It had rained on and off all day and we only got about 2 miles before it was 5.45pm and we stopped at a place Mike had contacted already. There was a paddock, but neither horse wanted to go in there and had to be forced. My waggon came to rest in a deep bog and I didn't know how I'd get out.

It was still raining in the morning and Polly was freaked out by the bog, not really trying to pull and at one point even rearing up in the shafts. 3 people came out of the house and with much pushing from them and Mike she managed to get the waggon out. She was in a nervy state afterwards though, and I felt she was fed up with me, however we set off and it was a good day. Talie had already gone to sleep and slept a long while before waking and amusing himself. Previously he'd lain or sat in his Moses basket behind the driving seat, but now he was getting more mobile and I hoped he wouldn't try to climb out.

Polly was annoyed with me. She kept nipping my arm and trying to knock my hand away when I was leading her. I could feel she hadn't the strength and fitness she'd had when we arrived in Glastonbury, and I hadn't seen much of her during those weeks when Anna and the other girl had been riding her. I wished we hadn't stopped in Glastonbury so long. After 7 miles I was getting tired myself, and half way up a quite gentle hill she refused to go any further and let the waggon roll back, fortunately turning it into a hedge. Mike got her going again by taking her across the road sideways. I was like jelly. How much was just Polly protesting and how much genuine weakness? I knew we had a really big hill to tackle the next day and wondered how it would be possible.

Quite early Mike asked a farmer if we could go in a field, so the horses had a nice dry one this time and we had the waggons on some hard standing. I went to a farm to ask if they could sell us some hay and the man didn't want much for it and brought it down on a tractor. I went for a walk with Talie beside a lovely river confluence full of tree and elemental spirits, feeling it was a place I'd love to sleep out one summer.

The weather became beautiful as we travelled on, although there was a cold wind. The fields were full of lambs and I was fascinated by trees, especially loving the pattern of hazel twigs as they grew, sort of flat and branching out at all angles with lots of catkins. We got past Wells without seeing any shops, tried to go the way Patrick had shown us, but found it very steep and narrow with Polly starting to freak again. Some passing people said the main road wasn't so steep, though it was longer, so we turned round and went that way. It was on and on and on and up and up and up. I went in front because it was better for Polly to make her own pace and keep her momentum going. There were places to rest, then on to another corner and more hill, on and on up into the Mendips.

Only towards the very end was she sweating and trembling a bit – what a valiant little lady! She had all her will back. The previous day I'd felt she'd lost confidence in herself, but now it was back and she almost did better than Rosie. In later years when I travelled that route by bus I marvelled at how we had ever done it. We stopped at the top where there was some nice hard standing, opened a gate and put the horses in a field. Nobody said anything. It was still quite early, but we couldn't ask them to do any more. Mike cycled back to Wells for some shopping and a man who knew Talley Valley stopped by and said he might come back with some paraffin. Richard and Juliet turned up, amazed at how far we had got, bringing something we'd had a blacksmith weld for us. A tiredness came over me which was a kind of pleasure. The moon was growing and getting very bright.

I woke more tired than I expected and it was hard to get going. My eyesight was sometimes really bad which made me feel distanced from the world. We were in dense cloud and the water from it dripped off the waggon. It had been a cold night with a heavy surface frost, but the wind had stilled. The man returned and brought me two cider bottles full of paraffin.

It was the most beautiful day with bright, clear sunshine and the horses were going fine as we travelled across moorland which reminded me of Derbyshire. I love being up high with a clear unrestricted view and a sense of wildness. The earth was very red here – a deep browny-red like roof tiles. We went on and got to a lake called Chewlake, went as far as we could before the verge alongside it ran out and stopped there. We could hear geese and ducks and everywhere the trees were covered in the purple and orange mists of ripening buds. It was idyllic.

We had come down off the Mendips on a long steep hill with the skid shoes braking us. Mine was by then only about half the thickness it had been to begin with and I doubted it would last the journey without having another base-plate welded on. Sometimes I carried Talie and he laughed a lot. He 'rode' me like a horse when he was on my back.

I went to a nearby house for water. Something on the gate rang a bell indoors. The people were lovely and asked me in, fascinated by what we were doing. They were very proud of their house, which they were gradually doing up, and gave us bantam eggs and apples.

Next morning I woke tired again to a brilliant white frost and wished time would stand still. The man from the house photographed us, saying travellers often stopped along that verge. Mike had now got a lot of literature, sponsorship forms and collecting tins from Oxfam and made a display about it on the side of his waggon. We went on to the Neolithic stone circles of Stanton Drew, which I'd never visited before. We took the horses up to a farm near the top and had a lunch break.

There was a cold wind as we walked round the stones. They felt strong and powerful and complete in their energy, reminding me of the Twelve Apostles near Dumfries, being solid and square and quite masculine. I got the impression it was a rather strange village: there was no parking anywhere, even though it must have had a lot of visitors, and the stone circles were closed on Sundays. I walked on to a kind of dolmen near a pub called the Druid's something or other, which seemed at odds with the churchy energy. It was a great place for a lunch break though!

As we travelled a big long hill on a main road, an RSPCA officer escorted us and stopped the traffic so we could make an illegal right turn onto a side road. We nearly got to Keynsham and stopped on a rather dangerous corner, but the owner of a plot next to it and a farm down the road insisted on us moving for our own safety. He helped push the waggons and we got the horses away from the road. Later he came and gave us hay and said we could return if ever we wanted to. We were now skirting round Bristol, so there was a lot of traffic.

That evening I found Talie had cut another tooth which explained why he'd been a bit grisly.

March 7th was a dull, damp, grey, tiring day with not such a cold wind and, when walking, I got very hot. I hadn't washed for days and felt smelly and sweaty and was longing to stop by a good water supply to wash myself and my hair and some clothes – and to clean the harness. Rosie was going at quite a pace and I could feel Polly getting tired and dreaded all the hills we still seemed to be encountering. We had a lunch stop, though knowing we had to go on again, I wasn't relaxed enough to eat. We must have done 10-11 miles in the end and it seemed too much for all of us. We were now looking for a place we could stop and have a day off.

It was dusk when we stopped. We had passed some wonderful stopping places, but where we eventually pulled up was rather grotty for the horses and very muddy. I didn't have the energy to cook and worried again that I wasn't eating enough or having green vegetables. The land we'd passed through had largely been grazing land, but the last bit was agricultural. There were troughs around and we sometimes got water from them, but only if they had a supply flowing into them.

It had been full moon and gently this one had come upon us, the light growing each night and becoming unimaginably bright. When I blew out the candle it was still light in the waggon and I could feel the strength of the moon flooding into me, yet at the same time I felt exposed, as though I were out in that light, naked on the land. Now it was waning and I dreaded the coming of the darkness of no moon, of not being able to see in the night. It was a strange fear, very primal, a lack of comfort turning me in on my self.

I woke most mornings to lie in the light for a while before getting up. Talie was getting into kneeling positions a lot and wasn't content to stay sitting. He did, however, spend a lot of time with his Fisher Price Activity Centre, a present he'd had for Christmas. It had lots of things to turn, twist, push and roll and was good for learning all sorts of dexterity skills. He played with it very seriously as though it was his 'work'. Mike fixed his roller brake. Some of the hair was coming off Polly's shoulders and she was a bit scabby. I willed her not to get sore shoulders, for then we would have to stop for two weeks to heal them and we just couldn't. That day we only went a few miles and stopped on a verge near a corner where there was a ditch and a kerb, so I just pulled off where I could. It was quite near the road and lorries kept speeding past, making the bender sway violently. It was nice to pause though, and the weather was reasonable for a while. There was a trough, so I did a bit of washing, washed my hair – and me, and yearned to sleep and sleep and sleep. Sometimes I could hear skylarks singing and wondered why Talie had to sit in the waggon most days listening to the sound of passing traffic instead of being in fields with the sound of birds.

I longed to be in Wales; this haul up round the Severn was a drag and we were in a strange part of the world where everything seemed nondescript. Mike said it was very foggy and wet outside.

Thinking about my tiredness, I wondered if it was my will which was exhausted, working so hard to keep everything alright, make everything work; that it was my will which kept us safe and protected us, my will which willed Polly up and down hills. I wondered why I could not draw strength from the earth, trust, and just let it be, but felt I couldn't let go, had to hold it all together in the moment, for if I didn't, everything would just disintegrate. It was how I had felt flying to Australia; that only my will kept the plane in the air, and that if I relaxed it would crash.

We had our day off. Early on a lot of lorries sped by, rocking the waggon violently, but it eased as the day wore on. I felt good when the sun came out, the fog lifted and there was a cool wind. I opened the front but felt I'd rather sit inside and watch everything from there than be outside in the carbon monoxide fumes. We were under a flight-path from Bristol airport and could hear the distant sound of the M5. The verges were littered with bottles and it was quite depressing.

I did more washing, being amazed at what you can do with a single bucket of water. How much we waste living in houses. I always kept some clean tap water for Talie's food. I oiled the harness and Mike went twice to Thornbury and got himself a gas cylinder. Talie and I went for a walk up the road to a common which he loved, looking at the colours of the buds getting fatter on the trees and listening to the birds. There were a lot of newly-laid hedges around, as though people were doing it again after a long time. It was a gorgeous sunset and I marvelled at what a beautiful country Britain is.

March 10th. It seemed all set for a lovely day, getting really hot quite early, but with a cool breeze, and I was almost down to just a tee-shirt. We got off at a reasonable time and both horses seemed to have lots of energy, especially Rosie, who went charging up hills, though Polly got a bit sweaty and puffed, but kept up. I was quite tired after 7 miles but wanted to carry on for if we stopped it was hard to get going again. Mike met a female friend of his going the other way in a caravan. We crossed the M5 (on a bridge) having crossed the M4 a few days before. We must have done a good 10 miles, turned off the A38 and came up a road looking for a place to stop. We saw a good patch on the other side of the road and turned round onto it. As we did so, both of Mike's shafts snapped! I parked mine, tethered the horses and we pushed Mike's waggon round with help from a man in the house opposite. Oddly, I

The waggon parked up in the snow at the end of Kevin Drapers track.

didn't feel at all concerned and we wondered whether we could get the shafts off Richard's waggon.

There was a lot of hair on Polly's collar and when I looked at her shoulders I found there were two bald patches on them and one was almost a sore and I had to face the fact that she couldn't wear that collar again for a couple of weeks. It was a horrible shock, but I had an odd sense of relief as well. The man in the house gave Mike a lift to a place where two friends of ours – Paul and Lizzie – were parked up. They had been planning to leave the next day, but said they'd come to visit. They were living as real travellers, in a caravan, doing scrap metal and with their horses in a box. They weren't into lending us a horse, though I half-wondered whether he might sell me one, but would lend Mike some shafts.

We reckoned I would have to have Atlantis pull my waggon, which I wasn't at all happy with. Otherwise I would have to get it transported to Lampeter and walk with Polly and my rucksack and Ros's tent. Strangely I felt less anxious and depressed than I had for ages. Faced with an actual crisis I tend to rise to the occasion and be fired up to solve the problem.

Next day Talie and I had a lovely walk into Berkeley, which was a sleepy little town with lots of useful things in it and I sat and ate chips on a seat, feeling as though it was a summer's day from my childhood or even a century ago and was just happy in the moment. Carrying Talie on my back meant I had to carry the shopping bags in my hands and they were very heavy. I can carry enormous weights on my back, but not in my hands. I got conflicting advice on the distances of various ways back and walked about a mile and a half with my hands in agony before one of the noisy lorries gave me a lift.

Mike soon returned from Nailsworth with Paul's mum and dad and the shafts. He and I talked and agreed we shouldn't have to cope with Atlantis. He already had lots of opportunities to do performances round Horsely and Stroud, but I had no motivation to do stuff there when we should be in Lampeter. We decided to somehow get the waggon over to West Wales so I'd be there for Pisces, then I'd come back, meet up with Mike and walk with Polly. It was a relief to have made a decision and the only way I could be in the right place for Pisces.

I talked to a local farmer who 'knew everyone', including people with low loaders, but he reckoned it would cost £100. I said I would see him next day and went to the phone on Mike's bike. The night was dark and my hands froze. I phoned a woman in Lampeter, and a man called Kevin Draper in Pumpsaint. She was hopeful of finding us a place to perform and he said I could put my waggon at his place and then move it on when the horses arrived. I went to bed hoping some sort of lorry or trailer which wasn't too expensive would turn up.

After another freezing night it was again a warm day and I went to see a scrap-metal dealer, but no joy there. He operated on trade plates carrying 'disabled vehicles'. I tried to persuade him that my waggon was disabled but he wasn't having any. He couldn't think of anyone non-haulage, so I walked down to a garage but they weren't much help either. I bought loads of chocolate, Wagon Wheels, and Walkers crisps, and ate the lot.

Back at the waggon I despaired a bit, and Mike went off to phone about his gigs, but the woman he was phoning had left. He went again later and the back wheel of his bike collapsed. I waited until 7 for the farmer who wasn't there either: I had to watch for the lights coming on in his stable when he went to feed his horses. I started to cook supper but gave up and ate what I'd cooked so far, felt horrendously tired and went to bed.

Next morning I listened for the sound of animals being fed and went to see the farmer: no joy; his friend with transport would charge £300. My mind raced and I sat working out all possible computations, then Mike came in and we realised that unless we could get transport from the people Paul and Lizzie were parked up with, we'd have to stay where we were until Polly was better.

As soon as we knew, I'd go off to Lampeter, so I was there for Pisces, while Mike did a gig here, then I'd get back in time to set off again with the horses.

We moved the waggons into a field as Mike didn't feel secure by the roadside, being really afraid of gangs of blokes setting on us and beating us up. It was interesting how we had such different fears. I felt content in the field, not thinking about the future. We were next to race-horses, cows, sheep and birds.

Later Mike and I talked about the Taliesin story and the possibility of performing it at Lampeter when we finally got there. I wasn't getting much sleep as I seemed to lie down, be interrupted from a couple of dreams and then it was dawn and I'd had no rest.

In a cold wind next day I set off for Berkeley and a woman gave me a lift for the last mile. I visited a man who made and repaired harness and was extremely helpful, giving me a piece of leather to reinforce my trace and even trimming it for me and saying we could use his workspace if we needed to. I had fish and chips again sitting on the wooden seat and Talie sat on it too. I suddenly fancied a weird cake thing which seemed to be made of layers of fat, flour, sugar and currants. It was very doughy and un-risen and I wondered if I had been meant to cook it. I so enjoyed sitting there with my little son, feeling happy even in the cold wind and reading in the chip paper about Princess Margaret in Mustique.

When I was nearly back at the waggon a lorry carrying broken cars came by and I thought it was the local scrap man. It stopped and I wondered if he'd had second thoughts, but a woman got out and I realised it was Lizzie – with Paul. They stopped by for tea and cream cakes and I explained my problem. Paul then said he would take me to Lampeter the next day for £30 and a drink!

After they left I was in a great state of excitement, thinking the Universe worked in mysterious ways. I made some phone calls. I could take the waggon to Kevin Draper's, though he didn't know how I'd get it up their steep track. Paul would come at 7am, and I hoped the waggon would go on his truck and wouldn't fall to bits en route. Walking back from the phone the sky was extraordinary – some parts blue and white and sunny with lots of interesting colours, but other areas had dark clouds and moving veils of grey hanging from them and spirals of white like whirlwinds.

I walked round the magical field we were in, which had huge fruit trees, some bearing bunches of mistletoe. It felt like a privilege to have had time there and I gave thanks for it.

March 15th – the Ides of March! Paul came at 7, backed the lorry into the field, tied ropes onto the waggon's 4 axles from his hydraulic crane and lifted it onto the lorry. All the hazel benders compressed but nothing seemed to break. He had great fun mocking my anxiety and that broke the tension because obviously there had been risks. He only tied the front and back of the waggon and the four wheels by rope, not a chain in sight, and he and his mate joked about the wonders you can do with baler twine.

And after all that – we went over the Severn Bridge. I was terrified, but everything was fine. We called in to Chepstow where they were now stopped, saw Lizzie and set off with his mate Carl in another truck, as they were hoping to pick up some scrap to make the journey worthwhile. Through the beautiful Welsh countryside we travelled and I thought what a wonderful journey Mike would have. The plan now was, that if his woman friend came back to help him, he would travel with Polly in tow, so I wouldn't have to go back.

Somewhere along the way I lost the candlewick bedspread which had hung at the front of the waggon all winter long, being my windproof door, but didn't seem to have lost much else. Some of the plastic tarp came unstapled, but Paul spotted it and tied it underneath. We eventually reached Kevin Draper's place near Lampeter and drove the waggon up their track a little way, but could go no further; then they used Carl's ramps to get the waggon down – at a 45 degree angle. I walked up the track while they did it and couldn't watch. Kevin said the wheels bent, but I didn't understand what that meant. I seemed to be in a relatively safe spot, though Kevin did frighten me with comments about vandalism.

I gave Paul £40 and he was happy with that, and I hoped they got some scrap on their way back. I felt spaced out from going so quickly from one reality to another; from England, over the Severn and right across to West Wales. When I sorted the waggon out I couldn't see much damage, except the strings tying the hazel which had come loose, and of course the bedspread; but Kevin's wife Chris kindly gave me some curtains to replace that. I was astonished how it had survived the journey.

Kevin and Chris were very good to me. I had been put in touch with Kevin, a human dynamo, because he knew a lot about the Pumpsaint terrestrial zodiac. We talked for ages about the journey and journeying in general as they were very excited by it. Sometimes it was good to talk with people who actually understood what we were doing. I had supper in their house, and went back to the waggon for the night.

I was hoping we would find somewhere a bit more permanent to park up in the following few days, somewhere the others could be as well when they arrived. A woman called Helene Hess had found one place, but it was over the other side of a mountain. I thought we might have to go on Llangybi Common, which had been 'reclaimed' and lived on for some time. There was a possible performance place, but it wasn't in Lampeter itself.

So, my tiny Taliesin and I were back in Wales. I felt somewhat insecure, but happy to sleep in my dear waggon after all it had been through. It was really cosy and warm and though there was more snow and a gusty wind it was in a reasonably sheltered place. I hoped Mike would make it ok.

It snowed a lot in the night and I woke to an incredibly beautiful world of white. The snow was dry and the wind blew it up into great whirlwinds with the fields below slowly appearing like shadows as the snow was blown off them.

Kevin took me into Lampeter, which seemed a long way from his house (Ffarmers). We went to see the place where we could perform and it seemed silly not to be parked up near it. We looked at Llangybi Common, but I was worried about security there, and then to a place which was up a mountain and down a steep, narrow, rough track and miles from the performance place.

Later I sat with the setting sun streaming into the waggon, the snow now all gone. Up at the house I got a phone call from Monica and arranged to spend the Equinox with her. As I returned there was a new little lamb with a fresh umbilical cord hanging down calling for its mother. We listened to the bleating of the tiny new lambs, and to the birds, and then it snowed again, this time softer and wetter. Grey clouds moved along the valleys and I knew I'd done the right thing in getting there while it was still Pisces and that everything would work out. The most amazing thing was that Kevin was a Pisces.

We woke to the rising sun and what sounded like the croaking of a frog. There was no traffic noise, only the occasional scream of a low-flying jet. My 'roof' had become flat and collected puddles of melting snow which dripped through. It was Mother's Day and here I was a mother again with my tiny boy. I wanted to be in touch with my three other children, but Kevin and Chris were doing so much for me I didn't feel I could ask to use their phone for personal reasons. They had 3 children and Talie enjoyed being with them and having a wonderful time in their baby bouncer. It was a glorious afternoon, the hills looking like soft, rounded flesh; the earth like a living body, so alive, so comforting, so protective, that I wanted to nestle into her and thought maybe I should live there a while when the journey was over. It felt more like home than East Anglia.

We went to see the performance place – Barn on the Farm in Bwlchwernen Fawr, Llwynygroes. It was indeed a barn in the courtyard of a farm with a green square outside. The people said that for the period we were working there we could stay with the waggons and horses, so I thought maybe it would be ok on the Common before then moving to the Barn, though I'd need a tow. I doubted Polly would be able to do it when she arrived after such a long time not working. Slowly things were falling into place.

Piscean Kevin took us to a wonderful site- a large lake with several islands in the middle. He stood on a narrow bit of unstable bank with low overhanging trees, took my wooden Pisces zodiac sign and without much room to move his arm back threw it out into the water. Something – was it wind or some other force – picked it up and carried it and it flew and flew and flew right out to one of those islands where it finally came to rest. It felt like magic. To me the island was a golden and green Spring maiden.

We visited a lovely couple who lived in the centre of the Pumpsaint zodiac to see if I could stay there. They were a bit dubious, but said I could if I got desperate. Kevin had sorted out a device which meant he could tow the waggon up his track to be near their house, as it would be more secure there. It also meant he'd be able to tow me to the Common, as I'd have to get there before Mike arrived. The Barn people said the Common people often worked for them.

We moved the waggon up to the house and I felt happier leaving it there while I went off to Monica's. The plan was that I would return on the 21st and babysit for them while they went out; and the following day I set off to hitch to Fishguard. It took an hour and a half but got easier after Newcastle Emlyn. From there I got to the cottage where Monica was living with her partner Keith Motherson and her son Leif.

March 20th. Spring Equinox. They now had a car, as Monica was learning to drive. We headed off for St. Davids, she driving for a bit before I took over. We went up a cliff searching for somewhere we could look down on a cave and rock which Monica wanted to draw. Up we climbed in a near-raging wind which was coming off the sea and knocked us over twice. We climbed high along the edge of the towering cliff where any fall or unsureness of footing would have been disastrous. Sometimes the icy wind lashed sideways and I shielded Talie from it in my arms as it stung needles into our faces. What an Equinox! We looked down from the high cliff to the raging sea crashing on the rocks beneath, huddling for a moment in a little dip, then went to see the cave. Monica sat there and I had no idea how she could draw in that wind and rain. It was a dark slit of a cave with a huge troll-like rock woman hunched before it, and is a vision still etched into my memory.

The wind was unmerciful and Talie's cheeks began to turn blue, so I returned to the dip and huddled with him until Monica had done, when we returned by a slightly less dangerous path. At first the car wouldn't start, but a party of

239

geology students on a field trip gave us a push and we drove to a bay we had previously visited when Talie was 4 days old. There was now snow in the rain and wind and it felt like a purging, a clearing out, a stark blowing away of everything: I hoped just the negative. Swedish Monica, who thrived in such weather, said it would blow away a few cobwebs.

On the beach I found a place of stillness behind a great rock. In the grey sand I drew a cross with a circle round it – a symbol of the Universe and the four directions, which is now echoed on Hot Cross Buns. I marked the centre with gorse which is the Spring Equinox tree in the Beth-Luis-Nion calendar. The West was to the sea, marked with a stone; the East connected me to those in East Anglia, so I marked it with a flint I had carried in my pocket all the way from Norfolk, making the link East to West as the sun rose and set on that Equinox day. In the North I placed a stone from where we were and in the South one of the quandong stones from the tucker the aborigines had given me from behind the house at Uluru. I also had a flint from Dunwich in Suffolk where we had celebrated the previous year's Equinox on the beach – so the circle was also my past year. Circles, many circles in the one. And I encircled the whole with my Ininti beads.

We sat with it a while making the connections – East to West, North to South, and the still centre. At that time I knew we had the will and the power to create peace and harmony in this tortured world–if we will. I had dreamt of watching the sun set into the sea, but there was no chance on this wild day. I photographed the circle and Lynne and I used the image for our exhibition poster in the October of that year.

I walked round the setting three times sunwise and three times moonwise. Monica did her own meditation, placed her sheela-na-gig talisman in the centre and we sang "We all come from the Goddess...". We felt the sun, even without seeing it as everything grew brighter and very still.
I left the gorse, all but one bud; I left the flints; I left the quandong stone; I took the stone from the West and the stone from the North and one for the year and put them in my pocket. The tide was coming in and nearly cut us off and the snow fell thick and fast all night. Back at their house the electricity failed and we sat by candlelight.

I phoned the Drapers who said there was so much snow they couldn't get down the track. This meant they weren't going out and didn't need me to babysit, so I said I wouldn't go back just then but to East Anglia for a few days. Monica, her friend Val, and I hitched to Nevern where there is a yew tree which bleeds sap which looks like menstrual blood. It was peaceful in the churchyard where a completely rotten tree had fallen in the Equinox gale. It lay like a universe unto itself – covered in life: ivy, lichen, black fungus, insects, and filled me with wonder. Later a man sawed it with a chain-saw, and inside me something

240

screamed. The stillness which had been broken only by the great black rooks circling the trees above was now rent by this murderous sound. The tree was rotten and should have been left to moulder back into the earth like the bodies in the graves. The violence of the chainsaw deeply upset me – it was like sawing limbs from the dead. A chainsaw massacre! I walked with Val to seek the beautiful red/pink flowers of some trees which I thought were Scots Pine. They had triple-spiral cones.

The yew trees were like great old hags. All I could see that day were the spirits, the beings of trees; young beings within the old. The flow from the bleeding yew was very slight just then: a stickiness in the opening, like a first menstruation.

Gently the dark moon turned.

We set off to walk to Newport but a woman gave us a lift, got a bus to Fishguard, had chips and tea, and went to a pub where men were sitting around singing and playing music like something from long ago, from some old farming community. Back at Monica's I had a bath.

Next day Keith Motherson gave me a lift to the main road and I hitched to London in six and a quarter hours, then got a coach to Norwich. I was able to go to Brentwood Farm and spend a lovely evening with Tiffany and Saffron. They'd bought me a huge box of chocolates for Mother's Day. I was so happy and it made up for the hurt I'd felt before in not seeing them.

Going to a camping shop in Norwich I bought a good tent. It weighed 3lbs 12oz and was supposed to stand up to strong winds. (It did and I'm still using it.) I also bought a down sleeping-bag and the man showed me how to put the tent up. It should have come to £214.45, but as the tent had been on display in the shop the man charged me £190. It seemed like a good investment and having them gave me a sense of security, as I could carry everything and go off and survive on my own. Talie was 9 months old by then but swears to this day that he can remember this whole event really clearly.

I had my money in an account which paid interest monthly (the rate was 9.5% then) into my current account and this is pretty much what I lived on. Returning to London we got a coach which again had videos, refreshments and a hostess. Back in Wales, Aida Birch met me and took me to her house in Neath for the night. I had another bath, washed my hair and did some washing. Aida gave me a copy of the Mabinogion then drove me back to Ffarmers.

I sorted the waggon out, including some stuff which I was going to leave at Monica's. Chris washed more of my stuff, including a blanket, I babysat for them and Talie had his 6th tooth.

The next day Kevin was going to tow me to Llangybi Common. I woke feeling very nervous, not so much of the tow as of being on the common. I hadn't heard from Mike, didn't know where he was, and hadn't been able to discuss it with him. I had no idea what frame of mind he would be in when he arrived or who he would have encountered en route.

I talked with Kevin about what might happen next on our journey. He and Chris had been inspired by it and by my writings of previous journeys and had dreams of what they would do in the future.

They too wanted to travel with horse and waggon and he said they would buy my trolley when the journey was over. I suggested that, as part of the deal, they could meet me wherever I ended up, collect the waggon and take my stuff to Monica's, where it seemed I would initially stay. I didn't know what to do with Polly, but was thinking I might journey with her as a pack-horse.

The tow was fine. I'd found a blacksmith and had an extra bottom put on the skid shoe. It was heavy but would last longer. Reaching the Common I felt a bit freaked out, the rain and wind not helping. With Kevin's van we could only pull the waggon on to the edge of the common and I wondered how I was going to get off. We knocked at a few caravans but the people didn't seem very friendly, then a traveller woman told us (nicely) not to park up near her. They were already asking if we had anything to sell and I was feeling uncomfortable and that I couldn't handle it there. I could have coped with stopping a couple of nights if I'd been with Mike and the horses, but not on my own. I didn't feel I'd be able to go off and leave the waggon, even to post a letter or make a phone call. I chickened out.

We went up to Bwlchwernan and I asked if I could stay there and they agreed, though it took a lot of manoevering to get the waggon into a spot which was sheltered from the wind. The people there offered all their facilities and I was extremely happy, feeling again that Talie was protecting me and making everything turn out right.

When I re-read the Taliesin story in preparation for devising our forthcoming show, I was fascinated by the magic of it. Talie himself was no longer content to play alone, being frustrated and bored by the space in the waggon. When I put him on a floor he was beginning to crawl.

I phoned the Secretarial Agency and heard that Mike had called a couple of days before saying he was having a lot of trouble with his waggon and not making the progress he anticipated. I then phoned Richard, who needed to decide whether to do some harrowing with Atlantis or come to us. I tried to persuade him to come to us.

April 1st. The wind and rain continued and everything was damp inside as well as out, so created a kind of rain-forest condensation cycle and I dreaded discovering how wet the floor must be getting. I sat in the Barn for a while, getting the feel of the space. Talie seemed quite frightened by it and I wondered whether he could see things I couldn't. Someone then took me into Lampeter, which I grew to like, and I got the leaflets which Kevin had designed photocopied and put a few of them up, even though there was still just me there and no show yet. It was too wet to pick up some materials for a mask-making workshop we were scheduled to do in a few days' time and I hoped some masks would come out of it to be part of the show. In the time of preparation before the journey we had been taught by a super mask-maker, but I'd been so heavily pregnant I hadn't taken much of it in – and now it looked as if I might have to run a mask-making workshop on my own. Perhaps I'd even have to do the performance on my own!

The wind grew even wilder, blowing onto the 'flat' side of the waggon. It was like serpents of the air raging wild; strong and powerful snakes with long, twisting, muscular bodies: all force and pure energy. At first there would be stillness, then the sound of wind coming from far off, nearer and nearer, faster and faster, roaring through the trees, and then upon us, whipping, lashing, roaring, pushing us with its power and fury, this way, that way – wild, coiling, twisting, raging air. Then it would pass, its sound roaring back through the trees. I'd catch my breath and relax a little and then would come another one; all over the air they came. I felt we had nothing to withstand them should they choose to destroy us, but they just displayed their power so we shouldn't forget how puny we are – and in the face of nature, so is all we create. I thought of men at sea, tossed like toys and blown by these serpents of the air. "Peace" I wished the serpents, wondering whether they came from the wildness of our own ragings, our uncontrollable and unfocussed energies. Peace, wind, peace.

The very air was wet. Even when the wind blew and it wasn't raining, the air was a damp cloud. A woman who had promised to bring boxes for the mask-making came by, but had forgotten them.

The local shop had no cardboard boxes, saying everything came in blister packs nowadays. I phoned the secretarial agency again, but they'd had no further word from Mike. They seemed rather off- hand – due no doubt to Richard not having paid their bill.

The long light evenings were still strange to me as I sat late with the front of the waggon half open. Another wind blew up, seeming to come from all directions. I thought what a good old structure my waggon was and how, in the previous few weeks, I had gained an enormous respect for hazel, and that maybe I'd done it a great injustice in thinking it might snap under the force of the wind.

Rain, rain rain, pouring in everywhere – and then Richard came! We exchanged so much news. He brought a letter from Mandy, who had heard I was going to be travelling with Atlantis and wanted to buy Polly. This made me feel very strange. Kevin wanted to buy the waggon, now Mandy wanted Polly...maybe what I did next was all being decided for me.

The next day we rushed into Lampeter, rushed back late and didn't really know how to start the workshop. The children who came were quite small but somehow we managed to make some really nice masks and in the end it was all quite successful, however we had a long way to go before we had a show. Richard slept in a loft above the theatre workshop.

I could sense the full moon and felt meditative anyway so next day we sat in the loft with a candle in Phillipa's goddess candle-holder, incense and a sprig of blossom. I let what would come to me. At first I was with a circle of women and could feel hands clasping my wrists in a tight grip, then the energy of the moon flowed down into me and the strength of the earth flowed up. I did some Tibetan purification practices and felt negativity clear out of me, the land being purified as well. We discussed the approaching performance, trying to understand the symbolism of the story and how we could manifest it.

Next morning we had a lift to Lampeter and in another mad rush bought materials for making props for the show including some bamboo canes which turned out to be riddled with woodworm. The weather at last was clearing, with blue sky and a dry wind. The sun was hot and there was a rainbow later.

Back at the Barn we slowly got on with making the shape-shifting animals. We created cut-out shapes of birds and fish with long tissue tails which we fixed onto the poles and they did the most amazing things when they were whirled around. Each shape-shift represented an Element so we laid them around a circle in the appropriate places. It took ages, but the light evenings meant we went on and on and didn't realise how late it was.

Then Mike came! With his friend and his waggon and both horses. He was very, very tired. The tractor towed them up the hill and he put his waggon in a field. He'd had a horrendous time. It had flooded with rain the whole time and his waggon was completely saturated. The roads had been incredibly busy and twice they'd nearly had a serious accident. Many hills had almost proved too much for Rosie, who seemed to be getting 'hill-shocked'. Polly had been awful, not wanting to go behind Mike's waggon and breaking everything they tied her on with, and having in the end to be led by his friend, and still being awful. They were really sick of her, and indeed with everything. He didn't want to go on any further with the journey.

The horses went in a field near my waggon, with a tiny Shetland pony. Just walking a short way with Polly made my heart sing. I had forgotten the power of what I felt being with her; something which really had remained just potential, and which the circumstances of the journey had prevented from allowing to fully develop, and now probably never would. I realised I loved her in a very profound way. She was a female, a horse, a fine spirit, a being who I respected enormously.

I still didn't know what my future would hold, even what would happen the following Tuesday when we were due to leave. It was all going round and round in my head. I didn't know how we'd get the show together – but I knew we would.

It was slow getting going, with Mike tired and ill, and there was a funny atmosphere all day. I knew once again they were talking about me behind my back and I was sick of it.

And somehow, sometime in the evening, I made my decision. It was quite sudden and not like making a decision; it was just that there was no longer a decision to be made. A whole massive weight was lifted from me and I felt clear and light and there was no longer any confusion. Mike made yet another nasty remark and it cut through everything like a knife. It cut any doubts I had been hanging onto and my path was clear.

From that point on, Talie and I would travel alone. We would travel as we could to catch up with the time of the zodiac, and then we would walk. I lay a long while that night with the presence of a whole new life ahead of me.

PART 3: WALKING

Chapter 17: Aries, Anglesey.

Monday April 8th 1985. It was Richard's birthday and now Aries, but we were still physically in Pisces. Somehow we would have to get to Anglesey, even if briefly.

This was the day of the Taliesin performance. After giving Richard a horse-brass of a man in a coracle we had our final run-through. We laid out our 'set' - with a paraffin stove and saucepan for Cerridwen's cauldron. The straw bales were piled up at one end of the room so the audience sat on them in tiers, making it a good performance space. Around 3.30 Monica, Keith Motherson and Leif turned up, then a load more audience, so we had a really good crowd.

The story very briefly is that the goddess Cerridwen has 3 children – a handsome son, a beautiful daughter and a very ugly son – Afagddu. To make up for Afagddu's faults Cerridwen sets about brewing a potion in her cauldron, which when done would contain three special drops to make him a wise poet full of insight. She collected all the right herbs at the right times of year and phases of moon and began the brew, which had to be stirred for a year and a day before it would be ready.

She chose a young boy, Gwion, to carry out this task. On the last day, as he was stirring – perhaps a bit excitedly – a dollop of the brew splashed onto his hand, burning him, so he put his hand in his mouth to cool it. Of course, instantly, he received the three drops which had been intended for Afagddu and in a moment had all wisdom, insight and vision. They also enabled him to see that Cerridwen knew it was he who had received them and he raced away as she began to chase him.

He now had magic powers, so changed himself into a hare, but Cerridwen changed herself into a greyhound. Gwion plunged into a river, becoming a fish, but Cerridwen became an otter-bitch. Gwion leaped a waterfall and changed into a crow but Cerridwen followed him as a hawk. Just as she was about to catch him he fell onto a winnowing-floor and became a tiny grain of wheat, but Cerridwen as a red-crested black hen gobbled him up. Immediately she became a woman again and returned home, now pregnant with Gwion, carrying him for 9 months. When she gave birth he was so beautiful she couldn't bear to kill him, as had been her intent, so put him in a leather bag and threw him into the sea. Not far away was a weir owned by Gwyddno. He had one son, Elphin,

246

The Draper family on the trolley, now stripped of its blue tarpaulin and all my possessions - no longer our home

who, although he was good and honest, never had any luck. Every May Eve a huge haul of salmon came to the weir and this year Gwyddno gave Elphin one chance to prove his luck was not all bad; but that night no fish came and all Elphin caught was the leather bag. When he opened it, out came the beautiful boy with a shining forehead. "Look – 'Radiant Brow'" said Elphin, and in Welsh this is 'Taliesin' and from that moment was how he was known.

He took the child back to his father, crying at his lack of luck with the fish, but the child spoke a wonderful poem, as he was now the greatest of poets. "What are you?" asked Elphin, "A man or a spirit?", and Taliesin replied with more verse. There followed many adventures, Taliesin proving himself more valuable than any fish, for after defeating other great poets and enabling Elphin to win a race on an old nag, Elphin and his wife gained a crock of gold which never grew empty.

Our performance was just the right balance between the simple essence of the story, some magic, and a presentation perfect for the children in the audience. Talie (with a star on his forehead and dressed in a sparkling pointy hat and white scarf the Drapers had given him) gave an absolutely brilliant performance. When he was asked whether he were man or spirit he gave the dirtiest laugh imaginable and the audience fell about.

Afterwards I spoke to Monica, explaining what was now happening and asking whether Kevin Draper and I could take the contents of my waggon to her place, and felt things were starting to get arranged. I still hadn't been able to contact Mandy about Polly, but trusted that was going to work out as well. We had a nice evening in the loft, relaxed after the show, having proved we were a good working team - now we were no longer travelling together.

The next day was sunny and my waggon was towed back to the Drapers'. With mixed feelings I realised it would be my last journey with it. At last I spoke to Mandy and heard she was sorting out how to get Polly back to East Anglia. I started to dismantle the bender from the trolley: my home of the previous few months ceasing to exist; then had a great surprise – Helen, who had been looking after Daisy in Suffolk, turned up with her daughter Kate. Daisy and Helen had given each other enormous confidence – the horse with laminitis and the woman with an artificial leg. She wanted to buy Daisy! I was amazed at how so many things were just falling into place.

It was difficult to remember Helen's leg, as she walked and drove her car quite normally. I explained how we needed to visit Anglesey while it was still Aries, and persuaded her to drive us up there with Aries Richard.

April 11th. We set off North, pausing at Bedd Taliesin, the burial place of the famous bard. This is an ancient dolmen/quoit in a powerful area overlooking the sea - a place frequented by the bard, full of his wisdom, knowledge, inspiration and magic. The child Talie sat on the stone, his eyes watering in the wind and I wondered who Taliesin had been. Was it one man in one lifetime or many; was it a title, as Merlin might have been; was it one soul travelling through many incarnations; or a series of lineage bearers? It felt like a place where he had sat, gazing out over the water with a hill behind him; someone who was the land, the hill, the sea, the wind and the rain, the clouds and the storms, the sun and the colours of the sunset. Someone who was the east, the south, the west and the north – and the still centre, the Cauldron of Inspiration; who was the air, the fire, the water and the earth; who knew all things and was all things. And now this Taliesin babe was here, he who challenged my fears and conjured up all the help we ever needed.

We stayed overnight with Justin and Lucy from the Walk For Life. Their son Joel was similar in age to Talie and it was lovely to see them together. We continued our drive up west Wales; a wild ride after the pace of horses. It was green and wet and full of lambs as we sped past huge mountains, torrential streams, vegetation of vibrant red and orange and powerful sunsets. Over the bridge we went to Mon, the Mother. It was wet and cold with an icy wind which later turned dry, blowing the sand off the beach. It was strong and powerful, with nothing gentle about it, and I felt small and weak, realising how much I still had to prepare before tackling the rest of the Journey on my own. Anglesey reminded me of the Isle of Lewis – up there hundreds of miles to the north.

We first visited Bryn Celli Ddu (The Mound in the Dark Grove), an ancient chambered cairn, so skilfully built, as are all these Neolithic structures. It enclosed a great stone pillar, which reminded me of the slab in '2001 A Space Odyssey'. I didn't connect with the place as I had hoped, maybe still being too rushed from the car-ride, and couldn't quite 'place' it in my internal map of the land. Kate said poems came into her head, the words of which were totally appropriate, but couldn't be remembered when she came outside. Richard felt the pillar drawing energy down and sending it up, as opposed to that of a circle which spins round. I had the concept of a three-dimensional symbol like a cup-and-ring mark or Aboriginal carving, wondering whether the energies acted in the horizontal and vertical at the same time.

We went on to Barclodiad y Gawres (The Giantess's Apronful), another chambered cairn carved inside with zigzags and other Neolithic patterns, and I found this one extremely potent. Outside the wind was wild, but inside there was calm and silence and strength. I felt exhilarated, as though I were inside a great nurturing, maternal being, her arms curved round to enclose us in the still darkness – the strength in death which one would enter and never leave. Outside the nearby grass was soft and I longed to have it for a bed, but we slept at a camp-site after supper in the 'Wayside Cafe', this being our first cosy night in the new tent. Richard helped me put it up and I hoped I'd be able to do it on my own in future.

Next day we returned to Barclodiad y Gawres, which is poised on an edge, overlooking the ocean. It was again a powerful experience and in there I felt connected to some of the Orkney sites, which it seemed to resemble, in particular feeling close to the women of Skara Brae. We remained there a long silent while and the place came into me and I was one with it and knew I could always return in spirit, if not in body. Helen said we looked beautiful, as though we had been there for ever. Talie 'talked', knowing so much but not yet having the words to share his knowledge. Again I had that sense of 'brownness' which I'd had at Avebury and as my eyes became accustomed to the dim light I saw the subtle patterns carved on the stones, though, as Richard suggested, they seemed more gently rubbed into existence by the constant movement of fingers. It was a place for the transition of life to death, for the

Richard with the Aries sign and gorse bush on Anglesey

attainment of the Tibetan 'Body of Light', re-integrating with the elements; a place for shamanic journeying – for death and rebirth.

This was what we had come for, what the Aries of our journey needed and I was completely fulfilled. It was also a good practical lesson in how much I had to sort out before going it alone, and an acknowledgement that I feared doing so. It became clear to me that when I had sorted out my possessions, the waggon and Polly, I must return through Anglesey to travel from there to Ireland.

The 'plan' of the Gipsy Switch just said 'Ireland' but I was now sure I must go to the Hill of Tara in County Meath for the Taurus of the journey. Cuchulain, the Tain, bulls, Taurus – it all fitted. I became, though fearful, very excited. Richard took the wooden Aries sign and placed it in a bush of blazing yellow gorse. There was wool everywhere, from the Aries sheep and on Kate who wore a wonderful jumper with the picture of a hill and sheep on it, totally reflecting the landscape we were in.

We returned through a land of vivid russet and brilliant green: old wet bracken, beech leaves and new spring grass manifesting as a goddess spirit of place with

250

wild auburn hair and a gown of vivid emerald with russet trimmings and here and there powerful gashes of purple-grey. Torrents of water rushed down mountains, turquoise and dark green – returning to the sea.

Back at the Drapers Helen and Kate left us. Over the next few days I finished stripping down the waggon. Everything was wet, the blue plastic reluctant to come off, still wanting to be my loyal home. I presumed I was sad somewhere inside myself, but wasn't really feeling it, instead being excited by all that lay ahead. We slept several nights in a pig-sty loft, a place I would have loved as a child. I visited Polly each day, giving her apples and carrots and an amazing mash which was supposed to help her nerves and coat. She was very happy in the field, free and un-tethered, though extremely muddy. It seemed such a long time since we had arrived in that part of the world when it was covered in snow. Now the days were hot enough to lie out lazily in the sun.

The nights troubled me though, my fears returning. Over the dark moon I needed to sleep with the light of a candle, as though to keep the darkness from entering me and 'eating my soul'. The dark seemed very dark, as though I myself was the dark, and panic would fill me.

April 19th. Another beautiful, glorious day. I got my last few things loaded into Kevin's van and we set off for Fishguard. I left the waggon, which had passed through my life for a moment and left dear Polly, to whom I felt so deeply connected, finding it hard to contemplate not travelling with her again.

The plan was that two horse dealers, one from the west and one from the east, would travel and meet somewhere in the middle of the country to exchange horses. Polly would go with the one from the west and be taken by the other to East Anglia and Mandy.

We drove to Monica's. In the van the children climbed over my stuff and broke Talie's Moses basket, but it felt as though he would never need it again. At first Monica was a bit appalled by how much I had ("How much more is there?!"), but they cleared out a shed and put some of it in there, more under the stairs where I hoped it wouldn't get damp, and the rest in an upstairs room.

It was a massive shift. Although I had been travelling all over Britain, my base had always been in East Anglia where my daughters were, and with son Kevin in London. Now, suddenly, for the first time in my life my base was in the west. This was where I would return to when the journey was over, though I had no idea what I would do after that. It was a big event in my life and I experienced something fundamental inside me shifting – the perspective from which my 'internal map' functioned maybe. I was missing and longing for my older children, feeling that they and Talie were all I had in the world. No parents, no partner, and though I had friends, they were often transient and not

251

a secure base, very few of them in East Anglia by then. I realised I must not be dependent on anything outside myself – that the base must be within me.

April 20th – 28th. We shifted into Taurus and should have been on our way to Ireland. I was preparing myself, studying maps of where we would walk for the next few months, reading a book called 'Brigantia', doing some work in Monica's garden and working out all I would need to take with me yet be able to carry. Talie played outdoors and developed a terrible nappy rash. He didn't seem very happy, wasn't his usual self, almost as though 'Talie' had gone away and I had another little boy with me.

Jill and Talie at the razorwire around Stonehenge: Women Reclaiming Salisbury Plain week.

April 29th – May 5th. There was to be a Women's 'Reclaiming' walk from Avebury to Stonehenge, crossing the MOD firing range. Monica persuaded me to go on it before I set off and it did feel an important thing to do. We hitched to Avebury and walked around, meeting other women Monica knew. Towards evening we went to Silbury Hill, the pregnant belly of Mother Earth. I lay down to sleep on her in our new down sleeping bag, remembering the times we'd slept there before, especially when Talie was a few days old, and gave thanks. At one point in the night I woke in the presence of what I can only describe as Faerie. The dawn was misty and I took Monica to the Swallowhead Spring, where she had never been before.
Later in the day women gathered to picnic at the foot of Silbury. The police said they couldn't camp there and fifteen minutes later at least a hundred of them were on the top of the great hill. There was a focussed energy and a

reclaiming of so much lost: a beautiful, strong experience with all those women: all with one intent. I felt ritual was not necessary, that the gathering of women on the Beltane night was enough, but with Talie asleep in my arms I moved with the drumming and singing. The wind grew strong and after a while I went down to sleep on the 'ledge', a little lower than the top, sitting at first and just being with the place itself.

Next day we began the walk. I talked with many different women, some I'd known before, some new, and Talie was carried by many of them. It was a long and exhausting trek but so good to be back in Wiltshire, in an intimate relationship with the earth, the land, the sky and all that is. I successfully put up the tent for the night, pleased to find Phillipa there, camping beside us.

The following day began with endless meetings. The famous inspirational author and political activist Starhawk was there – not wanting to lead, but finding women wanted her to. I stuck with Phillipa, unsure of the energies of some of the other women. We reached the firing range and the red flags were flying, indicating active exercises – and somehow were suddenly a great line of singing women: through the first fence and then the second. A mass of running, snaking serpents all over the place, encircling the police, breaking, joining, going this way and that; long strings, tiny fragments. The police kept trying to arrest women but other women wouldn't let them. Women teemed everywhere, and then the order came "let them go". They stopped their firing and their practising for war; their little boy games. We walked across Salisbury Plain and reclaimed it, at least for a while.

It was a powerful day, crossing that land, sensing our own power and the power of the earth - yet the land was ravaged with shell craters, her flesh torn to pieces, though she lived on as best she could and grass and flowers still grew. But there was a strange air of death and it wasn't like walking across a wild unspoilt moor.

We split into groups round small fires that evening. One woman, a friend of Monica's, made some remark to me about my being on the fringe of things – a 'fringe' person, and this hurt me to my very core and I wondered why she had to take that attitude. I hadn't expected that from a woman. It was one of the worst things anyone could have said to me. I was, in fact, at the very heart of real things, but there were some strong personalities about and some 'famous' women vying with each other for position. It was interesting to observe, but not very enjoyable to be around.

Each morning it was I who was up first, making up the fire and having a bit of joyful solitude before the others rose. Next morning there was a huge circle, a raising of energy and a grounding. There was much confrontation, with lines of police arresting women. They tried to arrest me but when they saw Talie, let me go. At one point an Australian woman with an aboriginal message stick walked up to another police line and it just dissolved. We walked past barracks and lame cows with enormous hanging udders and reached the Stonehenge car-park. For a long time I gazed at the stones through razor wire, then slept in our tent.

Next day was a kind of personal preparation and in the evening we went to the gate, and were through it, over it, under it, and in with the stones. I have never liked Stonehenge much but, honoured, that night I saw faces in those stones; of the old ones, the ancient lineage of Britain, the spirits of the stones, there before they were shaped by the hands of man. I walked round the earth bank, and found myself back in a time before they were there.

There were so many women, but amongst it all Talie and I made our own journey. I walked the earth-work moonwise, balancing our sunwise journey round the land. I gave the place small elemental objects – feathers, a stone, sacred water, ash from our fire; then the orange moon appeared from the clouds as it went into an eclipse. What a night. Everything felt complete. I didn't want to sleep there and returned to the tent and lay in a state of sweet bliss. The next morning I felt I had gained great inner strength for my journey.

One of the great things of those few days, after that winter with men who so lacked understanding and support, was quite simply just that of being with women. Help was there without my asking: all women, whether they had children or not, understood. Always there was some woman to carry Talie if I needed, always some woman checking that everything was alright, that there was nothing I wanted. No-one actually did much very often, but that awareness, understanding and caring did so much for me and for my preparation to move off alone. I felt ready.

May 5th-11th. I went to East Anglia for the last time before setting off on the walk, saw a lot of friends and met Tiffany in Norwich the day after her birthday. She was very thin, which worried me. We bought her some clothes. I met up with Mandy, who now had Polly. A lot was spoken and acknowledged between us. She had been the source of much of the 'stuff' being talked about me behind my back and admitted it had come from her jealousy; but it was a pity I'd had to go through so much to get to that point. I met Nick from Dunwich and we drank champagne. I returned through London, seeing son Kevin, but not having much time alone with him.

A long hitch back to Fishguard and Monica's. I did my final packing and prepared for the walk. Having sorted out all I needed I then had to halve it. Talie had developed a bit of a cough.

Chapter 18: Taurus, Ireland

May 14th. The rucksack wasn't as heavy as I had dreaded. I carried it on my back, Talie in the Snugli on my front and a small bag in one hand. (This very soon became a bag in each hand.)

Monica walked with us to the main road and we caught the bus to Fishguard where we had lots of tea. It was very hot and I was already sweating profusely. We said goodbye. Monica was quite sad to see us go and kept saying things like "You may be back sooner than you think", which wasn't very encouraging! My plan was to hitch to Anglesey and then get the ferry to Ireland, but this first day I was aiming to stop off with Justin and Lucy, about half way up the west coast of Wales.

I got a lift to Cardigan, but from there on the hitching became hard – many short lifts with long waits in between. A strange mist (which I now know was haar) came in from the sea, making everything dark and weird. One lift was from a man with a bandaged stump instead of a leg and I was amazed that with such a problem he showed concern for others. We then had a lift from a family of Irish Travellers, which surprised me as I hadn't thought they would give lifts. The woman of the family asked if I'd ever been on 'the big boat', which I took to mean the ferry, and had I been to Ireland. As always, they wanted to know if I'd got a house, and because I hadn't I was ok. But I made a big mistake. I boasted that it never rained when I was hitching, and as soon as they dropped me it started to rain heavily and relentlessly. I foolishly got out on a by-pass, and had to wait there until I got a lift back to the main road. We sheltered under a tree before getting a lift half-way, but then had to stand for ages on an exposed lay-by in absolute disbelief that people could drive past a baby in that rain. In the end a man took us right to the door.

I woke with the light and became aware that Talie's breathing was a bit laboured, his eyes were glazed and he was rather hot. He slept again and woke cooler but was panting a bit all day. He was off eating solids so was feeding a lot from me, which was exhausting. We were almost back on the journey at last, and now this had hit us. Although I was worried, he was my fourth child and I had enough experience to know when a child was seriously ill.

Lynne and Hilary called by and we had a meeting to discuss the exhibition we were planning in London after my journey was over.

The next day Talie didn't seem so bad. It was a beautiful day with clear sun and a real summer heat, so I left quite soon. There were butterflies, daisies and dandelions and everything was lush, seeming to have grown abundant in the previous few weeks. It was a fresh, clear, intense, spring greenness, the leaves on the trees fully out after so recently having been swollen buds.

Justin and Lucy told me of a homeopath in Machynlleth, so I set off there to get a remedy for Talie, but when the first lift came it was to Bangor, so it seemed I was meant to go straight up the coast. The driver suggested I walk over the bridge onto Anglesey, so I did, and it was the right pace by which to approach the island, especially after our previous rushed trip. Doing it on my own feet made it a real part of the journey, and this time I had a proper sense of the place: Mona, the Mother of Wales.

I was letting my immediate plans be formed by the lifts. The first was to the turn-off to Bryn-Celli- Ddu, but a woman who was going near St. Gwenfaen's Well, which I wanted to visit, picked me up next; however she ran out of petrol so we went to her place for a coffee and a meal. Her husband ran the Post Office for RAF Valley and said we could camp in their back garden if ever we went back. Her daughter drove me to a place near the Well, but because Talie was tired I went to a tiny camp- site where we were the only people staying. It was a glorious evening and so different from the Aries visit, with birds singing and the sound of cuckoos. There were also midges and mosquitoes, but I took a homeopathic remedy and wasn't too badly affected. I felt it to be a blessed island – a holy island indeed.

I had a hard night with Talie, but he seemed better in the day and everything else made up for the difficulties. The woman in the house at the camp-site gave me coffee and looked after Talie while I had a wash. They told me how to find the Well and I realised I wouldn't have found it if I'd tried the previous evening. I left my pack at the camp-site and the man said he'd give me a lift to Holyhead.

The Well was beautiful, high on a cliff with the sea visible in the distance. Sheep, gorse, rocks, stillness – and RAF planes! It had a forecourt with stone seats, and round the back, steps down to water which seemed to have endless depth. It must have much lore attached to it, though I knew none of it, but could sense the silent presence and energy of the Old Ones, who would have sat gazing into the still waters, their energy even more powerful when the place was dark and windswept at wintry dark-moon times.

As I arrived, an old man who I'd watched walking on the headland gathering things in a sack, called out "Remember, I had a tryst with you here a hundred years ago and she never turned up". He then disappeared over the headland, his sack on his back.

I returned to the camp, sat in the hot sun and was given a cup of tea. I washed a t-shirt, hoping I could dry it sometime. The man drove me to Holyhead. Talie was wonderfully good on the ferry. As I sat there I decided to return to Liverpool when the Irish trip was over. The crossing was as calm as a mill-pond and the boat full of aged American widows.

It was only when I reached Dublin that it hit me I was in a foreign country, even though everyone spoke English. I hadn't brought much money and realised I wouldn't be able to get any from a bank or Post Office as they were all different – and the money itself was different. (This was long before cash machines). So I had to make sure I kept enough for the return fare.

I was in a strange city without a clue as to where I was, although that's how I feel in most cities. I would have liked to stay the night in Dublin, shop in the morning and then go to Tara, but had no idea where I could find cheap accommodation or a camp-site. A cab driver said he'd take me out of town, but wouldn't tell me how much it would be and I felt suspicious of him so said no. I kept asking people the way to Tara and they all said "Tara, County Meath?" and I wondered if there was another Tara, but I eventually discovered a bus that passed within a couple of miles of it, and got on that. The driver had never done the route before and a passenger had to tell him where to stop.

I walked about a mile. My load was beginning to feel heavy and it was getting dark, though the sunset was incredible, so as it was still another mile to Tara I found a magical place to put up the tent for the night. I was very excited to be in Ireland, and in Taurus – the Gipsy Switch coming right again.

Talie had been wonderful the whole time, but when he now fed, he had a whole breastful, and then sicked it up again in a projectile vomit, emptied the other breast and sicked all that up too, so I was getting worried about him becoming dehydrated. I didn't think I had enough food to last until the Monday (this was a Friday) when I hoped to get to Navan, but had to trust in something turning up. We were there. We had got to Ireland. What I was doing wasn't easy, but I was doing it.

The night turned colder and I woke to a mist of rain, but managed to get Talie to eat something. Outside I realised from looking at the map that we'd slept in Rath Maeve, a magnificent ancient earthwork, to which we'd unknowingly been led. I packed up the tent although it was wet – often it was easier to pack when wet, though heavier to carry. The morning was hot and humid, but it didn't seem far to Tara, and once there I went straight to a little shop where I was able to buy guide books and chocolate, but no actual food. There was, however, a cafe at the back doing teas and scones, so I thought I wouldn't starve.

Asking the lady where I could camp she said "Oh, anywhere on the hill". How wonderful, I thought, good old Ireland. I picked a sheltered place to the north, left the rucksack and walked over most of the earthworks, amazed at how extensive they were. It was acknowledged as an ancient pagan pre- Celtic site and I could sense the place as it had been before anything was constructed. I felt enormously fulfilled in having got there. I sang the Tara theme from 'Gone With The Wind' and realised the place had actually 'called' me for decades. I had read the Cuchulain story during my last weeks waiting for Talie to be born and if he'd been a girl I would have called her Tara.

The concrete statue of St. Patrick seemed so out of place there and I was pleased to see woman-symbol graffiti on his plinth. I felt a great serpent-power in myself and in the land and was sure Patrick didn't banish them but just sent them to sleep: maybe the time was now right for them to wake and rise. I carried the power of the women at the Stonehenge eclipse and felt I must do a serpent ritual at dark moon, which was the next day.

We went to the churchyard near the site, where there is an ancient stone with a carving on it which is probably a sheela-na-gig. I thought it looked more like a horned figure, but that it must be the crescent moon on her head. She was very smooth, as though often touched.

I was tired, had a rest and felt that, for all his being sick, Talie was getting better. In the evening we had another walk to more parts of the site and I climbed The Mound of the Hostages, a chambered cairn which must be the oldest structure there. It had a locked gate so I couldn't go in but could see spiral carvings on the stones inside and would have liked to draw them. I wondered if there was a key and where I could get it.

We slept early. I loved our cosy little tent and Talie had a better night. I just lay and let the energy of the place flow through me. I felt so connected to Tara, not as though I had been there in some previous life, but as though it still held the living essence of the Celtic world – an essence which we must once have had in England but which has now gone, overlaid by too much else which has come since. Before this I had always felt most strongly connected to Neolithic and Palaeolithic times in England rather than to the Celts. I wondered why Christianity had taken over so easily in Ireland and whether the beliefs which were there before, had already degenerated by the time it arrived.

It was a dull, wet, windy day, which didn't matter, though it would have been nice to sit out on the grass and dry some washing. I had a very swollen right hand, which I thought must have been caused by an Anglesey mosquito rather than an awakening Irish serpent, but who knows. After a while we went to the cafe. The lady had just finished milking her cow and made me scrambled eggs and lots of toast and a pot of tea for only £1.30. She said it had been a terrible night and she'd worried about us and sat us by a warm radiator. I wished I had brought the wet washing.

We went for another walk in the wild windiness and then back to the tent where Talie had a long sleep and I was able to get on with a lot of writing. When he woke we played for a while then I thought it was time for tea and scones to eke out my paltry bit of expensive food. This time I took my washing and dried it on the radiator. The place got very busy and I left, feeling quite full up.

Now it was time for my 'serpent-awakening' ritual which involved encircling various parts of the site, walking moon-wise round things with the energy of the Stonehenge walk and willing the serpent energy of the emerald isle to wake again and re-empower its women. I moved to the Mound of the Hostages: the silent, deep heart of the place, and began to encircle that too – three times round each place it had to be. On my first circle, as I came round to the far side, the figure of a woman suddenly emerged from the thick mist, appearing to be faerie or the manifestation of some ancient being, but she said she'd seen me pass by her house on Friday and was amazed I was still up there in that weather and would I come back for tea? She apologised for not coming sooner, but the day before she had buried her father and it had put me out of her mind.

I had to go. I had to pause my ritual, promising I would come back later to complete it. Something had been conjured up and I had better go with it. She drove us to her house. She was Doreen, her husband was Harry, and they had four boys: Stephen, Vincent, Edmund and Michael, and a little girl Elisha. We sat in their warm kitchen and I was interested to see that they burned peat brickettes which had been shaped by machine. Talie played with the children and their toys, we had a wonderful supper and talked until it got dark.

They wanted us to stay the night, but with the tent and all our stuff on the hill and my ritual incomplete, I felt I had to get back. Harry drove us there; me in borrowed socks with a flask of hot water and teabags. I took some things to the tent, noticing a car parked nearby, then went to the Mound to complete my ritual, feeling it all must be done on the dark moon.

Back in the tent it was warmer than the night before and Talie went peacefully to sleep. It was still a bit light and as I lay musing I became aware that the parked car was still there. I began to have some unusual fears, almost as though I was picking up on things which had happened there in the distant past. At first I became afraid of rape and then began to fear someone coming in the dark with a huge iron bar or sword to beat or cut us to death through the tent, stabbing us through and through. I also feared a fanatical Christian would see me as a witch - a heathen, evil woman alone with a child - and would want to

259

destroy me. I felt people had been watching my ritual and known what I was doing.

These fears were so unlike how protected I normally felt, but as the dark came I relaxed, though the car didn't go for ages. I became more myself, curled up and slept. Talie had a better night; still waking and coughing at times, but with much longer, peaceful times in between.

I dreamed of the Banqueting Hall being full of men eating and drinking and dressed in brown; part of a degenerate, male-dominated society. I was there in some important capacity, wanting something vital to be discussed, but realised it was hopeless and walked out. It was like a memory from the last days of the place, as though I had started to peel back layers of time. Who knows what I would have dreamed had I stayed longer and peeled back more layers.

I woke to rain and cold and wondered how I would get everything packed up, so waited until the rain stopped and Talie could sit outside, then folded the tent up very wet and very heavy.

We had camped near some hawthorn trees. Hawthorn is the tree of the May time of year in the Beth-Luis-Nion calendar, so I put the wooden Taurus sign in one of them and felt pleased that for once the sign was in the right tree, adding power to the circle we were turning round the land.

I felt our time at Tara was complete, so bade it farewell without going up the hill again, and walked back the way we had come, past Rath Maeve, where it had turned from fine and hot to cold and wet, and back to the house of Doreen (which was called Maryfield), needing to return the things she'd lent me. She had gone back to bed; the tiredness of the previous few weeks having hit her at last, so I felt a bit awkward, but she was insistent on giving me breakfast. I had a wash and changed our clothes and she washed and dried all our things. We had lunch and talked. I was fascinated by how an Irish Catholic woman sees the world but didn't get into any arguments with her about things I saw differently.

The news that day was that a 1000lb bomb had exploded near Newry. 20 seconds before it went off a party of schoolchildren on their way to Newgrange had passed by that very spot. I found it interesting being with an Irish family as we heard such news, which they abhorred, though in such situations I often felt embarrassed at being English.

My washing was done, the day still cold, windy and wet. I was going to leave, but it was getting late and Talie suddenly seemed to be in agony from his sore bum. He still had the nappy rash, which I didn't seem able to clear. As they had previously offered us a bed for the night, I asked if we could stay as I no longer had the energy to get off again on the journey.

We had a lovely supper of cabbage and potatoes and went to bed really early. Talie slept well and I slept like a log. At one point Doreen brought me a cup of tea, but I didn't wake, even though Elisha banged the door. While there, Talie had crawled properly for the first time and a neighbour of theirs had called by asking if I were 'the woman from Tara', and I had talked of faeries with Harry. We had been shown such extraordinary kindness. May such people of the earth be blessed.

May 21st. Harry took me into Navan, which had been somewhat out of my way. I spent a good time there, discovering Irish supermarkets and stocking up a bit, and getting myself prepared for the rest of my time in Ireland.

I set off out of town and got a lift to Sclane. The man stopped and showed me Sclane Castle – "where the stones were". Oh, how interesting, I thought, only to realise he meant the Mick Jagger variety. From there I decided to walk, as it seemed I was now on a pilgrimage.

Surprisingly, the day cleared and got warmer and warmer. Everything was so green – the emerald isle indeed, ripe and rich. Lambs here were bigger and older than the tiny new ones in Wales. The hawthorn buds were near blooming and there was a sense of plenty. I felt ashamed at knowing so few of the wayside plants, aware that we used to live from this wild bounty, and now most of us have forgotten how – and I had just been to the supermarket! I thought of how, in parts of England, farmers and builders were destroying more and more of nature's wild offerings – no hedgerows, no verges, no wild patches; but there in Ireland something was not quite lost. I noticed how they cut the stems of ivy to make it die and stop choking the trees, kinder and less savage than some of the things I'd seen in England – like flailing hedges to bits.

Talie's eyes had become bloodshot the day before, and were now a bit mucky. He seemed to be going through everything possible just then – he who had always been so healthy, especially through the winter.

We got to Knowth, one of the great, ancient chambered cairns of the Boyne Valley, only to find it under excavation and not open to the public. I was shocked at the devastation wrought by the archaeologists – great long strips of it having been cut up and wrapped in black plastic. There was a viewing platform you could climb so you could watch the destruction. It seemed like a violation and really upset me. Knowth is one of the major Neolithic sites in the world, yet they had just sliced it all up. It wasn't good enough for them to say they would put it back so it looked the same – it had been constructed in subtle

Knowth under excavation

harmony with the energies of the earth and universe, and once tampered with that cannot be restored.

We had a bit of lunch and one of the archaeologists came over for a chat, but I didn't challenge him about anything as I just didn't know where to begin. I had romantically imagined the Neolithic sites in that area to be on a big open plain so you could see each one and walk from one to another, but it was all just roads in a modern landscape.

We walked on down a lane to Newgrange and suddenly everything I was carrying seemed to weigh a ton and I was in agony. I couldn't find the way in at first as it was all very 'Stonehenged' though nothing to how it is now, when you can only get there on a bus trip. I had been partly prepared, but it was a shock to see it fenced off, with an entrance gate where you had to pay, and coachloads of children and tourists. It was also a shock to have to join a group to go inside the cairn with a guide and listen to her ridiculous speculative drivel, which was rather like that of the coach drivers at Uluru. However I was feeling too physically and emotionally weak to challenge the silly woman, who was insulting not only the ancient people who had constructed this wonder, but also those of our own time who wish to experience the winter solstice sunrise entering the very heart of its incredible chamber. Maybe it's better now. I hope so.

Inside, the place was overwhelming, with amazing carvings made by stone on stone with such astonishing skill, and the extraordinary way in which the interior of the place had been constructed so that the beam of the midwinter

262

sunrise shines right down the deep passage, illuminating the wall carvings as it moves – what learned and sophisticated people they must have been.
I went outside and sat by a tree in the cold wind, my scarf round my head, feeding Talie and feeling like the woman in Monica's beautiful painting – 'Corn Mother at Newgrange'. Two men came and photographed us, as though we were some kind of mythological beings.

Newgrange was such a powerful experience, yet it was weird to meet it in such a touristy context, with one part of me in the present and another back in the Neolithic. I was overawed by what must have been a great temple, manifesting a peak of perfection and attainment, reflecting the people's absolute state of being. I had not realised there was so much carving inside, executed so perfectly, and wondered whether much of it had been done by women. Why is it always assumed to be by men?

I wrote "White mounds in a green land; crystal glinting in the sunlight and moonlight – and then the midwinter sun shines in along the long curved tunnel to the very heart and depth of the mound. The turning point; the moment of vision and initiation; out of darkness into light'. Imagine being in there for weeks before that moment, in total dark retreat, deprived of all sensory stimulation but for touch as one fingered the patterns carved into the stones. Did they cover the light-box until that moment when sunlight seared into the very core, or did they watch day by day as it got nearer and nearer? Maybe none of the living were ever in there, only the spirits of the ancestral dead. I was full of reverence for its great carved stone basins and felt the energy of the ashes scattered on them. Did they fill the chamber with sound as well as light? What is the sound of the midwinter sunbeam?

Were there all-night circles of chanting people surrounding the mound? Does the moon also shine in there? Do moonbeams caress the triple spiral as well as the sun? We are the elements; we come from the elements and from the stars. We return to the elements and re-integrate with them. We have the power of the elements because we are them."

I had hoped we could sleep near Newgrange, not having realised it was in a compound, shut up at night. They had even closed off the 'back' of the mound so you couldn't walk right round it to see all the carved kerb-stones. I set off walking again, really tired, and rejected several beautiful green road corners which would have been perfect if we'd been with the horses, and eventually 'hopped' over a gate and set up the tent in a field, near a hedge, without asking permission, feeling too tired to do anything else. It was a glorious evening and we slept well through the rest of it and on into the early night, but then Talie started crying. I was concerned that people passing by would hear him and tell us to move on, but it was fine. The inside of the tent was dripping with condensation, but at last I realised I could see the dawn coming and we slept a little more.

May 22nd. I woke properly, wondering whether we were in Gemini now, concerned about Talie not being completely better, had a headache and thought I too might be dehydrated. But there were birds in the laden Spring trees, insects and dew on the grass and a promise of blue sky in beautiful green Ireland. I wondered why Irish people spoke English and presumed that at some point in the past they had been forced to. Talie was 'not himself', even rejecting a banana. He was crying and crying and his poor little eyes were all red and swollen. It was difficult to pack up, but I managed and, rather hot, bothered and distraught set off and realised we were only a few yards from Dowth. There were 'No Camping' and 'No Picnicking' notices everywhere but it was beautifully peaceful to walk around, though it was shut. If circumstances had been different I would have sat there for hours, but with Talie unwell I couldn't relax, so hungrily drank in the intense experience of the huge mound. I was very, very full of this time in Ireland although it had been so difficult, with such a lot to overcome, feeling I had been working against some negative energy. I didn't think this was my imagination, and thought I had been pretty strong in dealing with it.
I walked on, through lush verges and hedgerows full of mists of cow parsley, and came to a big green corner where I sat for a rest as Talie slept, realising I couldn't go on to other parts of Ireland as I had intended. I had done everything I had come to do on this part of the Gipsy Switch and could return in the future to see other ancient Irish sites. I thought I should move on to somewhere Talie could get completely better before we began our walk proper. I reckoned I could get to Dublin by 9pm in time for the bus to the ferry and with distance, digest the intensity of this Irish experience.

It was 1.10pm. I got up and began to walk. I photographed cattle in the Boyne Valley – the cattle of the Cu Cuchlain tales; the Taurus cattle of the Gipsy Switch journey. I had taken no photographs of Talie in Ireland. I wasn't documenting the Gipsy Switch journey as such, rather marking the first year of Talie's life, and this bit of his journey was missing.

I hitched a few lifts then got a bus to Dublin. I'd dithered about getting it, wandering around on a by- pass which was still being constructed as I recall. A couple offered to take me if I'd pay for petrol, but I had to make them an offer. I thought they were travelling people and felt pressurised, and when they eventually asked for £5, I said 'no, I'll go by bus'. The bus was £4.10.

On the bus I had a monologue about Irish history directed at me by a strange Irish-Jewish school- teacher. He carried my bag into the bus station and I put it in the left luggage. My 4-hour wait went quickly as I had cups of tea, wrote postcards and walked to a letter-box while Talie slept. His eyes were badly gunged up and I thought it was an infection he had picked up in Ireland as several women told me their children had had it.

We got the bus to the ferry. I'd worried they might not take an English cheque, as I hadn't enough cash left for the fare, but they did and once on board I found a really comfy seat in the TV lounge. Coming over from Holyhead we'd been on a Sealink ferry, but this one was a B&I which I much preferred, as I felt more like a human being on it. On the Sealink I had felt like a commodity, with no regard given to the comfort of passengers or the problems of travel. Talie went to sleep. My milk was very low, what with all the walking in the heat and him constantly suckling then sicking up half he drank.

We were headed for Liverpool as I didn't want to go backwards on the journey. I was hoping we might be able to stay with John Lacey (Bruce Lacey's eldest son) in Todmorden, bus up to Cumbria, catch up with the journey and then just walk.

I had a comfortable night and both of us slept well. I had tea and porridge for breakfast, then we were off the boat and in Liverpool. I felt more relaxed, Talie's eyes were a lot clearer and he seemed more 'himself'. I had managed to spend most of my change and came back with only one Irish pound note (this was before the Euro). I phoned John and he said it would be fine to stay. He is someone who has given us a great deal of help over the years. I had to work out how to get to Todmorden, asked around a bit and eventually got a coach to Manchester, another to Halifax and then a bus to Tod. By the end I was hot, tired, smelly and had had enough, but I phoned John and he came to collect us. What a relief.

I had a bath and there was much good conversation. I realised I had been carrying too much and needed to sort it all out and post some back to myself in Wales. I also realised I must get a little stove before I set off again, and needed time to study maps, write letters and gather my strength for the next onslaught. I fantasised about getting an old battered pram that I could push my stuff in instead of having to carry it, but this remained a fantasy. (I didn't imagine pushing Talie in a pram). It was a joy to sleep in a warm, soft bed, but Talie was full of phlegm and I had a bad ear which popped and leaked fluid. What a couple!

May 24 – 28. It was a good and very necessary break. John drove me around and didn't get impatient if I dithered and was indecisive. I got some homeopathic cough mixture which Talie loved and spoke to a homeopath over the phone. She advised me to give him Ipecac. It seemed to work and he managed to cough up a lot of phlegm and became much more his old self. He'd lost a lot of weight, but had been quite fat to begin with. He also seemed to be straightening himself up in readiness for walking, and in the midst of crawling madly about everywhere, stood up tall for the first time. His bad days had been a sort of crisis and not only did he get better, but changed a lot, turning from a baby into a little boy – as though, as we were about to set out on this new phase of life, he had entered a new one of his own.

I got a little stove; not Camping Gaz, but an aerosol one where the cylinder screws and unscrews from the stove bit, so I could pack the different parts separately in the rucksack. John even managed to get me a discount. Ireland had been a good trial run and I had realised I needed to boil water for Talie's food – and for tea! We watched a lot of John's films, including some of my other children when they were young.

We went for some walks, including one to a stone called Churn Milk Joan, which I felt had something to do with Brighde. It's legend was of a milkmaid who had died there and been eaten by foxes. We visited a friend of John's who asked "Is this yet another one of your sisters?",seeming unable to grasp the complexities of the Lacey family (Bruce has 9 children) nor to really believe all the women he turned up with really were his sisters. But, no, I was his father's second ex-wife.

Another day we drove over moorland. We went to Ilkley Moor and visited a place called White Wells where a man gave us information about the carved stones on the moor, and walked to the Swastika Stone which I had long wanted to see. I was impressed by the siting of these stones, this one high, overlooking a valley. We found a cup-and-ring-marked stone in a beautiful copse, on a raised mound between two branches of a stream, then went over more of the moor to the Badger Stone. I felt the carvings on these stones were incredibly old, from long before the Neolithic; from a hunter-gatherer culture, a nomadic aboriginal way of life before farming and settlements. Part of a British Dreaming Path.

We walked on, trying to find a circle of stones, asking people we passed for directions and walking on and on and on. I got very tired, and even John got tired, but Talie had a lovely ride on my back. When we found the circle I was disappointed. It seemed to have been interfered with, stones being propped upright, maybe having fallen or not even having been there originally. I was exhausted and my knee started to hurt – I hoped it wouldn't give me trouble in the coming days. We had somehow experienced the weird, still, 'darkness' of the moor, having been in deep silence with just the sound of birds calling from the sky. We walked on and came back to where we'd started – a good though long and tiring day.

Whilst at John's I had my first ever chip butty, and, looking through a copy of Exchange and Mart, saw there were properties for sale in Wales and the Western Isles for £8,000 - £9,000, a price I could afford. I still had no real idea what I would do on a permanent basis when the Journey ended, but having known since 1982 that I must live on Lewis, now became sure that the dream could become reality.

I painted a smaller version of the Gipsy Switch sign which had been tied on the back of my waggon, this one to go on the back of my rucksack.

On our last night there Talie looked at me with the eyes of a newborn, full of ancient wisdom and pure spirit. It was to be a new beginning.

Chapter 19: Gemini, Appleby

May 29th. I woke to glorious sunshine and knew this was the day to be off. My left knee was quite strained from Ilkley, but I bought a crepe bandage and hoped it wouldn't turn into a bigger problem. The Ilkley walk had been about as far as I could go just carrying Talie, never mind all the luggage, so I realised I had overdone it a bit in Ireland and had to take the walk ahead gradually and break myself in gently, as we had with the horses at the beginning of the journey. At some point on this stop I had weighed me and Talie in the Snugli, and it was 10 stone 10lb and I wondered what just I weighed.

At lunchtime John ran us to Burnley and we got a bus to Preston, then a coach to Keswick. I was following the trail of my 1982 journey, yet with so much in my life having changed. I felt like an open sunflower. Talie and I, even just travelling on the bus, achieved a perfection I found hard to explain. It was how I had always imagined our life would be, yet had never quite been before: a magical togetherness. We reached Keswick. The Ladies in the bus station was shut. I had some chips and still disliked the town and the whole touristy thing round there and didn't expect a lot of help, worrying slightly about getting a constant supply of food and nappies.

So, at last my little boy and I were back properly on the Gipsy Switch and beginning our walk. We were going to be walking for about three and a half months – first to Appleby to coincide with the Gipsy Horse fair, then across the Pennines to Durham, down to York, down even further to Lincoln and on another 15 miles to where the Gipsy Switch had actually begun when Richard and Mike, Rosie and Polly were parked up at Sudbrook.

We walked up the hill to the Castlerigg stone circle – the blue heart of Albion on my 1982 journey when I had received such love from the rounded stones and the earth herself, and I was again overcome by the beauty of the place as I brought my little Gemini babe there for the first time. We lay down to sleep by a wall, surrounded by sheep with curly horns and little lambs. Last time I had been there with a field of bullocks, and on the way up the hill had hoped that this year it would be sheep, and there they were. In other places the lambs had grown big, but here they were still small and frisky. At last Talie was crawling on grass. We didn't sleep in the tent, just out in the open, as it was so warm and dry. I felt totally blessed by everything, and that everything around me was blessed. Skylarks sang above, crows flew, bees buzzed, black beetles crawled. More and more lush grew the wayside vegetation, with little white flowers like stars; and streams that trickled by as we walked up the hill. A few weeks

Taliesin with the Gemini disc on Appleby Fair Hill

before dandelions had been abundant, crying out in unpolluted places to be made into wine; now the heads had turned to seeds and blew in the summer breeze. What we were doing felt momentous and I hoped for strength and protection.

Talie had a really good night and slept long into the morning. I woke to see the red sun rise in my eyes and lay a long while as it warmed us. Now at last we had only ourselves to consider and could pace the days as best suited us. All around were mountains and sheep and, a little walk away, my beloved stone circle, and that day was one of the most perfect of my life. I was so happy. Talie was wonderful, playing with flowers and everything around him, very aware, noticing it all and so cheeky and playful. We had a lovely relationship again, as though we were doing this together, sharing the experience and both enjoying the pace of it. We set off when we were ready: a bit of a walk, a bit of

269

a rest with him out of the Snugli to play, then another walk and so on. If he was asleep when I stopped I'd leave him in it and that gave me the opportunity to write, or I might take it off and just lie him down.

It was perfect weather – sunny and dry but with a breeze so we didn't get too hot. I still wished for an old pram so I could be like a gipsy woman, pushing all our stuff and carrying Talie on my back, but as I was carrying him on my front and the rucksack on my back it balanced well. I now had a bag in each hand and that balanced even better. My load was too much for perfect enjoyment, but it was ok. It was lovely off the main roads, with long grass, tall trees, leaves, flowers, birds and butterflies, though every so often a great demon screamed through the valley, causing Talie to look at them in disbelief. He was eating much better now and his illness seemed completely over. We came eventually to an area of unfenced road and found a lovely little place to stop. Several times we were visited by a dozen or so heifers which fascinated Talie and he stood up bravely as if to protect his mother from the great beasts. The moon rose in the blue sky, the sun set over the mountains and we went to sleep. I felt as though we were living as we should at last, though still wishing we could live from the land and not be dependent on shops.

It was lovely taking our time in the morning and not rushing off. This was a beautiful road to walk, small and quiet, up hills and down dales, Talie talking to cows whenever we saw them. On and on we went, pleased to find a footpath to save walking an extra mile. We got to a place marked P on the map. I'd aimed for it as it meant Post Office and I hoped it would be a shop as well, but the P was just a little window in a woman's house, though she said there was a shop in Penruddock. The pub wouldn't serve me coffee at 3.30pm, but I was actually losing the inclination for caffeine. With my little stove I could make myself two teas in the morning and the rest of the time seemed satisfied with water. The main road was new, but they had left the old one where it used to be, so I walked that and it was beautiful. We could have stopped there, but I wanted to get near Penruddock for the shop in the morning, so continued and finally stopped on a verge which sloped down away from the road, overlooked a valley and was a perfect place to just sit gazing. Talie spent a long time talking to cows through a long-disused gate.

We seemed so tucked away and the roadside so quiet that I thought we might as well stay there and we lay down quite early. From time to time people walked by, then a bit later a car pulled up and a man rather cautiously asked if we were alright. It seemed that one of the walkers had been terrified and thought we were a body. I reassured him that we were alive and well and he said he owned a caravan site down the road and if we wanted to call in for a wash and water in the morning that would be fine. I resolved that in future, in such situations, I would prominently display the sign on the back of the rucksack to allay such fears. I'd got so used to stopping on verges with the horses that it seemed perfectly natural to just lie down and sleep on one.

Looking back on all this over 30 years later I think maybe it would be more difficult nowadays, what with mobile phones and people easily calling the police etc. Society has radically changed and I am grateful I was able to do this while I had the chance. At that point I felt my whole life was perfect, I could ask for no more and hoped it could continue like this for as long as possible. Walk a little, rest a little, eat a little, play a little. We walked honouring the body of the blessed earth with every step we took.

I was glad Talie had been able to rid himself of his illness with homeopathy, as he had not yet had any 'straight' allopathic medicine, and I thought this would help his body build up its own natural resistances. I was pleased he hadn't needed any antibiotics.

We lived each day as it came among those beautiful mountains – green nearby, fading to blue in the distance, glaciers having shaped the rounded land. The moon grew fuller in the blue sky and gazed down on us. The greenness was golden in the setting sun, like a time of youth before the rich mature ripeness of harvest-time.

The days were so drawn out by then and there was a magic in the length of them. A great wonder filled me. It didn't seem long since the deep darkness of winter when every tiny lengthening of day was a miracle. In winter one cannot imagine the length of a summer day. Now the growth of light was beginning to slow down towards the pause of the summer solstice and I rather dreaded that turning, when we would move once more towards the shrinking of days and the coming of the dark. Annie Macleod had once said of the summer solstice "Today is the first day of winter".

But we had a few weeks to go yet!

Saturday June 1st. We set off quite early and walked into Penruddock, the caravan site being too far off the road to visit. People in cars don't realise how far distances are to walk, especially with all I had to carry. In Penruddock I found that yet another P was just a house with no shop. I asked a man who was gardening where the nearest one was, but it was miles off our route, so I asked if I could leave my pack in his garden while I hitched into Penrith which, although it was 6 miles away, was accessible as we were right by the A66. He agreed and I quickly got a lift, though it was strange to be in a town after the open roads. I realised that from now on our route would have to be determined by the accessibility of shops. I could carry food for no more than a day or two plus the contents of small packs of nappies, and was only walking about 3-5 miles a day.

I got the next map, which we would soon be walking onto, and enough food for both of us to last until the Monday. I could only get a small size of nappies and hoped they would fit him now he was thinner. (He had been in toddler size at 5 months). In a supermarket a girl short-changed me a pound, but I tried to get over it and not let it spoil the happiness of the journey. I found a place to sit and eat as much as I could so I wouldn't have to carry it, which I did whenever possible, drinking fresh milk and eating perishable food as well. I then walked to a roundabout and two women drove us right back to Penruddock, which was miles out of their way. I collected my pack, thanking the man and his family profusely.

I took a route down towards a lake, which I think may have been Ullswater. We usually found lovely places to pause and rest, and here there was a little quiet spot by a river with sunlight dappling us gently through the trees. I had to fit a lot of the shopping into my rucksack, having already learned not to carry even a single sheet of paper that I didn't need. I opened each packet of nappies and fitted them individually into spaces here, there and everywhere in the pack. I removed the inner packets of baby food from their boxes, opened them to squeeze out the air so they too would squash into small spaces. I got better and better at all this as the walk continued.

I could have walked further, but it was getting touristy and perhaps I was more tired than I thought, having learned to stop before I got really exhausted. I found a flat bank high above the road with long grass, a holly bush and a hedge of trees to hide us, yet open to a field on the other side. It wasn't overlooked by houses and was a really secret, faerie place. I had never noticed holly in flower before, so that was a new treat, and there were lots of bumble bees around it. Even 3-5 miles was hard work and I found I needed about 12 hours rest a day. I would thank the spirits of each place we stopped for sharing it with us, and thanked the animals and birds, the grass and the earth herself and hoped we wouldn't crush the plants too much as we lay on them.

It was lovely to wake in that little nest. We took our time and I even changed and had more of a wash than I had for a few days. I didn't have many clothes and needed to find places where I could wash the dirty things. Talie had more than I, but not that many, so I had to keep him as clean as possible. We walked beside the lake on a busy road, then on to Pooley Bridge on a path round the bottom of a hill which had an ancient 'fort' on top. It was steep and high and impossible for me to climb carrying Talie and the pack, but I acknowledged it's presence as an ancient site overlooking water and walked around it.

The town was busy with tourists. It was hot with not much of a breeze, but I found a nice cafe and we sat outside for a cheap meal and tea, which eked out the rest of the food I was carrying. Talie ate baked beans and a potato, so certainly had his appetite back.

Walking on, I had to stop frequently because of the heat, and my knee was playing up a bit. I rejected a beautiful wood as a stopping place and went on another mile, eventually finding a little walled corner of a field, lying on nettles so as not to damage the crop. Earlier in the day we had seen the first fields cut for hay. I had stared uncomprehendingly at the stripes in them before realising what it was.

We were now in a high and uninhabited area. As Talie slept I lay a long while suddenly overcome by a deep longing for the Western Isles. Approaching midsummer I realised I was about as far North as I was going to get that year and, beautiful as it was, I was aching for that special magic of midsummer in the Islands when the nights don't actually get dark. I had left Ireland with the smell of peat smoke in my nostrils and it seemed to carry me further North that night, and any doubts I may have had about where I should live disappeared.

As the sun lowered I watched the clear blue sky with an occasional streaky cloud looking as though it had been painted on. I felt the cool breeze of evening come and lay among the nettles and listened to the mounting cries of some large birds which I couldn't identify, regretting my lack of knowledge of them. The sky darkened and the moon rose, then I slept as she shone her brilliance down on us.

She would be at her fullest during the day, so the following night would already be waning. I found it hard to believe it was a month since the full moon at Stonehenge, but now marvel at all I had done in one short month. I was on the high moors of North England and my whole being felt clear as we approached midsummer. There had been bits in the roads which sparkled like diamonds in the sunlight.

June 3rd. The moon was full at 04.50 and it became a slightly strange day. Talie woke earlier than usual while I was still tired, then when we were nearly ready to leave he fell asleep – with his little bare legs and bum in the sun. When he woke again we set off. It had been such a beautiful place to stop, yet I 'beat myself up' for not making nettle tea or having dandelion leaves in my sandwiches, though I did think that if dandelions are diuretic it was maybe not such a good idea to eat them while lactating.

Things seemed to have changed a lot even in one day. Previously the hawthorn had still been in bud, but now, after one night, it was in full bloom, the hedgerows laden with white blossom as though they had burst forth for the full moon. The Gemini goddess danced in her striped dress and had may blossom in her hair.

Getting to Askham, we sat on its lovely village green for lunch, and I thought of how the place must have been a century, or even 50 or 60 years before -

busy and full of people. Now it was silent and empty, with everyone presumably commuting elsewhere to work.

Walking on we could now hear a motorway and railway and an unpleasant atmosphere pervaded everything. We did however walk past a 'long cairn'. It was in a tangly wood through a fence, so there was no way I could fight my way to it, but I could see it lying there among the trees – an old hag winter body clothed in summer green, sleeping gently and waiting for the dark to return. It felt strong and as though it knew we were there.

We crossed the motorway on a bridge, rested, then passed under the railway and onto the road to Great Strickland. It had some welcoming verges and a good spot by a stream, but I didn't feel we had gone far enough, so carried on. We came to a river, went into a wood and prepared to stay, but Talie really didn't like it and we started to get bitten by mosquitoes. There was the sound of what I thought was gunfire, but may have been bird-scarers, and it felt awful, so we left. I didn't feel like going into any of the fields round there, so found a bit where the fence had been moved back from the road to make a kind of corner and put up the fly-sheet with the Gipsy Switch sign on it. Initially Talie wasn't happy inside, not having been in it on this part of the journey, but later settled. When we went to bed my leg was hurting and only then did I start to take Arnica and put 'strain ointment' on it and wished I'd done so sooner. Earlier a man had wished us well, and I dreamed of walking a labyrinth with a stone path, needing to get Chalice Well water, though didn't feel I was in Glastonbury.

In the morning Talie was happy again, but it was a strange area, with something darkly ominous and foreboding about it and felt the same until we got near Great Strickland. There was a nice lady in the shop there who talked of how good it was to have a child years after having your older ones, as she had one who was a teenager by then. She was the first person to ask if we were 'going to the fair' (Appleby). It was going to be bigger than usual; some special anniversary.

We paused to eat a tin of peaches, which Talie was very into, and semolina, which he wasn't. It was good to not carry full tins, but of course I always had to carry our bags of rubbish, including Talie's used nappies, until I found a bin. The day was cooler, but muggy and cloudy. People were getting nicer and nicer as we got away from the tourism of the Lakes and there were quiet roads with potential places to stop. The hedgerows were full of colour – vibrant purples, blues, yellows and white. The green was changing – no longer the light, bright green of spring but darkening as everything thickened and reached the peak of green abundance, but not yet the deeper colour of late summer when the fruit comes. The hawthorn flowers hung heavy, profuse and creamy white, in contrast to the earlier blackthorn blossom which had been like delicate snowflakes. There was a lot of activity in the fields, a lot of grass being cut for silage. Where it lay in stripes it was hay, but where they took it straight off it was for silage. There were more and more fields each day where the grass had gone, leaving a white- green among the dark. It was as though the earth were being given a strange punk hairstyle, shaved in patchwork.

A man stopped by and gave me £1 for Oxfam. It rained in the night, but we got wet from the condensation in the tent. Talie woke around 4am, but soon slept again. I knew the time from the chime of a village clock. Gradually the cool of evening would come, grow, darken into moonlight, and soon lighten into dawn. It was a time to reflect that we must not waste a moment of our lives.

There was no more rain and we rose and packed up methodically and systematically, having developed quite a routine. Talie would play while I got on with things, and I'd got him doing the washing- up in a large margarine tub I used as a kitchen sink. While I packed up the tent he played with the tent pegs.

My load was light with no water and no food and it seemed a pity to have to buy more and burden myself all over again. Everywhere we went people admired Talie's tan and assumed we were going to Appleby Fair. It was much cooler; dull and silent apart from the machines making silage – huge round rolls wrapped in black plastic. There were so many sweet bird songs, but the delicacy had gone from the plants which were now in the bloom of full-blooded summer. The previous day there had been rabbits running all over the roads.

At one point I sat on a bridge for a rest with Talie sleeping in my arms. A policeman stopped by and ran me through his computer, probably because I was getting near the Fair. He was ok when I showed him my leaflets about the journey and didn't seem to have a criminal record. I think I had my driving licence with me as ID.

Walking down a quiet road we came to the end of the verge. It was getting cold and windy, so I stopped and put the tent up, although it was only 3.15pm. It was the softest patch yet we'd had to sleep on. Another policeman stopped by and I got ready with my story, but in his free time he was a back-packer so was interested in my tent and gear and was very friendly. I worried a bit about cars pulling off the road in the dark, not seeing us and running us over and thought I should get some reflectors and sew them on the tent.

Later a vehicle stopped and I could see its lights. There was a pause and it took me a few seconds to realise that some of the tent pegs had been pulled out. I was pretty pissed off and shouted something out about them being stupid, and they drove off, but then a minute later there was a lot of giggling and more pegs pulled out. I was even more pissed off and rushed out, but there was no-one to be seen. I wondered if it might have been the faeries! Fortunately all the pegs were lying on the grass so I was able to put them back in while holding Talie, who had by now woken. It made me realise how vulnerable I could be, so decided that in future I would either sleep hidden right away where no-one could see us or be in very obvious sight of habitation. That place was neither. I didn't fear anything further and we had a good night. I also decided not to put the sign on the rucksack or tent until after Appleby, as it now seemed rather pretentious. It might well have been travellers doing it – taking the piss.

June 6th. Well, this was it: the day we would reach Appleby. We had made such good time we were getting near earlier than I had planned. It was a cold morning and not pleasant so we stopped when I found a seat rather than sitting on the wet ground. As we got closer we saw our first waggon come trotting up a hill and into a field. It made my heart lurch as, for all the joy of our walking, I did miss being with the horses. I had always imagined arriving here and being part of Appleby with our own ponies and waggons, so it was strange to approach on foot and I felt somewhat apprehensive. For the first time I felt alone and wished I was with a group.

We got to Appleby by midday. It was early closing, but I did my washing in the launderette. An old man there kept telling me I shouldn't be carrying such a heavy load and that I would pay for it later.

There were hordes of travellers everywhere and it was strange not being one of them. They made their own law at Appleby – for just that one week, and it reminded me of how we had passed through London with our horses. They all stared at me as though I was from another planet and I seemed as much a curiosity to them as they were to the tourists.

I got fish and chips and we sat on the riverbank eating them. Two women talked to us. They thought I was mad. They gave Talie a Penguin biscuit and 50p. Later, two girls came and gave me their "buy a lucky charm from a gipsy" spiel. They were only young but came out with the age-old lines of "I've got to buy food for me children" etc and "Me mother's just made 'em" (the charms). I gave them the 50p for persistence, and the charm was a tiny yellow sweet! I promised Talie I would replace his 50p, but decided to keep the sweet because you can make anything 'lucky' if you want to.

I was getting cold sitting by the river, having to summon the courage to walk up to the Fair site. I hadn't known before arriving that this was the very day they gathered, coming from all over the land, being allowed there for just that one week. I had a cup of tea, walked around a bit more, then plucked up courage and went to the site. On the way I passed groups of men who were calling out things about my being alone and not being with a bloke. Up and down the road they raced on wild horses, as did old men with ponies and traps – up and down, up and down – and there were great loaded pick-up trucks with children spilling out of every crevice.

I walked onto the site and the power of the hill hit me. I asked a man if it was ok to go over the back and put my tent up. Everyone seemed amused by me, but not actually able to work out exactly what I was.

I went over the brow of the hill away from everyone and only put the fly-sheet up. Some boys came over and sat chatting and playing with Talie, who wanted to go off with them and be a true gipsy lad. I wondered whether they would hang around and become a nuisance, but they were really nice and when I said I had to put the baby to bed, went straight away.

It was good to lie hearing the whinnying of horses again, but I felt overwhelmed. The hill was such a powerful centre, like a great mother calling her children to her. From all over the land they were coming, following their traditional paths as they had for centuries, maybe even for millennia: year after year, generation after generation – all those routes leading to this one hill. It seemed a confirmation of something; a great tribal gathering, an affirmation that they are still doing it, and I recalled that strange 'memory' I'd had of a great ancient gathering on Windmill Hill in Wiltshire.

Maybe they are ancient Dreaming Paths they are following, the original purpose lost. Now our journey had joined theirs, however lightly, and maybe ours had been one of theirs long ago. Everything felt vast and timeless. I remembered how travelling people had accepted us when we were with our horses, glad to see people still doing it, however 'green' we were. I thought of how the tourists would come for a few days and then when it was over, how badly the travellers would be treated again. I thought of what Talie and I were doing, that you could still walk and stop and sleep on the land. It felt important to claim that right and keep something ancient alive. There on the hill was the gathering of those who had been doing it longest, and we were there too – in the Gemini wind on the Fair Hill.

We slept on the hill and merged with it. The evening and night were peaceful, calm and quiet with no noise from the site and no hassling by dogs, donkeys, children or men. They were all up early, exercising their horses and it was good to hear the sound of sledge-hammer on tethering stake again. I gave Talie the wooden Gemini sign and he sat outside as I packed up, playing with it and some Fair Hill stones. It was magical and shamanic, as if he knew what he was doing. When all was packed I put the sign deep in a gorse bush, near to where we had slept. As with the others, I knew it may not stay there long, but it was the placing of them which was important. Their energy and significance passed into the earth and what then happened to the piece of wood was unimportant.

At the end of the journey, when the circle was complete, the energy of the circle would remain.

It was slightly drizzly as we walked back down towards the town. A woman in the most fantastic chrome caravan I had ever seen, with windows like house windows, called me over, gave Talie a biscuit and said if ever I didn't want him any more, to give him to a gipsy. She said she'd worried about us sleeping out on the hill in the wind and had thought of asking her husband to make me a shelter at the back of their van. I said we'd been fine. Like all the others who spoke to me, and like the Aborigine women, she kept asking me where my husband was. They seemed unable to understand a woman being on her own through choice.

I felt a sense of acceptance that morning. The children didn't laugh so much and I was no longer fair game for being sold a charm. I had slept on their hill and gained some level of respect from them, no longer just a punter. As with the Aborigines, I knew I couldn't photograph them, or what was going on there.

For all that, I still felt alone. It would be several days before the Fair was open to the public and I remained overwhelmed by the energy of the whole gathering. If I had been with even one other person it might have been different. I didn't feel I could leave the tent up with our things in it, so would have to carry my whole load wherever I went, both down to the town and around the site. It didn't seem likely I would meet anyone I knew and felt I couldn't stay there all those days on my own. I wrote at the time that I chickened out, but looking back I don't think I did at all.

I made some phone calls and heard that an acquaintance had been in an accident, so decided to spend a few days with them, then return for the main Fair days. I felt like a wimp, but it had all been a bit too daunting.
June 11th. We went back to the Fair. The rainfall had been colossal; no longer those lazy, hazy days of flaming June. It was still pouring, but my heart was high. Talie and I were working as a team now, each doing our own bits of magic. I put most of it down to him – looking after his old Mum and himself. I was sure Lizzie and Paul would be there and specifically asked Talie to help us find them easily and not have to search the whole site in the rain. As we approached the Fair entrance a voice called out "Jill" and it was Lee, a friend of a friend of a friend of theirs, and he told me where their caravan was. A weird shiver went through me when things like that happened.

The site was incredibly wet and muddy and there were loads more vehicles, people and everything than there had been when we left. There was now a track with vehicles on either side of it, leading right to the space where we had slept, and their van was near that spot, which again gave me a shiver. They weren't there and their van was locked, so I just sat in the rain, covered in plastic, glad to be back, and to have someone to sit and wait for.

They returned after a while. They had left their horses in Scotland and just come with the van and their dogs. I had a chat with them and a cuppa and a bit to eat, then Lee looked after Talie while I put the tent up in the mud. I had to put the inner bit up to keep us warm and secure, but couldn't tell which way the wind was blowing and it was hard to find a place where we'd be comfortable and wouldn't be run over by vehicles in the dark, but I managed it somehow.

It was very windy, blowing side-on to the tent, but we were fine and snug. There was a massive amount of rain in the night, and in the morning, although we were surrounded by puddles, I found I had instinctively put us on a raised bit of ground, like a little island. In the evening I had been loath to close up the front, for the sight of the cloud and mist hanging low over the dark Pennines was excitingly beautiful. Yes, the Pennines were in sight and we were about to cross the spine of Albion.

The inside of the tent got saturated, even underneath both us and the sleeping bag and I didn't know if it was a leak or condensation. We would have to live with the warmth of damp wool and feathers for a bit. When Lizzie and Paul were up I left Talie with them while I packed. They were soon going to move off. Maybe if they had stayed I would have too, but it was so wet I felt I couldn't cope with being alone with a baby and all our stuff in that situation. However, Gemini Talie and I had spent another night on the Fair Hill.

We walked down past many stalls. I looked unsuccessfully for something for Talie's birthday, but was fascinated by all the harness for sale – and waggons and carts and gigs and trolleys and many two- wheelers. At the Post Office in town I collected mail from all over the place and after a pot of tea in a cafe, once again got fish and chips and sat on the riverbank to sort out all the post, as it was no longer raining. There were lots of lovely letters and quite a few things for Talie's birthday. I bought him a really tiny iced cake, knowing it would be just the two of us for his birthday next day. How different it would have been had Square Wheel Theatre come to Appleby Fair.

The day intermittently brightened, though still windy – very much an Air sign. The town was teeming with tourists, travellers and horses – some being washed in the river, lots being shown off with snazzy harness and more being ridden and driven up and down. I found myself listening to their hoof-steps as many of them weren't shod. Heading north for Alston our route away from the town took us back past the Fair site and along a road which was closed off for the horse selling. Up and down the horses were ridden at breakneck speed, wild

manes, tails and feathers flying, the riders crying out so you'd get out the way. Man and horse, boy and horse and sometimes girl and horse.
What energy of horse. What horse power.

A man we had met when travelling with our horses recognised me as I passed by on foot and asked if we had any of ours there: people had always wanted to buy them. I had to tell him I no longer had mine and was now walking on my own, but it had been fantastic to be recognised by him.

We left all that behind and the wonderful road carried on – miles of wide verges full of tethered horses, and green and tall cow parsley where there were none. The sky was dynamic – dark clouds followed by white, then blue sky and sun and always the powerful wind. I wanted to put some distance between us and the Fair site so passed a few good stopping places and made the decision to do a few more miles a day from then on, as I was getting stronger.

We got near Long Marton and saw a patch of grass off the road leading down to a gate. The clouds were gathering and it was about 5pm, so I thought we had better stop. I went to a house opposite for water and asked whether it would be alright to camp there. The man said "yes, it's common ground", but as I walked away he called me back. "No, come and stay in our loft". He showed me to a wonderful loft over a barn – with a bed in it. His wife came in and said "No, we've an even better place", so we ended up in a little out-building which they had done up for their many frequently- visiting grown-up children and their families. There was running water and an electric kettle and I was thrilled to bits. I had wanted Talie to wake up on his birthday somewhere safe and secure, so we could fully enjoy it. He went to sleep and it grew dark. I thanked the earth who looked after us and hoped I could do the same for her. It was nearly a year that Talie had been by my side and I felt totally blessed.

June 13th 1985. Talie's first birthday. He woke at 5.30am, as if he knew there were exciting things awaiting him. The sun shone in on us and it looked like it might be a nice day. He opened his presents, enjoying all the shiny wrapping paper, and especially liking the toy from Kevin, which was a plastic thing of circles within circles which spun round. Lynne sent a brown teddy, a bit like a koala, some beautiful bells on rainbow ribbon and a badge which said 'Merlin the Immortal'. Richard and Juliet sent the story 'Taliesin and Avagddu', a photo of me very pregnant at Thorpe Fair, a lovely card, a marble like a tiny crystal ball and some balloons. There was a rainbow one which I blew up and tied to the rucksack where it flew all day. He played with it a lot every time we rested and it only popped when we finally stopped for the night. Some travelling children we passed asked for it and I said "no" and felt mean. I should have given them one of the others, but they were packed away and not easily reached.

Taliesin on his first birthday where we camped near the spine of Britain.

I had a fragment of Polly's hair with me and had intended to leave it on the Fair site, but decided not to and kept it in my coat pocket for the rest of the journey. It had been to the Fair and that felt enough. I worried something might have happened to it on the hill which might then have affected her. I had the same feeling when Lorye gave me the beautiful metal horse with its great curved neck when we left Glastonbury. I had wanted to hang it up in the waggon, but couldn't bring myself to hang it up by its neck.

We left the lovely people. They said we could stay another day, but I felt we should get on as we had only just started after our break. It was a very Gemini day again: sometimes dark clouds gathered and threatened rain and storms which never quite manifested; at others there was blue sky, white clouds and sun. When it was dull and the grass was wet we only had short rests and I didn't feel as properly relaxed as I had in the long hot days when we began. However, at one point I sat by a wall and went into a light trance, placing myself at the top of the Egg of the journey and seeing it as a glowing white crystal beneath me, a beautiful experience. The woman we had stayed with told me there was a place near St. John's Chapel where there were geodes.
The greenery was darkening even more and the fields were lush. There were stone walls some of which were brick red; but there were fences and hedges too. There were verges for quite a way out of Appleby, but now I felt I should only camp on them when all else failed. I didn't want to sneak into the lush

fields as the grass was a crop we might damage. I was thinking I should ask at farms now.

Well, this was Talie's first birthday. The lovely people had given him an apple and an orange, but I hadn't given him anything yet. We were just together and that was beautiful. The day brightened as it wore on and we found a quiet village with a big green at lunchtime and I thought it a good place to have his 'tea party' in case the weather wasn't so good later. He enjoyed his teeny tiny cake and other sickly things, including some Smiths crisps: a lovely gentle little party. The village was huge and rectangular with a large green in the centre which had animals grazing and the feel of something unchanged about it.

Walking on we somehow went farther than I had initially intended, then sat by a river as Talie talked to cows across the road. When I got to a village about a mile before I was meaning to stop I thought I had better get some water, asked a farmer if he had a field we could go in and he said there was a Common up the back. That seemed too good to miss as I was by then feeling quite tired. It was wild and huge, a sort of heath with grass and gorse. We sat in the lovely sun and played as I slowly put up the tent, good to feel secure and relaxed for his birthday night. A woman came for a chat and asked if we wanted anything and as it happened we didn't. We were wearing all our dirty washing and it was too difficult to take off. We lay down to sleep at around the time of his birth the previous year. What a year it had been, and now we were in the foothills of the Pennines.

We woke to a tent soaked in dew, both outside and in. I loved it there so much and took my time, lingering over the packing and the sun dried everything. It was a fascinating village with a particularly ancient quality I'd not encountered anywhere else. It had some place into which they used to herd livestock and close it over, so they were underground when the marauding Picts came by! This green also was used to graze ponies and goats. The village centre was set back off the road, so it took me a while to find its little Post Office, where I sent some stuff back to myself in Wales. Every little made the load lighter, and included the maps we had now walked away from.

Once again the day would sometimes get hot, then cloud over and be cold, so I didn't know whether to wear my coat or not. It was heavy and when I didn't wear it I tied it across the top of my rucksack. We came to another village for lunch. There was no shop, but it had a little pub called 'The Sun' so I had Guinness and crisps and nuts. It became gloriously sunny, so we sat on the high green, looking down on the surrounding land. A grocery van came round, and I got a few things, including a tin of 'Goddess' fruit salad, which I couldn't resist. The woman who had chatted with us the previous night rode by on a

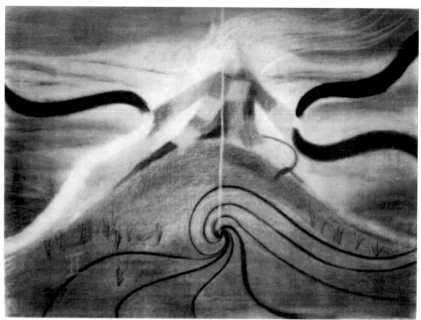

My image of the Horse Mother of Appleby

bike and told me of a wind which occasionally reached 100mph and had been known to blow a cow from one side of a field to the other. She was a mine of interesting information!

It clouded over again and, after clearing some rubbish from the green, we set off. I was beginning to sense Talie getting a bit bored on my front and wished I could carry him on my back so he could watch more, but I didn't see how – without that old fantasy pram! We passed a campsite in Ousby, but it was small, full of caravans, no tents, and looked very posh, so I walked on and found a river with interesting places beside it. There was a bridle-path signed, so I went through some gates and up the path a bit out of sight. The field was grazed so I didn't think anyone would mind us being there. It grew cold so I put the tent up. Outside it was incredibly still, with mists rolling over the fells towards us and even into the tent. It was so silent I could actually hear the mist. No traffic. No planes. No machinery taking in silage. Just a rare bird and a few sheep. The tent was filled with the pungent perfume of crushed yarrow.

Once again we took our time leaving, waiting until the sun dried things that were wet from the mist and dew. It was so peaceful that the mile and a half to the next shop felt easy and we sat for ages on the grass eating lunch and the 'Goddess' fruit cocktail. Later we passed a place called Tod Hills which had

283

lots of little mounds and I wondered if they were ancient. Distance is strange: sometimes I seemed to get along faster than possible, then a short bit would take ages. Suddenly we were on the next map and I almost expected to see a line on the ground where the edge of the map was. We sat by a river, then got water from a place called Hazel Rigg and I wondered what a Rigg was, what a Heaugh and what a Clough.

We went up an unmade track, rather like Wiltshire's Ridgeway Path, so steep it was almost as much as I could do and I had to stop often, sometimes after only a few yards. We were ascending the Pennines at last. It was hot and sunny with shadows of clouds and areas of light moving like patchwork across the hills. We got to an A road. It would have been too hard to continue straight up the track across the fell, so I went on the larger road, but it was quiet without much traffic. I found it easy to walk and got along fast until we reached another public bridle-path and settled near that feeling pretty secure. It was wild land, and as the evening came the sparse traffic stilled to nothing. There were snipe in the night and the eerie sound reminded me of the Hebrides. I thought this was probably the best bit of the walk and I must savour it. It was my kind of landscape – bare, rugged, high, overlooking the land for miles around. We were up in the clouds.

Next morning those clouds came rolling down. I climbed a steep path and came upon a cafe, like an oasis in the desert. It was on a 'beauty spot' where cars parked and people sat and looked through their windscreens at nature. I had a proper sit down and a meal. Talie ate some chips and beans and crawled up and down and met lots of people, which made him happy. I deposited a heavy load of rubbish in a bin, cleaned my teeth, went to the toilet, got water and set off again.

This part was along the main road, but it was peaceful and almost like those in the Islands. I was stopped twice by people in cars: a woman from Newcastle paused for a chat and good wishes and gave Talie a Twix, then two women from Hexham gave us money for Oxfam. It was an exhilarating day and I didn't feel tired even though it was cold and windy. We had great stops, looking out over the valley and fells and I didn't suppose there would be many more days as good as that, and indeed later in the day it got more occupied with some fields, so I took a back track and found a walled path to nowhere and camped there, having asked a neighbouring farm person, who felt sure it would be ok.

It had a beautiful view with only the sound of lambs and birds, but, because it was wet there were a lot of slugs - enormous black ones, some 4" long or more and I'm afraid they are one of the few forms of life I find repulsive. The tent was light and transparent in the setting sun and I didn't have my usual feeling of security and had some weird dreams. I decided to pause at St. John's Chapel, which would be the high point of our midsummer.

It was warm and cosy and we took our time next morning. The slugs surrounded us but weren't too much trouble as once again we seemed to have found a solitary dry patch to sleep on. We walked down into Alston, which was pleasant and very hilly. I was fascinated by the change in accent of the people. Where we had been at the weekend they had spoken a Cumbrian? Lancastrian? -type lilt, but now already had that NE/Durham/Geordie-ish accent. We went to a cafe and had lunch, then to a launderette, which provided a poor wash for the money it charged. At the Tourist Information Office I got the next map, but not the one after, as I hadn't yet decided which way to go. It was dull and dreary, so I sat under a bus shelter to sort out all the shopping and had to stop Talie playing with discarded cigarette ends. A couple gave him 20p, I had another tea, which was a bit of an indulgence, then set off again. The wind was really cold and there was light rain, and a lot of the route was up hill. I now had an enormous load and was hoping my shoes would last until Durham.

After a while I had to change and feed Talie, sitting on wet grass in the rain, so thought "this is far enough" and asked at a place which might have been a farm. I was unsure of the area as there was a nearby hotel and I thought they might be snobby, but a woman said I could go over in the meadow under some trees. It was hazardous getting there, through long grass, stones and fallen trees and I didn't want to fall or get a sprained ankle. I wasn't sure if I'd ended up in the place she meant, but found a nice flat bit and set up the tent while still wearing Talie in the Snugli, which was quite an achievement. We had to zip up the inner to keep the slugs out, but had a still and cosy night. I continued to have intense dreams, including one about three old women, one of whom was teaching me about leys and energy lines projected out into space; where the energy nodes were planetarily, and where they were in the universe. I felt my dreams were either involved with or coming from Lynne, though I couldn't explain why.

It had been a peaceful Dark Moon but I was hardly aware of it darkening those nights as they themselves were light. The hillsides were all grazed now and there were no more lush pastures being cut for silage. The green was darkening even more and Nature already felt ripe.

Chapter 20: Durham, Cancer.

June 18th. The gas cylinder on the stove ran out. How fast the water boiled on the new one! I had to work out how long the old one had lasted so I could plan when I'd need another. There were lots of slugs again and Talie was playing with them. I tried not to go 'ugh', but at least he wasn't trying to eat them.

The walk towards Nenthead wasn't at all what I had expected from the map – it was open and wild and beginning to look like old mining country with many reclaimed slag heaps, and though everything was now covered by grass, heather and sheep, it had the shape, somehow, of having been turned over by the hand of man.

Nenthead was, I supposed, an old mining village. I bought 2 days provisions and ate some, sitting outside the shop, where the people were very friendly. I then got confused, because my map said I was on the A689 but the road signs said it was the B9243. I thought I must be on the wrong road or they'd built another one somewhere, but it just seemed to have changed its number.

We climbed a steep hill which was 1 in 5 for a mile and a half – up, up, up. There was a glorious view – wild and free with unfenced roads. At last, after many stops, lots of sunshine and being able to direct a lorry driver with the use of my map, we reached the top and a (somewhat battered) sign which said County Durham. I was thrilled to bits and picked some heather from the spot.

We lay there in the sun, full of our achievement and very happy. A frog came to visit and sat with us. Talie couldn't see it because it was so well camouflaged as it snuggled down into the heather and didn't move. I was surprised to see one so high up, but didn't know much about the life and habits of frogs.

This was the cusp of Gemini and Cancer – air leading to water. After a while it grew colder and too windy to stay up there for the night, so I walked down the other side of the hill, which immediately became 1 in 5 again. At the bottom of the steep bit I sat and wrote, and at 5pm realised I loved the place so much I would go down to a nearby river and set up the tent there. A sign had said 'St. John's Chapel - 6 miles'. Talie was a bit cold, so I put the tent up over him and he liked that. The sun came out and the evening was long with just the sound of the beck and not much traffic, so we had another contented night beside water as we approached Cancer, which seemed an even more watery sign than Pisces.

The early morning was sunny and Talie played outside with stones and earth and no nappy on. I wanted to collect wood for a fire, but it was too difficult with him at that age. Being near flowing water would have been a good opportunity to boil some for washing clothes, but I couldn't afford to use my little gas cylinder for such things; however I used some of the river water to wash up and wash some knickers without having to use precious drinking water. It began to cloud over, so I packed up. We seemed to have got into a routine of getting up about 7.15am and off at 10.30-11.00. I was so glad I had stopped there. Talie paddled his feet in the river before we left.

It was mostly downhill all day, wild and lonely and wonderful.

We passed a place with a great wheel and had a rest looking down on it. It was by a Visitor Centre and I was curious to know what it was. Parties of tourists were being shown round – some were Americans who called out "Hey, man" and "Peace, man", presumably at me. I didn't respond to being called 'man' and wondered what sort of world we lived in where 'peace' had become a term of mockery. Later I found the structure was the Killhope (!) Wheel, and these were lead mines, so was glad I hadn't gone down, imagining the ghastly conditions men must have worked in and wondering how many had died from lead poisoning. I thought how much mining still goes on in other countries with miners sometimes forced to work themselves to death. I didn't like the feeling there.

On we walked, still wonderfully high and free, and the road mysteriously turned back into the A689. We sat while some lovely Highland-looking cows and calves walked past, grazing the verges. On and on I walked, starting to come down and down through a series of villages, the first of which was indeed called Cowshill, and had not only a good little shop but litter bins and a toilet.

I was now on a gap between maps and felt strange being in a bit of land which wasn't on one, not knowing what was coming next. It was odd how I felt such need for maps, having to know exactly where I was all the time and only able to do that from a map. I stuck to the main road, as it looked as though it would take a huge effort to climb up the back way which might be a bit posh anyway. I accepted that this bit of my journey was rather towny and villagey.

At Ireshopeburn I felt I couldn't go much further. We'd had a rest in a playground where Talie had a good crawl, but there was a lot of litter and no rubbish bin, and some workmen who seemed to think we were weird. I turned off the road and found a grassy footpath beside another river. There were dog-walkers and fishermen and it was near some houses, but I didn't think anyone would mind. I went to a nearby museum for water and met some nice ladies in

'Rucksack on my back, Talie on my front': how I walked for 3½ months. At Ireshopeburn (photo Malcolm Humphrey).

there, so decided to visit it the next day. I was beginning to feel the need to stop somewhere for a day or two, and had to decide where to be for the Solstice.

It took me a long time to sleep, but at last I went off into peacefulness. I still had strange dreams, including one searching for a little white figurine carved out of ash which I had sent to Lynne in Australia, only in the dream she was a life-sized statue, and may have been alive.

We woke to a sun that was hot and strong and sat outside. There had been some comings and goings of dog-walkers and suddenly a man asked me if I'd like a bath and breakfast. His wife had passed me several times and told him to come and speak to me. I leapt at the chance, awed at the kindness of people we were meeting. These were Mavis and Malcolm Humphrey. He'd had open-heart surgery two years previously, but was up a ladder mending the gutter. There was also 'Dad', a sprightly, wiry chap who was 85 and deaf, but building a greenhouse. Mavis cooked me a wonderful breakfast with loads of tea and it was great talking to her, properly explaining my ideas. I had the impression it was an area of many interesting and aware people. I thought theirs might be an old railway house and even that there might once have been a railway going through their garden.

I had a gorgeous bath, with pink bath crystals, and washed my hair and some clothes. Mavis gave me a booklet about the area, we exchanged addresses and I kept in touch with them for years. I felt full of joy as I left, and went to look round the museum. A woman followed me all the time, which aggravated me and meant I didn't spend as much time looking at things as I would have liked. I don't know what she thought I was going to do. There wasn't much on pre-history, though there had been Mesolithic finds on the heights. There were lots of beautiful minerals and crystals, and I wondered where the geodes were. Malcolm came and took some photographs of us and later sent me some prints. I think they are the only pictures of me carrying Talie and the rucksack with the two bags in my hands.

It got cooler. We reached St. John's Chapel with its wealth of shops selling everything I needed. Some mail had been sent on from Appleby, but sent back to the Sorting Office as they had just put 'Jill Smith, St. John's Chapel' on it and not c/o the PO. They managed to trace it and it was going to be returned. I bought some food and sat on the green. There was a funeral going on, but everyone seemed very friendly.

I decided to walk up a track to be high for the Solstice and found a place with a stunning view of the surrounding hills. I spoke to a farmer and ended up talking to him for easily an hour; about cows calving and all sorts of things. I was surprised to learn there was almost as much intervention in calving as with humans giving birth. He told me lots of calves get stuck in funny positions and have to be delivered by caesarian. He was in awe of the female vet – "Just a slip of a girl like you" - who quite happily sliced into the side of a cow and yanked out the calf. I set up the tent and the sun set gloriously hazy and red. The farmer had said that when it was misty it wasn't going to rain.

Over a year previously, Square Wheel Theatre, making its preparations for the great trek round the land, had looked at the map and seen St. John's Chapel as the central northern point and designated it the place for the Summer Solstice – and now, a year later, it was just Talie and me who were here, high up on hills overlooking the valley. Everything had slowed down as we moved towards this day: long, long days awaited the pause, before the pendulum swung back towards winter again. It was high, crystal clear and pure. Just being was perfection.

June 21st. Summer Solstice. It got very windy in the night and kept me awake, then rained at dawn, so the time of sunrise was grey, misty, rainy and windy, with no sign of the sun. However, I felt strongly connected to Glastonbury Tor, as though there were a powerful line of light joining us, and we were as much there as where we were physically. At other times during the day I felt joined to Callanish and the Sleeping Beauty mountain. It was a day when one seemed to lose the confines of one's own body and be everywhere at once. I felt tired and every so often went off into a kind of trance, not being fully there for the whole day. At the moment of Solstice (10.44am) we were just in the tent, but the tent seemed to become the whole universe.

Later we had a joyful walk down into the town, though I had to be careful near the bottom not to miss my footing. My letters had come and several of them gave addresses of people in Durham where we might be able to stay, which was great news.

We walked higher up the hill and higher and higher into the mist. There was no sun so we just looked down onto the cloud-filled valley and a grey sunset. The day had been so simple and strong and I got a clear sense of the power of place as it had been before man tapped and channelled it, and was now beginning to destroy it, and something in me wanted to weep and rage with impotence at not being able to stop that destruction. Once, all things and beings had related to one another and I wondered how we could re-kindle in violent hearts the awareness of how things had once been and could be again.

As the Solstice night approached the pendulum swung away from the pause, and we lay and listened to the wind. Only the curlew had cried in the day and now there was just the haunting sound of the snipe, an occasional lamb and a distant lowing and I wondered whether the overdue cow had calved. There was wet grass and slugs beside the stony path, but shelter from the dry-stone wall. There was red clover, yellow king-cups and I had seen pink hawthorn, so slow to come, now fading and falling already.

I woke early, really refreshed. The wind had stilled and the cloud filled the whole valley. It had been good having a day of rest and I got off early, anxious to get beyond Stanhope and beginning to want to reach Durham. When we got back to St. John's Chapel I did more shopping and managed to cash a backlog of child benefit coupons without any problem. I waited for the chippie to open, thinking it good to eat something before walking, but it was almost too filling. There was nowhere to shelter and we sat beneath a tree on a seat covered in bird droppings.

We left St. John's Chapel, the Solstice behind us: the 'first day of winter' and it seemed we'd hardly had summer. Now we were descending. I loved the still long days and wished we needn't spend so much time shut up in the tent and it could be like those first few days again. It was hard to have rests as the ground was wet and it was threatening rain, so on we went, passing a caravan site where I got water. The fields were lush and managed and it began to feel middle-class and no longer wild.

It started to rain heavily and I went up a path to a spot I thought good for us camp, but there were broken walls and a pony came through, hassled us and chewed the rucksack, so I changed my mind, packed everything up again and went back to the road; but she followed us down and I got scared of being kicked. I thought 'you'd never think I'd travelled with a horse until recently'. How strange to be seen off by a horse.

I searched for another path which was marked on the map but didn't exist in reality, then saw a patch by a river, wandered into a farmyard to ask, saw no-one and went towards the water, but immediately a man appeared and asked where I was going. He obviously didn't want us there and suggested a caravan site a mile and a half away. When you only walk 5 miles a day you can't go one and a half more when you are so tired you need to stop.

We came to a Blue Circle cement works. There was a patch of ground outside a fence which was planted with trees, so I went in there and hoped no-one would turn me off. I'd felt edgy and wound up all day, probably because we'd come down from the high ground into the valley where the energy was very different. We'd heard gun-fire all day and now being near a cement works with its related quarrying made me feel they were tearing the flesh from our Mother's body.

However this spot, if we were left alone, was pretty amazing, with long undergrowth which I hoped wouldn't be hurt too much by our lying on it. Because of the slope of the ground the top of the tent, low at the best of times, was even lower than usual. There were a lot of insects and I expected to get bitten. As on most evenings, we only had the fly-sheet up, not the inner part of the tent which had a floor to it. There were also a lot of snails – that morning a snail had got into our cheese and eaten some. It was very, very damp and I was hoping we would soon find somewhere I could relax and feel secure, and wondered whether I should go up into the hills again.

We had no trouble at all from humans and didn't get bitten too much, the only upset being that Talie rolled over in the night and squashed two snails. Sorry snails.

I woke at 5.15am, still feeling edgy. There was a shift change at the quarry at about 7, even on a Sunday. I got on the road by 9, which was our earliest yet, and wondered whether the cement company owned all the land round there and the farmers were tenants. Many buildings looked derelict, or as though they were used by people from outside the area.

We found a quiet corner where we sat and had breakfast. I turned off our back road in order to go into Eastgate, hoping for a litter bin, and found a comfortable bus shelter where we sat a while.

Oddly, the main road had a nicer feel to it, but I determined to stick with the back way. There was a sign to a hotel which did bar meals and said 'children welcome', so I thought I'd try it for a cup of coffee. On the way we met a man who started to chat. He was from South Shields, but his son owned the hotel and had owned a lot of the surrounding land, though he'd now sold much of it off. He carried my bags and walked me to the hotel, taking us in to the part where they lived and giving me two mugs of tea. The son was a bit taken aback and the daughter-in-law never appeared, but Talie had a great time playing with the grand-daughters, Andrea and Emma, who gave him a Matchbox toy car (a Rolls-Royce Silver Shadow) which he was thrilled with. They said "We never play with cars" in that awful way little girls do. I hated how children were indoctrinated into gender roles so early in life, and remembered being a little girl playing with the boy next door. We used to have fights because he wanted to play with dolls and tea-sets whereas I wanted to play with cars and planes.

The grandfather walked with my bags back down to the road junction, chatting a while and giving me his address, saying I could stay any time I was in South Shields. He was so friendly, yet all the time kept going on about how he'd never liked women and hadn't had anything to do with one for 32 years.

After he left we sat a while on the cut grass. I decided to explore paths round the river for a possible stopping place, and finally found one leading to a disused quarry, and once there, wandered around until I found a place which felt safe. It was very windy, but there was a dip which provided some shelter, and though out of the way, was overlooked by a house on the other side. It was on old tarmac with about an inch of topsoil and mossy grass which, though perfect for sleeping on, was no good for sticking tent pegs into and I hoped they wouldn't be pulled out by the wind. However, on the flat surface there was more room in the tent than usual.

Talie went to sleep at about 3.30pm so I wrote a lot and the wind dropped.

In the night I dreamed I was somewhere immensely high, on a pinnacle of rock on top of a mountain. Up there was a kind of house and in it lived a woman-being who had others looking after her, like worker bees tending a queen. She was a being of amazing power and I had come to see her and was granted audience, and was in great awe of her. Her face was somewhat like that of a frog – a dark, brownish-red colour, flat and large with tiny eyes at the side, no nose and a huge flat, wide mouth at the bottom. She had flat things the same colour instead of hands and was dressed in dark green silk and satin, a bit gipsy-like, with drapery round her head. She was in a kind of small boudoir behind some curtains. I didn't feel subservient to her in any way and she seemed to share something with me (but when I woke I couldn't remember what). Then the people in the village below, who hated and feared her, rose up and began to dismantle the mountain, so that her house became more and more precariously balanced on shaky rocks and stones which were held up by wooden supports. In the end it became chaos and everyone fled, and in the melee I saw a mask lying on the ground. It was the woman's face, made from rubber.

We were up early again. I packed all the dirty washing together, aware I was taking a gamble on there being a launderette in Stanhope. I left some stale bread for nearby sheep, or whatever other beings wanted it. We walked into Stanhope – and there was no launderette – and no map. I did a sketch of the route ahead from a large atlas in a shop, did my shopping and had a cup of tea. I did some washing in cold water in the Ladies, but it had just been cleaned and left with water all over the floor, so everything I put down got soaked.

It was still early and I just wanted to keep going and not stop until 6 or 7 in the evening. We passed Frosterley, having been on a back road beside a railway line where we'd had some peaceful stops drying the washing on a fence. The rest of the day the wet stuff was tied on the rucksack to blow in the wind. We got to an awful A road, so I just kept on and on, walking on the road itself, because walking on a grass verge with a heavy load is difficult – you hardly lift your feet off the ground and any unevenness trips you or throws you off balance. This meant I had to keep my eyes constantly on the traffic, not enjoying the surrounding countryside.

Near Wolsingham I thought I'd had enough so asked a farmer, but he wouldn't put me on any of his land because the lads were shooting pigeons and he wouldn't want us to be shot. Or so he said. He directed me to a place further down the road, but when I got there it was beside a much traversed picnic area, and had signs saying it was private and belonged to an angling club. It was still before 4pm and I felt we'd be vulnerable there, as there were parked cars nearby which always seemed to hold the potential for something nasty.

After sitting coldly in the aptly named Windy Nook Picnic Area, I set off for Wolsingham, which still provided no map. I chose an incredibly long, steep hill out of the town, which was nearly as busy as the A road, and not seeming able

293

to rest just kept on and on. I got a pain in my diaphragm/stomach area: the only time I'd felt any physical ill-effects other than in knees, ankles and feet, but I nearly reached the top.

Up there I found a good place to stop, beyond some trees beside a wall. I had to put the tent up sideways so that, although it was level lengthways, the width was sloping down the hill. It was quiet, full of bushes, and with a lovely view. We had very little room, but were warm and cosy. I had been in a strange state all day, with this relentless drive to keep going, and must have walked twice as far as usual – 8-10 miles.

June 25th. We slept well on the slope, though there were many slugs. One had slid (slugged?) over Talie's face, leaving stuff like Evostick, and one may have been in my hair for it was hard to comb. Otherwise all was fine – a blessed place.

A wonderful day followed. The sky was blue and the sun came out, there were white clouds and it felt like summer again. We walked to Tow Law and suddenly I felt I was in the North East. It was so different from the towns of the previous day – everyone was friendly, helpful and supportive and cafes had signs saying 'flasks filled'. I sat in the sun for lunch and two really nice men came to talk to me. I tried to phone Griff in Durham, the contact who might be able to find us somewhere to stay, but the phone was broken. I sent him a postcard instead.

A shopkeeper said it was only 9 miles to Durham, but I found that hard to believe. The worst thing about being off the map was not knowing distances. I set off again, once more feeling great to be up on high unfenced moor where I could see for miles. The weather was beautiful and some men in a car stopped to give me money for Oxfam.

As I went on, the landscape changed into one of fields, some being cut for silage and others with crops, and there were no verges to the roads. I got to a point just outside Cornsay Colliery at 5pm, having taken it easy after the marathon of the previous day and only done four and a half to five miles. I felt sure we would reach Durham the next day.

There was a triangle outside some fences where I thought we could camp and sat there a while in the sun, then thought that maybe, if I asked, I could go just inside the fence. I walked down to the farm and the man said I could go in a lush meadow by a stream. I was so grateful and happy. We spent the evening sitting outside and at last all the washing was dry. It was good to feel really secure and relaxed, but oddly it wasn't such a comfortable night. I was a bit cold, as I'd taken a few layers off when I was hot and hadn't put them on again.

294

Here I had another dream: I was watching a feature film being made about aborigines. They were real people doing real 'stuff', but in a landscape 'set'. There was a major gathering and ritual going on in a kind of village. I was staying with some people and went for a walk, finding myself in the actual landscape which the film set had been of. It was a profound experience to walk through the physical landscape in which I had seen so much going on in the film. I came to a huge clearing among hills, which was where the village and ritual had been. It wasn't like the parts of Australia I'd been to, more like England with woods and clearings and paths. I came upon two rows of corrugated shacks painted peeling green. They were like rows of stables facing inwards, but the doors were all closed. One on the left opened and this oldish aboriginal woman stood there staring at me with her black sparkling eyes. I was carrying a plastic Bambi model, orange and white, long and thin, and about 6" high. She said "you watch, he won't be with you for long" then pointed to another open door opposite and said "you'd better give it to him". Inside was an old aboriginal man sitting and working at something, like an old craftsman. He wore dark clothes and a brown hat with a floppy brim and was white-haired. He looked up at me with those same black, sparkly eyes. I gave him the Bambi, not knowing why or what he would do with it. I returned to where I was staying, later setting out with the boy and girl of the family to return to the place and get the Bambi back. When we got there it was all shut up and I didn't know which one was the old man's door as you couldn't see the doors when they were shut. There was something you had to call out to make them open. How could I call the old man and get the Bambi? You couldn't just go and knock and ask, you had to say the right thing and then he would come out. I really had to get the Bambi back, but didn't resolve it and Talie woke me up and was in a grisly mood. I was concerned about the Bambi. Talie hadn't been in this dream, though he was in most of them now. Was he the Bambi (little deer/dear?) who wouldn't be with me long?

In the morning we watched the man at the farm making silage. He had a huge square container and as more and more grass was put in it he went over and over it with a tractor, compressing it down.
We walked up a steep hill to the P.O. at Cornsay Colliery and people kept telling me a different way to go, but the Esh Winning route was flat. They said Durham was eight and a half miles and I wondered if I could do that in a day. Now I was near I wanted to get there. The sun was hot, and with no wind I was sweaty.

It was strange not knowing where I was, in the sense of distance. There was a beautiful unfenced bit with woodland beside it, but the whole area was hopeless for road signs. Most junctions had none, or old ones which had broken off or pointed in the wrong direction or were completely covered by trees; or really old ones which were so faded they couldn't be read unless you went right up to them. I kept asking people how far Durham was, but got completely different estimates. Now people drive everywhere they have lost the ability to judge distance.

We got to Esh Winning, but somehow cut through without seeing the centre. Clouds gathered and I was very hot. We got to a bus shelter just as there was a downpour, but it soon cleared. I was phone hunting, but for miles they were all out of order – one of the gathering signs that we were approaching the city. There was more rubbish, more graffiti, no seats in the bus shelters, bits of dumped metal everywhere, smashed glass in phone boxes, smashed phones....

On I went with no road signs to even tell me if I was on the right road, but the buses had Durham on the front. I got to Ushaw Moor: still no phone, so I sat on the grass, already tired, and felt I was overdoing it: 5 days walk in 3 days. After all that time I had developed blisters. The insides of my shoes were a mess and I thought they were decomposing. A nice district-nurse type person stopped for a chat as we were outside a clinic with lots of pregnant women going in and out.

In the next village at last there was a working phone. I made contact with Griff of Peace Action Durham, and found he was setting something up for us. The drive to get to Durham was relentless - and then suddenly there was a place I recognised. Floods of memories came back as though from a past life, which in a way it was. In the early to mid-'70s I'd come here several times with Bruce and my children, doing Community and Performance Art events at the Durham Light Infantry Museum and Arts Centre. It had been a good time then in the arts, with lots of Regional Arts Associations having money to spend on events such as ours. We had visited many places in the North East, but particularly Durham.

I pushed myself almost beyond limit, past the peace flower bed with its CND symbol in the centre of the roundabout by the viaduct, reached the peace paintings on the walls of the houses in Griff's terrace, and finally came to Griff's house. I couldn't find it at first and was in tears because I was so tired, but eventually I was there and had a lovely welcome. I had hoped to actually stay in the city, but it had been arranged for us to stay in Esh Winning! I had a bath and tea and coffee while they went out to the Woodcraft Folk, then Griff drove me back to Esh Winning, where there was a party going on. Lots of women talking to me thought I was mad for doing the walk and couldn't understand why it wasn't dangerous being out in the country. I realised people had come to fear the countryside itself, as if it had some inherent danger, whereas if you are aware of the specific dangers there might be – and they aren't from the actual countryside – then you can avoid them.

Talie was beside himself with joy to be with people, children, babies and toys. This was another whole terrace of Peace People, and we were to be 'passed around' them. Nicola, the woman who was organising it, seemed an interesting person and was a Cancer in this Cancer of the Gipsy Switch.

It was strange to be precipitated from 'out there' into such a different reality, and in the heart of an alternative peace community. I found it hard to sleep, being too warm in a soft bed!

June 27th – July 3rd. In fact we stayed most of the time with Barrie Ormsby, who 'fell in love' with Talie. It was quite awesome to be with Talie sometimes, and experience the way he 'charmed' people. He often seemed to me like an old wise being, and other people picked up on it too. We saw a lot of the friendly people round there during our stay and felt highly supported. I love Durham and went into the city almost every day, bought another pair of shoes identical to the previous ones (some kind of Hush Puppy), more socks, and did practical things which I couldn't while travelling. I did lots of washing, collected my post and sent some, bought more maps, sent stuff back to Wales and planned the next part of the journey. I heard that Richard and Juliet had had a baby boy (Sharma) in June.

We seemed to bring the sun to Durham. I had carried a sun flag in my rucksack all the journey so far, Sandra having asked me to carry it for luck, as she was soon to move to Durham. She was a Cancer and I felt strongly connected to her while there and she was a deep part of this section of the journey.

I found it important to locate the sacred centre of the city, which was the heart of our Cancer on the Gipsy Switch journey. At first I was drawn to the cathedral on a huge mound almost completely surrounded by a huge loop in the River Wear. I was awed by the patterns on its pillars – diamonds, zigzags and spirals – which echoed the Neolithic carvings we had so recently seen in Newgrange. I felt sure that this had always been a sacred site. The legend is that the first church was built there because they had been led to the site by a cow, which made me think of Brighde/Bridget.
Now, the grass outside the cathedral was pristine with precise stripes and 'keep off the grass' notices. I bonded deeply with how the place must have been before anything was built there, as though the buildings were transparent or in another reality.

As I visited more often, I saw the 'mound' as an island and a giant pregnant belly. I walked the path down by the river moonwise, beginning my Cancer ritual, which I intended to complete on the full moon. I perceived the river as a serpent encircling the mound and later learned there are legends of a dragon or worm in those waters. This was where I must leave our wooden Cancer sign.

We were now on the east of the country, 'coming down' the land from this point on, with the year past its peak, already descending towards the winter and south. The coming full moon felt strong, yet we had not seen it wax, the night skies having been so cloudy.

On its eve I felt drained and even Talie seemed strange, looking pale, with his brilliant blue eyes turned grey. I carried out my second moonwise perambulation on this dull, grey day. The river was smooth and calm and there were few people about. There were clear reflections of trees and I was deeply aware of the immense volume of its water and its deep looming sides. I was working at a very profound level, 'healing' the place, which seemed damaged by patriarchy and the harmful energy of the modern world. The sound of a man's footsteps followed us a long way, but I didn't look round. Everything felt negative, so I took it on and came through. It was hard work, but the sun came out, the sky cleared completely for the first time in weeks, and there was a glorious sunset.

July 2nd. Full Moon. At the actual moment of full moon I just stood holding Talie and felt its radiance shine into us. We went into Durham and made our third moonwise circle of the womb-eye-land. There were many people in punts on the river and strolling round the paths and I walked as near as I could to the water all the way.

In the evening we returned with Nicola, crossing the bridge from the University and walking until we found a holly tree and bare earth down by the still water. Holly is the tree of this time of year in the Beth-Luis-Nion calendar. Everything was still, silent and warm. We drew a circle in the earth, a circle which was the universe. At the east we put sweet apple incense, at the south a candle the colour of the river, at the west a jug of river water and at the north a stone which Nicola had brought from Findhorn. In the centre we put 3 roses from Nicola's garden, then traced the zodiac signs round the outside, putting the wooden Cancer sign in its place and leaving a gap for Leo as we hadn't been there yet, putting Sandra's sun flag there instead. I had a vision of each place and travelled the whole journey again in my mind. The silver-white moonlight filled us and I sensed everything being connected and part of one great whole. We were surrounded by huge green trees rising high above us and the deep, still water beside us, silent but for the plopping of fish. The summer sky was still partly light from the setting sun as we spoke our wishes and gave our thanks and sat there a long while. We passed the flag round the elements and asked that Sandra should easily find a home in Durham. We dipped the Cancer sign in the water of the serpent river as the incense went out, then slowly removed the objects until only the candle burned. I took the Cancer sign and in the almost dark placed it in the holly tree. Leaving, we felt we had reclaimed the place. It had been notorious for attacks on women, and girls arriving in the city were warned not to go there. As we returned to Esh Winning we saw the great moon rising higher and purple in the sky. I realised how low she was in the summer now and that we were only 2 years off the next southerly major moon standstill, when the moon would rise at its lowest for 18.6 years.

Thursday July 4th. I could so easily have settled for ever in South Terrace, Esh Winning. I had seen Griff the previous day and given him Sandra's sun flag. He hung it in his window and left it there until she had a home in Durham. The time there had been intense and I felt it would take me days to get over it.

Nicola picked us up and drove us out of the city to Shincliffe. We had a drink and sat outside a pub, then went with her about 2 miles to a busy C road. It was great to be 'seen off' for once. She gave us a crystal – the sort you hang in your window – and tied a piece of red thread which had been to Greenham round my wrist, then left.

I anticipated the next part of the journey being strange as we needed to wend our way between cities. Stopping had affected me and I felt unfamiliar with the journey and with the reality of our life in it, was nervous and couldn't relax. It was a straight run down to York without a break and felt quite daunting. We turned a right-hand bend and headed south. Things were now agricultural and reminded me of East Anglia. I felt I was heading 'home' except that East Anglia wasn't my home any more. I walked on a bit after Nicola left, found a yellow-arrow-signed footpath and went over a stile into a field of sheep. We were near the road and within the sound of the A1(M), but it felt good and I hoped the farmer wouldn't mind.

The peak was passed: flowers withered and even a leaf or two; plants and grasses were going to seed; ash keys hung in green bunches; there were pink and white roses in the hedgerows and the deadly nightshade was in flower. There was a paleness in the fields where the hay had been taken and some verges had been cut. I had seen baby apples swelling on trees and there were flies and crickets in the muggy damp. It was all a lesson about life – the rising to the peak, the descending, the maturing and ageing which in the ripening and bearing of fruit is all part of the cycle. In the modern world we see ageing as a failing instead of just a changing. We need to see our own ageing selves once more as ripening and bearing the fruit of wisdom.

A lot had changed in a week. I asked for protection and strength.

Chapter 21: Moving down to York and Leo.

When I woke I felt I'd had enough and didn't want to go on with the journey any more, possibly affected by things the women in Esh Winning had said. It was a misty but warm morning, and soon the sun broke through and we sat outside for breakfast. What a joy it was to sit on grass and feel it was still summer as we watched the surrounding field with its old plough ridges and shorn sheep with their new wool already growing. We set off on a lovely, quiet road, and suddenly I was completely 'in' it again, and a great strength came flooding back into me.

It grew hot and humid, the sunshine hazy, and we went through a very magical area and came upon an extremely ramshackle and decrepit pub on top of a hill. The door was open, so I went in to ask for water though the place smelled of woodworm killer. A woman called down through a locked door and told me to fill my container in the Ladies. Next to the pub were some caravans and I wondered if they were travellers. It was all a bit faerie round there.

The miles seemed to drop away and I felt I was getting even fitter and stronger. We sat on a seat and drops of rain seemed to form out of the air. At the first village the women in the shop knocked 35p off my bill – and took my rubbish! There were so many wonderful people in the world and I felt I wasn't giving much in return. But Talie was, for fleeting glimpses of him seemed to give people enormous happiness.

However, this was a very man-made landscape and we passed a fully operational colliery. It began to rain – at first lovely summer rain, but then much heavier. Talie was in his waterproofs, but I couldn't bear to put on my coat, determined it was still summer. At a town we sat in a bus shelter and a strange woman couldn't understand I was on a journey, didn't want to catch a bus and didn't actually have a destination on a daily basis. She enquired in a hushed voice if I were 'short of money'. I asked if there was a cafe and a man said a pub down the road would do me tea. I had a whole pot: 50p for 4 cups.

Outside the rain had stopped and the sun was shining again. I had to decide whether to continue on the very busy B road, which was quite built up and not likely to provide much for the night, or onto a C road which was a mile and a half longer. I chose the latter.

We paused on wonderful wide verges which would have been perfect for the horses, but this C road, though beautiful, was busier than some A roads, with lorries continuously thundering by. Eventually I started to look for somewhere to stop, rejected a few potential spots which felt strangely vulnerable, and plodded on until I saw some farms ahead, deciding to ask at one with chickens outside. The woman saw me coming and opened the door. She asked her husband and he agreed we could go in what was virtually their back garden. It was a patch of grass with young fruit trees and chickens and looked as though it had recently had a horse in it. I was thrilled to be somewhere I wouldn't have to worry about anything. She put the kettle on and I filled my billie and had a cup of tea. She adored Talie and gave him three biscuits, then kept coming out, bringing me first a pint of milk, then a cup of tea, then a bowl of water to wash him in and then another tea and some sandwiches and two eggs to boil for breakfast. I felt we must be doing something right to be so looked after. She said we could stay the weekend if we wanted a rest. It was tempting, but I felt we'd only just set off again and must move on. I had easily done seven and a half miles and was quite blissed out.

It was a bit cold in the oddly disturbed night. I made tea in one of their china mugs, as it tasted better than in my plastic one. It was a joy to have plenty of water and not have to eke it out. I started a new gas cylinder to boil the eggs, leaving a bit in the other for making tea. We were invited in for tea and toast and marmalade and Talie had a good crawl on the floor and got fussed over. A wind blew up, the sky being sometimes blue and sometimes cloudy. I was a bit confused when packing up, and this wasn't helped by the lady incessantly warning me of the dangers of camping out, as it somehow undermined the strength of my personal protection and my relationship with the spirits of place. I reckoned people in cities were constantly bombarded by negative news from the media which made them afraid to go outside their front door unless it was straight into a car. I believed fear itself creates danger, breeding an ever-growing downward spiral of negativity which can actually cause unpleasant things to happen. I felt the media had a lot to answer for.

I didn't enjoy Sedgefield. Most people were nice enough, but some just stared without saying anything. We sat on the green, but the wind was a disturbance and I couldn't relax. When the sun went in it no longer felt like summer and the wind was a powerful energy all day. I had looked forward to the C road, but found it depressing and became rather downhearted. It was a Roman road and I had visions of military troops marching along it, then of the Old People, who felt like 'my' people; slaves forced to walk the road in chains with no water to drink. I felt tired, with little strength in my legs; lost and alone and out of contact with all those I knew and loved. This was unusual for me, for normally I felt closely connected to people, no matter how far I was from them physically.

After the wonderful wild areas I'd walked through, this was flat and managed and almost like being near London, or at least the worst bits of Norfolk. The fields were full of crops and there were no animals. There's a feeling of life when animals are on the land, and in the people who look after them. The crops grew in regimented rows like the Roman soldiers – the earth once more forced to unnaturally over-produce by the use of chemicals which killed insects, worms and wild natural plants; and for what? To create grain mountains while the other half of the world starved. It was desolate and cut off from nature, the roads fenced so I had no access to the land. I walked a narrow strip of tarmac with speeding cars at my side and nature beyond my reach. I sat in the long grass by the roadside, the child sleeping in my arms while the wind blew in the trees above, but everything else felt wrong. I realised what I was experiencing was actually the pain of the abandoned earth, and determined to give her all the love I could.

I thought that with no secret corners it might be hard to find somewhere for the night round there, and approaching Great Stainton noticed a rough paddock and a farm with grassy bits, so went to ask. Three young men sunning their oiled torsos in the garden came over with rippling muscles and told me that all their fields were full of bulls, which I knew was rubbish. They said the paddock wasn't theirs but belonged to people over the road. I asked there and a girl said "yes, of course" and gave me some water. I walked back to the paddock feeling great and went to the far end where the thistly grass had already been cut. All my negativity dissolved. The paddock was surrounded by tall hedges which included elder, grasses about 4ft tall and loads of flowers, insects, bees and not too many slugs. We sat playing, but there was a lot of gunfire. I couldn't tell whether it was pigeon-shooting or bird-scarers. It had turned beautifully sunny when we arrived and we were protected from the wind.

We woke properly at 6.30am. Talie was rather grisly and seemed to be starting a cold. I had to cuddle him a lot, which made packing up difficult, but managed it in the end. There was no hurry. The nearby village was surrounded by grazing land, though I never saw any cattle. It was physically similar to the previous day, but more pleasant. I somehow missed a pub, where I had hoped to leave some rubbish and get crisps or something snacky, but it was lovely weather – blue sky with clouds and a gentle breeze to break the heat. I felt much happier but Talie just wanted to lie on me and not play. We came to a quiet section where I would have felt happy camping on a verge, but felt I should go further and went on through another village where we rested in the shade.

Of course, the next bit of road was busy again and as it got late I had to start asking, though everything round there looked like factory farming. I walked up a path past a paddock of sheep to an empty house, loads of machinery, chemicals and a general air of un-cared for desolation. Round the back I found a man in a Land Rover. He was quite suspicious, seeming to regard me as a hippy or potential squatter, asking me what time I'd be off and so on, but said "ok, anywhere round the back, but keep away from the buildings". He did, however, show me the water tap in the pig-sty and said "let it run a bit". I chose a spot behind some large rolls of straw on an area which might once have been lawn, but was now overgrown and roughly cut. The man said there were rats in the straw, as though trying to frighten a silly woman. At one point he'd almost let me go in the house – "You couldn't make it much worse than the girl who's just left", though what I could see looked perfectly spick and span – but thought better of it, and I'd have probably been accused of all sorts if he had.

Talie went straight into a fitful sleep for 12 hours. I didn't worry about rats, just bagged the food up better than usual, reckoning we and the rats were on the same side in that environment. I didn't think country rats would bother us if they could help it, being more afraid of us than we were of them. Never heard a squeak of one. It seemed oddly fitting to be in a place full of chemicals in that strange damaged landscape. Although on our way to Leo, we were still in Cancer time-wise. Our Cancer had been full of the earth's pain and man's rape of the land: first the mining and now this agri-business.

But the tent was full of the perfume of pineapple-weed.

In the morning, after a night of rain, Talie was more his normal self and we set off for Middleton St. George. From the map I had thought this would be a sizeable town with lots of shops and cafes, but it was simply two villages with a lot of houses. I sat on a seat and a man gave me a pint of milk – perhaps he was a milkman going 'off-duty'. I wandered round the few shops and managed to get yogurt and baby food but no bananas, and the only nappies were too small. I got fish and chips though, and sat eating them in a playing-field. Talie crawled about and had a yogurt and half a chip.

I carried on and kept asking people where a bridge I was aiming for was, but none of them knew. For once the pack felt excruciatingly painful and heavy. At first I wore my coat, but the sun came out so I tied it on the rucksack where it was a nuisance. Some men on a golf course told me of a path which would cut out a lot of the convolutions I'd planned in order to cross the river – the serpentine, sinuous, Tees - yet somehow it felt important to take my winding route. We crossed the river south to north in order to carry on travelling south, and in so doing entered North Yorkshire.

Here it was all a bit posh, though there were wide verges in an avenue of trees, with old iron fences which I much preferred to barbed wire; but as it went on I passed several places with 'Private' signs. I saw a wide cut verge on a bend with a house opposite and asked if they would mind my putting a tent up there. The lady said why didn't I ask their neighbour if I could go in the field next to her, through a little gate. I left the pack in her garden and asked the neighbour: no problem. The lady's son carried the pack into the field. Talie was very tired and I had to hold him while I put the tent up. It was by now very hot.

The lady offered me a cup of tea, which was heaven. I asked for hot water to wash some clothes and she gave me some with Persil already in it, (I normally carried a small amount of washing powder in a plastic bag) so Talie and I sat on the grass and did the washing. It was amazing that a day which had begun with rain and no hope of drying anything, and a dirty clothes bag already beginning to smell, should end with everything dry and the clothes washed. The lady brought out tea, two cakes – and a banana (Talie's favourite food) – and I was amazed at how we were provided for, feeling we must be in tune with something and hoping all these helpful, giving people would get their just reward. It was a pretty idyllic spot without much traffic, though we were under the flight-path from Tees-side Airport and saw a few huge ones go over. I couldn't really believe in aerodynamics and how those massive machines stayed up in the air, yet we had gone to the other side of the earth and back in them. Talie felt a bit feverish and I hoped he wasn't going to be ill again.

It turned out to be a hard night. He cried a lot and was sick. He became a bit panicky, trying hard to explain how he felt, but not yet able to talk. I took him outside for a while and he seemed to come back into himself. Back in the tent I sat singing to him until he slept, then had to slip down without waking him into a position where I too could get some sleep, and had the horrendous experience of seeing 5 enormous black slugs crawl over the inside of the tent only a few inches from my face. At one point in the night I woke and felt my chest wet, as though my full, unsuckled breast had leaked, but when I touched it I found it was a SLUG!

He seemed reasonable in the morning, though quiet and needing lots of cuddles. I had woken from a dream where I was about to catch a coach to Callanish. The lady, Mrs. Severs, asked us in for tea and toast and marmalade again. I packed up, we said goodbye and she gave us an apple and another banana. It had rained a lot in the night and I supposed that was why the slugs had been out.

At last we were on a really quiet little road. I took my time and relished it, sure it would be busier later. At our first stop I found two large slugs at the bottom of the food bag. They had been at the trail mix so I had to re-bag it and throw some away. We continued through glorious countryside which either had long grass on narrow verges or very wide ones, and once again I thought what a dream it would have been for the horses. Talie was ok, though his eyes were heavy-lidded and he was quiet.

It did still feel like summer when the dull days grew hotter, but now there were signs, usually near rivers, saying 'Private land, Keep out', 'Private woodland, Keep out' and even 'Pig unit. Keep out', and many indications of battery farming.

After a coffee in a pub in a little village (Hornby) we turned left, stopped going south and headed east for a bit. Immediately it was better: flat and open, making it possible to see way into the distance. The blue Cleveland Hills were getting nearer.

The colours were changing. The grain was ripening by the day, to a paler green and then yellow. The whole landscape began to have that late-summer tinge of yellow-gold and there were types of butterflies I had never seen before. The previous day I had passed a house with a small field beside it in which there was a pump and had seen communal pumps on village greens, surprised there were still so many around and wondering how recently they had been used. I was enjoying the area, for all the agri-business of the farms.

I spied a rough bit over the way and spoke to a tractor driver coming down a track. He said it wasn't his, but suggested I ask his boss who lived a little way back. I walked to a bungalow where a man told me to go to the farm opposite and he'd phone and get them to meet me and tell me where to go. At first he was going to put us in a field they were going to spray, but decided on one they'd taken the hay off. We sat in the sun for a while and gradually the family came to visit us. There were 7 of them, though I didn't see them all. They brought me a cup of tea and the two bosses came to look at the curiosity! Talie was glad to see all these people even though he was tired.

We had a much more normal night with lots of sleep, though it was cold because the sky was clear. In the morning we sat outside and I was bought tea twice. One of the girls played with Talie as I packed up. Earlier he'd been taken to visit cows, pigs, chickens and the girl's mother.

The elderflower by the wayside was beginning to smell beautifully strong and is one of my favourite perfumes. I was really happy on those quiet roads. The hills ahead loomed larger and nearer, we crossed the A19 and a man stopped and gave me £2 for Oxfam.

I felt it would be silly to push myself on to Swainby, especially as I was aiming for a camp-site shown on the map, not knowing whether it would actually be there. I wanted to camp somewhere for a couple of days, so I could leave everything and go unencumbered to a nearby town to get stocked up for a few days in the Cleveland Hills. I was tempted to ask at Doddle Farm though, simply because I liked the name, but went on a bit further.

The first place I considered for the night looked a bit posh, but there were children playing outside and the man showed me round the back to a nice grassy bit which had goslings and sheep in it. He talked a lot and started advising me of all sorts of other ways over the hills from that which I had planned. The children played with Talie and I got the tent up. The wife returned. She was a physiotherapist and invited me to tea. She seemed to think my route was fine and told me it was an old drove road.

She went out and the man talked incessantly for hours and I couldn't get a word in edgeways. He told me of his life as an animal dealer, which meant he bought and sold stock rather than having all the hard work of breeding and rearing them. He then regaled me with horrendous tales of his exploits in the SAS, where he had dealt out death in quite a personal manner. He was now part of a kind of 'secret society' which was stronger than the Masons and which included police. He seemed to have a quite desperate need to talk about it. Part of me wondered whether any of it was true and he was a fantasist, while another part thought it was true and had unhinged him a bit.

He also told me of a girl who was attacked on the route I was contemplating, but it had been 4 years previously. As with the man and the rats, it felt as though he was just trying to frighten a woman. I emerged at last with a very tired Talie and bedded down. Not long after I had dozed off I was woken by something hard banging me on the head, only to find it was the nose of a hedgehog. I pushed it out and put some food on the grass to entice it away. I had never imagined hedgehogs would come in the tent. It really did feel that this was the journey of a lifetime.

July 11th. There were no more hedgehog visitations in the night. We were up at 7am and into the house at 9, where the man derided me for my length of sleep. They went to bed at 1 or 2am and got up again at 5 or 6. Well, I didn't! Especially carrying all I was, walking and breast-feeding. The day was rainy and windy-cold, with both of us wearing coats. As I walked, the man drove past in his camouflaged Land Rover. It was an agonising day just going two and a half miles. Talie had a slight rash and I wondered if it was some form of allergy. I knew it wasn't measles or chicken-pox as my other children had had those, but have since wondered whether it might have been German measles.

We reached Swainby and I was relieved to find the campsite did exist and was behind a pub. Some elderly Yorkshire people looked after Talie while I put the tent up, including the inner part to be more secure. We went for a walk and found it was a pleasant little touristy village with a well- stocked shop. We walked up to an old castle where I sat in the wind and wrote letters.

The next morning we got the bus into Stokesley, where it was market day. I got all the things I needed for the trek into the Cleveland Hills and North York

Moors, though it was all going to add to the weight I was carrying. I bought a paperback – 'Callanish' by William Horwood – the story of some eagles who escape from a zoo. When we got back Talie spent some time in the old couple's caravan, twiddling the knobs on their radio. I got worried about a little nanny goat which the pub had acquired the previous day and tethered for 24 hours on a short rope with not much to eat. I gave it some ash and elder and later the old man cut the top of a hawthorn hedge and they moved the goat to let it have the trimmings. We went for another walk where a river-bank had signs saying they'd been sprayed with weed-killer, so there was no chance of sitting and watching the water.

Talie went to sleep at about 5pm and slept for 13-14 hours. More people arrived and there were children playing outside a long time. It was a shame Talie missed them, but his sleep was precious. I read the whole of the 'Callanish' book, just finishing as it got dark. It was a lovely story and made me resolve to return to Orkney to visit the Tomb of the Eagles. (Talie and I finally went in the year 2000). The book made me cry, and cry for Lewis and the fact that I now hadn't been there for 2 years. I had been lacking in emotional strength a bit, but reading the book made the power of Callanish flow through my heart and I slept wonderfully well with long dreams. In one of these I went twice by plane to Australia, where I was working on a performance with Lynne. Then, although she was still there, I was back in Britain and couldn't face flying again, so we did the performance like that – with Lynne in Australia and me in England.

In the morning it was wet, but I knew it would be fine later, so didn't pack up straight away. Just as I was nearly ready, Talie fell asleep, so I explained to the lady in the next caravan, asking her to keep an eye and ear out for him while I went shopping, posting the 'Callanish' book to a friend. I returned just as my happy little boy emerged from the tent and the lady and her daughters entertained him while I packed up. She made me a cup of tea and then we left.

I was really looking forward to this next bit. It was hot, dank and humid going up the first hill and the uncut verges grew plants taller than I was and there were thistles with purple flowers which were almost as high. Then we were out of the flat, lush, cultivated plain, rising onto high, rocky moor and silence. It rained again but we came to 'Chequers' which sold tea and scones and when we emerged the rain had cleared and it just got better and better. I was back in my kind of landscape.

After sitting for a rest and hearing strange noises like a chain-saw, we came across some Territorial Army lads on an exercise, in a camouflaged hide with a noisy generator. They'd been watching us approach through binoculars and couldn't work out what we were. They were fascinated by us and gave me a mug of coffee and a tin of peaches and Talie some chocolate and sweets – all in regulation army wrappings. I didn't discuss my feelings concerning 'war games', presenting the positive aspect of what I was doing, but did say how awful it was that the MOD owned places like Salisbury Plain which had once been full of ancient sites. One of the lads was quite understanding about it.

We climbed higher and higher, walking an Ancient Way with tumuli alongside, and passing a long barrow which was at least Neolithic. There were mean patches of short, cropped grass and an abundance of heather. It was silent except for the buzzing of flies and the distant hum of one small plane. It was warm and now it was my body which sweated, whereas the previous summer it had been the horses'. I was carrying more water than usual because it was a long way to anywhere I'd be able to get any. Tied on the pack I had a big, brown, plastic, barrel-shaped container which had once held apple-juice. It held a gallon, but water is so heavy I could never have it completely full.

As it was a fine day, there were many parties of walkers: many of them young people in shorts and shirts, but all carrying transistor radios, and I wondered if they were afraid of the silence or if they needed a sound-track to experience the moors. The sky was getting dark when we camped down in a little hollow far from anywhere. We were high and clear and overlooking the land around us for miles.

It was a night of heavy rain and a lightning storm some distance away but we were safe, dry and cosy, waking to low cloud shrouding us in mist. It was a day of stillness. At first the mist hung, mysterious and damp, the skies grey, but then came the haze of heat as the sun burned through, though there was still mist over the distant hills. There were birds swooping around, but I wasn't sure if they were swifts, martins or swallows. It was wonderful to have just read the 'Callanish' book and now be in this high moorland, though I wasn't expecting to see any eagles. However, I knew that even that wild heathery moor was man-created.

It was initially hot with a breeze and lots of people out walking, but soon clouded over and gradually got colder with a strong wind. The mist descended again, but it was so good to be walking away from roads; so good to be walking an ancient way slowly, feeling the presence of the Old Ones, the ancestors, so near and so strong. I breathed it deep, for I realised it would be our last taste of the wild and high on this journey.

We stayed on the drove road when it became made-up, but the land around changed into farmland, no longer the open moor. I couldn't rest or relax in the cold, so we only had brief pauses and I pushed myself on and on.

Talie seemed to have reached another stage in his development. In the morning he was climbing little hills and loved playing in puddles. I had to keep the balance between not stopping him have fun, yet not letting him get so wet and muddy I couldn't get him dry and clean. For a while there were lots of planes towing gliders overhead. The last bit of straight road seemed endless and quite hard. We passed a large electrical installation, soon after which I called for water at some cottages with lots of children and a very young baby. I was told that the farmer lived in the house round the back, so went and asked. He wasn't exactly over-friendly, but matter-of-fact, showing me into a 21- acre field where the hay had been cut and was lying to dry. I picked a spot which felt quite special - at the edge, near a gateway, down a hill a bit to try to get some shelter. At first I just put up the fly- sheet, but it was so cold and windy I put up the inner as well. I liked to leave the flaps open at night so I didn't feel too cut off from the landscape outside.

I packed up as the farm workers turned the hay. I didn't feel hassled, just made sure Talie wasn't near the machines if they came close by. I tried to work out where the drove road went, for the made-up road seemed to turn away from it. We got to a tourist centre which had refreshments, so I had a few and Talie crawled about and chatted to people and played with an occasional bicycle pedal. I was constantly amazed at the inappropriate things people offered him, like small sweets he could have choked on; and here a man stuffed half a Twix bar into his mouth and couldn't understand why he wasn't ready for the other half 30 seconds later. If I refused things for him people thought I was mean.

I got a booklet on the Hambleton Drove Road, which was what we had just walked, and found it was at least Mesolithic, and used to be part of the way from Scotland to the English Channel. That part was the only section not now metalled over.

The tourist information lady phoned the next village and found there was a shop, so I decided to go straight down past a huge landscape white horse. The hill seemed to be 1 in 4 for a great distance, which was why it was such a tourist spot. It was an almost sheer limestone cliff with a view for miles. This was the Kilburn White Horse. For many years I had been very involved with the south England ancient white horses, such as Uffington, which were carved into chalk hillsides, and traditionally ritually scoured every 7 years, but didn't like the more recent ones which had been carved in the 18th and 19th centuries. The ancient ones flowed with the contours of the land, but the later ones had just been plonked onto hillsides, looking stiff and bearing no relationship to the landscape. Some, such as Westbury, had been carved on the sites of more ancient ones, completely eradicating them. This one seemed to be made from concrete and I found it an abomination. (However, we returned when Talie was about eight, and he was thrilled with it.) We passed a gliding club on the edge of the cliff, obviously where they'd all been coming from the other day.

We got to Kilburn, but the shop had very little. The majority of these village shops only stocked tinned stuff, with no fresh food: no bread, no cheese and certainly no fresh fruit – only things with a very long shelf life. It was a far cry from the days of real old village shops and I was continuously shocked by the fact that everyone, even in the '80s was supposed to have cars and be able to drive into towns or out-of-town shopping centres. I felt deflated, having come off the high land, down from the moors and into a posh touristy area. Lots of people were speaking to me, though.

I went on to the next village and sat looking at the map and trying to work out where to go next. There were three alternative routes, so it wasn't an easy choice. 1 or 2 went to a town called Easingwold, but seemed out of my way. Other routes looked quieter and one went over Elphin Beck, which seemed auspicious if you recall the Taliesin story, so I decided to go that way even though the road didn't look all that promising. When I stood over Elphin Beck two German women spoke to me and gave me £3 for Oxfam. Somehow the 3 gold coins in my hand felt significant.

I asked a man coming out of a field about places to stop and he told me to go up to the Priory farm. I spoke to the farm manager who said it was ok with him but I should ask Sir George over the road. Sir George was out with the family and the dog in the grounds and said "yes", so back to the farm I went and was shown a field and the tap. It was nice grass, though I was concerned it might have been sprayed, as there were lots of oddly black nettles and withered 'weeds' and some oily substance in some of the puddles, but there was a white horse in the field beside us. I looked at the map and realised we could get to York on Thursday evening. (It was now Monday).

Next day, after sitting and writing letters, I finally set off at 11am, just as the sheep were brought in to the field. There were more hills as we walked and I kept seeing different views of the concrete white horse. The next village had a lovely green, but a very nervous postmaster who looked as if he thought I was about to murder him, though he sold me a few stamps. It was a posh place, and on a downhill pathway on a blind bend there were narrow barriers you could only just squeeze through, perhaps to stop bikes and skateboards, but what about prams, pushchairs and wheelchairs, which would have to go out in the road to get past it?

I had a positive phone conversation with Brian Larkman of 'The Ley Hunter' magazine, about places to stay in York and trusted it would all get set up for us. It was still windy and again I just went on and on, not wanting to stop anywhere for long, though we did have one pause in long grass with pretty bits on top, so Talie couldn't see the road, which he had a tendency to head for. We got to an ancient-feeling village called Crayke, on a hill with a castle and church on top, so I sat on a seat near the castle before going into the village where I had hoped to spend some relaxed time. It had a nice green, but in such a cold raging wind I couldn't face sitting long, and the pub was shut so I couldn't even get a coffee. I'd had about enough for the day and it was only 3pm. The women in the shop were nice, but I was finding most people round there really weird, and was indeed finding the whole area weird and wondered if it were the York commuter belt. Coming up the hill I had encountered a woman, passed the time of day, and been totally ignored.

All the possible stopping places near there were a bit like small-holdings only not quite, looking more like battery farms. They had a horrible vibe, so I continued on down a long straight road where one part of a verge had wheat growing on it, and wondered whether it was another bit of the old drove road. I was tempted to camp there, but had no water.

I was getting desperate. On the map there seemed a strange lack of farms and I contemplated changing my route, but at a corner saw a place with lots of thoroughbred horses. I found the owner, who looked at me strangely and said "where do you want to go"? then "anywhere over there", which wasn't very clear. I asked him if there was a water tap and he said "yes", so I had to ask him where it was. I went into some long grass by an old hut, so wasn't where any machinery or vehicles might go, and away from some caravans where employees were living. 'Oh well' I thought, 'it's not a verge'.

The man was lunging horses in a circle and Talie was fascinated, wanting to go near them. We played a bit, but a tom cat came and sprayed the tent and then enticed Talie off down a path. I washed the tent and had to bring him back several times. He wanted to play with the soft earth path, but I thought it dirty and probably full of cat and dog shit. He liked playing with stones and grit and sandy stuff, and though feeding himself with bread and biscuits, never put any non-food things in his mouth. I was anxious to get on, not really enjoying the journey any more, but felt I must take it easy into York as I was pushing myself too hard and had all sorts of aches in my body. I was expecting the countryside to change and, unusually, doubting my choice of route over this bit. I had seen a road sign saying 'York 15 miles'.

I woke at about 6.30am. The man came by and asked if I needed anything. He said he'd not heard a squeak from Talie and what we were doing must be teaching him to be independent and not given in to like most children were those days. I was ready to leave by 8.30, the earliest yet, but my body was beginning to creak at the joints, and my back felt odd, so I knew I really should be careful: maybe it was to do with the weather making it difficult to have long rests. We got to Huby, which was mostly modern brick and suburban, but the people in the well-stocked shop were friendly: when I asked if there was anywhere I could get a cup of tea they made me one!

I phoned Brian Larkman and heard he'd just about got things arranged, and would meet us when we arrived in the city. I thought I'd make York the next day, though it would be pretty hard. I was half an hour too early for the pub and was longing for somewhere to sit and relax, so went on and found a little back lane with a group of trees which gave enough protection from the wind for us to sit a while. Things kept dropping from the trees. Maybe they were acorns. The limestone hills had risen from the flat lands, then were gone. The earth was changed now: dry and fine and dark. I got the sense of Lincolnshire even though I was not yet in York.

The year was turning further. The elder smelled sweet and powerful as we walked down sheltered lanes. The verges were lush and the hedges enclosed the perfume. There was a dank, damp, pungent smell which rose from the bottom of very tall plants in the uncut hedgerows and there was the tangy smell of ageing, bruised nettles. The barley was turning from pale green to ripening gold, yet the hay was still being taken in. There were baby horse chestnuts blown from the trees, never to mature, and we'd also seen baby birds dead in the roads and hedgehogs flattened by cars. It was a strange summer, where we had to shelter from the cold wind in order to sit and rest.

The track got more and more beautiful and the verges were incredibly wide, so this was surely more of the 'Ancient Way'. Something seemed to remain there, something of the very old, something as yet untouched. In the sheltered spots the sun was occasionally warm, and then we reached a bit which made me ecstatic – a soft wide verge where we rested a long while, at last able to relax. I wanted to camp there, but knew I should hate myself the next day for not doing the extra mile.

The going was really hard. My body hurt: my back, knees, ankles, feet, elbows, shoulders and neck, but this pause was one of the most beautiful times of the whole journey, and Talie and I had one of the most wonderful days we'd ever had. There were feathery seed-heads of grass he played with and flies which he tried to catch. Who needs toys? We were having such fun together. It was like summer should be, like life should be. When we moved on we did go nearly another mile.

Occasionally a solitary poppy would look at us sadly as we passed, as though wondering where were the blazing red fields of the past, and why was it the sole survivor of the herbicides? Are not its seeds food as well? Sometimes there would be a little cluster of them, keeping each other company, but they seemed bleached, washed out, their colour faded. Then we saw a line of them clinging frantically to a barbed wire fence; clinging hard in a thin red line. Someone had mown the verge, though it was by now only 2ft wide, and the dying poppy petals lay like pools of blood and those that could, clung for dear life to that barbed wire fence.

The verges ran out and I headed for another farm. Not being sure where the house was I went to the next one, but it may have been quite separate. It was 'The Forge', with a man making ornamental iron-work. A woman came out and said we could go in their back garden. She wanted proof of my identity, which was fair enough, but it was the first time I had been asked and seemed evidence that we were getting close to the city. They had a dog chained up and I was warned that it bit. I picked a rather nettle-y patch, which deterred Talie from his wanders to see the chickens.

It was dark moon night and I was awake at the time it turned – a beautiful, gentle, nurturing energy; but the night was torn apart by night flying. I didn't know where it was coming from and it seemed to be the most colossal exercise imaginable. I realised a lot of people in an area like that would not regard it as a nuisance and a violation of the night, but proof of 'our lads keeping us safe'. I was sure that was what a lot of people's concept of defence was – as if the good 'lads' could catch the nasty Russian H-bombs before they went off; not that they were likely to be 'our lads', but USAF. I thought it was more a public relations exercise than necessary practise and found them silly (and very expensive) games – 'look what I can do with my big machine'.

The woman was quite nice and let me use the toilet and took my rubbish and I felt physically better as we set off. There was a last quiet bit and then we were on four and a half miles of a very busy B road into York. In a way it was worse than an A road because it wasn't so wide and I really had to keep my wits about me. It was a long slog and not enjoyable, just a question of getting there. Just once, though, we saw a small field with poppies scattered amongst the corn. Maybe it was organic.

We stopped at a pub for coffee and sat in the garden. Talie crawled about, having to avoid a girl who was cutting the grass and had a look at some guinea pigs and rabbits in a run.

We carried on...and on... and on into York. My entrances into cities felt so triumphant, yet no-one knew. I felt there should be cheering hordes of people and bands playing, but I just walked in on my own and only I knew what a triumph it was. I phoned Brian and waited for him by the Minster among the throngs of tourists. I bought a souvenir paper of the previous year's Minster fire. It was fire in the Leo fire place of our journey and reminded me to be extra careful in this area.

Initially Brian took us to the house of his friend Claire Hewitt, who wanted to meet us and have us stay a few days. She was hugely pregnant and due to give birth shortly, needing some reassurance from seeing Talie and I living as we were.

Claire Hewitt with her 'pregnant pot'

Months before we had set off on the Gipsy Switch, I had been invited to speak at 'The Ley Hunters Moot'. This was a regular gathering of people who read the earth mysteries magazine 'The Ley Hunter'. At the time I had no idea how I could do this while on the journey, but it turned out it was going to be in York – and right at the time when we would be there anyway. Brian was organising it, so was 'looking after' my well-being in the city. Following our stay with Pisces Kevin Draper in Pisces, and Cancerian Nicola in Cancer, it was no surprise to find that not only was Brian a Leo, but shared my birthday.

July 19th – August 2nd. We stayed in York two weeks. It was a difficult time and not as enjoyable as Durham. At some of the places we were put up I felt awkward, and it was only after leaving I learned people had been paid to have us stay, and this produced a very different dynamic from situations where they specifically wanted us to share their homes. But the first few days were beautiful with lovely pregnant Claire. To be in the presence of that special energy of a woman about to give birth was a privilege and a joy. She already had a daughter, Rowan, whose birthday was the day after mine, and now Claire's fullness seemed the perfect manifestation of the time of year, reflecting the ripe earth about to give birth to its harvest. Claire was a potter, and I photographed her with a 'pregnant pot' she had made. (She is now a story-teller and clarsach player and lives in Scotland).

We stayed with a succession of people, moving in an arc round the outskirts of the city, so from each place there was a different route into the centre. We also moved nearer and nearer to the Knaves Mire, an area of grass where horses still grazed. An ancient place, the traditional York Races were still held there. The old gallows was on one side, close to a traditional mark-stone. We heard tell of a Gipsy Oak on it, hoping to find it and hold a Leo picnic with lots of other Leos, but this never came together. The last house we stayed in had a horse on the gate, so we were never far from horse sites as we paused here on the Gipsy Switch.

As for the day to day; for quite a while I had a really bad leg, so the excursions into the city were painful and tiring. I went in nearly every day because the city was challenging me to find its sacred centre. It was so obvious in Durham, but York defied me for a long while. I didn't like York. It seemed to have no centre, no heart, just a criss-cross jumble of streets teeming with tourists and it was only in the last few days that I could walk into it without the use of a street map.

I felt nothing for the site of the Minster, nor for the Castle Mound, nor another mound – Baillie Hill, though they were all special in their own way. Brian took us for a walk round the old city walls and that helped, for in encircling the city I became less overwhelmed by it, though I was surprised that, as a Leo, I felt so little connection with the Leo place of our journey. Slowly, though, I became aware that the sacred centre must be the confluence of two rivers which joined and flowed into one, creating a female Y-shaped piece of land between them. This was known as St. George's Fields and there had once been a Templar church there. Some sort of pattern was emerging.

I gave my talk at the Ley Hunter Moot. I thought a lot about what I wanted to convey – about Journeying and the links between people and the land, and was determined to just talk and see how it came out and not write a 'script'. I found the 'Ley Hunter' scene very male dominated, very intellectual and scientific in its approach, though it was beginning to swing into a more balanced, experiential direction, particularly in men like Brian, who was open, receptive and aware of the female. He had long been fascinated by all things Aboriginal, seeing the similarity between their symbols and those on our own ancient stones.

I was told I was only the second woman who had ever spoken at a 'moot' – the other being Mary Caine. I hadn't had much experience at giving talks in those days, and had no slides to show, but gave myself six out of ten for trying. I think my talk rang a few bells with people and didn't feel I had disgraced myself entirely.

One rainy morning Brian and his wife Dot took us on a walk along the York ley. This was an alignment of many points within a small distance in an exactly straight line and included the river confluence, St. George's Fields, the mound, several churches and the Minster. It was my first walk right down to the very point where the two rivers met and walking towards it, with the land narrowing and the swift-flowing water on each side getting closer, I found the movement of energy intense. It definitely was the sacred Leo place of our journey.

We came to Lammas, the last of the 8 major festivals on this circle of the year. It is now mainly celebrated on the eve of the 31st July and on August 1st, but surely anciently would have been on the ripe full moon nearest to those dates. It is the celebration of the earth giving birth to her harvest. Fruition.

In previous years I had mainly shared these times with the powerful energy of women, but here it felt fine to celebrate it with Brian – two Leos celebrating our own time of year at our place on the land. He had flu, but drove us out of York itself to a mound called Duggleby Howe and it was a great relief to get out of the city. It had been a dull day, heavy and overcast, but as the sun set, it was vast and blood-red on the horizon: a sudden gash of birth-blood through the clouds.

It was darkening as we reached the mound, the biggest tumulus in Britain (Silbury Hill not being a tumulus) at 24ft high – the Great Mother's pregnant belly rising from a field of sugar-beet. We walked between their rows, the leaves flapping against our feet and legs. There was a space round the mound where white stones caught the last of the light and we walked around it moon-wise. On the west there were trees – elder and hawthorn, where someone had made a camp. I struggled through and Talie lost a sock, then we spiralled up the mound in three turns. It wasn't frequently visited and the grass grew thick and tall with many flowers.

At the top we sank down into the centre, making a hollow in the grass. It was now dark. I sat and fed Talie and it seemed so fitting, to sit on the belly/breast of the earth to feed my child.

We drank warm pear juice. A solitary star appeared right above us in the dark cloud-streaked sky. We made a 'corn-dolly' from the standing grasses and she felt very alive, carrying the energy of the mound and the surrounding land. In her hair we placed ears of green barley, wheat and oats from a field where there were 3 megaliths. Musk incense burned to the east, an orange Leo candle to the south, a bowl of pear juice to the west and a bowl of sunflower seeds to the north. In a shop I had looked at many shells, tempted to buy a spiral one, but thought that here a spiral shell should be a snail, so bought 2 cowries with purple backs, because these are female, vulval symbols. I put one in the body of the corn dolly and it dropped right down, deep into the roots of the grass, into the earth itself it seemed, taken into her for her own.

The Full Moon turned as we made the dolly. I felt connected to others in a network over the land who were focussing that moment into change: to bring about some alteration in consciousness in the powers that be which would stop

316

us from hurtling headlong towards destruction. I slipped gently, peacefully, beyond the bounds of self and spread into a whole world unity. I sensed dancing at Silbury, and Callanish flashed in and out like the moon between the clouds. I had the physical sensation of holding hands in a circle of women. There was simply the sense of being a vast space, with the land stretching endlessly, and the earth being well. Not a thought, just a state of 'well-being'. On cue, a snail appeared, spiral-shelled, at the front of the lady. The moon came through the clouds and shone on her.

After a while we packed up and left. I took the ears of grain and one cowrie. We left the candle (something I wouldn't do now), the pear juice and the sunflower seeds in offering. The lady remained standing with the other shell deep within her. We each took a bite from a sandwich and left the rest there – for the faeries or the spirits of place. We gave thanks for the bounty of the earth and wished that she might continue to provide – but for all her children.

We descended and walked, under the moon, through the squeaky-leaved field. It was so good to have met that mound, the pregnant belly on the east of the Gipsy switch.

We returned to York. Brian slept in his car while Talie and I lay in a room with candlelight and incense, slept, and woke as the first light of dawn began to colour the sky blue-green.

We went down to the river confluence in the clear dawn while the city lay silent. In a cold wind Brian gathered wood. There was a hollow in the stones which now cover the land where the rivers meet. In the south, over the joined rivers, the clouds formed the shape of Glastonbury Tor, ridges and all, but without the tower. I drew the Zodiac round the depression in the stones (lacking chalk I used Brian's paracetamol) and placed the wooden Leo sign in its rightful place in the circle. Brian made Leo fire which burned wonderfully in the centre, the place of transformation. We circled it 3 times sun-wise, and stood gazing a long while into the fire as it was fanned by the wind. I hoped it would be a fire of purification, burning away all the negativity in the world and within ourselves.

We left the little fire still burning, and from the edges I took some of the ash. Brian found an excellent place to hide the Leo sign. Now all the signs had been placed in a giant circle round the land. I wondered how many were still physically there, maybe all, maybe none. It didn't matter. They had been placed.

The circle was complete. All I had to do now was close the gap – Leo to Virgo again and on to where Mike and Richard had begun the journey nearly a year before. Later in the day I returned to the spot and the ash was still there in the undisturbed circle.

August 2nd. Friday. It was our last day in the city and I made my preparations to leave. Since April Talie's nappy rash had waxed and waned, sometimes almost going and sometimes so terrible I needed 6 hands to change his nappy, as I not only had to keep him from tearing himself to shreds, but stop him getting cream on the tapes which closed the nappy or they wouldn't stick. Because of this he could rarely be without one, even though I felt fresh air would be the best cure. I had been told of umpteen remedies, tried them all, but to no avail, so in despair went to a doctor, only to be told it wasn't nappy rash at all, but thrush, and given a steroid cream which cleared it up in no time. If I'd known what it was sooner I could have found a homeopathic remedy.

In the late afternoon I went to the coach station to meet Saffron, who had come up from Norwich. She had travelled with us at the beginning of the journey and now, a year later, had come to walk with us for a week and to be with me for my birthday.

August 3rd. The morning seemed a mad panic, working flat out from 7am to be ready by midday. The longer I stopped somewhere the harder it was to put it all back together again. Claire's husband, Robin, came and drove us to their house. Their little boy, Tam, had been born and we looked at the wonderful photos of his birth. He seemed quite a faerie child and the Leo babe of our journey. We had tea and soup and then Robin took us a little way out of the city and put us on our road, leaving us near Gypsey Corner.

Chapter 22: Down to Lincoln and Virgo again.

At last we were walking again, back with the earth again. There was strong wind and a little rain. We stopped at a playground where Saffron and Talie had great fun on swings and roundabouts. It was so good having her with us.

We walked on and on, and as we passed a house were called back to have tea with a very interesting family: the man worked in child language development and played wonderfully with Talie, one of their daughters had lived a year at Greenham, and they said we could stay the night so we accepted. It was extraordinary how often this happened just as we'd set off after a pause at a city or 'place'.

We ate spinach and broad beans from their garden, then slept in an empty flat where there was a blind cat, so though not yet sleeping out on the sweet earth, we were almost magically provided for.

In a room with giant flowers painted all over the walls we had breakfast with the mother and the two daughters, Tamsin and Jane. Tamsin was just back from living in Greece.

It was a cool day in which we crossed a few rivers. We sat on a seat at one point and maybe disrupted an old man's Sunday ritual, for it looked as though he usually sat there. Sorry, old man. When the time came to stop, we asked at a place which wasn't really a farm, and got a refusal, so went down the road a bit and set up the tent on a verge under an oak tree. There was a lot of rain, but the next morning was fine and everything was dry by the time we set off. I thought Saffron was very brave to come. It was a way of life for us, but unusual for her and she must have trusted me. I was so happy she had wanted to come.

It turned dull with an intrusive wind. We unsuccessfully tried one village for a shop, but it was a strange, dead place with the only living things in it being us sitting on a triangle of grass. Once again I thought how alive these villages must once have been. We tried to make a short-cut to Bubwith, but lost the track half way and came out somewhere that wasn't a short-cut at all. Still, it had been nice to be off roads for a while and find a lovely sheltered place out of the wind for a rest.

At Bubwith we finally did some shopping and sat on the grass to eat lunch, though rain was once again threatening. We were all very tired, so I asked at a farm which looked promising, but was just told to go to a pub by a river down a track. We didn't, but found a grassy patch beside the river instead. It had 'Private fishing' notices up... but we weren't fishing. Saffron and I were both having vivid epic dreams, mine having a lot of deep involvement with very clear people (mainly men) who I didn't know at all in my waking life.

Tuesday, August 6th. Hiroshima Day. The day we had at last set off from Ditchingham the previous year. It felt like a lifetime ago, and for Talie it more or less was. In the night I had become intensely aware of this day and linked with Peace People all over the world. It was a quiet place, with little fields and wetland plants and lots of willow and reeds on both sides of the road.

We looked for something marked on the map as a fenced but unmade up road, but it was totally overgrown and the end filled with an enormous pile of manure, making it impenetrable, so we had to go a longer way round. After lunch there were sudden storms and violent downpours. A man offered us a lift, but we didn't have anywhere to have a lift to. For some strange reason we just walked along the A road in the teeming rain, laughing our heads off and getting soaking wet, though we kept Talie completely dry.

We turned a corner onto a C road, which actually had lots of lorries trundling down it, and, as Saff wanted to change her wet clothes, decided to camp on the verge again. We huddled under my sheet of plastic, then managed to get the fly-sheet up. The previous night I'd put the inner up too, as it was potentially very sluggy, but it had been stuffy and cramped with all three of us inside though beautiful to lay there with my two youngest children sleeping beside me. The journey was different with Saffron with us, the time with her going too fast. However, Talie was behaving strangely: bad- tempered and grisly and wanting his own way all the time and getting quite angry when he didn't get it – not at all the usual wondrous little Taliesin!

There were berries on everything now. The land here was flat, the harvest had begun and I had come full circle. I recalled the whole of the previous year, never having had such an intense experience of one turning. Back to where we had begun, yet so much having changed: the same but different. Children had been conceived and born and many people I knew were moving. There was no stability; nothing was constant but the cycle of the seasons, and man had the power to destroy even that. I had a vision of candles lit all over the world and wished for there to be no more bombs and the whole earth to be healed. As I lay on that earth and watched the sun set with two whole separate people born of my womb, I wished for there still to be a world for them to grow up in. The hedgerows offered what she was allowed to, but in the fields the machines tore an unnatural over-abundance from her. Again.

We woke at 5.30am and got on with the morning's business. From the map it looked as though it would be nearly all A roads and Goole and towny things

Round Britain through Goole

ROUND Britain walker Jill Smith passed through Goole last week on the last lap of her journey to Lincoln.

Jill and her fourteen-month-old son, Taliesin Rainbow Smith, left their home in Suffolk on August last year to join a group of people in Lincoln from where they progressed on their journey with the aid of horses and wagons. However, when the party reached Wales, the majority of people dropped out of the group leaving Jill and Taliesin to continue the route alone until recently when Jill's daughter, Saffron Lacey joined her for a short period in order to celebrate her mother's birthday.

The walk, which is in aid of Oxfam, is a traditional year-long route known as The Gypsy Switch and is at least one thousand miles in length. Each area of the journey corresponds to a time of the year and zodiac.

Since the beginning of the route, Jill has averaged five miles per day and has travelled through Cambridgeshire, Essex, through London, across Tower Bridge to Kingston-on-Thames, Wiltshire, Somerset, round the Severn to Lampeter, up to Appleby, through Durham and to York. She has also visit Ireland.

Jill said all the places she had visited on her journey were of interest in their own right. She was also very grateful for the kindness which had been shown on her travels.

At the end of the walk, Jill plans to stage an exhibition in London during the last two weeks of October consisting of various photographs and drawings which she has collected on her way.

and we needed to do a lot of mileage, but I was hoping to end up somewhere interesting. Talie was back to his normal self and being very good, so we were off at 8: the earliest yet. The A road wasn't so bad and we had views of a motorway bridge across the flat lands. (The M62). We crossed the River Ouse, crossed the motorway and were in Goole.

I quite liked Goole. Things got a bit strained between Saffron and me as we decided what to do and in what order, but it got sorted and I decided to go into Scunthorpe with her on Saturday to bid her farewell. We had a micro-waved chip butty in a cafe - and the most incredibly huge jam tarts. I got some money from the bank, as I always did when I came across one, and worried about how little there was left. I had my capital in a building society and the interest was paid into the bank monthly, and this was what I tried to live on, but the rates, which had started high, were going down and my income was shrinking rapidly.

Two women from the local paper stopped us. They had been searching all over town for us, wanting to do a 'piece' about our journey, and I was surprised really that it was the first time this had happened. We went to their office and had coffee while Talie played with their rubber stamps and got red ink everywhere. A girl non-interviewed us and a man took photographs.

The rain got worse. We walked through dockland and stopped to watch a swing bridge move out of the way for a barge, then sat on a bank as the weather improved, later walking beside the river. To stop for the night we turned inland and approached another farmer who wasn't very helpful, though he did give us water. It was strange how I'd rarely been refused when it was just me and the baby, yet when there were two women – albeit that Saffron was only 16 – we always seemed to be. However, we found a perfect place behind trees, and had a lovely evening with Saffron sitting outside reading teen mags. We had seen our first ploughed field and there was grain in the roads again. The ripe corn was the colour of Talie's hair.

The next day felt like summer again, so rare this year. We took it slower and got off later, walking flat land and straight roads in the sun and wind. It was good to see vegetables growing and the whole area had a sense of community: farming folk and children on bikes and even a travelling family. It was a good part of the journey, crossing the marshes from Goole to Scunthorpe, having faith we'd get across and not come to a dead end or a deep, impassable ditch. It was hot and humid with Saffron not feeling too well, but we carried on, resting often.

Following paths marked on the map, we passed a Fison's peat-works, the strange 'mining' of this precious commodity so different from the Hebridean people cutting their own for fuel, taking only what they needed. Here whole

322

landscapes were being ravaged. During one rest Saffron fell asleep and Talie drew all over her best white shirt without my noticing. Sorry, Saff.
We had a long walk on a disused railway track, a line for miles of Rose Bay Willow Herb; and saw a heron. I would have liked to camp here, but Saff wanted to go further, concerned about reaching Scunthorpe by Saturday. Where we finally stopped was still on the old line, but where it had been ploughed into the edge of a field. For a while I didn't feel relaxed and some lads threw stones at the tent, but I spoke to them and they said they thought it was some of their mates. I believed them.

Next day was my birthday. Saffron gave me some lovely little things – some pottery toadstools, a Womad badge with a lion on it and a CND badge she had made – all in a cracker which we pulled. Tiffany sent some earrings with a Tibetan quality and a Leo lion card. As a special present, Talie took his first three steps.

As we had a lot of rubbish we walked into a town (possibly Crowle), which took ages. We found no nice cakes for my birthday and weren't in the Goole Times (We were in the following week), but had a lovely day, with a wonderful walk across dykes and along paths and banks. Our route led us through one farm where in the middle of the track I found a tiny horseshoe, and a hare ran across the flat, drained peat marshland. Straight roads, straight drains, straight banks and straight ditches. We saw a patch of waste ground with brilliant yellow flowers and the vivid russet-red heads of seeding docks – a blazing cloak of Leo fire.

We looked for a bridge across a drain which was marked on the map, but not physically there, so had to walk a long distance out of our way to another one. We were discouraged by a man who told us we couldn't get through that way, but had faith and kept on and we could. The drains were deep and sheer-sided, and if we'd come to an un-bridged one there would have been no other way to cross.

At last we were near Althorpe, where the harvest was heavily under way. We needed water, so I called up to a man driving a gigantic machine. I had forgotten how big they were – monsters almost as high as a house. He climbed down and took me into the farm buildings, purpose-built for agri- business: lots of buildings, but no house, just a small office. We stopped near there for the night, in long undergrowth near a power station, tall pylons and great electric cables.

Up early, at first it all went according to plan, which was to get the 9.15am bus to Scunthorpe so we would have 2 hours to say goodbye over a celebratory cup of coffee, not having come across a pub on my birthday. But we sat at the bus-stop and no bus came. I got very agitated, especially as we missed a train we

Saffron and Talie with the tent on the way to Lincoln

could have got instead, but got the next train an hour later – just as a bus came! Saffron's time with us had seemed so short, and now it was over. At the bus station, an old acquaintance turned up, so our parting wasn't as planned, but we had a little while over a cup of tea, then saw her onto the coach. Bye, Saff, it had been lovely.

We spent the weekend in Scunthorpe, staying at a strange establishment which I realised was mainly B&B accommodation for homeless people. I had then to get myself back into journeying just with Talie. Every time I unpacked the rucksack everything seemed to explode out and fill a space four times the size. When I came to pack it again I had to have faith that as it had all come out, it must go back in, and eventually it did, but I felt daunted by the luggage at first. Saffron had carried a bag and other bits and pieces, so my load had been lighter; now I had to carry it all again. As soon as it was on me it was ok, but getting it on was a task. I got a bus to the edge of town, and my little boy and I were on our own again.

There were two different experiences of the journey: being with Saffron was one thing – lived very much on the day-to-day, ordinary level, but when it was just Talie and me it shifted onto another level, as though I were in a slight trance all the time, in a slightly other reality, a more spiritual state of being. The time with Saffron had been precious, but at times I had felt a failure as her mother. I couldn't have the conversations with her about my own feelings which I would have liked, and if I mentioned something more spiritual, she would come back with some mocking remark which made me shut up. I wondered why I couldn't share the real experience of my life with my daughter, and it was that which made me feel I had failed.

It was good to be on the road again. It was all such an adventure and the journey was our 'home', each day a complete entity unto itself. As we set off I could 'see' the whole path we were tracing on the land, like a circle of light laid on a living map of the landscape. This was the day of the Perseids – the meteor shower from the constellation Perseus and I recalled my birthdays at Waylands Smithy, lying at night watching the shooting stars.

Already there were road signs to Lincoln. We were now in the hazel time of the Beth-Luis-Nion calendar, their leaves tipping branches red and yellow, heralding the autumn colours to come. Leaves were dark green now with a kind of ageing coarseness. High summer was shifting to late summer; nature was ripe and full and in the process of giving birth. Rowan berries were blazing orange, and green berries formed on the brambles. The land began to roll gently after the peaty flat. We walked a little of Ermine Street, which I'm sure was an ancient nomadic way, long before the Romans.

It was a lovely day, the weather pretty good too. I was in a state of bliss again, as though everything once more were perfect. I thought then that in the future I might become a true nomad, for it was how I felt most right, and though life didn't work out like that, even now, when out with the land, still camping in the same little tent, I feel re-connected with the 'real' me and experience that bliss again.

We crossed another motorway – the M180 – whose sound had accompanied us for a while, then only did about 4 miles before it was time to stop. As I walked on, the strap of the rucksack broke but I mended it with baler twine – always carrying some for emergencies and collecting old bits which lay by the roadside.

Calling at a farm, a nice lady said "yes, go in that stubble field". She was very friendly, and so was her husband, who looked by later. Everything was back in the flow again. I wondered why no farms would give us a place when we were with Saffron, yet now it was once more just the two of us it was fine. Was it simply the nature of the area we had passed through, or were people somehow afraid of a woman and a 16-year old girl? I had felt more secure camping on verges with Saff, and now I needed them, farms were again helping. Strange.

We were on a slight hill overlooking the surrounding countryside, the sort of outlook I thought I would like to live with: up a bit with a hedge and trees behind us. It was a beautiful evening and we sat outside without a worry in the world. Talie wanted me to walk up and down, up and down the stubble rows, holding his hand. We fell asleep with the tent open, and I woke in time to get my coat and his socks in before there was a storm. Not so much rain, but lightning and thunder. It was very near, but soon passed.

There was no hurry so we set off quite late. I'd hoped to see the people at the farm, but they were out, so I left a note. I felt strong mentally, though it was a tough day physically. I sometimes forgot that, as time went on, Talie was growing heavier! We walked a beautiful stretch of Ermine Street where there was very little traffic and wide verges. I would have been happy camping anywhere along there, especially on a bit which had grass growing in the middle of the road, near a level crossing where they kept the gates open for the trains and closed to the road, only opening them for a rare car which came by.

It was hard walking into a strong wind all day as it slowed me down and made the pack feel heavier than ever. On the map I saw a footpath which was an easy way into Redbourne, but when I got to where it should be there was no signpost and it was across a potato field. I didn't feel like trudging through that, so continued on the road, which then changed, the verges disappearing, the energy becoming horrible. There were some woods I didn't like the feel of and lots of fields and agri-business crops. My energy slumped and I felt vulnerable.

I asked a man in a tractor if I could go on a tiny bit of grass, but he wasn't very friendly and said "ask the boss", who was off my route, so I carried on along a busy B road, hating everything and again feeling I was experiencing the pain of the violated earth. A man spraying potatoes (keep away from potato fields at that time of year) had a friendly word but was no actual help, so I trudged on, feeling anger at the despoiling of the land. I felt part of the land and vulnerable because they were assaulting her. I didn't feel safe.

I approached a junction with an A road, and realised I'd have to carry on and miss Redbourne. Some farms were marked on the map and I headed another mile towards them. Little wooded places near the junction didn't feel safe. As we headed away from the sound of the A road, I felt slightly better, but we were still on a busy and noisy C road. There had been a lot of 'Private Keep

Out' notices and even one which said 'Alarm. Mines'. There was another woody bit along this road, but they were the sort of places where solitary men in cars lurked, and I had labelled them 'wankers paradise'. We had rested near one with Saff and there had been a porn mag lying in a puddle.

Everything felt totally alien and I felt like an alien in an alien world. The two farms turned out to be businesses with no friendly farming families, but notices on the front saying Such and Such Company. There was no heart. Man here felt as far removed from the living earth as he could possibly be.

I couldn't go any further. There was a bit of verge with young trees growing on it and I decided to stop there. It felt ok once the tent was up and we were inside. Sometimes it was good to stop at such places as it was a form of reclaiming, but I had to work hard to make it feel safe. I usually wove a basket of protective light and energy over the tent: that night it was a crackling white cone. The traffic eased.

At about 8am something drove by and a man shouted out "Get up, you lazy cunt". Apart from the fact that I'd been up for hours, no-one could call what I was doing laziness. I felt deep sorrow, for it seemed symptomatic of the area. How unhappy a person must be to even have thoughts like that about a tiny, ordinary tent by the roadside. If I saw such a thing I would think it was a couple of lads on holiday, not someone being lazy, and our tent didn't look hippyish or anything. I was sorry for the man; he must have led a very unsatisfied life.

I started to read Mary Caine's 'Glastonbury Zodiac' out loud to Talie, who found it hilarious, and was sure the zodiac was something I would continue working with after the physical walking was over. Her book was a shamanic journey of death and rebirth; of King Arthur travelling to another realm to be healed, waiting to return when needed: dying, but not dead.

The tent was covered with little snails which I had to remove in order to pack it up. The wind made the pack very heavy again. We got to Waddingham, where the chippie was closed, but which did have some reasonable shops, and sat on the green to eat. I was getting concerned about my diet of chemical-filled junk food, but it was often all I could get. I longed for fresh organic vegetables and rice and things which would give me proper vitamins and minerals.

There was a lovely expanse of mown grass, but Talie insisted on crawling up and down a bit of road, and I had to keep pulling him back from a bridge over a ditch. As we set off we passed a tree planted in 1902 to commemorate the coronation of Edward VII, and I was interested to see how much a tree had grown in 83 years. At one point I sat under a tree to be out of the wind, half covered by my raincoat. It rained heavily and there was some thunder, but I wasn't very aware of it as I seemed to have 'gone off' somewhere. (But I came back!)I gave a stale loaf to a donkey, not liking to throw food away, and if I have to, trying to give it to some living creature, even if only insects and worms, because we couldn't really do without them.

Even my coat and scarf were now heavy with rain. I walked a tarmac path which had weed-killer sprayed on either side and felt I was walking between two lines of poison and death, unable to understand how people could use such stuff.

After another village, there was a wide verge and hardly any traffic where I would have loved to camp, as it felt safe, but it was too early to stop. Further on everything went misty with driving rain, so we sheltered under another tree and I nearly set up there. I was hoping the wide verge would continue after Bishop Norton, which we were approaching, so walked on in the rain and said "now what we want is a friendly farmer's wife to take us in, or at least someone to ask us in for a cup of tea", but it didn't seem the area for that sort of thing. We needed water and saw a family in a kitchen doorway and asked for some, and not long after were having a cup of tea, and as I went out of the door to leave, the offer of a bed for the night! It blackened over for more rain, so I said "yes", and was shown to a lovely room with a lattice window. There were three little girls and loads of toys; we had a bath and I washed some clothes. The people were from Yorkshire, though I think we had entered Lincolnshire by then.

With them, I looked at a map and found Sudbrook, where Richard and Mike had stopped for Virgo the previous year and actually begun the journey. It was about 20 miles south of Lincoln, and was where I must go to close the physical circle.

I also discovered that the Lincolnshire Wolds, about 20 miles to the east, were like moors with grass and sheep. I would have gone that way had I known, but from the map couldn't really tell they were there, or how I would have got over to them, though I had felt I should be more to the east on that part of the journey. This was the only time I really felt I had planned the journey wrong, and was probably why I was feeling so uncomfortable where I was, but – it was the journey I had ended up travelling and I couldn't change it now. The 'egg' of the Gipsy Switch circle was turning out to be a very strange and bumpy shape.

I had been feeling the bad weather was the earth fighting back at mankind, but wondered whether it had done agri-business any harm, even though I had seen a lot of flattened wheat-fields. It was probably hurting the small farmers most – if there still were any.

The people gave us breakfast. The lady said that often there would be rain and clouds all around, even quite close, but they always had a little patch of blue just above them. "The sun smiles down on us" she said and I wasn't surprised: they were such open, warm and friendly people.

It was fine at first, but still incredibly windy. I was walking almost due south and the wind seemed to be coming directly at me, pushing against me and making me feel I was carrying twice the load and walking twice as far, but I managed about 5 miles by the end of the day. For the first part we were still on lovely wide verges with practically no traffic and I got to a village and sat on the grass by a wall. I read the Mary Caine book, which was hard to follow at times, but was taking me further in my understanding of what I was doing. More doors of perception were opening as I was closing the circle.

I found a village with 2 cafes. A coach-load filled one, so I went to the other, which was enjoyably simple and quite primitive. Refreshed, I carried on. There were more lovely verges, lots of sun, lots of dull bits, lots of wind and it was really hard going. I was on the Lincoln map but wouldn't get to Lincoln until Sunday. (It was now Thursday). A man in a Telecom van stopped for a chat. He'd just walked from Cumbria to Robin Hood's Bay and told me of the Ramblers Association's 50-year anniversary walk round Britain: the Jubilee Walk. I had heard of it before, as someone had asked if I were on it. He told me more about the Wolds, that there was a Viking Way, which is an ancient road, and another called The Blue Stone Way, which is Neolithic. I kept wondering why I hadn't known of them and why instinct and intuition hadn't drawn me to them, as it had to the Hambleton Way. I wondered why I was walking a straight line and not the curve of 'the Egg'. I didn't like to feel I was 'wrong', but had to trust that for me and Talie, the way we were walking was right. I would tell others walking The Gipsy Switch to go on the Blue Stone Way in the Wolds.

Suddenly it all changed to hedges and no more verges, with big machines in big fields, though not quite as awful as before. The wind was taking me into some non-ordinary level of reality and it was impossible to remain totally in the mundane world.

It was raining when I found a rough patch with trees in the corner of a wheat field and decided to stop there, wanting to find somewhere that evening without having to ask. After the previous night indoors, and with Lincoln getting near, I felt there would not be many nights left to be out, at one with the energy of place. It was very windy in the tree-tops, one of which was a willow. Sometimes it rained and sometimes the sun shone, but it wasn't hot in the tent. The road was fairly quiet, with only the sound of local farm traffic and it felt good there. The earth had become a russet colour and the previous day I had seen the first smoke from burning stubble. We had been given some fruit and Talie had a great time with a peach, eating nearly all of it.

August 16th. Dark Moon. I had a strange night, somehow not wanting to sleep. All night long the powerful wind raged in the tree-tops and I lay for hours in a kind of trance. Everything seemed to have become a dark pool of oil which was all matter and all directions, including up and down.
Although I observed it and entered it, I was it. It seemed like the entrance to the Otherworld, to a shamanic journey. It was still, yet it was alive. There was movement without movement being visible–with ripples spreading out from the centre in concentric circles, the edges blurred into nowhere and everywhere. I began to make the journey down. Nothing was clear. It was a dark grey mistiness with everything only just formed, or partly formed, only partly clear. Grey, dark, indistinguishable shapes were distant and I had no sense of progress. I gave up, feeling it wasn't the time to go, as if it didn't want me that time, so stayed in the presence of it a long while with no thought. I felt connected to many other people the world over and to many stone circles. It was a powerful experience and I wonder what that place might have been in the past.

Talie was restless, waking and feeding a lot, exhausting me, and when we woke quite late I found I had a pain in my right breast: a touch of mastitis after all that time.

We went slightly off track to post a letter and got asked in to tea with a lady and her grand-children and when we left she gave us cake, scones and sandwiches. Then the weather turned stormy and we kept having to shelter under our plastic sheet. Talie got tired, but wouldn't sleep and was very grisly, but at last went off and slept right through torrential rain as we lay under the plastic by the side of the road. Some people in a car stopped to see if we were alright: I suppose, again, that we might have looked like a dumped body. My breast was very painful.

When the rain eased I walked on, and in the distance saw some horses and a traditional waggon parked on the verge of a side road. I wondered whether they were real travelling people, 'new agers' or even weekenders on holiday. I more than half expected the latter, but no, when I got close I found they were real gipsies. I spoke to the woman and asked if they would mind if we camped further down the same verge. She directed me to a house up the road saying there were "two old women who've got a barn, they'll help you". I did as she said, but one 'old woman' wasn't very helpful at all, and I didn't think I'd get much joy from a nearby farm, so went further up the road near some trees, where I felt safe. I set the tent up in some very long grass and got everything inside before Talie woke up.

The gipsy woman cycled down twice to see if we were alright, and tried to persuade me to go back near them, but having got completely set up and, feeling exhausted and actually quite ill, I declined and thanked her and hoped she didn't feel her hospitality was being rejected. She made me promise that I would turn to them if I had any trouble and go for tea with them in the morning. My breast was very bad and I had a fever, felt sick and couldn't eat. Talie didn't sleep for hours, but was cheerful, playing a lot and enjoying himself, and largely allowing me to just lie there and feel ill.
Eventually we both slept and I had a peaceful night.

In the morning he was still happy and I wanted to stay there all morning, but packed up and walked down the road to have a cup of tea with the gipsy man, the woman already out 'calling'. The first thing he asked me, as they always did, was "do you have a house". He quickly made a new fire and it was so good to sit by an open fire again with an old kettle boiling over it, then drink tea from beautiful, delicate, patterned bone-china cups and saucers like those my grandmother used to have. I talked with him a lot about horses and waggons . Theirs was a real traditional gipsy waggon with metalled wheels (no rubber tyres) and geraniums on either side of the door. They stayed a lot in Lincolnshire and had been stopping at that spot for 30 years. He also said it felt 'safe' there. He told me where I could get work picking peas, something I had always fancied doing, though people said it was excruciatingly hard and pretty soul-destroying.

He had a rabbit in a hutch, 4 finches in a cage, 2 dogs and 3 horses. They also had a flat-bed trolley with a whole lot more gear on it, including 2 bikes. They were the first travelling people I'd seen on our journey who didn't have a motor. They'd brought up a family in that waggon, but they were all off with their own families now. It made me feel good sitting there with him, because at that time I was also on and of the road, even though I no longer had a horse. It strengthened and confirmed something inside me. Talie played with the latch on the rabbit hutch.

We walked into Wilton, did our shopping and had fish and chips and peas sitting on a seat in the rain. I met the gipsy woman in the street. She was out with an old pram just like the one I had dreamed of. She gave us her blessing, which meant a lot. In those days I blessed people and knew it was real, because the energy of the earth which protected us would reward those who helped us. She had left me a pair of shoes at the waggon, but I couldn't carry the extra weight, so didn't take them. I hope she didn't mind.

It became sunny, hot and humid, and I sweated buckets. I was amazed to be asked into yet another house for more tea. Later, Talie slept as I rested, sitting among thunderflies and spiders. A woman on a bike stopped for a chat and told me there was a camp-site on the other side of Lincoln. It was already getting late and I hadn't done much mileage as I didn't have much energy that day.

The thunderflies got worse and I had to stop every few yards to wipe my face with my scarf, almost rubbing my face raw. At least Talie had his back to them, so wasn't bothered by them so much. It all felt like a hard slog, taking ages to get anywhere, like walking in a dream and not moving. I just walked, stopped, wiped my face, and didn't have any major breaks. I wanted to get near Lincoln so I didn't have far to walk in the morning, not wanting to reach the city tired. I went up a track marked Public Footpath, determined to ask at a last-hope farm, but came to a grassy bit on top of a hill and knew I could go no further. Feeling curious, I walked on to what I thought was the farm, having left the pack but taking the near-empty water bottle, but as I neared the buildings they looked like ordinary houses, and reaching them I found they were at the end of the track and there was no reply and no water.

I returned to the pack and realised the spot I'd been curious about was where the farmhouse had once been, but was now just a pile of overgrown rubble. I moved back from it to set up as it was getting late, and it was almost sunset by the time we slept. We had walked through an area which had sheep and nice meadowy bits, and this energy had been reflected in the people.

Sunday August 18th. I took it easy getting up. I had cream in my tea, which made it a bit curdly, and cream on my breakfast, because it was all I had. Once we left the track we were on a long road of middle-class suburbs which reached almost to the Cathedral. Early in the morning there had been church bells and I imagined how it must have been when London was small and Dick Whittington sat on Highgate Hill and heard Bow Bells, and it felt exciting and I looked forward to it. But it soon became 1985 again, with its endless roar of traffic, though it wasn't a bad road on the whole. We 'hit' the nicest part of Lincoln, meeting the Cathedral and going to find the Tourist Information place, where the lady was helpful, confirming the campsite and giving me the times of the buses which would take me there.

We had lunch at a place which didn't want Talie crawling on the floor, so I sat outside and fumed a bit, but he enjoyed feeding himself with peas and dropping them on the ground. I became nostalgic for some of my favourite caffs of the British Isles, like the Gaytime in Bungay, Suffolk (which later changed its name because it felt awkward about it).

I found an ex-churchyard with lots of grass and a path made of old gravestones, the lettering now worn away by the passage of feet. It made me realise how transient it all is, and wonder at the point of gravestones: a century or so and they're a path. I couldn't really relax there, though, as Talie kept making for the road. He was getting to be quite hard work, entering a phase which I feared might get worse when he walked more, though it might be better when he could talk and understand more of what I said. I did however think it would be one of the most exciting times, with much to unfold as he explored new experiences, and that I must try to stay in his reality. We went to the campsite and had a cuppa and awful sickly things at a refreshment place. On the wall was a hanging from the Northern Territory in Australia, and with amazement I realised that we'd been to nearly all the places on it.

I only put the fly-sheet up over ground which was covered in green sycamore seeds. We went for a walk by a lake, before returning to the tent. It was a pleasant place and better to be out under trees than in a house and a bed, even though we had to listen to the radio and inane chatter of two nearby youths having a fry-up.

August 19th, for a few days – Lincoln. We made contact with Paul Boizot and Trina, who were readers of Pipes of P.A.N., the magazine I'd been writing pieces about the journey for, and stayed with them a few days. It was a pause to collect mail from the P.O., replenish those things which can only be

purchased in towns, get clean and spend a little time with what I found to be a very pleasant city, loving its steep, winding roads. The sacred siting of it seemed to be a river between two cliffs – quite a female image again.

When we went to the Cathedral a tremendous wind blew up on a relatively calm day. I didn't go inside properly, but was fascinated by the ancient patterns on the outside, including some female symbols – especially a diamond shape with a protuberance in the centre.

It was a peaceful time, as I sensed we were nearing the end of our journey – a gentling of ourselves towards that end. It was strange, after all we had travelled and lived through, that it should be coming to a close, and that we were closing the circle. Everything was strong and calm and un- extreme. I felt the Virgo of the Gipsy Switch had already been 'done' the previous year, and that in Lincoln there was no need to 'do' anything, other than just be with the place and the time of year.

And the event which marked the time and place for me was that I bled for the first time since Talie's birth. It was only a little bleed, but I was astonished. Was I fertile again – in Virgo? Did it mean I had ovulated 2 weeks before? It felt sacred and special and I wished for ritual and celebration and to be with a group of witchy sisters, but there was just me and the earth and the journey and I knew I must somewhere give the blood to the earth in thanks.

It was a very special day with that different energy which is outside everything in everyone else's life around you – that special reality you are in when you are

333

born; first bleed; first have sex; first know you have conceived; give birth; the day you are close to a death and, I suppose, the day you die. We don't acknowledge and celebrate these great events of life enough these days. I would at that time have quite happily slipped gently into menopause, as I was so fulfilled by Talie, but it seemed, there in Virgo, that I was still full and ripe and I felt that the journey was my self.

Chapter 23: Closing the circle.

Around Friday 23rd August. It was beginning to feel like September as we set off from Lincoln, heading for Sudbrook, and everything felt different. Something fundamental had changed and nothing was the same. Each section of the zodiac had had its own distinctive character, but this was a whole change of energy.

It was wonderful to be on the road again: Talie and I together with the land, knowing it was something we must try to keep doing as he grew older. But now the physical journey was coming to an end it felt as though this last bit need not really be done; that it already had been done on some other level of reality, so the physical moving of it was unnecessary, yet I knew this not to be true.

The physical acting out of it was the confirmation, the affirmation of those other realities. It had been vital to walk this British Dreaming Path, to turn this great circle in physical reality, so that in all other planes of reality it would go on and on.

We were on the last bit of the Viking Way before it became a B road. It was beautiful, far better than I had expected: miles of track like the Ridgeway Path in Wiltshire, and once again I felt this was a sacred path which had been there long before the Romans came.

August 24th. I hoped to get to Sudbrook later, so this would be our last day of journeying on the Gipsy Switch, but the Switch would continue, the circle would remain on the land and keep turning. The road was clean and honest and helpful and provided shelter. I wondered whether Richard and Juliet and their baby would be there to meet us. Or anyone else. I was just wanting this way of life to go on and never end, but I knew it must and hoped there would be more journeys ahead.

We crossed the A17. In previous years, on my own, I had often hitched down from Callanish, and at Newark got onto the A17 across Lincolnshire to Norwich. I had crossed this track many times and not known of its existence and not known that one day I would walk it like this, and with Talie. It had rained a lot in the night and now there was a fresh wind and from time to time a blue sky. I couldn't understand that summer, so rarely had it had the 'feel' of summer, and there wasn't even the sense of 'late summer' now. There was the first breath of Autumn, though the true Autumn was a long way off. These past few months had felt like little more than - just 1985.

When we were with Saffron we had seen oats growing and now I saw oats being harvested, and the straw was unimaginably golden, but the barley straw, normally gold, was a dull beige that year. Most of the barley was in, but the wheat still stood, a lot lying flattened by the wind and rain. I had seen saplings planted and growing strong, man realising that he had gone too far in his tearing up of hedges and woodland. They may have been planted to save topsoil, crops and income, but it seemed a step in the right direction, putting a hold on all the mindless destruction.

Nature lay beige and brown, with a little flash of gold here and there where the sun shone, but after that wet summer, much was still green. Many cut verges had grown strong again, like Spring though with ripening berries. I hadn't really felt the earth warm that summer and could not see there being a glorious autumn. There was just a damp coldness which would gradually ease to winter. I began to feel the need for a jumper and Talie was in his coat again though his knees were still bare. The clouds were fluffy; some white, some black. I had to get on; hoping it would not rain on that last day.

And so we came to Sudbrook, which was not at all as I had imagined, and I thought how silly it was to imagine places before one had seen them, though it's hard not to. We walked up a long road with an enormous sense of completion; of returning to the beginning, of closing the circle, yet it was strange that Talie and I had not been here before.

It was such a momentous achievement, what we had done – and yet no-one around me knew. Even more I wanted hordes of cheering people welcoming me, willing me on the last few yards, with bands playing, television crews filming, but there was nothing. Only Nature knew that we the humans had turned the circle of the year on the land as the sun turned through the zodiac in the sky. Only we knew we had marked that zodiac on the land, our microcosm reflecting the macrocosm above. It felt like a coiled spiral, rather than a flat circle, for every turning, though repeating and strengthening the pattern, has its own differences. Something moves on.

We eventually found the house of the man who owned the 15-acre field. It took him a while to remember Mike and Richard and the waggons, but slowly it came back to him though he thought it several years before, and I pondered how differently each of us experiences time. I asked if I could camp in the 15-acre field, but he said it was full of mushrooms and he'd had a lot of trouble with mushroom-pickers going in there.

I hadn't known he ran a camp-site for caravans at the back of his house and put people with tents in his front garden, so there we were, our little green fly-sheet up for the last time on the Gipsy Switch on his close-cropped lawn in the company of his cats. It was good to feel safe, close to water and toilets and we

Richard, Juliet and Sharma in the Lincolnshire field where The Gipsy Switch began and ended

walked to a local shop and back. It all had a sense of unreality, as though we were passing by on some other plane from everyone else.

Sunday August 25th. We explored the village, saw the hall where they performed 'The Golden Box and Other Stories', but did not find the field. We sat outside the tent – and Richard walked into the garden with the inevitability of a much-run film. It was not an anti-climax, just an acting-out of some great cosmic reality.

I packed up the tent and joined him and Juliet and their baby, Sharma, in Ruby, the car who had been given a new lease of life. They thought it ridiculous to come all that way to meet us, but it had to be, it was part of the script, the end of the story. Richard took me to the field. We walked right round it and took photographs of us in it: Sharma, who had been conceived and born during the time of the journey, and Talie who had grown from a few weeks old baby to a near-toddler in his first year of life. The Virgo sign was no longer in the hawthorn tree, but its energy was there. The circle was complete.

And so ended this physical encircling of The Gipsy Switch, but it has no end and no beginning. We had opened something up, re-awakened something which had slept a long while. I hoped, and still hope, that others will make that journey, finding their own paths between the given points on the circle, the egg. The circle was in me; the circle was on the land; and the circle was in the heavens; it was done. Blessed Be.

337

Epilogue

We had a picnic in a Lincolnshire earthwork, then Richard and Juliet, having nowhere else to go, went to Nottingham where they knew people from the Lakenheath Peace camp. Although I felt precipitated away from the journey too quickly, I knew I needed the lift and went with them. What then? I was not ready to go back anywhere, and simply had to go straight to Callanish, to take Talie there for the first time.

For a year the journey had been our home, each day with a purpose in walking the next few miles round the circle. Now it was over and I felt homeless. We were homeless. And everything I carried seemed doubled in weight.

It was the late summer Bank Holiday and we travelled in hot, crowded coaches which ran late, nearly missing connections, but it all worked out and at last we were on the ferry to Lewis. I was going to the only place which felt like home. From the ferry we saw the most glorious, vivid arch of a rainbow back over the land we had left and saw the sun set into Lewis as we approached it.

The following day we hitched to Callanish, one lift being from Jan Gold, who became a good friend for ever afterwards. We camped at the old place north of the village, which was still beautiful in those days. Talie crawled about, exploring, and I was full of joy to see him there. We visited Annie, who was enchanted by him, and were checked up on by her sister Ishbel. At the stones I realised this was the real end of the journey and the place where I could focus and get a perspective on the whole of the previous year. It was also a beginning, for I knew we would live there.

On the night of the full moon we watched and waited, walked and waited, and when it finally shone through the clouds were alone at the stones: filled with their energy which went right through us and all the way round the earth. A circuit was complete and our journey was grounded.

As the moon turned, so did the weather. Ishbel checked on us again, and as our tent began to fill with rain, told Mary from the nearby new house, who came and asked us in for the weekend. As we shared their home that Sunday her extended family gathered and we met her brother-in-law (the now late) Simon Fraser: lawyer, estate agent and crofter. I spoke of how I wanted to live on Lewis and he said "You seem the kind of person who could make a go of it" and that sealed it for me.

Worn out.

In Stornoway I got details of houses for sale and found there were still some I could afford. The real decision was made then – that it wasn't a dream, but a reality. It just needed to be made to happen.

I returned to East Anglia, sorting out a lot of my possessions at the place where my caravan had been looked after. The people there wanted me to get rid of it, so I found a scrap dealer who would take it away, but not before Talie had a few nights' sleep in it. I was upset that some of my belongings had been stored outdoors under a carport and others were scattered round their garden. I was chased, attacked and quite scared by their Jersey cow, so it all became a somewhat unpleasant experience. I got rid of a lot of stuff, some of which I now regret.

I sent all the money I had collected to Oxfam. I think it was about £35. It doesn't sound much these days but was just what people passing by had given me when they saw the notice on my rucksack. Mike sent some in as well.

As part of the sale deal of the trolley I persuaded Kevin Draper to move me and the remaining stuff over to Monica's place in West Wales, as she had been the only person to offer me somewhere to stay when the journey was over. But I got a call to tell me that her youngest son, Leif, had been killed in a road accident while in France with her, and later her eldest son Sean was diagnosed with cancer, so she went to stay with him in Bristol.

339

Talie and I lived in a tipi in the front garden of the house in Wales and I wrote my first brief tale of the journey (later published in a small booklet by the people who did the Pipes of PAN magazine). I went to London, staying in a room in a house where people had glandular fever, and did 12 pastel pictures of the journey in 10 days, while suffering from something like flu. These were shown in an exhibition I had with Lynne at the Showroom Gallery in east London, where I also created an installation and did a performance of the journey.

We spent a strange winter in West Wales with Keith Motherson, Monica's now ex-partner, and their friend Val Remy, and then in February 1986 I went to Lewis, with Val coming to help, rented a flat, hired a car for a week and went searching for a home, looking at the few places I could afford. The nights were cold with frozen snow, but the days were bright and sunny with blue skies. At some places we viewed Talie wouldn't even be put down on the floor, but as we walked down a hill in Gravir, South Lochs, he was singing, and in the house – Tigh-a-ghlinne – he ran around in the sunlight which streamed through the windows, and I knew we had found our home.

Purchasing it was a long-winded struggle, but in June 1986 I hired a Luton van in Haverfordwest, and with Saffron coming to help, drove round the country picking up the bin-bags and cardboard boxes full of my possessions and finally moved into our corrugated-metal, ex-Church of Scotland mission house and hall in Gravir, our home for the next 10 years.

I have written about those years in my book 'The Callanish Dance' (Capall Bann 2000).

In 1996, with no money to repair the increasing number of things going wrong with the house, and with Talie aged 12 and us both needing a somewhat different life, I sold it and moved to Glastonbury in Somerset. Every year of the next 12 we went back to Lewis at least once and I felt more like an Islander living away for a while than someone who had left.

In Gravir I had home-educated Talie and with the time to pursue his own interests he had become a really good artist. I had developed my own art-work, having an exhibition in the hall every summer, and wrote a lot of poetry and magazine articles.

In Glastonbury Talie went to school for the first time aged 13. It was tough, but he stuck with it and got 2 As and a B in GCSE. He went on to Strode College, Somerset College of Arts and Technology and finally to the Exeter campus of Plymouth University, gaining various diplomas and a Foundation Degree along the way to a BA in Design/Illustration. I wrote my 2 books (the other is 'Mother of the Isles' Dor Dama Press 2003), created and sold a lot of art-work,

340

exhibited, gave talks and slide-shows and attended various Goddess Conferences.

Neither of us really fitted in down there, my heart still being in the Islands; and in 2008 Talie moved to Norwich and I returned to Lewis.
From the moment we lived in Gravir, the nature of our journeying changed. We still camped out in all weathers, turning the circle by going to the same places at the same time of year – year after year after year, but we never made any more long landscape journeys apart from one round the chalk white horses of southern England, where we found people still as hospitable and helpful to a woman and an nearly-9 year old as they had been to a woman and a baby.

One thing I had learned, though, is that given time I could walk anywhere. As long as I could cross the Minch from Lewis to the mainland I could walk 10 or 20 miles a day and get anywhere in Britain. I could walk to Norwich. How quickly you can walk 100 miles when you do 10 or more a day. When I camp out now in the same small green tent, I realise how normal I feel and come alive in a different way from when I am in my house, much as I love it, and realise that if I got things together to keep me warm and dry I could soon get back into sleeping out with no tent if the situation arose.

It seems sad to me that the concept of walking from one place to another through the landscape appears now to have died out and strikes people as strange and unusual; as though I did something extraordinary. In all of our past until very recently, it was how most people got about, and was not thought 'strange'. Those who walked were accepted by those who did not, often given food and shelter before moving on – as did so often still happen to us.

When I was young, in the '40s and '50s, there were many 'tramps' for whom this was a way of life and they were not looked down on in any way. I was reminded of this when reading an article in the Guardian by Robert Macfarlane (A Dream of Leaving 21/6/14) in which he refers initially to the long distance walks in 1933 of Patrick Lee Fermor and Laurie Lee, the first from Holland to Constantinople and the latter through London to Spain.

He refers to the inter-war years when there was a 'culture of vagrancy' with many 'long-term professional tramps' who walked as a way of life, and also those desperate and unemployed, who clung to some vestige of their former lives by polishing their shoes and carrying bags of tools. These were 'those who had no choice' and who 'barely held life together'. Macfarlane contrasts these with 'the wilful wanderer' who walked for the joy of walking and experiencing the landscape. Often these were artists, writers and musicians who had homes to return to, and I would class Macfarlane himself among those.

341

Where would I put myself? Well, I was a 'wilful wanderer', but certainly with the Gipsy Switch, had no home to return to, the walk being our home.

My point here is that until very recently it was an accepted way of life or travel to walk long-distance from one place to another, sleeping outside or finding what shelter one could, and I feel sad that even in the years since my journeys, attitudes have changed and we have become more and more dependent on vehicular transport, mobile phones, computers and GPS. But I do believe for all that, that it is possible to travel as we did, moving the human energy through the ancient dreaming paths, and I would love to hear from others who have done so recently.

I felt I owed it to my younger self to write this story in all its everyday reality, for that is what people have asked for. I hope you have enjoyed it.

Postscript

Talie is an intriguing, as yet un-published illustrator, in his own time studying and writing about the mythology and legends of Celtic lands, also researching Norse and Anglo-Saxon myths. His web- site is www.taliesinsmith.co.uk. Saffron got a degree in drama and is now a performer, singer and has her own business making creative furnishing pieces from vintage fabrics in north Norfolk: www.paffronandscott.co.uk; www.thesweetbeats.co.uk. Tiffany got a degree in Ecology, a PGCE, became a primary teacher, department Head, and for a few years ran a pub with her husband in Norwich. As I write she is teaching in a school in Malaysia. Kevin got a BSc in Combined Science (Geology with Biology), a PGCE, became a teacher and is now Head of a Primary School in Leicester. My website is www.jill-smith.co.uk.

With my move to the Hebrides and all the younger people going off into very different lives, I lost touch with most of the others who had been on the Gipsy Switch and the Walk for Life, though I am in occasional contact with Richard, Juliet, and once in a blue moon, Mike. This has been my story: they have their own stories to tell.

Praise for 'The Gypsy Switch'

"Very readable...very honest, extraordinary and inspiring."
Simant Bostock, artist and sculptor

"Jill has an extraordinary gift for magical storytelling...with an enviable
economy of language she manages to convey another world to us - one in
which enchantment, myth and mystery aren't marginalised but imminent...She
weaves this vibrant untamed reality with the one we recognise as 'everyday' in
a way that is authentically convincing and deeply affecting..."
Poppy Palin, author, artist and illustrator

"Jill's book has inspired me to believe that the quest to find ourselves in this
modern world is both doable and desirable. It's not about money, or success but
recognising the beauty that is all around us and the earth's ability to teach us
what we truly need."
Karen Taylor, partner in 'Working to Recovery'

"Jill's latest book, following her on the year's journey of The Gypsy Switch, is
not only engaging, but an historical archive of a pivotal time in empowerment
through campaigning action. The physical journey is interwoven with a deeper
journey into her inner landscape, revealing a seldom travelled pathway through
deep, demanding and unpredictable territory, becoming a celebration of one
woman's relationship with our mother-land. A journey I delighted to share page
by page."
Janet Jenkins, co-owner of Harvest Moon